JEWISH REVENGE AND THE HOLOCAUST

PERSPECTIVES ON THE HOLOCAUST

A series of books designed to help students further their understanding of key topics within the field of Holocaust studies.

Published:

Holocaust Representations in History: An Introduction (2nd edition), Daniel H. Magilow and Lisa Silverman

Postwar Germany and the Holocaust, Caroline Sharples

Anti-Semitism and the Holocaust, Beth A. Griech-Polelle

The United States and the Nazi Holocaust: Race, Refuge, and Remembrance, Barry Trachtenberg

Witnessing the Holocaust: Six Literary Testimonies, Judith M. Hughes

Hitler's "Mein Kampf" and the Holocaust: A Prelude to Genocide, John J. Michalczyk, Michael S. Bryant, and Susan A. Michalczyk (eds.)

The Holocaust and Australia: Refugees, Rejection, and Memory, Paul R. Bartrop

The Roma and the Holocaust: The Romani Genocide under Nazism, María Sierra

Israel and the Holocaust, Avinoam J. Patt

The Holocaust in Eastern Europe: At the Epicenter of the Final Solution (2nd edition), Waitman Wade Beorn

Forthcoming:

Sites of Holocaust Memory, Janet Ward

The Perpetrators of the Holocaust: The Folly of the Third Reich, Nathan Stoltzfus

Britain and the Holocaust: A Continuing Relationship, 1933 to the Present, Tony Kushner

Hitler and the Holocaust: History, Responsibility, Legacy, Manuela Achilles

JEWISH REVENGE AND THE HOLOCAUST

HISTORY, MEMORY, AND IMAGINATION

Laura Jockusch

BLOOMSBURY ACADEMIC
LONDON • NEW YORK • OXFORD • NEW DELHI • SYDNEY

BLOOMSBURY ACADEMIC

Bloomsbury Publishing Plc, 50 Bedford Square, London, WC1B 3DP, UK
Bloomsbury Publishing Inc, 1359 Broadway, New York, NY 10018, USA
Bloomsbury Publishing Ireland, 29 Earlsfort Terrace, Dublin 2, D02 AY28, Ireland

BLOOMSBURY, BLOOMSBURY ACADEMIC and the Diana logo are trademarks of
Bloomsbury Publishing Plc

First published in Great Britain 2026

Copyright © Laura Jockusch, 2026

Laura Jockusch has asserted her right under the Copyright, Designs and Patents Act, 1988,
to be identified as Author of this work.

For legal purposes the Acknowledgments on p. x constitute an extension of this copyright page.

Cover design by Design Holborn
Cover image: Czech political prisoner Zdének Syrovátka of Buchenwald near Weimar, Germany,
identifies an SS guard from the Buchenwald subcamp Wansleben, shortly after the US 3rd Army
had reached Buchenwald on April 11, 1945. The photograph was taken by Harold M. Roberts of
the US Signal Corps on April 14, 1945. © PJF Military Collection / Alamy

All rights reserved. No part of this publication may be reproduced or transmitted in any form
or by any means, electronic or mechanical, including photocopying, recording, or any information
storage or retrieval system, without prior permission in writing from the publishers.

Bloomsbury Publishing Plc does not have any control over, or responsibility for,
any third-party websites referred to or in this book. All internet addresses given in
this book were correct at the time of going to press. The author and publisher regret
any inconvenience caused if addresses have changed or sites have ceased to
exist, but can accept no responsibility for any such changes.

A catalogue record for this book is available from the British Library.
A catalog record for this book is available from the Library of Congress.

ISBN: HB: 978-1-3504-4926-8
        PB: 978-1-3504-4925-1
        ePDF: 978-1-3504-4927-5
        eBook: 978-1-3504-4928-2

Series: Perspectives on the Holocaust

Typeset by RefineCatch Limited, Bungay, Suffolk
Printed and bound in Great Britain

To find out more about our authors and books visit www.bloomsbury.com
and sign up for our newsletters.

For Omer, Alma, and Leo

A Day of Revenge!

And I tell you, brothers, remember what I say:
The sole comfort and consolation
Will come, you hear? The day will arrive,
That brings us revenge!

Revenge for our suffering and pain,
For blood spilled by our torturers,
Revenge for those about whose skeletons
No human being will ever know.
Revenge for deeds unknown in Sodom,
For mothers, orphans, widows,
Revenge that the blood of millions of victims
Will demand from underneath the earth.

Man will awaken, no doubt about that,
To see the horrors of war and
As one of our prophets, he will loudly proclaim:
Revenge! I'll take revenge!

The day will come, oh, I hope and believe
I see it, brothers, arrive from afar,
It will bring us, like Noah's dove
A message of peaceful times.

Lagiewniki, January 5, 1942*

---

* Mordecai Gebirtig, *S'brent:1939-1942* (Krakow 1946), 27; translation from Yiddish by Laura Jockusch.

CONTENTS

List of Illustrations	viii
Acknowledgments	x
Introduction: Rethinking Jewish Revenge and the Holocaust	1
1 **Paranoia and Elimination: Revenge in Nazi Propaganda and Genocidal Practice**	25
2 **Responding to the Apocalypse: Jewish Revenge during the Holocaust**	79
3 **From Wartime Desire to Postwar Fantasy: Jewish Revenge after the Holocaust**	149
Postscript: Jewish Revenge in Postwar Film	223
Conclusion	231
Sources and Bibliography	245
Index	269

ILLUSTRATIONS

1 Testament of twelve Chelmno prisoners, April 1943; Yad Vashem Archives O.6/343; courtesy of Yad Vashem Archives — 9
2 The "Storm Song," with lyrics by Dietrich Eckart and music by Hans Gansser, in the *Liederbuch der Nationalsozialistischen Deutschen Arbeiter-Partei* (Munich: Zentralverlag der NSDAP, 1938), public domain — 34
3 "Jewish Cry for Vengeance!," front page of the Nazi publication *Der Stürmer*, no. 4, January 1939; USHMM Photo Archives # 31520; United States Holocaust Memorial Museum, courtesy of Virginius Dabney — 36
4 Men reading *Der Stürmer* at a display box, Worms, 1935; display boxes typically featured the slogan "The Jews are our misfortune" and this one also says "With the *Stürmer* against Juda [i.e. the Jews]"; Bundesarchiv 133-075; courtesy of Bundesarchiv — 43
5 A page from nine-year-old Horst Schlegel's letter to the editor of *Der Stürmer*, April 9, 1943; Leo Baeck Institute Archives, New York, Bernhard Kolb Collection AR 360, series V, Stürmer Files; courtesy of Leo Baeck Institute — 52
6 A Nazi propaganda poster depicting a photograph of Herschel Grynszpan, Berlin, 1938; USHMM Photo Archives # 32663; courtesy of United States Holocaust Memorial Museum — 81
7 A defaced *Der Stürmer* display box in Sankt Peter, Baden-Württemberg, c.1933; the slogan "the Jews are our misfortune" was manipulated to read "the Jews are our fortune"; USHMM Photo Archives # 18523; United States Holocaust Memorial Museum, courtesy of Miriamne Fields — 82
8 The words "Jews, revenge!," written in blood on the floor of an apartment belonging to one of the 800 Jews murdered by Lithuanian nationalists in Vilijampole (Slobodka) June 25–26, 1941; photographed by George Kadish; USHMM Photo Archives # 04640; courtesy of United States Memorial Museum, copyright George Kadish — 104
9 Yiddish inscription on the walls of the Vilna prison: "For Ponary we will take revenge! May 2, 1943"; photographed by George Kadish; USHMM Photo Archives # 29932; courtesy of United States Memorial Museum, copyright George Kadish — 107
10 Diary of Michal Kraus; Michael J. Kraus Papers, USHMM Accession No. 1995.A.1067.1, file 5 Diary IIA 1945–1947; United States Holocaust Memorial Museum, courtesy of Ilana Kraus — 127
11 Ohrdruf survivors demonstrate torture methods to highest ranking American generals General Dwight Eisenhower (center),

	General Omar Bradley (second from the left), and General George S. Patton (left), April 12, 1945; USHMM Photo Archives # 63511; United States Holocaust Memorial Museum, courtesy of National Archives and Records Administration, College Park	155
12	Letter from George Patton to Dwight D. Eisenhower, April 15, 1945, mentioning the revenge killing of a former SS guard who had posed as a prisoner when the US generals toured Ohrdruf three days earlier; Dwight D. Eisenhower Presidential Library, NAID #12007734; courtesy of Dwight D. Eisenhower Presidential Library	156
13	A group of survivors and soldiers from the 11th Armored Division of the Third US Army view the corpse of a camp guard killed at the liberation of Gusen, Upper Austria, May 12, 1945, photographed by Sam Gilbert; USHMM Photo Archives # 82868; United States Holocaust Memorial Museum, courtesy of Wilfred McCarty	158
14	Survivors in Dachau berate an SS guard captured by US troops, April 29, 1945. USHMM Photo Archives # 82952; United States Holocaust Memorial Museum, courtesy of National Archives and Records Administration, College Park	171
15	Mock tombstone for Adolf Hitler, Landsberg, Purim 1946; Yad Vashem Archives # 1486/1431; courtesy of Yad Vashem Archives	179
16	Photograph of a banner in the Landsberg DP camp with a cartoon illustration of Hitler hung during a celebration of the Purim holiday, 1946-1948; USHMM Photo Archives # 69498; United States Holocaust Memorial Museum, courtesy of Rita Friedman Hattem	180
17	Jewish DPs dress up as Hitler and Goebbels for a Purim play at the Feldafing displaced persons camp, 1946–1948; USHMM Photo Archives # 39919; United States Holocaust Memorial Museum, courtesy of Allen Rezak	181
18	Poster displayed in the Landsberg DP camp, decorated with an image of two Jews throwing a copy of *Mein Kampf* into the fire; Landsberg, 1946–1948; USHMM Photo Archives # 69492; United States Holocaust Memorial Museum, courtesy of Rita Friedman Hattem	182
19	A survivor dressed up as Hitler in the Landsberg DP camp, Purim 1946; Yad Vashem Photo Archives # 1486/698; courtesy of Yad Vashem Archives	184
20	Young mothers take their infants for a stroll in the Landsberg DP camp, *c.*1948; USHMM Photo Archives # 96460; United States Holocaust Memorial Museum, courtesy of Dorit Mandelbaum	186
21	The memorial at the Waldfriedhof Gauting, Germany, today; photographed by Tamar Aizenberg; courtesy of Tamar Aizenberg	203

ACKNOWLEDGMENTS

This book would not have been possible without the help of many people. My dear colleagues at the Department of Near Eastern and Judaic Studies at Brandeis University have given me invaluable encouragement and support, especially Dar Brooks Hedstrom, Yuval Evri, ChaeRan Freeze, and Eugene Sheppard. I would like to acknowledge, in particular, Sylvia Fuks-Fried for her insightful feedback and advice on the entire manuscript. I am equally indebted to Elisabeth Gallas and Kim Wünschmann who read and discussed drafts of chapters in our priceless transatlantic support group.

I would also like to thank all those with whom I had fruitful conversations about revenge over the years: Elyana Adler, Natalia Aleksiun, Omer Bartov, Nicolas Berg, Max Czollek, Havi Dreifuss, Gali Drucker Bar-Am, Dani Eshet, Gabriel Finder, Alexandra Garbarini, Amos Goldberg, Hank Greenspan, Atina Grossmann, Tomaz Jardim, Aurélia Kalisky, Sharon Kangisser Cohen, Ellen Kellman, Eva Kovács, Alexandra Kramen, Lisa Leff, Tamar Lewinsky, Wendy Lower, Dan Michman, Stephen Naron, Philipp Nielsen, Avinoam Patt, Edith Pick, Devin Pendas, Shulamit Reinharz, Sharon Rivo, Lisa Rivo, Mark Roseman, Alexandra Szabo, and Carl Weinstein. I am grateful to the engaged audiences who enriched my thinking through their questions as I presented this research at the Tauber Institute's Colloquium in Jewish Studies, the University of North Carolina at Chapel Hill, the University of Hamburg, the Vienna Wiesenthal Institute, Central European University, Yad Vashem, and American University in Paris.

This project was made possible with the generous financial support of the Theodore and Jane Norman Fund, the Tauber Institute for the Study of European Jewry, the Mandel Center for the Humanities at Brandeis—which sponsored a pathbreaking faculty writing retreat in May 2022—and the Fortunoff Archives for Holocaust Testimony at Yale University where I served as William Rosenberg Senior Scholar in fall 2024. As always, I owe greatest debt to the Albert Abramson family for making my scholarship and teaching possible and for fostering a fruitful professional partnership between Brandeis University and the United States Holocaust Memorial Museum in DC. Although long out of graduate school, I remain always indebted to my teachers and mentors, Hasia Diner, David Engel, Atina Grossman, and Marion Kaplan.

Thank you also to my student research assistants Tamar Aizenberg, Hannah O'Koon, Carey Slaeker and Sarah Wintner, and to the Gilda Slifka summer interns at the Hadassah Brandeis Institute, Annabel Morrisová, Meghan Paradis, and Sivan Piatigorsky-Roth.

I owe special thanks to Joel Golb for his careful reading, honest and thoughtful feedback, and thorough editorial work. I would like to express my sincere appreciation and gratitude to the anonymous reviewers of the book proposal and manuscript and to Rhodri Mogford at Bloomsbury Academic, for taking on this project. Thank you to

Hayley Buckley, Amy Brownbridge, Gabriella Cox, and Merv Honeywood for bringing it to the finish line.

I am also indebted to the many knowledgeable and helpful librarians and archivists who have supported me over the years at the Brandeis Library, the Center for Jewish History, the Fortunoff Archives, the United States Holocaust Memorial Museum, the USC Shoah Foundation, and Yad Vashem among many others. While every effort has been made to trace copyright holders and to obtain their permission for the use of copyright material, if any have been inadvertently overlooked, I will be pleased, if notified of any omissions, to make the necessary arrangement at the first opportunity.

Friends and family listened to my forays into the topic of this book over the years; I would like to express my gratitude to Bärbel Buchelt, Naomi Frankel, Helen Przibilla, Dorothea Salzer, and Alma Yannai-Shani; to my mother, Vera Jockusch, to my mother-in-law, Sara Offen, and to the Offen family; to my cousin, Beatrice Szameitat, and to my uncle, Alfred Kalmbacher.

And most of all, I am unendingly grateful to Omer, Alma, and Leo who are my everything—I dedicate this book to them.

INTRODUCTION
RETHINKING JEWISH REVENGE AND THE HOLOCAUST

In Leonhard Frank's 1949 novel *Die Jünger Jesu* ("The Disciples of Jesus"), Ruth Bodenheim, a young German Jewish survivor, returns from Auschwitz to her hometown Würzburg and avenges the murder of her parents. She kills the Nazi official who had beaten her mother and father to death while rounding up the family for deportation. A local German court tries Ruth for murder. The jury empathizes with her rage and acknowledges that a far greater injustice had motivated her deed. Ruth is acquitted.[1]

Frank, a non-Jewish novelist and playwright who had received international acclaim in the interwar years, had escaped Germany after Nazi students burned his works for their socialist and pacifist messages in the May 1933 book burnings. He spent the war years in exile in Switzerland, Great Britain, France, and the United States, returning to West Germany in 1950. As a socialist opponent of Nazism, refugee, and returnee, Frank was highly sensitive to the intricacies of the postwar moment in Allied-occupied Germany. His novel depicts how local Nazi functionaries evade denazification, revive old networks, rebuild political influence, and regain power. Yet he also portrays German citizens who recognize the wrongs of the recent past and seek to build a better future: some do so by redistributing material goods stolen from those who profited from the Nazi regime, giving the goods to its victims or people otherwise in need in the war's wake. Frank vividly describes the struggles of a Holocaust survivor living with loss and trauma, in an environment where some Germans are former lovers and friends but most are former perpetrators. In Frank's account, Ruth, who managed to survive as a prostitute in the camp brothel, uses artwork to process her trauma of sexual exploitation and victimization as a Jew. But only her revenge brings some closure and return to life; it allows her to rebuild her relationship with her prewar sweetheart, take care of her younger brother, and adopt the orphaned infant of her best childhood friend who died in childbirth. Frank's novel is a classic revenge tale: the victim of a historical injustice commits a premeditated violent act against the perpetrator and achieves emotional satisfaction. The moral imbalance produced by the perpetrator through an initial act of injustice is restored to a kind of moral equilibrium. Although the revenge cannot bring back the dead, by letting the source of the injustice suffer for his initial deed, it memorializes the wrongdoing along with its victims. Ruth's revenge act is cathartic; it is also the only way she can go on living and normalize her relationship with her German environment.[2]

Frank's powerful fiction captures early postwar German fears that surviving Jews would take violent revenge for the destruction of European Jewry. He invites his readers to empathize with the young German Jewish survivor and see the Nazi past and postwar reality through her eyes. While Frank's understanding of the Nazi "final solution," and specifically of Auschwitz, was fragmentary at the time and his rendition of Jewish suffering focused on sexual exploitation as a symbol of powerlessness, victimization, humiliation, and shame,[3] his story nevertheless made the desire for revenge after the Holocaust relatable. He even seemed to suggest that revenge—kept in check by a functioning justice system—was necessary to achieve historical reckoning and societal reconciliation.

Although Frank perceived and conveyed real emotions that prevailed among both Germans and Jews in the early postwar period, there seems to be no historical record of a survivor's revenge killing of a Nazi perpetrator that was then adjudicated by a German court. German fears and fantasies of "Jewish revenge" by far outweighed the revenge acts that Germans actually suffered at the hands of Jews. Frank offers an overly benign portrayal of ordinary Germans' empathy for the Jewish victims and survivors of Nazi crimes. Postwar judiciaries were staffed with former Nazis; and in domestic court cases related to Nazi crimes, both the legal staff and the broader public generally empathized with the defendants in the dock, not with their victims. It is unlikely that a real trial before a German court of a Jewish avenger-murderess would have ended in acquittal.[4] Frank's fictionalized German response to Jewish revenge was perhaps meant to be prescriptive, to suggest how Germans ought to respond. His positive stance in respect to revenge as a response to the Holocaust may have been an expression of his own ambivalence toward returning to Germany from exile, with Ruth being Frank's alter ego. In reality, the story of Jewish revenge in the shadow of the Nazi "final solution" and German responses to it is far more complex than Frank suggests. It merits careful analysis.

Revenge—inflicting pain in return for suffering pain—is an anthropological constant in the response to real or imagined grievances. Such grievances may vary from actual or perceived humiliation, dishonor, and shame, over betrayal and injustice, to injury, violation, and atrocity. Revenge is unique to humans; not even our closest relatives in the animal kingdom practice it. Thus, desires and practices of revenge have preoccupied humans across periods, societies, and cultures; and they remain a contested topic. Despite the moral stigmatization and the quest to contain and overcome revenge, it remains ubiquitous in politics and popular culture and informs quotidian human interactions.[5]

Revenge denotes a wide range of different emotional, cognitive, and behavioral phenomena: it may refer to a personality trait—i.e., a person's tendency to cultivate feelings of revenge—or an emotional state caused by a concrete traumatic event, and a variety of behaviors triggered in response.[6] There are semantic distinctions between revenge and vengeance. Revenge tends to refer to direct payback against an individual wrongdoer for the sake of the victim-avenger's personal satisfaction. Vengeance, for its part, tends to signify indiscriminate payback on a collective more loosely associated with wrongdoers, in the name of a more abstract principle of the greater good; it can take the form of, for example, a punishment on behalf of divine justice.[7] Both revenge and vengeance may result in acts of retribution and retaliation. While retribution seeks proportionality in the response to a wrong and is guided by moral principles, retaliation follows the logic of talion, where the response reciprocates the wrong as a form of punishment. Closely related is the concept of what German denotes as *Selbstjustiz*, "self-justice," vigilante justice or vigilantism. Vigilantism is not simply revenge aimed at inflicting retaliatory harm; here a wrongdoer's guilt has been assumed or established, but the legal authorities are presumed to fail to duly punish, so that victims take punishment into their own hands.[8] These different concepts are often used interchangeably as their distinctions are not clearcut.

Although there is a wide range of revenge phenomena—from feelings, over thoughts, fantasies, plans to actions—societal discourse and cultural representations tend to reduce revenge to negative social behavior: violent, brutal, bloody, excessive, and disproportionate acts that threaten the social-political order—indeed society's moral fabric—because of their potential to generate ever more violence. Revenge is thus morally condemned, socially stigmatized, and often prosecuted as a criminal offense. Modern societies tend to see revenge and justice as opposites. Branding revenge "barbaric" and "primitive," something deviant that "the others" engage in, these societies present a celebratory self-image: that of having overcome a principle of revenge and replaced it with a modern justice system, with centralized state power possessing an exclusive right to exact just retribution. But such shared focus on revenge as violence tends to ignore the fact that revenge does not necessarily have to be violent, excessive, and disproportionate. Indeed revenge may remain within an individual's realm of feelings. It may never lead to any outward-facing behaviors; and if it does, these behaviors are not necessarily violent. More often than not, revenge finds expression in nonviolent acts, or remains imaginary. Hence revenge does not inevitably generate an uncontrollable spiral of violence; it may in fact also discourage further escalation by reestablishing a balance of power built on deterrence. As an individual response to trauma, revenge may have some short-term benefits as it may help individuals rebuild their self-efficacy, self-esteem, and sense of justice and security.[9] In the long term revenge may have negative effects on individual health and social relations as it may become an addiction. Moreover, revenge for perceived grievances may also serve as pretext to violate alleged enemies and reverse the roles of victim and aggressor.[10]

Scholars of a wide range of disciplines have destigmatized and historicized revenge by acknowledging its importance as a post-traumatic response. They have suggested that in the aftermath of the mass violence of oppressive regimes, wars, and genocides, vengeance-connected emotions and vengeful acts are a primordial human response by victims and those who identify with them. Over time these emotions lose their rawness, decline but do not disappear, while victims tend to channel them toward a search for justice and reconciliation—and perhaps also forgiveness.[11] Historians of law and transitional justice have emphasized the advantage of legal frameworks and processes over vigilantism and proposed narratives of development and progress in "staying the hand of vengeance"[12] with the help of legal institutions and prescribed rules and responsibilities and a quest for fairness.[13]

In this book, I will consequently understand revenge in broad terms: as an act through which someone who has suffered (an actual or imagined) wrong retaliates upon the individual or group who inflicted the wrong. Through the act, the avenger regains agency, changing from a suffering to an acting subject. Revenge is thus experienced as self-empowering; it restores a balance that the avenger believes has been disturbed by the wrongdoing. The vengeful act can be but is not necessarily violent; it does not even need to be acted out but can remain a fantasy. Whether manifest as an act of violence, taking non-violent forms, or remaining a fantasy expressed, say, as artistic creation, it has the same emotional benefit for the avenger, restoring a sense of honor, self-respect, and empowerment. Time and temporality are crucial factors in this process because revenge is always *reactive*, its response to past acts of injustice or atrocity often aims at preventing the atrocity from reoccurring in the future. Vengeful acts of any kind derive their identity and meaning solely from reference to a preceding wrong. The avengers communicate that reference to the perpetrators and those who identify with them, as well as to those who identify with the victims; for otherwise the vengeful actions would be random. Revenge therefore combines different temporal axes; it is backward looking and forward looking at the same time, while also being a means to cope with the present. And by its very nature, it is intrinsically connected to memory, reminding perpetrators of their deeds while commemorating victims by bringing them into the present. I thus understand revenge and justice not as opposites but rather as intrinsically connected, as two different ways to gain redress after an injury: one that is direct, personal, and extra-legal, the other indirect, depersonalized, and mediated by an institution and a code of law. For individual victims, revenge and justice may in fact be deeply entangled: for some, taking violent or non-violent revenge on perpetrators is experienced as a form of justice; for others, bringing perpetrators to justice is experienced as a form of revenge.

Exploring the manifestations and meanings of revenge—and with it, also of justice—is particularly complicated in the case of mass atrocity. All mass atrocities beg philosophical questions involving the kind of revenge that can possibly satisfy the pain of the victims and survivors, the kind of punishment that can be proportional to the crime of the murder of thousands and millions. But things are conceptually complex and affectively charged in the case of the Holocaust—not because of its enormous proportions as a transnational genocide, but also because of the distinct history of antisemitism and its perennially manifest trope of "Jewish revenge."

"Jewish Revenge" as an Antisemitic Trope

Over centuries, stereotypes of Jews and Judaism as possessing a "vengeful mindset"[14] have served to other and dehumanize the Jews as a collective, as well as to justify anti-Jewish violence.[15] As an aspect of such a broader dehumanizing process, essentializing fantasies about Jewish revenge reveal much about the non-Jews who hold them, little about Jews and Jewish culture. On a historical level, it is non-sensical to distinguish uniquely Jewish forms of revenge from other, non-Jewish forms: Judaism and its texts were shaped by its neighboring cultures; Christianity and Islam emerged from Judaism. Like other organized religions, the sacred literature of Judaism has many injunctions for and against revenge: injunctions that reflect a struggle to contain the human impulse to answer injustice with vengeance and propose legal and ethical frameworks to prevent an uncontrolled exaction of revenge.

In the Hebrew Bible, revenge is part of a larger set of acts of retribution aimed at redressing different kinds of wrongs. Accordingly, the biblical Hebrew texts have several terms denoting the complex of vengeance, including *nakam* or *nekamah* (revenge and vengeance; the Hebrew does not distinguish between the two), *netirah* (resentment), *gmul* (retaliation), *shilum* (reparation), and *gemilat ha-dam* (literally, redemption of the blood).[16] As in many other ancient cultures, revenge in ancient Judaism was part of a justice system; the practice was strictly regulated to prevent the emergence of cycles of violence. The Hebrew Bible thus distinguishes between appropriate and inappropriate forms of revenge—depending on context, it can be either an obligation or a transgression. The sometimes contradictory approaches to revenge and retribution in different books of the Hebrew Bible reflect a development from tribal custom to Mosaic law. Vengeance is appropriate if it serves to punish legally punishable crime, for example murder,[17] but that retribution is meant to follow strict rules and prescribed limitations.[18] These furnish proportionality, preventing the aforesaid open-ended cycle of reciprocal violence. For example, God punishes Cain with expulsion for murdering brother Abel; but God blocks any human revenge cycle by threatening to avenge whoever kills Cain seven times over. And whoever kills Cains' descendent Lamech is to be avenged seventy-seven times.[19]

Disproportionate personal acts of revenge are often condemned in the Hebrew Bible. One example of this is the story of Dinah, daughter of Jacob, who is raped by Shechem, son of Hamor, king of the Hivites. When Dinah's brothers Simeon and Levi take revenge by killing not only Shechem but all the Hivite men, they are scolded by Jacob, their father, for a disproportionate act that will generate more enmity and bloodshed.[20] The Hebrew Bible also stipulates the proportionality of retribution. Although the principle of "eye for eye," first laid down in Exodus,[21] is commonly understood as a quintessential formula of revenge—and indeed often seen as the essence of "Jewish revenge"—it was actually about the proportionality of a crime and its punishment, namely that the punishment cannot exceed the severity of the original crime. While the rule is not meant literally, it situates biblical Judaism within the general culture of *lex talionis*, which answered an injustice between humans by reciprocity and which was also common in Babylonian and Roman law.[22] Moreover, biblical literature identifies human revenge as inappropriate if it stems from personal rancor—"You shall not take vengeance or bear a grudge against any of your people, but you shall love your neighbor as yourself"[23]—an individual quest for settling scores, and committed out of cruelty.[24] Human vengeance is legitimate only if it is commissioned by God and humans function as God's agents in exacting *his* revenge on the enemies of the Israelites, as Moses who takes revenge on the Midianites.[25] Vengeance then is mainly a divine prerogative which humans should not challenge: "Vengeance is mine, and recompense, for the time when their foot will slip," says God in Deuteronomy 32:35.[26] It is God who steps in to save his people and punish its tormentors through his vengeance: either in the very moment of powerlessness and suppression—as for example by sending the plagues and drowning of the Egyptian army in the Red Sea[27]—or after the fact, in the form of apocalyptic vengeance in the distant future.[28]

However, despite these constrictions on revenge, biblical literature also includes passages that call for the killing of Amalek or the Amalekites, a nomadic tribe and archenemy of the Israelites, as revenge for their attack on the Israelites on their way out of Egypt (Deuteronomy 25:18).[29] While in Exodus 17:8–16 God vows to destroy the Amalekites, in Deuteronomy 25:19 God puts this task on the Israelites. Similarly, prophet Samuel (1 Samuel 15:3) conveys to king Saul God's order to blot out the Amalekites—men, women, children, and life stock—which rings like ethnic cleansing or genocide to modern ears.[30] This story—as the countless other violent passages of biblical texts—reflects little historical veracity and should not be taken literally. In post-Biblical Judaism the divine command to smite Amalek did not occupy a central place compared to the many other divine commands that comprise the Jewish tradition.[31] Yet the biblical figure of Amalek as a symbolic, timeless enemy of Jews is nevertheless deeply rooted in Jewish cultural imagination—supplemented with other villains most prominently Haman of the Book of Esther—and it was often invoked as a response to persecution in times of political powerlessness.[32] This tradition notwithstanding, relying on God to exact revenge remained dominant in post-Biblical Jewish culture. Rabbinic texts encourage humans to strive after God's qualities such as love, mercy, forgiveness, and justice but not after his vengeance.[33] At times of persecution and violence, Jews turned to God with pleas for divine vengeance on behalf of his people against its enemies.[34] Thus Judaism resolved the threat that human impulses to respond to injustice by exacting revenge can put to the social and political order by restraining human action and reserving revenge for the highest religious authority and to the cultural imagination.

From early Christianity onward, Christian proselytizers promoted a claimed difference from and superiority to Judaism of their faith, offering pejorative descriptions of Judaism and the Jews.[35] Revenge served as a central element in this process. Through the centuries, Christian polemicists have developed narratives that defined Jews as worshipping a "God of vengeance," and Christians as worshipping a "God of love." Within such narratives, Christians were presented as practicing neighborly love, compassion, and forgiveness, by contrast with Jews. An apparent paradox was at work here, since Christianity was built on Judaism and its scriptures, adhering to the same God, the core ideal of neighborly love and mutual care emerging from the Hebrew Bible (for example from Lev. 19). The Christian gospel argued that injustice should not be retributed measure for measure, "an eye for an eye," but be answered with endurance and forgiveness—"Do not resist an evildoer. But if anyone strikes you on the right cheek, turn the other also"[36]—so that evil could be transformed into good. Christianity nevertheless maintained the concept of divine vengeance for individual human sin.[37] Thus both Jewish and Christian biblical literature proposed tempering the human impulse for vengeance, relegating vengeance to divine authority.

In any case, throughout the history of organized Christianity, we find the presence of revenge as a central aspect of the Christian approach to Judaism and Jewry. It was present, for a start, as Christian revenge *upon* Jews.[38] Within Christian anti-Judaism, the Jews have been blamed, collectively, for Christ's death at Roman hands; purported collective and congenital Jewish responsibility for deicide has served as a justification for discriminating against, persecuting, and murdering Jews: mistreatment tied to the idea that the Jews were thrown into exile by God for rejecting Christ, thus meriting divinely sanctioned, righteous vengeance.[39] To be sure, the phenomenon of Christian revenge on the Jewish collective for alleged deicide contradicts Christianity's basic theological tenets of neighborly love and individual responsibility.[40] Yet, as the writer Susan Jacoby observes, "The charge of deicide as a rationalization for the 'just retribution' inflicted on Jews offered a legitimate outlet for the vengeance that was, in most other circumstances, prohibited to those of the Christian faith."[41] Still, Jacoby further indicates, "turning vengeful impulses . . . away from the society the religion wishes to preserve" so that it is directed against those not accepting the favored faith is not something specific to the Christian churches. Rather, it is the result of an alliance between religion and political power.[42]

Although the political power of the Christian churches gradually declines from the early modern era onward, religiously grounded anti-Jewish stereotypes did not. To the contrary: they were supplemented by secular antisemitic stereotypes of a social, economic, political, cultural, gendered, and biological-racist nature. In this context, within the entire range of ideas that non-Jews held about Jews, their supposed character traits, thoughts, and actions, motifs focused on revenge *by* Jews remained strongly present. Even when, as in the wake of the French Revolution, Jews were granted equal rights with non-Jews, narratives of Jewish vengefulness reinforced the image of Jews as evil, backward, alien, untrustworthy, and disloyal—hence to delegitimize their belonging to one or another nation while legitimizing discrimination and mistreatment. Racist antisemitism fueled these culturally embedded stereotypes, adding a biological dimension: Jews were now deemed innately incorrigible because of "racial" traits, including vengefulness.[43]

Building on this virulently antisemitic legacy, the Nazi regime made use of the vengefulness motif to justify anti-Jewish policies that moved from ostracization to mass murder. Revenge rhetoric here served to reverse the roles of victim and aggressor, the Germans portrayed as victims of a Jewish aggression that justified German aggression against the Jews.[44] As German perpetrators victimized Jews, they understood themselves as *avenging* wrongs imagined as having been inflicted by Jewish hands: from a defeat in World War I blamed on the Jews, to, more generally, Jewish power, influence, and ideas (liberalism, democracy, communism, capitalism, pacifism), onward to Jewish war-mongering and the theme of Germany having been driven into one more "Jewish war," and finally to Jewish responsibility for partisan and other anti-German resistance during the new World War. In this way, genocidal measures against the Jews were justified as righteous revenge for claimed wrongs against the German nation; and at the same time, Nazi perpetrators used fear of future Jewish revenge to justify ever more radical persecution, culminating in indiscriminate mass murder of Jews. Similar antisemitic ideas motivated non-German collaborators across Europe. Especially in areas of eastern Europe occupied by the Soviets prior to the Germans, anti-Jewish violence by local non-

Jews was spurred on by perceived "Judeo-Bolshevism" and a desire to take revenge on Jews for their alleged alliance with communism.[45]

These ideas outlived the Nazi regime; they took on an independent afterlife in the postwar era. Influenced by an ideologically grounded perspective on Jews and Jewry, a fair number of people in Germany and throughout formerly occupied, mainly eastern Europe continued to imagine themselves victims of conspiratorial Jewish power, wealth, aggression and vengefulness: they feared that Jews would return to take back their property; they blamed military occupation and communist rule on Jewish political power and international dominance; they saw themselves as victimized by trials and tribunals that were the result of "Jewish vengeance"; and they resented Jews for reminding them of theft, betrayal, collaboration with German occupiers, and involvement in genocide. In the postwar moment, such sentiments were especially strong among Germans reading the experience of defeat, occupation, war crimes trials, mass rape, and ethnic German expulsions from eastern Europe as products of "Jewish revenge," despite the absence of any evidence that Jews were the source of any of these developments. Rather than acknowledging collaboration in the victimizing of European Jews and demonstrating empathy for Jewish suffering, many Germans focused on themselves as perceived victims of the Jews and their imagined power.[46] A residue of such feelings and concepts keeps resurfacing, in Germany but also elsewhere in Europe, and even on a more global level, with Holocaust remembrance and calls for historical and legal reckoning perceived as evidence of Jewish vengefulness and an inability to forget and forgive.[47]

Any inquiry into the history of revenge, as theoretical concept, emotional state, and behavior, during and after the Holocaust must take antisemitic projections of this sort into account in telling a complex, multi-layered story. In this book, I will consequently integrate two complementary perspectives. On the one hand, I will analyze the anti-Jewish mythology of "Jewish revenge": a complex of ideological projections for the most part disconnected from historical Jewish actors; on the other hand, I will explore different kinds of revenge phenomena that Jews in different places during and following the Nazi German genocide actually engaged in—this without drawing any alignment whatsoever between Nazi ideas of Jewish revenge and actual revenge by Jews on Germans and their collaborators for Nazi crimes. Moreover, this is a work of historical scholarship on Nazi Germany, the Holocaust, and its aftermath. It does not seek to tell a global history of revenge in relation to political violence, armed conflict, and genocide broadly; nor does it seek to analyse the uses of "Amalek"-rhetoric in Jewish cultural imagination throughout the ages; and it does not seek to explain revenge phenomena of the present.[48] Rather, it seeks to understand the multifaceted historical manifestations of revenge as they pertain to the complex, transnational historical event of the Holocaust in its own right.

Presence and Absence of Jewish Revenge during and after the Holocaust

A great variety of historical sources suggests that many Jews in Nazi-occupied Europe, trying to confront and process the unfolding persecution and mass murder, also either addressed the possibility of or engaged in active forms of revenge. The concept of revenge was present in emotions and fantasies expressed in diaries, poems, songs, and jokes. It was present in letters, last wills, and wall inscriptions. Addressing relatives, friends, or indistinct groups of Jews who might survive the war, those safe outside the sphere of Nazi occupation, or future generations, calls for revenge were meant as imperatives for the future, those issuing them having few expectations of survival. We see this in, for example, a handwritten Yiddish note from April 1943 that Polish investigators discovered after the war at the site of the dismantled Chelmno death camp; between December 1941 and July 1944, the SS would murder at least 172,000 people, mostly Polish Jews from the Lodz ghetto, at Chelmno: twelve Jewish prisoners, temporarily kept alive for work in the camp, listed their names and places of origin. Anticipating their own deaths, they informed any living relatives of the Jews of Lodz that all the deportees to Chelmno were "murdered in a very cruel manner. They were tortured and burned. Farewell. If you survive, you must take revenge."[49] Appeals such as this one, did not specify how revenge was to be exacted, when, where, on whom, and in what form. But it was clear that revenge was to be taken by others and in the future, the writers feeling impotent to exact it themselves.

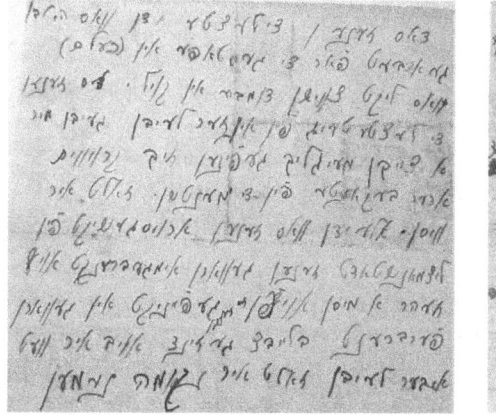

Figure 1 Testament of twelve Chelmno prisoners, April 1943; Yad Vashem Archives O.6/343; courtesy of Yad Vashem Archives.

At the same time, there were acts of revenge in the real here and now, violence carried out by Jews upon Nazi perpetrators and collaborators at execution sites and death camps. On October 23, 1943, for example, Franceska Mann (aka Manheimer-Rosenberg, 1917–1943), a Jewish dancer from Warsaw, killed SS-Oberscharführer Josef Schillinger, one of the SS guards supervising the undressing of the women who had arrived with Mann at Auschwitz-Birkenau and were about to be sent to their deaths. Mann reportedly lingered while undressing, using the appeal of her body to entice a pair of guards and blindside them. Using her shoe-heel, she attacked SS-Oberscharführer Walter Quackernack, seizing his weapon to shoot at him and Schillinger. While Mann missed Quackernack, she managed to kill Schillinger. Mann and all the women around her were immediately shot and killed by other guards.[50] Such acts of vengeance were last-resort actions by Jews who had realized their death was inevitable and immanent; the avengers and other Jews around them were almost always murdered on the spot, so that we mostly know of such acts not from the avengers themselves but from the rare surviving witnesses.

There was also plotted revenge that was attempted and was either aborted or simply failed, or else ended up in the realm of fantasy, as was the early postwar case with *Nakam*, a group of survivors led by poet and partisan Abba Kovner and his wife, partisan Vitka Kempner. In 1945–1946, Nakam developed a plan to kill six million Germans by poisoning the drinking water of four major German cities—bringing the classic antisemitic fantasy of Jewish well-poisoning to life in an act of poetic justice—and drenching the bread delivered to SS officers in American custody in arsenic. Abba Kovner's arrest by the British in Egypt in December 1945 having put an end to the water-poisoning plans, the group then targeted the SS men, at Stalag 13 outside of Nuremberg, but the bread they poisoned in April 1946 merely caused symptoms of food poisoning. These failed plots were exceptional in their radical nature and intended scope—there were many small-scale and spontaneous revenge acts. In the extremely brutal and lethal final months of World War II and its immediate aftermath, there was a great deal of grassroots-level violence targeting Nazi perpetrators (mainly camp guards), random groups of Germans whatever their former roles, and other European nationals who had been Nazi collaborators. A body of research has confirmed that vengeance was part and parcel of the transition from war to peace.[51]

If revenge is a universal human response to trauma, political conflict, and mass violence, and was widespread across early postwar Europe, why would Jews not have engaged in revenge? Jews participated in violent retribution—but did so alongside much larger numbers of non-Jewish camp prisoners, forced laborers, POWs, resistance fighters and partisans, and displaced people from across Europe in an extremely violent period. Some early postwar observers noted that given the enormous scale of the murder of Europe's Jews, revenge acts were an intuitive response. Yet, forming a contrast to many German voices expressing fear of Jewish revenge,[52] they also observed that the number of acts of revenge by surviving Jews fell short of these fears. The American Jewish psychologist David P. Boder interviewed 130 Holocaust survivors across Europe in the summer of 1946. With some bewilderment, he asked Otto Feuer, an Austrian Jewish survivor of Sachsenhausen, Dachau, and Buchenwald why it was "that when the liberation came and the Americans still did not have things in their hands, why did the prisoners behave so well? Why didn't they go out and say burn cities nearby and . . . take revenge?" Boder felt a need to justify his question, explaining that it was "just a kind of a human question that sometimes my temperamental American friends ask";[53] in this way he indicated that it was not really his question, but rather that of the audience for whom he was gathering interviews with a wire recorder. The life-world and experiences of this audience, he felt, were so distant from what his interviewees had endured that he needed to mediate between them and the audience. After an interruption, Boder further explained his question as one "that I hear so often. How is it that the liberated prisoners behaved so well, did not get hold of arms, did not shoot the SS, did not go out to demolish the nearby towns like Weimar, although I think the Air Corps, the Air Force has done that. What accounts for that decent behavior?"[54] For Boder, then, there was a widespread absence of revenge among Jewish survivors; and he found the alleged restraint surprising yet also honorable.

Similarly with American Jewish businessman Ira Arthur Hirschmann. Having served on the War Refugee Board and helped rescue Jews from Romania during the war, he would then work as a special envoy for the United Nations Relief and Rehabilitation Administration (UNRRA), reviewing the situation of Jewish Displaced Persons (henceforth DPs) in occupied Germany. Speaking of Jewish survivors he encountered, Hirschmann indicated that the fact "they did not turn upon the Germans living so much better than they, these who were indeed the conquerors, and not the vanquished, and tear them limb from limb, seemed to me incredible self-restraint."[55] This view was also reflected in the words of Saul Kussiel Padover, another Jewish observer, travelling through newly liberated Europe with the US Army while working for the Office of Strategic Services and trying to come to grips with Nazi atrocities and destruction. "[A]mazingly enough, there was no rioting and little vengeance," Padover noted, adding that the liberated prisoners were "generally so orderly, comparatively speaking, that I was almost ashamed of them. I expected a St. Bartholomew and I witnessed a pilfering."[56] Boder, Hirschman, and Padover all sensed that desire for revenge was justified—this in the context of unprecedented mass murder, together, it would seem, with a failure to properly pursue war crimes prosecution for the sake of gaining Germany as an ally in the emerging Cold War. But each was surprised that postwar acts of Jewish revenge on Germans fell short of what they had *expected*—and that for the most part, survivors chose not to enact revenge.

Decades later, the claim that Jews by and large refrained from revenge resurfaced, although now in a very different context: that of what Annette Wieviorka has called the "era of the witness," when survivors had moved from the periphery of public attention to its center and had gained status as moral authority figures.[57] Some of the most prominent Holocaust survivors claimed they had refrained, as a matter of conscious choice, from the use of violence against Nazi perpetrators, instead finding other ways of coping with their wartime experiences. As Elie Wiesel noted in 1978:

> On behalf of the dead, we sought consolation, not retribution. In truth, the lack of violence among these survivors warrants examination. Why deny it? There were numerous victims who, before dying, ordered him or her who would survive to avenge their death.... And yet ... with rare exceptions, the survivors forced themselves to sublimate their mandate for revenge.[58]

And Simon Wiesenthal, another prominent survivor, while dedicating his postwar life to hunting down Nazi criminals, insisted that he was not motivated by vengeance: *Justice, not Vengeance* is the title of his 1988 autobiography.[59] Even Nakam leaders Abba Kovner and Vitka Kempner declared in the 1970s and 1980s, however credibly, that they never meant their plan to be successful and had always only championed Jewish revenge as an *idea*, a *fantasy*.[60] "Ordinary" survivors, individuals without the renown of Wiesel, Wiesenthal, Kovner and Kempner, would often insist that they never sought vengeance. For example, in one of her many interviews with the United States Holocaust Memorial Museum, Regina Spiegel, a survivor of Auschwitz and Bergen-Belsen, insisted, like Wiesenthal, that her motivation was "justice, yes. Vengeance, no"—that she had not *wanted* to engage in revenge for their suffering.[61] Other survivors rejected revenge given the sheer proportions of the Holocaust. "I have not played with these ideas," noted Eva B. (born in 1924 in Berlin), in testimony she gave to the Fortunoff Archive at Yale in 1979. "I have not really, somehow, had dreams of revenge. It's too big. How do you revenge yourself on that?"[62] Still others rejected revenge as un-Jewish, as incompatible with Jewish tradition and culture; in particular, the biblical commandment "Thou shalt not kill" remained just as valid in the face of the catastrophe of European Jews.[63]

To be sure, such insistence underscores a discrepancy between some of the historical evidence and the witness-narratives that emerged. Why this contradiction with a range of sources indicating that during the war and after some Jews carried out acts of violence against Nazis, many others at least expressing vengeful feelings? For one thing, it appears that raw and unfiltered emotions lost their edge with mediation, which is to say over time. For another thing, language and intended audience mattered, as in the early postwar years survivors were more likely to raise the topic of revenge in Jewish languages and convey it to Jewish audiences. This was especially the case in survivor circles and networks: in relating traumatic experiences in non-Jewish languages to non-Jewish audiences, revenge would be elided as a contaminated theme, morally fraught, primitive, and contrary to modern society's pursuit of justice, hence stigmatized in public discourse. Analyzing Elie Wiesel's autobiographical writing, Naomi Seidman has shown that his 1956 Yiddish memoir *Un di velt hot geshvign* ("And the World was Silent") contains many candid expressions of rage and desire for revenge, together with frustration about general non-Jewish indifference toward the fate of Europe's Jews.[64] These feelings were edited out of the 1958 French version, *Nuit*—to be then published in English as the famous book *Night*—which instead presented an image of embodied suffering and endurance. Assuming such a survivor-persona was, in Seidman's words, "Wiesel's ticket into the literature of non-Jewish Europe."[65]

As popular culture came to valorize victims and survivors, rendering them into what Carolyn J. Dean terms "moral witnesses,"[66] narratives of valor, endurance and perseverance, loss, trauma, resilience, and rebuilding against all odds stood at the center of attention. Public discourse sanitized negative emotions felt by survivors, emotions such as anger, hate, frustration, bitterness, resentment, and aggression, prioritizing narratives of suffering and endurance. That left little room for survivors to articulate an emotion as contested and morally stigmatized as revenge. Some witnesses simply did not mention it, perhaps from simple discomfit, perhaps because after the passage of decades, revenge no longer seemed relevant to the complex life story they wanted to convey. Furthermore, acknowledging vengeful feelings was inhibited by various fears: of the potential negative impact that discussing revenge might have on the status of survivors as victims of an unprecedented mass crime; of negative stereotypes about Jews regaining legitimacy; of an undermining of accountability for Nazi perpetrators. In the latter respective, we should not forget that in the early postwar years and later, former Nazi perpetrators often accused survivor-witnesses of fabricating their accounts—and of doing so from, precisely, a desire for vengeance. Not only was this argument self-serving in the courtroom; it also replicated conspiratorial views of Jews that hailed from the playbook of Nazi propaganda.

Thus, any nuanced historical analysis of revenge and the Holocaust needs to differentiate between revenge as perpetrator justification and as victim response, between violent and non-violent acts; between feelings that lead to deeds and those that remain fantasies never to be actualized.

Some widely read Jewish accounts of the Holocaust contain revenge motifs—however marginal or vaguely expressed they might be—that seem to have gone unnoticed. Millions of readers around the world accorded Anne Frank's posthumously published diary canonical status for its universally applicable "lessons" on victimhood, youthful innocence, and feminine purity. With Frank's account ending before she experienced betrayal, arrest, deportation, and death, readers could connect to her without having to confront the murderous reality of the Nazi "final solution" and the Jewishness of its victims. The most widely cited line of her book, "in spite of everything, I still believe that people are really good at heart,"[67] written on July 15, 1944, just three weeks before the inhabitants of the secret annex at 263 Prinsengracht, Amsterdam, were arrested and deported, affirmed unrelenting belief in human goodness and universal humanism. We can only speculate that the traumatic experiences that were to follow at Westerbork, Auschwitz-Birkenau, and Bergen-Belsen—where Anne eventually died of typhus at age fifteen just six weeks before British troops liberated the camp—might have fundamentally shaken her belief in humanity. In her penultimate diary entry, dated July 21, 1944, Anne rejoices at the news of Claus Count Schenk von Stauffenberg's attempted assassination of Adolf Hitler: finally, not only "Jewish communists or English capitalists" but even the top German military brass "would like to send Hitler to a bottomless pit" she kvelled. Upon further reflection, Anne determines that the military plotters against Hitler who were now being punished by death did not deserve her sympathy because after all they only intended to establish a "military dictatorship and make peace with the Allies" so that they could "rearm and start the war again in about 20 years' time." Anne toys with a vengeance fantasy: "it would be easier and more advantageous for the Allies if the impeccable Germans kill each other off, it will make less work for the Russians and the English."[68] These vengeful sentiments, however boisterous and playful they may have been, are absent from the icon Anne Frank; indeed, revenge fantasies seem incompatible with her postwar public image as hero, martyr, and virgin.[69] The same is true for other Holocaust icons—for example, Victor Klemperer. An elderly academic trained at the universities of Berlin, Geneva, Munich, and Paris, Klemperer became most famous for his keen analysis of Nazi language and his meticulous diary writing.[70] Born in 1881 to Jewish parents in Landsberg an der Warthe, Prussia (today Gorzów Wielkopolski in Poland), Klemperer had converted to Christianity on the eve of World War I for the sake of his academic career; but in 1935 he was forcibly retired from his chair in Romance languages at the Technical University of Dresden for his "non-Aryan" descent. Although the "non-privileged mixed marriage" to his "Aryan" wife Eva (née Schlemmer, a pianist, painter, and translator) gave Klemperer some protection, he nevertheless suffered poverty, humiliation, forced labor, harassment, and arrest, along with constant threat of deportation to Theresienstadt or worse, Auschwitz. The Klemperers were forced to room with other mixed couples at a designated "Jew house" in Dresden before roaming around southern Germany passing as a bombed out "Aryan" couple. Klemperer's diaries offer a detailed, insightful, and nuanced account of the unfolding catastrophe. Occasionally Klemperer, the keen observer and chronist of life in extremis, also contemplates desires for revenge.[71] When in May 1942 Nazi authorities prohibit Jews from either holding pets or giving them into the care of non-Jews, the Klemperers put down their beloved eleven-year-old tomcat Muschel to spare him from being collected and killed by the city authorities. Muschel functions as the Klemperers' Ersatz-child and their mission to bring this animal through the war is vital for their resilience and ability to cope; therefore Muschel's death at the behest of the Nazi state has deep symbolic meaning for the couple.[72] On May 22, 1945, two weeks after Germany's capitulation, Victor Klemperer noted in his diary, writing from destroyed and American-occupied Munich: "Curious conflict within me: I rejoice in God's vengeance on the henchmen of the 3rd Reich—'today is the anniversary of Muschel's death' said Eva on the twentieth, and I: 'Every hair on his thick little fur has been paid for by a German life'—and yet I find it dreadful now to see the victors and avengers racing through the city, which they have so hellishly wrecked."[73] Does voicing thoughts like these, in all their ambivalence, make Victor Klemperer vengeful? Do they seem to call into question any of his measured analyses of the historical moment he witnessed and endured? Do Anne Frank's feelings of anger and animosity toward Hitler and the Germans undermine her love, optimism, and belief in humanity? Certainly not. On the contrary, these feelings are not only humanly relatable. What is perhaps even more important is that analyzing their presence in the historical record only enriches our understanding of the past and its historical actors and they are thus highly valuable to any humanist in pursuit of nuance and complexity.

Nevertheless, the striking absence of revenge as an openly discussed topic in later postwar decades also appears to endow it, paradoxically, with an indirect presence. For some survivors there seems to have been a *need* to negate revenge—something going well past merely not mentioning it at all—as unimportant. For some, at least, located between the lines of what was said there was surely a struggle with possibilities of revenge in an effort to confront the Holocaust and its abiding trauma. Some will have felt a need for such negation because revenge violated ethical convention; to those located in different life-worlds or born after, it was difficult to explain why vengeance seemed justified and indeed desirable. And as suggested: how could survivors speak of revenge without giving fuel to the worst, abiding antisemitic stereotypes: those deeply entrenched in a long history of Jew-hatred, figuring prominently in Nazi propaganda and perpetrator-rationalization, and possessing a vibrant afterlife in the postwar period?

Introduction

Toward a New Understanding of Jewish Revenge and the Holocaust

Scholarly inquiry into revenge during and after the Holocaust was held back by the same inhibitions and concerns.[74] As the psychoanalyst Shamai Davidson observed in the 1980s, after decades of working with Holocaust survivors, "Revenge was dreamt of again and again and fantasied in all stages of the Holocaust. . . . The fantasy of revenge was an existential leitmotif aiding in survival, but however vivid it was in imagery, it was rarely manifested in action."[75] But eventhough starting already with Raul Hilberg in the 1950s and continuing to, most recently, Evgeny Finkel, Holocaust scholars have typologized different behaviors and survival strategies from evasion, coping, compliance, over cooperation and collaboration to resistance,[76] few scholars have confronted the phenomenon of revenge, and those who did so honored the above-outlined self-representation of Holocaust survivors. In 1996, philosopher Berel Lang thus noted that "the most notable aspect of the place of revenge in the aftermath of the Shoah is its absence – both as a topic of discussion and before that in its occurrence."[77] Although articles by Lang and later Jael Geis and Mark Roseman have offered a nuanced tableau of wartime feelings of revenge that led to few postwar revenge acts besides some taking symbolic form,[78] historians did not delve into the topic until now. There is, however, one notable exception to this general picture: the topic of "national revenge" carried out by individuals motivated by strong Zionist feelings.[79] The case of the Nakam group and its failed revenge plots has garnered much attention, most notably in a recent meticulously researched book by historian Dina Porat.[80] In addition, starting with Quentin Tarantino's 2009 film *Inglorious Basterds*, in both cinematic and TV productions popular culture has taken up a counterfactual representation of wartime and postwar Jewish revenge. Although most if not all of these representations both sensationalize the topic and lack historical nuance, they can also be said to prepare the ground for historical analysis, venturing a foray into uncomfortable and contested areas that historians have been generally loath to investigate for nearly eighty years. In Germany, a younger generation of mostly Jewish authors, spearheaded by Max Czollek, has explored the manifestations of Jewish rage in an effort to shake up public discourse in a society that has grown all too comfortable with its own rhetoric and performance of *Versöhnung* and *Vergangenheitsbewältigung*—reconciliation and mastery of the past.[81] While there continues to be a popular fascination with Holocaust vengeance themes in film and literature, historical knowledge of the Holocaust is declining (especially among millennials), and the generation of survivors and perpetrators fades into history, scholars are ready to revisit the topic of Jewish revenge during and after the Holocaust. This study is part of a new surge in scholarly interest.[82]

Until now both in scholarship and popular culture, the focus has been on violent revenge—on acts or plots aimed at *murdering* Germans—and on avengers who saw this as "national revenge," which is to say on people who were Zionists and on combatants in the anti-Nazi resistance. As Shai Lavi and others have stressed, revenge ideas were vehicles for national self-assertion and closely connected to the quest for nation building and the path to sovereignty in Yishuv Palestine and the early State of Israel.[83] But during the Holocaust "national revenge" was only one among many motives,[84] a perspective focused on it leaving largely unexplored many other manifestations of revenge as both concept and behavior: non-violent, imagined, attempted, aborted, and rejected revenge, as well as revenge of a symbolic or indirect nature. As the Holocaust unfolded and afterwards, revenge served various functions for Jews with different backgrounds in different places and different times. One did not need to have a nationalist-Zionist worldview to have revenge fantasies; one did not need to be a partisan to undertake a concrete act of revenge; and one did not need to be religiously observant to reject revenge for ethical reasons. We will thus need to explore the multifaceted ways in which a diverse group of Jews engaged with revenge, and how that engagement changed over time.

By contrast with the relative paucity of scholarly literature on Jewish revenge during and after the Holocaust, there are many discussions of the different forms Jewish *resistance* took as the mass murder unfolded.[85] This difference would appear to at least partly reflect the fact that in any historical context (not just that of the Holocaust), resistance and revenge are subject to differing moral judgment. Resistance is seen as honorable and often heroic; it is discussed with pride and admiration, celebrated and steadily commemorated. Revenge, on the other hand, is seen as at best a morally fraught, problematic, ambiguous phenomenon. But in fact, in our context the relationship between resistance and revenge is much closer, more intricate than such after-the-fact moral assessment would suggest; answering the very question of whether an action is one or the other will depend on the subjectivity of the historical actors and the historical particularities involved. We will thus also need to look closely at the relationship between revenge and resistance, with a focus on how the idea of revenge was made use of by the historical actors themselves: What did they consider to be revenge, when, and under what conditions? And how was it tied to or distinct from what they considered resistance? What function did revenge acts and ideas fulfil for Jews during the war? And how did Jews' attitudes to revenge change after the war and over the postwar decades?

In their ideas and actions, the Jewish individuals discussed in these chapters will reflect a wide range of perspectives, extending over differences in age, gender, social background, ideological outlook, location, and wartime experience. Since their ideas and actions were a response to what Germans and their collaborators did to European Jewry, we will also look at the thoughts and deeds of perpetrators: both fanatic believers in the Nazi cause and less ideologically committed "ordinary Germans," and some non-German "bystanders."[86] Although Germany will be a central geographical location, that fact stands, inevitably and crucially, in relation to the transnational nature of the German mass murder, with examples of different manifestations of revenge drawn from across the Nazi empire. Importantly, in conceptualizing different—concrete and more abstract— manifestations of Jewish revenge in this perspectival framework, I am staking no claim to being exhaustive; I do not wish to offer, as it were, a catalog of revenge acts, but rather to address salient issues emerging in relation to this neglected aspect of Holocaust historiography.

Introduction

Over the past decades, the history of emotions—in other words, inquiry into feelings; how they are expressed and regulated in a given point in time and political context and what they reveal about social and cultural norms—has provided new tools for analyzing the phenomenon of revenge. In exploring the topic in the framework of the mass murder of European Jewry, I have drawn on a rich body of sources: early and more recent, archival and published, written, oral, and visual. These sources include letters, diaries, and other such personal documents from both victims and perpetrators; historical newspapers, memoirs, court records and memorial (*yisker*) books, together with written, oral, and audio-visual testimony; photographs, historical films, and feature films; fiction, poetry, and songs. Most of this material is not mainly about revenge, the theme only emerging or being addressed in passing. In this respect, it is nevertheless striking that although some of these sources have been widely read and used by historians, the revenge acts and fantasies embedded in them have been broadly overlooked.

Notes

1. Leonhard Frank, *Die Jünger Jesu. Ein Roman aus dem Deutschland der Nachkriegszeit* (Amsterdam: Querido Verlag, 1949); film version: East Germany 1965, *Chronik eines Mordes* (dir. Joachim Hansler, with Angelika Domröse as Ruth).
2. On Frank's biography see Katharina Rudolph, *Rebell im Maßanzug. Leonhard Frank: Die Biographie* (Berlin: Aufbau, 2020).
3. Many early postwar renditions in fiction and film used sexual exploitation of women and men as a symbol of the Nazi persecution and mass murder of the Jews. Examples are the 1948 feature film presenting a Jewish perspective on the Holocaust and postwar displacement, *Lang ist der Weg*, where one of the main characters, the German Jewish survivor Dora, alludes to sexual abuse; the 1953 Hebrew-language work of fiction *House of Dolls* by Ka-Tzetnik (Yehiel Dinur), the story of a woman who works in a camp brothel (its "joy division") and his 1961 *Piepel* about the sexual exploitation of a young male concentration camp inmate; Gillo Pontecorvo's 1960 film *Kapo* (the main character hides her Jewish identity, becomes a Kapo, and sells her body for food); and Otto Preminger's 1960 film *Exodus* (based on a novel of Leon Uris; the story of Holocaust survivor Dov Landau, who has been emasculated through sexual abuse).
4. For example, Jewish survivors who were tried in German and Allied courts for having denounced other Jews in hiding in an attempt to evade deportation received harsh sentences with little understanding for their duress. Similarly, although non-Jews engaged in black market activities alongside Jews in postwar Germany, Jews received disproportionate sentences and there was an agitated public discourse about the black market singling out "Jewish criminality." See Doris Tausendfreund, *Erzwungener Verrat. Jüdische „Greifer" im Dienst der Gestapo 1943–1945* (Berlin: Metropol, 2006), 259–85; and Michael Berkowitz, *The Crime of My Very Existence: Nazism and the Myth of Jewish Criminality* (Berkeley: University of California Press, 2007), 145–219.
5. See, for example, Fabian Bernhardt, *Rache: Über einen blinden Fleck der Moderne* (Berlin: Matthes und Seitz, 2021); Susan Jacoby, *Wild Justice: The Evolution of Revenge* (New York: Harper & Row, 1983).

6. See Ira Gäbler and Andreas Maercker, "Revenge and Trauma: Theoretical Outline," Michael Linden and Andreas Maercker (eds.), *Embitterment: Societal, Psychological, and Clinical Perspectives* (Vienna: Springer, 2011), 42–69, here 47.

7. See, for example, Linda Ross Meyer, "The New Revenge and the Old Retribution: Insights from Monte Cristo," *Studies in Law, Politics and Society* 31 (2003): 119–42. Some scholars distinguish between revenge, retaliation, and redirected aggression, for example, David P. Barash and Judith Eve Lipton, *Payback: Why We Retaliate, Redirect Aggression, and Take Revenge* (New York: Oxford University Press, 2011), 4–6.

8. Vigilantism can have different connotations of "righteous avengers" on the one hand, and lynch mobs on the other: it may be that vigilantes come from the ranks of a persecuted minority and seek to punish those who have wronged "their people"; they take matters in the own hands because the majority society and its legal system have failed to recognize the crime and prosecute those responsible, as for example, in the case of the Armenian genocide and anti-Jewish pogroms after World War I. However, vigilantes could also be members of the majority society (i.e., white Christians) who lynch members of a minority (i.e., Blacks and Jews) for "crimes" that are only alleged and entirely imagined as they are grounded in the majority's conspiratorial and prejudiced views of the minority and the equally conspiratorial view that law enforcement and the judiciary cannot be trusted. See Carolyn J. Dean, *The Moral Witness: Trials and Testimony after Genocide* (Ithaca, New York: Cornell U.P., 2019), 26–60 and Erik Mortensen, "The Mode of Lynching: One Method of Vigilante Justice," *Canadian Review of American Studies* 48, no.1 (2018): 20–39.

9. Gäbler and Maercker, "Revenge and Trauma," 45–6.

10. Anthony C. Lopez and Rose McDermott, Pete Hatemi, "'Blunt not the heart, enrage it': The Psychology of Revenge and Deterrence," *Texas National Security Review* 1, no. 1 (December 2017), 69–88 James Kimmel, Jr., *The Science of Revenge: Overcoming the World's Deadliest Addiction—and How to Overcome It* (New York: Harmony Books, 2025).

11. See Stephen Benard, et al., "An 'Eye for an Eye' Versus 'Turning the Other Cheek'? The Status Consequences of Revenge and Forgiveness in Intergroup Conflict," *Social Forces* 102, no. 3 (2024): 1200–19; Kit Richard Christensen, *Revenge and Social Conflict* (Cambridge: Cambridge University Press, 2016); Trudy Govier, *Forgiveness and Revenge* (London: Routledge 2002); and Martha Minow, *Between Vengeance and Forgiveness: Facing History after Genocide and Mass Violence* (Boston: Beacon Press, 1998).

12. American chief prosecutor Robert H. Jackson in his opening address at the International Military Tribunal at Nuremberg, Nov. 21, 1945, see International Military Tribunal, *Trial of the Major War Criminals before the International Military Tribunal, Nuremberg, 14 November 1945-1 October 1946* [henceforth *IMT*](Nuremberg, Germany: International Military Tribunal, 1947–1949, 22 vols.), vol. 2, 99.

13. See, for example, Gary Jonathan Bass, *Stay the Hand of Vengeance: The Politics of War Crime Tribunals* (Princeton: Princeton University Press, 2000); William A. Schabas, *An Introduction to the International Criminal Court* (New York: Cambridge University Press, 2001); Ronen Steinke, *The Politics of International Criminal Justice: German Perspectives from Nuremberg to the Hague* (Oxford: Hart Publishing, 2011).

14. See Julian-Chaim Soussan, "Indeed, where revenge is necessary, it is a great thing," in *Revenge: History and Fantasy*, ed. Max Czollek, Erik Riedel, and Mirjam Wenzel (Berlin: Hanser Verlag, 2022), 47–55, here 47.

15. On this antisemitic topos see, for example, Gunda Trepp, *Gebrauchsanweisung gegen Antisemitismus* (Darmstadt: WBG 2022), 84–106, 166; and Monika Schwarz-Friesel and

Jehuda Reinharz, *Inside the Antisemitic Mind: The Language of Jew-Hatred in Contemporary Germany* (Waltham: Brandeis University Press, 2017), 28–66.

16. Edward Lipiński, "נקם, nāqam," *Theological Dictionary of the Old Testament*, ed. G. Johannes Botterweck, Helmer Ringgren, and Heinz-Josef Fabry (Grand Rapids: Eerdmans, 1999), vol. 10, 1–9; Haim Hermann Cohn, "Blood-Avenger," *Encyclopaedia Judaica*, ed. Michael Berenbaum and Fred Skolnik, 2nd ed. (Macmillan Reference USA, 2007), vol. 3, 772–3 and Joshua H. Shmidman, "Vengeance," *Encyclopaedia Judaica*, vol. 20, 498–9.

17. See, e.g., Gen. 9:6; all quotations from Hebrew Bible and New Testament follow the New Revised Standard Version, NRSV.

18. See, e.g., Num. 35:19–33.

19. Gen. 4:15–24.

20. Gen. 34:1–31.

21. Ex. 21:24–25; this is repeated in different contexts, for example Lev. 24:20; Deut. 19:21.

22. Morris J. Fish, "An Eye for an Eye: Proportionality as a Moral Principle of Punishment," *Oxford Journal of Legal Studies* 28, no. 1 (2008): 57–71 and Tikva Frymer-Kensky, "Tit for Tat: The Principle of Equal Retribution in Near Eastern and Biblical Law," *The Biblical Archaeologist* 43, no. 4 (1980): 230–34l; William Ian Miller, *Eye for an Eye* (New York: Cambridge University Press, 2006).

23. Lev. 19:18.

24. See, e.g., Prov. 6:34; Jer. 20:10.

25. Num. 31:1–21.

26. See also verse 43; other examples: Ps. 79:10, 94:1; Lev. 26:25.

27. Ex, 15; Deut. 11:4.

28. For example in Joel 3:1–21; Ezekiel 25:14–17; and Nahum 1:1–3.

29. Samuel Abramsky, et al., "Amalekites," *Encyclopaedia Judaica*, vol. 2, 28–31.

30. Gili Kugler, "Metaphysical Hatred and Sacred Genocide: The Questionable Role of Amalek in Biblical Literature," *Journal of Genocide Research* 23, no. 1 (2021): 1–16.

31. Marc Brettler, "Destroying Amalek," The Future of the Past Blog (University of Minnesota), published March 22, 2024, https://sites.google.com/umn.edu/future-of-the-past/blog/destroying-amalek (accessed Aug. 14, 2025); as Brettler points out, if taken literally, the Amalek story bears the danger of serving as justification for the indiscriminate murder of anyone declared to be "Amalek".

32. Avi Sagi, "The Punishment of Amalek in Jewish Tradition: Coping with the Moral Problem," *The Harvard Theological Review* 87, no. 3 (1994): 323–346; Elliott S. Horowitz, *Reckless Rites: Purim and the Legacy of Jewish Violence* (Princeton: Princeton University Press, 2006).

33. Admiel Kosman, "Vengeance in the Tanakh, Mishnah, and Talmud: A Brief Introduction," in Czollek et al., *Revenge: History and Fantasy*, 39–46.

34. Examples are found in the Book of Esther, in piyyutim, and in stories centered on the "purple robe of God"; see Israel Yuval, *Two Nations in Your Womb: Perceptions of Jews and Christians in Late Antiquity and the Middle Ages* (Berkeley: University of California Press, 2006).

35. Gavin I. Langmuir, *Toward a Definition of Antisemitism* (Berkeley: University of California Press, 1990) and David Nirenberg, *Anti-Judaism: The Western Tradition* (New York: W.W. Norton, 2013).

36. See Matthew 5:38–39; similarly Romans 12.

37. Jacoby, *Wild Justice*, 83.

38. This has been a justification for blood libel accusations and violence against Jews, see Deborah Forger and Susannah Heschel "Christianity and Antisemitism," *The Routledge History of Antisemitism*, ed. Robert J. Williams, James Wald, and Mark Weitzman (London: Routledge, 2024), 247–54, esp. 248–9; Magda Teter, *Blood Libel: On the Trail of an Antisemitic Myth* (Cambridge: Harvard University Press, 2020).

39. Jacoby thus speaks of the "longest-running revenge tragedy of western civilization" and "the paradigmatic western example of vengeance committed in the name of divine justice." Jacoby, *Wild Justice*, 68, 99.

40. Ibid., 99. There is also a long history of a Christian self-perception of victimhood and martyrdom at the hands of other religions, even if Christians were the majority and held positions of power and were victimizing other religious minorities; see Candida Moss, *The Myth of Persecution: How Early-Christians Invented a Story of Martyrdom* (San Francisco: HarperOne, 2013).

41. Jacoby, *Wild Justice*, 100.

42. Ibid., 69.

43. See, for example, Jeffrey Herf, *The Jewish Enemy: Nazi Propaganda During World War II and the Holocaust* (Cambridge: Harvard University Press, 2006) and Jacob Katz, *From Prejudice to Destruction: Anti-Semitism, 1700-1933* (Cambridge: Harvard University Press, 1980).

44. For the extended history of Germans defining themselves as perpetual victims, see Omer Bartov, "Defining Enemies, Making Victims: Germans, Jews, and the Holocaust," *The American Historical Review* 103, no. 3 (June 1998): 771–816.

45. See, for example, Jeffrey Kopstein and Jason Wittenberg, *Intimate Violence: Anti-Jewish Pogroms on the Eve of the Holocaust* (Ithaca: Cornell University Press, 2018).

46. See, for example, Norbert Frei (ed.), *Transnationale Vergangenheitspolitik: Der Umgang mit deutschen Kriegsverbrechern in Europa nach dem Zweiten Weltkrieg* (Göttingen: Wallstein, 2006) and Frank Stern, *The Whitewashing of the Yellow Badge: Antisemitism and Philosemitism in Postwar Germany* (Oxford: Vidal Sassoon International Center for the Study of Antisemitism SICSA, the Hebrew University of Jerusalem, 1992).

47. Often this perception of "Old Testament vengeance" emerges mingled with the claim on the one hand of having heard "enough" of the Holocaust and on the other hand comments on Israeli politics and especially Israel's relationship with its neighbors as alleged evidence of a distinct propensity for vengeance; see Schwarz-Friesel and Reinharz, *Inside the Antisemitic Mind*, 97–8, 107–8.

    At times, stereotypes of "Jewish vengeance" are used as an Israeli self-criticism coming from the political left, especially since October 7, 2023, and the war in Gaza, see, for example: Amira Hass, "Arriving again at the Cycle of Vengeance," *Haaretz*, Oct. 10, 2023; Carolina Landsmann, "In Pursuit of Revenge, Israel No longer Knows what it is thinking," *Haaretz*, Aug. 29, 2024 and ibid., "Israel Is Living in a Tarantino Film. We Have Become the Inglourious Basterds" *Haaretz*, Jan. 10, 2025; see also Sidra DeKoven Ezrahi, "My mother taught me Jews are above vengeance. The Israel-Hamas war is finally making me doubt her," *Forward*, Oct. 27, 2023. There are also strong voices from among the Israeli hostage families who explicitly reject revenge, see for example, Maoz Inon, "Hamas murdered my Parents. Six Months later Israel's War of Revenge threatens us all," *Haaretz*, April 7, 2024 and Sarah Wildman, "The Israeli Hostage who Refused to Embrace Revenge," *The New York Times*, June 10, 2025.

    The Israeli political right has a long embraced vengeance in its political rhetoric and practice; and it is a central component of settler violence against the Palestinian population in the occupied West Bank, see Adam Afterman and Gedaliah Afterman, "Meir Kahane and Contemporary Jewish Theology of Revenge," *Soundings* 98, 2 (2015): 192–217.

Internationally, the critique of Israel as "vengeful" has served to exceptionalize Israel and apply a double standard, ignoring that other countries, especially Israel's opponents in the Middle East, in particular Iran, are no less guided by vengeance. As are the actors in other ongoing armed conflicts such as Russia's war of conquest in the Ukraine or India-Pakistan's recurring confrontations around Kashmir. In addition, as the current moment of authoritarianism and anti-liberal strongman politics in the US, Europe, the Middle East and beyond shows: revenge rhetoric and practice are a global phenomenon.

48. Both Hamas' October 7, 2023, massacre of 1,200 Israelis and the kidnapping of 240 hostages as well as the Israeli government's ensuing war in Gaza—which has since claimed perhaps forty times as many lives on the Palestinian side—were rife with vengeance. Israeli Prime Minister Benjamin Netanyahu and other members of his extreme-right government have used Amalek-themed rhetoric to justify Israel's response and with it its war crimes and crimes against humanity in Gaza. This ongoing war as the Israeli-Palestinian conflict and the Arab word's conflict with Israel more broadly—in which all sides have made ample use of vengeance motives and acts—do not pertain to the history of the Holocaust and are thus beyond the scope of this book.

49. Yad Vashem archives O.6/file 343; English translation in Reuven Dafni and Yehudit Kleiman (eds.), *Final Letters from Victims of the Holocaust* (New York: Paragon House 1991), 119–20. Later, other prisoners left similar notes that also invoked revenge, see Shmuel Krakowski and Ilya Altman, "The testament of the last prisoners of the Chelmno death camp," *Yad Vashem Studies* 21 (1991): 105–23.

50. See Filip Müller, *Eyewitness Auschwitz: Three Years in the Gas Chambers* (Chicago: Ivan R. Dee, 1999), 87–8; the incident was reported by Auschwitz inmates, Jewish and (non-Jewish) Polish: Aharon Beilin's testimony at the Eichmann trial, June 7, 1961, The State of Israel, Ministry of Justice, *The Trial of Adolf Eichmann: Record of Proceedings in the District Court of Jerusalem* (Jerusalem: The Ministry 1993), vol. 3, 1263–4; Tadeusz Borowski, *This Way to the Gas, Ladies and Gentlemen* (New York: Penguin Books, 1976), 143–6; Zalmen Gradowski, *The Last Consolation Vanished: The Testimony of a Sonderkommando in Auschwitz* (Chicago: University of Chicago Press, 2022), 116; it became widely known among survivors, see Kirsty Chatwood, "Schillinger and the Dancer: Representing Agency and Violence in Holocaust Testimonies," *Sexual Violence against Jewish Women during the Holocaust* ed. by Sonja M. Hedgepeth and Rochelle G. Saidel (Waltham, Mass: Brandeis University Press, 2010), 67–79.

51. Richard Bessel, *Germany 1945: From War to Peace* (New York: HarperCollins, 2009), 148–68; Ian Buruma, *Year Zero: A History of 1945* (New York: The Penguin Press, 2013), 75–129; Tony Judt, *Postwar: A History of Europe since 1945* (London: Penguin Books, 2005), 41–62; Keith Lowe, *Savage Continent: Europe in the Aftermath of World War II* (New York: Picador, 2013), 75–184.

52. Fears of "Jewish revenge" have been addressed in Frank Biess, *German Angst: Fear and Democracy in the Federal Republic of Germany* (Oxford: Oxford University Press, 2020), 31–9; Peter Longerich, *"Davon haben wir nichts gewusst!": Die Deutschen und die Judenverfolgung 1933-1945* (Munich: Siedler, 2006), 263–310.

53. David Boder's interview with Otto Feuer, Aug. 22, 1946, Paris, Illinois Institute of Technology, Voices of the Holocaust, 00:39:11-00:40:14.

54. Ibid., 00:40:54-00:41:25.

55. Ira Arthur Hirschmann, *The Embers Still Burn: An Eye-Witness View of the Postwar Ferment in Europe and the Middle East and our Disastrous Get-Soft-With-Germany Policy* (New York: Simon and Schuster, 1949), 81.

56. Saul Kussiel Padover, *Experiment in Germany: The Story of an American Intelligence Officer* (New York: Duell, Sloan and Pearce, 1946), 343, 344. Similarly, Meyer Levin observed that most of the liberated concentration camp inmates he encountered "walked barren, too weak to carry or push even a little retribution," see Meyer Levin, *In Search: An Autobiography* (New York: Horizon Press, 1950), 264.
57. Annette Wieviorka, *The Era of the Witness* (Ithaca: Cornell University Press, 2006).
58. Elie Wiesel, *A Jew Today* (New York: Random House 1978), 126-127. Wiesel will reiterate this argument in his autobiography, idem, *All Rivers Run to the Sea: Memoirs* (New York: Schocken Books, 1995), 141–3: "Jewish avengers were few in number, their thirst for vengeance brief". For "metaphysical and ethical reasons," Wiesel writes, Jews "chose another path. Later this absence of violence among the survivors, this absence of vengefulness on the part of the victims toward their former hangmen and torturers was widely discussed."
59. New York: Grove Weidenfeld, 1989; see also Tom Segev, *Simon Wiesenthal: The Life and Legends* (London: Jonathan Cape, 2010), 18–19.
60. Dina Porat, *Nakam: The Holocaust Sturvivors Who Sought Full-Scale Revenge* (Stanford: Stanford University Press, 2022), 283–4, 297–8.
61. Interview with Regina Spiegel in "Justice Yes, Vengeance No," Holocaust Education, USHMM https://www.youtube.com/watch?v=hdDREztZZY (accessed Feb. 7, 2025).
62. Testimony of Eva B., May 2, 1979, HVT 1, Tape 2, 12:13.
63. For example, testimony of Brenda H., Oct. 13, 1991, HVT 877, seg. 9 and testimony of Aron S., Nov. 26, 1991, HVT 1936, tape 2, seg. 17.
64. Elie Wiesel, *Un di velt hot geshvign. Dos Poylishe Yidnṭum*, vol. 117 (Buenos Aires: Tsenṭral-Farband fun Poylishe Yidn in Argenṭine, 1956).
65. Naomi Seidman, "Elie Wiesel and the Scandal of Jewish Rage," *Jewish Social Studies*, New Series, vol. 3, no. 1 (autumn 1996): 1–19, here 15.
66. Dean, *The Moral Witness*.
67. Anne Frank, *The Diary of Anne Frank: The Critical Edition*, ed. David Barnouw and Gerrold van der Stroom (New York: Doubleday, 2003), 716.
68. Ibid., 717.
69. For an insightful account of the different roles Anne Frank has fulfilled, see Ruth Franklin, *The Many Lives of Anne Frank* (New Haven: Yale University Press, 2025).
70. Victor Klemperer, *The Language of the Third Reich: LTI, Lingua Tertii Imperii: A Philologist's Notebook* (London: Athlone Press, 2000) originally published as *LTI: Notizbuch eines Philologen* (Berlin: Aufbau-Verlag, 1947).
71. Klemperer relates a passionate debate with his Jewish acquaintance Paul Kreidl, who was "for a large degree of reconciliation *after* things change, for Christian renunciation of revenge; I on the other hand in favor of an eye for an eye for a tooth for a tooth." See Victor Klemperer, *I Will Bear Witness: A Diary of the Nazi Years, 1942-1945*, transl. by Martin Chalmers (New York: Modern Library, 1999), entry of Jan. 18, 1942, 8, emphasis in original.
72. Ibid., 52.
73. Ibid., 488.
74. For example, Ari Joskowicz, noted that "After the war, many survivors felt comfortable talking about their desire for revenge, even as historians were largely unwilling to broach such themes." See Joskowicz, *Rain of Ash: Roma, Jews, and the Holocaust* (Princeton: Princeton University Press, 2023), x. In her insightful 1983 inquiry into the human propensity for revenge over three millennia, Susan Jacoby claimed that it was "impossible to overestimate

Introduction

the importance of that singular event, the Holocaust, in reshaping the modern view of the relationship between justice and vengeance." Jacoby, *Wild Justice*, 53.

75. Shamai Davidson and Israel W. Charny, *Holding on to Humanity—The Message of Holocaust Survivors: The Shamai Davidson Papers* (New York: New York University Press, 1992), 74.

76. Raul Hilberg, *The Destruction of the European Jews* (3rd ed. New Haven: Yale University Press, 2003), identified resistance, mediation, evasion, paralysis, compliance (662–9) and Evgeny Finkel, *Ordinary Jews: Choice and Survival during the Holocaust* (Princeton: Princeton University Press, 2017) conceptualized cooperation and collaboration, coping and compliance, evasion, and resistance; neither explorations of the different modes of Jewish behavior include revenge.

77. Berel Lang, "Holocaust Memory and Revenge: The Presence of the Past," *Jewish Social Studies* 2, 2 (1996), 1–20, here 1; republished in idem, *The Future of the Holocaust: Between History and Memory* (Cornell University Press, 2018), 142–60.

78. It was Berel Lang who first suggested that there was a "displacement effect," namely instead of engaging in violent retribution, Jews sublimated urges for revenge and transformed them into symbolic forms, see Lang, "Holocaust Memory and Revenge," 3; Berel Lang made similar observations in his *Post-Holocaust: Interpretation, Misinterpretation, and the Claims of History* (Bloomington: Indiana University Press, 2005), 17–31. Other authors have continued along such lines: Jael Geis, *Übrig sein, Leben "danach": Juden deutscher Herkunft in der britischen und amerikanischen Zone Deutschlands 1945-1949* (Berlin: Philo, 1999), 207–87, and ibid., "'Ja, man muss seinen Feinden verzeihen, aber nicht früher, als bis sie gehenkt werden': Gedanken zur Rache für die Vernichtung der europäischen Juden im unmittelbaren Nachkriegsdeutschland," *Menora: Jahrbuch für deutsch-jüdische Geschichte* 9 (1998): 155–80; Mark Roseman, " '. . . but of revenge not a sign.' Germans' Fear of Jewish Revenge after World War II," *Jahrbuch für Antisemitismusforschung* 22 (2013): 79–98; ibid., " 'No Herr Führer!' Jewish Revenge after the Holocaust: Between Fantasy and Reality" in *Revenge, Retribution, Reconciliation: Justice and Emotions Between Conflict and Mediation, a Cross-Disciplinary Anthology*, ed. Laura Jockusch, Andreas Kraft, and Kim Wünschmann (Jerusalem: Hebrew University Magnes Press, 2016), 69–90. Other scholars mentioned revenge as one among many ways in which survivors, especially Jewish Displaced Persons, confronted Germany, see Margarete Myers Feinstein, *Holocaust Survivors in Postwar Germany, 1945-1957* (Cambridge: Cambridge University Press, 2010),114-119, 150, 155-156; Atina Grossmann, *Jews, Germans, and Allies: Close Encounters in Occupied Germany* (Princeton: Princeton University Press, 2009), 226–33; and Zeev W. Mankowitz, *Life between Memory and Hope: The Survivors of the Holocaust in Occupied Germany* (New York: Cambridge University Press, 2002), 235–42.

79. There have been several popular books on the topic: Michael Bar-Zohar, *The Avengers* (New York: Hawthorn Books, 1967); Rich Cohen, *The Avengers* (New York: Knopf, 2000); Michael Elkins, *Forged in Fury* (New York: Ballantine Books, 1971); John Sack, *An Eye for an Eye* (New York: Basic Books, 1993); Jim G. Tobias and Peter Zinke, *Nakam: Jüdische Rache an NS-Tätern* (Hamburg: Konkret Literatur Verlag, 2000).

80. Dina Porat's *Nakam* and her earlier biography of Abba Kovner, *The Fall of a Sparrow: The Life and Times of Abba Kovner*, transl. and ed. Elizabeth Yuval (Stanford: Stanford University Press, 2010).

81. In fall 2022, the Jewish Museum in Frankfurt am Main mounted an exhibition (curated by Max Czollek, Erik Riedel, and Miriam Wenzel) entitled *Revenge: History and Fantasy*, which looked at Jewish revenge in a historical trajectory extending from the Hebrew Bible to Golem legends and superheroes and onward to graphic novels and contemporary film. Geared toward a general audience, it was accompanied by an exhibition catalogue, public programming, and a podcast series. See Czollek et al., *Revenge: History and Fantasy*, available in German and English. See also

Czollek's *Versöhnungstheater* (Munich: Hanser 2023) and *De-Integrate! A Jewish Survival Guide for the 21st Century* (Amherst, MA: Restless Books, 2023).

Similar, though less polemical Jewish critiques of German "mastery of the past," see Achim Doerfer, *"Irgendjemand musste die Täter ja bestrafen": Die Rache der Juden, das Versagen der deutschen Justiz nach 1945 und das Märchen deutsch-jüdischer Versöhnung* (Cologne: Kippenhauer und Witsch 2021) and Yascha Munk, *Stranger in My Own Country: A Jewish Family in Modern Germany* (New York: Farrar, Straus and Giroux, 2015).

82. Parallel with the current study, two book projects are being prepared: Sebastian Schirrmeister's investigation of post-Holocaust revenge as a theme in Jewish literature in German, Yiddish and Hebrew, entitled "Legitimate Passions. Reflections on Revenge in post-Shoah Jewish literatures" (research project at the University of Hamburg); and Katarzyna Person's *The Hour of Revenge: Holocaust Survivors' Quest for Justice and Retribution* (Toronto: University of Toronto Press, forthcoming) which focuses mainly on Polish Jewish survivors in the aftermath of World War II. The current study, by contrast, integrates both the wartime and postwar periods and does not deal with literature per se.

There are two theses on the topic: Roni Lerner, *National Vengeance as a Component of Jewish Resistance during the Holocaust, 1939-1945* (Ph.D. dissertation, Bar Ilan University, 2018) and Anna Celina Guenter, *Jewish Revenge in Postwar Vienna* (MA thesis, University of Missouri, 2023).

Some scholarship has focused on testimonies as Margarete Myers Feinstein, "Reconsidering Jewish Rage After the Holocaust," *The Palgrave Handbook of Holocaust Literature and Culture* ed. Victoria Aarons and Phyllis Lassner (Cham: Palgrave Macmillan, 2020), 743–60 and Alexandra Kramen, "Justice versus Revenge, or Justice as Revenge? A Case Study of Holocaust Testimony" *AJS Perspectives* (Fall 2022), 80-81; and on film: Daniel H. Magilow, "Jewish Revenge Fantasies in Contemporary Film," *Jewish Cultural Aspirations*, ed. Bruce Zuckerman et al. (West Lafayette: Purdue University Press, 2013), 89–110 and Olivia Landry, "Jewish Revenge on the German Screen," *New German Critique* (2025) 52, no. 1 (154): 107–29.

There is also the dissertation project by Alexandra M. Kramen, "Justice Pursued: Jewish Survivors' Struggle for Holocaust Justice in Displaced Persons Camp Föhrenwald" (Clark University) which explores the relationship between revenge and justice in a local study.

83. See Shai Lavi, "'The Jews Are Coming': Vengeance and Revenge in Post-Nazi Europe," *Law, Culture and the Humanities* 1, no. 3 (2005): 282–301; similarly, Shahar Pinsker, "On Jewish Revenge: What might a people subjected to unspeakable historical suffering, think about the ethics of vengeance once in power?," *Aeon* (May 17, 2024), https://aeon.co/essays/what-role-for-revenge-in-jewish-life-literature-and-culture (accessed Feb. 7, 2025).

84. Doerfer, *"Irgendjemand musste die Täter ja bestrafen*, 80-99; and Tom Segev, *The Seventh Million: Israelis and the Holocaust* (New York: Henry Holt, 2000), 140–52.

85. Roni Lerner, *National Vengeance as a Component of Jewish Resistance during the Holocaust, 1939-1945* addressed that topic, but did so mainly through the lens of national resistance. I approach the theme in a broader sense, one in which national approaches are just one dimension.

86. In a recent book the legal scholar James Kimmel, Jr. identified some forms of revenge-seeking as an addiction that should be treated as such. One of his historical examples includes Adolf Hitler's revenge addiction that led to the Holocaust. While Kimmel's model is convincing overall, the historical examples of single dictators and genocidaires-in-chief raise the question of applicability to the broad range of perpetrators that are necessary to perpetrate a genocide. Therefore, the current study will look at a wide range of Holocaust perpetrators at the center and the periphery of the Nazi regime. See Kimmel, *The Science of Revenge*, 107–16.

CHAPTER 1
PARANOIA AND ELIMINATION: REVENGE IN NAZI PROPAGANDA AND GENOCIDAL PRACTICE

In July 1938, the editorial of the radically antisemitic Nazi weekly *Der Stürmer* ranted about how the Jews as a collective were plotting to destroy Germany. "But Jewry will be mistaken," argued editor Karl Holz. "It will blunder as it always has done when dealing with National Socialism. In the person of Adolf Hitler an opponent has arisen for which Jewry is no match and by whom it will be beaten again and again. Jewry will not achieve their aim." For those following Holz's logic, a Germany in Hitler's hands would seem to have nothing to fear. But Holz went on to say that the danger was far from over. Rather, quite to the contrary: "The 'Zionist protocols' might announce triumphantly the 'coming world war.' Full of hatred, the Jews in Germany might long for the 'day of revenge.'" Yet Holz also predicted the following: "This wishful thinking of the Jews will not materialize. On the contrary, the great revenge will fall on the Jewish people themselves, the revenge of fate, the revenge of justice, the revenge of the tortured non-Jewish peoples. The revenge will break loose one day and will exterminate Jewry from the surface of the earth."[1] Clearly, this revenge was going to be spearheaded by Germany and the Germans.

Holz here articulated a liberation fantasy of colonized and suppressed people and presented a scenario for taking revenge on the colonizers through genocide. To be sure, the scenario was built on an antisemitic fixation with no ground in reality, as Jews were not victimizing Germans or other non-Jews. Rather, the reverse was true—for the past five and a half years, the Nazi regime had been humiliating, dehumanizing, disenfranchising, plundering, and violating some 500,000 German Jewish compatriots; it had recently tested even more radical measures on the 190,000 Jews who had come under its rule through Austria's annexation. It would be another three years before the regime moved to the systematic mass murder of Jews across its power-orbit. But even if Holz's July 1938 article was still merely a genocidal fantasy and Holz, although a long-time member of the Nazi party and the Gauleiter of Franconia, was not a high-ranking political leader and central decision-maker, the article reflects a radical eliminationist logic already stamping Nazi thinking, propaganda, and policy making.[2]

According to that logic, Jews were aggressors; they suppressed, harmed, exploited, even sought to destroy and eliminate the Germans. Hence the Germans were the victims of the Jews; any measures the Nazi regime took against the Jews—be it legislation, segregation, expropriation, expulsion, forced labor, or murder—were acts of prevention, protection, and self-defense. They were necessary, even legitimate, since indispensable for German self-preservation in face of the threat of Jewish aggression. From the earliest days of National Socialist political agitation throughout the regime's existence, Nazi propaganda steadily engaged in such role reversal. Within this inverted logic—steadily conveyed by the regime's central figures and propagandistic outlets to a mass audience representing all social classes and walks of life—Germans were not accountable for what they did to Jews, who had, the propaganda went, brought it on themselves through aggression, wrongdoing, and genocidal intent. Germans, in other words, were averting the threat of annihilation by the Jews by annihilating the Jews, in a national struggle for self-preservation. Indeed, in the end the mass murder would be defined by those who perpetrated it as a necessary and legitimate response to a Jewish threat not only to the German nation but to humanity as a whole.

Revenge motives, showcased in Holz's editorial and countless other propagandistic texts, speeches, posters, and films, thus played a crucial role in the Nazi effort to instigate and legitimize the persecution and genocide of the Jews; they served as a compelling motivation and justification for a wide range of individual Holocaust perpetrators. With scrutiny, promulgation of the revenge topos emerges as serving three distinct yet interconnected and paradoxical purposes. First, Jewish revenge was here cast as a racial trait. Among the many other negative qualities that Nazi propaganda ascribed to the Jews as a collective, with the intent of racializing and dehumanizing them, branding them as simultaneously inferior and threatening, it also resuscitated the old stereotype of the Jews as inherently vengeful—one racial feature accompanying aggressive, bloodthirsty, criminal, and generally wicked counterparts. In short, and crucially: in declaring purported Jewish vengefulness a matter of biology, the Nazi propagandists disconnected it from German behavior toward Jews.

Second, Jewish vengefulness was also posited as a historical fact, indeed a law of history. In conveying their message of Jews' constant, racially grounded victimization of Germans, the propagandists formulated a random list of alleged Jewish-perpetrated historical wrongs; Jews were now identified as the historical source of all the problems and threats Germans were facing in the here and now. For this reason as well, all legal-political measures taken against the Jews were self-defense—and in a convoluted and contradictory way, the self-defense argument was mixed with calls on Germans to themselves take revenge on the Jews for their history of anti-German plotting, for seeking German destruction. Often, these appeals for vengeance were themselves accompanied by a certain concession: although, the message went, the Jews had been conspiring for centuries to destroy Germany and annihilate the Germans, the annihilation had not yet taken place and could be averted through pre-emption, obliteration of the Jews before they could themselves succeed. Hence that Germans were finally avenging the long history of Jewish aggression and harm was itself a matter of *historical necessity*; in line with this twisted pseudo-historicist logic, the consequent claim was that the regime was working to change the course of history, to ban the historical threat that the Jews were posing, for the sake of a better—"Aryan"—future. The two revenge scenarios—Jews as innately vengeful; Germans as needing to avenge themselves on Jews for being victimized by them—were mutually reinforcing; together they served to motivate and justify anti-Jewish violence and impeded ordinary Germans from feeling compassion for their victims of persecution and genocide.

Third, closely linked to the arguments about race and history was the propagandistic casting of Jewish revenge as a likely future development. In the framework of Nazism's delusional existential logic, because Jews were vengeful by race and had vengefully harmed the Germans in the past, and because the Germans were now defending themselves against the Jews, the Germans were menaced—so went the imagined metahistorical scenario—by *future* Jewish vengeance. The genocidal planning and policy—the targeting of every last Jew, in cooperation with non-Jews across the German-occupied and German-allied continent—thus needed completion; and it needed to be timely, because should the window of opportunity close, the incomplete destruction of the Jews and a lost war would catalyze Jewish revenge leading to the annihilation of the Germans by the Jews. The argument for anticipatory vengeance grew stronger as the Holocaust gained momentum between 1941 and 1945 and intensified after spring 1943 as the war took a toll on the German population at the front and at home. The argument was tied on the one hand to moral qualms, namely that Germans, whether they had participated directly or indirectly in anti-Jewish measures, were complicit in a mass crime. On the other hand, as the war unfolded there were growing fears of national failure and defeat. Nazi propaganda harnessed these emotions, painting a worst-case future scenario—again, should the war be lost, total annihilation of Germans and Germany through Jewish revenge. In this manner, depicting Germans as victims of future Jewish genocide, Germans were offered justification for participating in a crime aimed at leaving no survivors; they could, in fact, deem it no crime at all but self-defense, an existential necessity for the German future. This pre-emptive reasoning, annihilation *by* the Jews as future punishment for not finishing the task of annihilating the Jews, had the potential to harness even those Germans not ideologically committed to the Nazi regime. Imbued with self-pity and fear, it was a reasoning that challenged anyone potentially "too weak" to rise to the opportunity for national salvation being offered by the Nazi regime.

Susan Jacoby observed that a "particularly dangerous form of symbolic revenge" emerges when political movements seeking or wielding power and control

> persistently represent themselves as victims in need of redress. This type of symbolism reflects a paranoid mindset that may originally have been based on real injuries (the conditions imposed on Germany by the Treaty of Versailles, for instance) and eventually becomes an instrument for generating and manipulating a generalized drive toward vengeance.[3]

Nazis, Jacoby further notes, were

> masters of the tools of symbolic revenge. . . . The political symbolism of revenge is frequently characterized by a confusion of identity between victim and aggressor and by the transformation of vengeance into a positive social value. In public spectacles, the confusion is subliminal, but it can easily be transformed by totalitarian states into an explicit rationale for acts of rage and vindictiveness.[4]

Jewish Revenge and the Holocaust

That was the case with the Nazi regime's antisemitic rhetoric. That rhetoric might best be seen as articulating a form of *paranoid* revenge, avenging fabricated grievances that were entirely based on Nazi ideology's paranoid delusional structure. Against this backdrop, we will need to consider the sources and motivations for the German entry into such a structure: how could the perpetrators of a continent-wide, transnational genocide of millions of human beings have come to see themselves as avenging entirely imaginary crimes and injustices—as purported victims of imaginary past and future mortal enemies who were in reality simply unarmed and guiltless civilians, Jewish men, women, and children?

Nazi Antisemitism and Anti-Jewish Policies

Race was the central organizing principle of Nazi ideology, antisemitism its cornerstone. Jews were defined as a distinct race and the lowest in the hierarchy of races, even lower than the "subhuman" category that took in the Slavs. This was the racist core of a broader worldview within which Jews were the arch enemy among a large set of human beings which the regime declared to be enemies because of their biology, behaviors, or beliefs: the disabled, Roma, Afro-Germans, Slavs, homosexuals, political opponents, and Jehovah's witnesses.[5] In this respect, it is important to note that antisemitism did not always have the same prominent place within the Nazi movement as it developed. In its early days before Adolf Hitler's rise to power, Jew-hatred was muted or amplified depending on political, economic and social contexts.[6] Nevertheless, the centrality of an antisemitic agenda was clear to everyone who joined the movement. That notwithstanding, in the Weimar period not all voters came to Nazism because of its antisemitic agenda. Rather, many were drawn to the possibility of social and political change: to the movement's perceived care for the "little people," a social-welfare agenda prioritizing ethnic Germans, hence tied to its violent xenophobia and anti-immigrant stance; to its vehement anti-communism and historical revisionism; and—just as importantly and tied to all of that—to its call to do away with the Versailles Treaty.[7]

Along with seeming to hold the promise of such a sharp shift from hated Weimar liberalism and parliamentary democracy, the Nazi party also attracted a following by conveying a capacity for efficient organization, for offering what seemed like dynamic leadership with a prowess for achievement, and through an emphasis on cult and ritual that celebrated masculinity, patriarchal hierarchy, and militarism with marches, music, and speeches. In any event, nearly all Germans not especially drawn to National Socialism for its antisemitism nevertheless accepted it as part of a package deal. Starting already in the earliest days of fringe right-wing political agitation in the wake of World War I, in printed media, speeches, and, eventually, radio broadcasts,[8] Hitler and other central figures in the movement made repetitive, elaborate use of a rich arsenal of antisemitic images and ideas that was impossible to overlook for anyone in the reading or listening public.[9] Geared toward building an antisemitic consensus, the use of antisemitic tropes was stepped up at times, both in euphoria over military successes as well as in crisis over military and civilian losses and looming defeat.[10]

For a long time there was a discrepancy between what the Nazis said they were doing and what they actually did. Despite consistently dehumanizing rhetoric, the use of terms with genocidal connotations such as "removal," "eradication," and "extermination"— *Entfernung, Ausmerzung, Vernichtung*—early on,[11] the "final solution" was the outcome of a long and unsystematic process. In the prewar years, Nazi anti-Jewish policy was hesitant, experimental, and often contradictory. It oscillated between different sorts of directly violent action and legislative measures that defined, disenfranchised, and segregated Jews—measures that destroyed professional livelihoods, plundered property, arrested, incarcerated, and expelled German Jews from Germany. Aware of internal and international public appearances, the regime steadily tested the acceptability of the antisemitic steps they took, while Nazi leaders honed propaganda aimed at demonstrating the need to ban Jews from German spaces and purge Jewish culture from German life.[12]

Tropes drawn on by the Nazis often associated Jews with, for instance, animals (especially rats and pigs), bacilli and vermin, illnesses such as cancer and pestilence, and the devil; often Jews were branded with derogatory social terms such as riffraff, rabble, criminals. A consistent theme emerging in this rhetoric of hate was parasitism: Jews, the relentless propaganda went, were innately unproductive, profited from other people's labor, gained wealth at the expense of others to the extent of destroying their "hosts." Paradoxically, while denouncing the Jews as constituting a categorically inferior race, the Nazis also denounced them for being domineering and powerful: controlling everything from the media to the economy and entire countries, "international Jewry" thus defined as governing the world.[13]

In this way, incessantly circulating Nazi propaganda held the Jews responsible for all the problems of modernity and all its ideas and "isms"—and for everything that had gone wrong in German history. The salient trope here was a nexus between the Jews and Marxism, communism and Bolshevism—a nexus encapsulated in the term "Judeo-Bolshevism"[14]—but together with modernity and modernism, worldwide Jewry was also held responsible for capitalism ("plutocracy"), liberalism, feminism, pacifism, and democracy. Jews were vilified for having stereotypical Jewish features and maintaining Jewish ritual, and also for *not* being visibly Jewish, thus insinuating themselves into society in order to destroy it from within. They were propagandistically assaulted for keeping to themselves and maintaining racial purity, and also for threatening the racial purity of "Aryans" through "racial mixing." Notably, circulating luridly within the Nazi mindset and propaganda were fantasies about Jewish men as sexual predators, hyperpotent, and intent on defiling "Aryan" women and girls.[15] This entire range of antisemitic Nazi propaganda tropes was grounded in the proposal, made very early on already, of a distinct form of Jewish enmity toward and hatred of Germany;[16] and this served as a core element in the justificatory arsenal, all and any measures taken against the Jews being presented as a necessary, legitimate defense against them. On the one hand, then, Nazi propaganda emphasized that fighting the Jews was in Germany's national interest because the German nation was under threat. But at the same time, having defined Jews as outside humanity, the promulgated struggle against the Jews was universalized into a world problem: in a "life-or-death" struggle, Germany—so went the trumpeted claim—was doing humanity a service.[17]

Many of the tropes and concepts outlined here were not specific to Nazism. Rather, they were pre-existent and global. The Nazis reused old stereotypes, images, and even concrete measures; their propaganda drew on models going back at least to Martin Luther and onward into the nineteenth century.[18] But with their "final solution to the Jewish question," the Nazis did contribute something to the repertoire of Jew-hatred. In Raul Hilberg's words: "That was their great invention . . . [a] turning point in history,"—although, Hilberg emphasized, this was the result of a "logical progression" from earlier precedents, a progression that "came to fruition in what might be called closure."[19] This was, Hilberg observes, "something unprecedented . . . something new."[20]

Along with literally declaring Jews as occupying a space outside humanity, the Nazis consequently were the first to target the Jews in total, every Jewish person in their sphere of domination being denied a right to live, in a developing program of global genocide.[21] This process was undertaken with quasi-religious zeal: with fantasies of salvation, Adolf Hitler taking on the role of messianic savior, a man doing, in his own words, the "work of the Almighty Creator."[22] In this respect, Saul Friedländer has emphasized the "redemptive" quality of the Nazi aim to resolve what they viewed as the "Jewish problem" once and for all times.[23]

Particularly in Hitler's writings and speeches, but also those of Heinrich Himmler, Joseph Goebbels, Hermann Göring, and other central figures in the Nazi party, we find this genocidal mindset articulated early on as the seeds of an eliminationist logic: a call for annihilation of the Jews itself charged with revenge motives, the consistent victim-perpetrator role reversal. But with the concrete plan for mass murder—a distinct genocidal policy with a global trajectory—only evolving over time, the path toward mass murder amounting to what Karl Schleunes has termed a "twisted road."[24] In the six prewar years, the Nazi regime's anti-Jewish measures were marked by hesitancy and experimentation, oscillating between dehumanizing propaganda that posed the Jews as a threat, improvised legal measures that complemented forced emigration and "Aryanizing" plunder, and violent action. In the prewar years, the grounds were being tested for acceptance by the wider German public of more radical antisemitic measure—at this time "orderly" disenfranchising and ostracizing legislative action found greater public acceptance than straightforward violence, was less likely to stir up undesired empathy.[25] This was the period in which, in the course of its relentless defining of the Jews as aggressors, the Germans as their victims, the Nazi propagandists formulated a rhetoric of "decolonization": a call for "Aryan" Germans to "take back what is ours" in respect to power, property, and space, in preparation for "social death."[26]

As the prewar annexation and wartime occupation of territory brought ever larger populations of Jews under German rule, there was opportunity for more radical anti-Jewish action. Nevertheless, the path to mass murder only followed along failed "territorial solutions" that envisioned concentrating Jews in a reservation in eastern

Poland or else the island of Madagascar, or the interior of the Soviet Union. The war of extermination against the Jews would be closely tied to the war against the Soviet Union and the effort to conquer *Lebensraum* for ethnic Germans in "the east." Although the mass murder began with the June 1941 German attack on the Soviet Union, it took several months for systematic killings to also affect Jews outside Soviet territory; and it would be well into the spring of 1942 before it became a general policy for all Jews under German or German-allied rule.[27]

The development of the "final solution" was thus far less preordained, far less the result of Hitler's centralized decision-making, than was long assumed in the historical research, more the result of trial and error, gradually increasing radicalization, an interplay between different German agencies, and a division of labor between different kinds of perpetrators. Hitler set the tone, gave ideas and the general direction; but he allowed subordinates to work out concrete policies. While leaving room for improvisation and experimentation, this modus operandi also resulted in radicalization as a result of competition between different personalities working for Hitler and the overlapping responsibilities of different agencies for anti-Jewish policy—among these, the SS, the police, the party, the civilian sphere, and the military.[28] In occupied territory, local German agencies and civilian administrators had leeway in choosing what to do with their Jews. Ethnic violence by local non-Jews against their Jewish compatriots, especially pogroms and communal genocides in Lithuania, Poland, Romania, and Ukraine in the summer of 1941, contributed to an intensification of the pace and scale of anti-Jewish violence.[29] Once SS-*Einsatzgruppen* (mobile-killing squads), police, Wehrmacht battalions, and local auxiliaries had moved to the indiscriminate killing of Jewish civilians, the step from mass shootings to killing centers—there would be six in total—followed a logic of manpower, logistics, and the effects of mass shootings on the perpetrators' mental well-being. There was an operative difference between killing-squad perpetrators reaching their victims and murdering them en masse in open fields, on the one hand, and having the victims brought by train to mass-murder facilities run by the perpetrators, on the other hand, using an ostensibly normal bureaucratic manner, deceiving the victims about their planned fate until the moment of murder. With this operative development, a fewer number of perpetrators could murder a larger number—trainloads—of Jewish and Roma victims, turning them into ash over just a few hours.

Such industrial mass murder is often regarded as emblematic of the Holocaust as a whole; it is often identified with Auschwitz-Birkenau, the other five death camps—Chelmno, Majdanek, Belzec, Sobibor, and Treblinka—consigned to general forgetting, although Treblinka in fact left almost an equal number of Jewish dead as Auschwitz (900,000/1,000,000). Likewise, often forgotten is the fact that just over half the victims of the "final solution" died in death camps, the other half were murdered in mass shootings, and (both inside and outside Nazi-created ghettos and concentration and labor camps) by starvation, disease, and exhaustion, together with various other forms of violence.[30]

Although after the war, Germans who shared varying degrees of complicity in the systematic genocide tended to claim they had known nothing of it; but in light of the intensive prewar and wartime propaganda looking forward to a necessary annihilation of the Jews, the ample use of rhetoric and imagery centered around that event, the claim was by and large improbable. For the most part, it involved evasion of sometimes criminal, sometimes at least moral responsibility. It is the case that concrete information about actual episodes of mass murder and facilities to that end were carefully concealed from public circulation in Germany.[31] That notwithstanding, millions of Germans certainly brought together the propagandistic predictions with what they unavoidably saw unfold in Germany, and from what they heard from Wehrmacht soldiers, SS men, and police personnel on home leave—as well as from German civilians working or living near killing sites and from Allied radio broadcasts. The claim of ignorance was not least an expression of indifference to the fate of the Jews, and a reflection of the fact that the National Socialist regime had managed to sever existing social and emotional ties between German non-Jews and their Jewish compatriots. For most Germans, Jews had died socially long before they were murdered; they had indeed been defined outside of humanity, removed from a realm of human emotional and ethical obligation.[32]

As suggested, the revenge rhetoric forming part of this dehumanizing process was a crucial motivation for ideologically committed Nazis, including those actively engaged in implementing the mass murder of Europe's Jews. But the rhetoric also had considerable resonance among Germans who were not true believers, increasingly fearful of payback for what they themselves perceived, consciously or otherwise, as a shared national crime.[33] Especially toward the end of the war, fear of Jewish revenge was not only the result of indoctrination, but also partly an expression of frustration at the course things had taken, concomitant existential angst—and recognition of, precisely, German guilt.[34]

Revenge as a Theme in Nazi Genocidal Rhetoric and Practice

From the Nazi party's inception in 1919 onward, its leaders, like those of other right-wing political groups, built on the idea that Germany had been victimized in World War I. The country had, after all, suffered a loss of territory, a breakdown of the monarchy's conservative and patriarchal order, humiliation through the armistice and subsequent Versailles Treaty, a near Bolshevik takeover of power, and economic ruin. But for right-wing nationalists, the worst catastrophe of all had been the military defeat itself—caused, the perception went, by a "stab in the back" perpetrated by liberals, social democrats, communists, and Jews. Much of the Nazi party's raison d'être was thus liberation of the German nation from the Versailles Treaty's yoke and the disgrace of the Weimar Republic—together with taking revenge on Germany's alleged internal enemies, especially the Jews.

Already in a speech delivered in September 1922, Hitler accordingly noted the following: "We must call to account the November criminals of 1918. It cannot be that 2 million Germans should have died in vain and that afterwards one should sit down as friends at the same table with traitors. No, we do not pardon, we demand–vengeance."[35] Hitler's followers will have known very well who these enemies were. With such revenge rhetoric, Hitler and other prominent Nazis fashioned themselves into leaders of a revolutionary movement aiming to free Germany from a shameful past and take the nation into a brighter future, in the process exercising revenge on those deemed responsible for Germany's gamut of problems.[36] In this context, songs played a basic role in disseminating the movement's message to ordinary Germans while fostering an experience of belonging, community, and comradeship among the party's members. When the party still amounted to a politically insignificant fringe phenomenon, one song in particular accompanied the marches of its brown-shirted members: *Deutschland Erwache* ("Awaken, Germany"). Also known as the "Storm Song" (the *Sturmlied*), the lyrics were written in 1919 by Dietrich Eckart, Hitler's confidant and mentor and soon the dedicatee of *Mein Kampf*, under the impression of his reading of the *The Protocols of the Elders of Zion*. These lyrics were an antisemitic version of the revolutionary *Hecker-Lied*, written in 1848 to 1849 by Friedrich Hecker, a popular liberal-left agitator in Germany's 1848 revolution. During the Weimar Republic, the *Sturmlied* would gain great popularity in right-wing circles. Consisting of two stanzas, the "Storm Song" called on Germans to "rave, rave in the thunder of revenge." When "Judas" (i.e. the Jews) came to conquer Germany, the lyrics exulted, they would encounter "burning, martyring, killing"; the earth would "tremble, under the thunder of delivering vengeance."[37] Widely included in song books of Hitler Youth, the party, and the paramilitary storm troopers (the *Sturmabteilung*; the SA), the "Storm Song" was later overtaken in popularity by the *Kampflied*—the "fight song" or "song of struggle"—written by SA leader Horst Wessel in 1929. When, the following year, communist opponents of the SA fatally shot Wessel, Joseph Goebbels turned Wessel into a martyr; the song, renamed the *Horst-Wessel-Lied*, now became the dominant hymn of the Nazi party. Predictably, the *Horst-Wessel-Lied* itself revolved around the idea that Germans were subjugated, in bondage, but about to be liberated: "The day of freedom and bread is dawning!" exclaimed the second stanza, while the third predicted that "[b]ondage [*Knechtschaft*] will only last for a short time!"[38] And stanza five offered the following proclamation: "The SA swears, clenching hand to fist/ The day will come, when there will be revenge, not forgiveness /When salvation and victory will sound through the fatherland!"[39] Yet another song, in a 1934 song book for Hitler Youth, edited by Hugo Wolfram Schmidt, echoed this quasi-salvational vengeful historical mission: "And if at some future date the day of vengeance approached, and the Fuehrer calls us to war, then we will carry the Swastika out of misery and disgrace from victory to victory. We march at dawn towards death for Hitler's flag."[40]

Once in power, in its efforts to destroy democracy, dismantle basic rights, and crush the political opposition through new laws, paramilitary organizations, and penal institutions (the concentration camps), the Nazi regime phrased many of its anti-Jewish measures as revenge on the Jews. For example, the nation-wide boycott of Jewish businesses on April 1, 1933 was framed as revenge on "international Jewry" for "atrocity propaganda" that victimized Germany.[41] In calling for a boycott of Jewish businesses in Munich, notorious *Stürmer* founder and editor Julius Streicher, Gauleiter of Franconia, a fanatic proponent of violent action against Jews, fused that call with a variety of the revenge theme troping luridly on religious anti-Judaism: "I do not ask you whether you are Catholics or Protestants, but if you are Christians, then I tell you: Golgotha has not

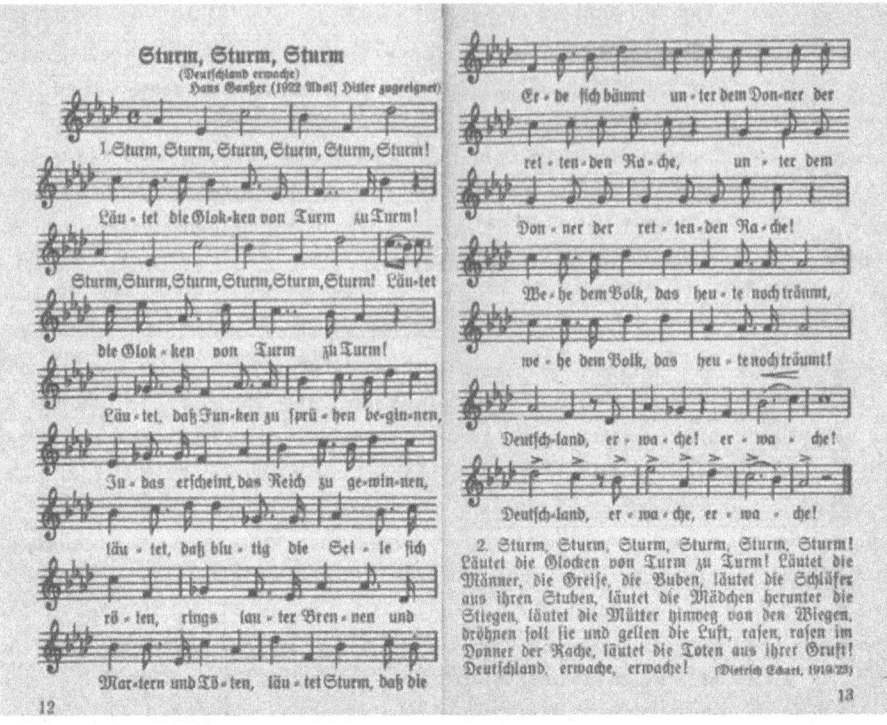

Figure 2 The "Storm Song," with lyrics by Dietrich Eckart and music by Hans Gansser, in the *Liederbuch der Nationalsozialistischen Deutschen Arbeiter-Partei* (Munich: Zentralverlag der NSDAP, 1938), public domain.

yet been avenged. But time brings its own revenge, and those who were responsible for Golgotha are already on their way to it."[42] Implicit here was the prediction that the Jews would pay for their sins with collective execution.

Revenge motives were also used in the context of the nation-wide pogrom of November 9–10, 1938 ("Kristallnacht"). Shortly beforehand, seventeen-year-old Herschel Grynszpan, a Polish Jewish student, had shot and killed Ernst vom Rath, a German embassy official in Paris; vom Rath was not a member of the Nazi party. The assassination was intended as vengeance for the suffering inflicted on many thousands of Polish Jews, including his parents, who had previously been living in Germany and now, under the threat of being stripped of Polish citizenship, had been expelled into an open area of the Polish-German frontier, where they were wandering around trapped, as Poland refused to take them in. Prominent leaders of the Nazi regime, especially Streicher and propaganda minister Joseph Goebbels, used the assassination as a pretext to organize nation-wide violence—propagated as a spontaneous expression of legitimate rage, and spontaneous German revenge for Jewish anti-German aggression[43]—targeting Jews, synagogues, Jewish businesses, homes, and property. The pogrom resulted in nearly a hundred deaths, and many more cases of physical assault, humiliation, and sexualized violence, with over 7,500 (perhaps even 10,000) Jewish shops destroyed and hundreds of private homes vandalized and demolished, and synagogues across Germany set ablaze, destroying 275 of them; over 25,000 Jewish men were arrested and transported to concentration camps in Germany.[44]

In her diary, the Berlin journalist and anti-Nazi Ruth Andreas-Friedrich noted that some Germans understood Grynszpan's deed, compassionately, as a "revenge-act of tortured Jewry on the Nazi regime."[45] She also noted that some of her Jewish acquaintances expected that Nazi propagandists would have vom Rath die whether he survived the attack or not, as "otherwise there would be no value. To avenge him, he would need to be mourned first. The greater the grief, the more fanatic the hatred."[46] In the pogrom's course, the destroyed fronts of vandalized Jewish-owned stores were smeared with graffiti such as—to cite from an American consular report—"'Revenge for the murder of vom Rath', 'Death of international Jewry.'"[47] When the Nazi party investigated twenty-six of its members for raping four Jewish women and murdering nineteen other Jews without clear orders and authorization, the party-court punished the sexual violence— by either party-exclusion or prohibition from holding public office—as a violation of Nazi anti-miscegenation laws; but it dropped most of the murder cases, on grounds that the perpetrators had no criminal motives. Rather, as recorded in the party-court's accompanying "secret report," the reasoning was that they had acted in good faith, interpreting the will of party leaders, especially Goebbels, who could have stopped killings but had made statements to the effect that even murderous violence was justified, even desirable.[48] The murders were, the report concluded, "motivated by hatred against Jews or in the opinion that vengeance ought to be taken for the death of Party Member von [sic] Rath upon the wish of the leaders."[49] Individual party members were not to be held accountable for these murders because "a series of subordinate leaders understood some unfortunately phrased orders which reached them orally or by phone, to mean that Jewish blood would now have to flow for the blood of Party Member von [sic] Rath," and that "the leadership did not attach importance to the life of a Jew, for example, not the Jew Grynszpan but all Jewry was guilty of the death of Party Member von [sic] Rath, the German people were therefore taking revenge on all Jewry. . . ."[50] Individual Germans were thus not meant to be held accountable for acting out of revenge, even if the action turned murderous.

In the pogrom's wake, propagandistic outlets portrayed Jews as aggressively vengeful, and as such, a menace to the existence of the German people. For the SS-periodical *Das Schwarze Korps*, Jews "not only secure their existence by committing crimes but . . . are furthermore intent on exacting revenge" and they had incited the nations to wage "a war of revenge against us."[51] Speaking the day after the pogrom to a large crowd of 100,000 Nuremberg residents,[52] Streicher used vom Rath's death to cast Jews as full of hatred and vengeance, now drawing on the trope of victim-aggressor reversal in life-and-death circumstances: "From the cradle," he exclaimed in a publicly delivered speech in Nuremberg, "the Jew is not taught, as we are, such texts as 'Thou shalt love thy neighbor as thyself' or 'Whosoever shall smite thee on thy right cheek, turn to him the other also.' No, he is told 'With the non-Jew you can do whatever you like.' He is even taught that the

Jewish Revenge and the Holocaust

Figure 3 "Jewish Cry for Vengeance!," front page of the Nazi publication *Der Stürmer*, no. 4, January 1939; USHMM Photo Archives # 31520. United States Holocaust Memorial Museum, courtesy of Virginius Dabney.

slaughtering of a non-Jew is an act pleasing to God." Streicher then offered "examples" of Jewish revenge from the "Old Testament" and Book of Esther:

> The Jew slaughtered in one night 75,000 Persians [a reference to the Purim story; more on the cited number below]; when he emigrated from Egypt he killed all the first-born, that is, a whole future generation of Egyptians. What would have happened if the Jew had succeeded in driving the nations into war against us, and if we had lost the war? The Jew, protected by foreign bayonets, would have fallen on us and would have slaughtered and murdered us. Never forget what history teaches.[53]

Drawing on ancient Hebrew narratives, Streicher's implicit message thus involved, here again, legitimacy: that Germany's November 9–10 violent and deadly nation-wide orgy of Jew-hatred was a legitimate counter measure to the threat of mass murder of Germans by Jews. This was also the message of the front-page article in the late-January 1939 edition of *Der Stürmer*. Written by the viciously antisemitic author and Nazi propagandist Ernst Hiemer, the article was entitled, "Jewish Cry for Revenge! The Ghastly Confession of a Jew." The accompanying caricature depicts Grynszpan as crucifying vom Rath with a caption reading as follows: "Crucifixion/ Will a world want to risk, for the sake of Judas/ The spilling of its lifeblood/ Whereby, once again, it will lose its best blood/ And Jewish sadism will triumph?"[54] We can note that *Der Stürmer*'s point—Streicher's lurid mix of modern and ancient Jew-hatred—is made all the more clear with the insertion of two additional crosses drawn next to crucified vom Rath. The periodical, Hiemer informed *Der Stürmer*'s readers, was in possession of a letter from a Palestinian Jew in Jerusalem that revealed Grynszpan's assassination to be part of a larger conspiracy by "world Jewry" to murder the German people. This meant, Hiemer warned, that the "Jewish problem" was "not yet solved, nor will it be solved when one day the last Jew will have left Germany. Only then, when world Jewry has been annihilated, will it have been solved."[55]

Der Stürmer was not an official Nazi party platform but was privately owned by Streicher; by January 1939 it had an estimated circulation of between 500,000 and 800,000 readers representing all social backgrounds and ages; it was also widely accessible as a wall newspaper publicly mounted in "Stürmer display boxes" across the country.[56] But *Der Stürmer* was no outlier. As Germany moved toward the war, the public rhetoric announcing annihilation of the Jews as retribution for claimed Jewish deeds became more frequent and explicit.[57] It came directly from Hitler: celebrating six years in office, on January 30, 1939 in a speech before the (nominal) Reichstag parliament in Berlin's Kroll Opera House, Hitler took up the theme of the Jews as posing a threat to Germany— and depicting them as, among other things, possessed by an "Old-Testament thirst for revenge."[58] Here, approximately seven months before Germany's attack on Poland, he blamed "world Jewry" for driving Germany into a war anticipated by the Jews. In this venue, Hitler adopted a distinctly genocidal tone, announcing, notoriously, that should the war turn out another "world war," it would result in the "annihilation of the Jewish race in Europe."[59] The speech was greeted by enthusiastic applause. At this point, there was not yet a concrete plan of annihilation. Nevertheless, functionally the speech was important not just as a threat. For in blaming a future war that Germany had been actively preparing (this at least since Hitler's 1936 Four-Year-Plan) on the Jews, Hitler could maintain an image of "pursuing peace" (as he had beforehand when annexing Austria, the Sudeten areas, and the so-called Protectorate Bohemia and Moravia)—Jewish aggression regrettably leaving no option other than defensive measures, for the sake of Germany. In rendering the idea of total Jewish annihilation conditional on the scope of forthcoming armed conflict, Hitler underscored the postulate that the annihilation would be a defensive measure: one meant to contain a conflict the Jews had unleashed. Here again, we find the claim of Jewry's responsibility for its own annihilation, annihilation as just retribution for wrongdoing, and Jews as posing a threat to both world peace and the existence of the German nation.

This message would then be carried forward, potently, in two notorious films propagating Jew-hatred released in 1940. *Jud Süß*, directed by the Nazi regime's most acclaimed director, Veit Harlan, at the behest of propaganda minister Goebbels, would be seen by some 20 million Germans and an equally large, enthusiastic audience elsewhere across Europe; along with helping mint public opinion, it thus would generate considerable revenue. Widely received as an artistically refined and realistic portrayal of the Jews,[60] it premiered at the Venice film festival, where it was awarded a Golden Lion. Goebbels would laud *Jud Süß* as "the first truly antisemitic film."[61] Himmler ordered it shown to SS and police forces in training.[62] Acclaimed officially and popularly in this manner, the film offered a viciously falsified historical picture of the famous eighteenth-century court Jew Joseph Süß Oppenheimer, who rose to great wealth and influence as a trusted financial adviser to Karl Alexander of Wurttemberg, a Catholic count. After Alexander's death in 1737, Oppenheimer lost protection and privilege. The following year, he was tried, sentenced to death by Protestant clerical officials on a range of charges (they included fraud, graft, and lechery), and hanged publicly, his corpse being left on public display for six years. Using famous German actors, Harlan's film made Oppenheimer's tragic history into a story about Jewish power, greed, wealth, corruption, criminality, discord-sowing, lecherous lust for "Aryan" women ("race defilement")—and vengeance.

In this way *Jud Süß* presents something like the full repertoire of antisemitic stereotypes. The revenge motif is established early on in the film, in a scene in which Oppenheimer has the house of a simple blacksmith, Hans Bogner, destroyed on account of the simple man's disagreement with his new tax policies. But occupying the film's center is the story of Oppenheimer's lascivious advances toward German non-Jewish Dorothea Sturm. After Dorothea rejects him and marries her fiancé—this following her father's refusal to grant Oppenheimer his daughter's hand, proclaiming "My daughter will not bear Jew-children"— Oppenheimer takes revenge by raping Dorothea. The scene, whose sexually explicit nature will have offended and titillated many viewers at the time, contains a dialogue between Oppenheimer and his victim in which she begs for mercy and begins to pray—Oppenheimer responding as follows: "Yes, pray to your God . . . we the Jews have a God too. It is the God of vengeance. And eye for an eye, a tooth for a tooth."

Although Süß rapes a married woman, previous scenes suggest the marriage has not yet been consummated. Unable to cope with the shame, Dorothea drowns herself, the local population then blaming her death on Oppenheimer and crying out for capital justice ("The Jew must go!"). Oppenheimer is seized and tried, the revenge motive reemerging when the court asks Dorothea's father to weigh in on the sentence. He declines to do so, explaining "an 'eye for an eye,' that isn't our custom." The court now sentences Oppenheimer to death—but not for rape, rather, in harmony with Nazi "race" laws, for having slept with a non-Jew; then he is hanged. *Jud Süß* does not, however, conclude with the hanging, but with a scene depicting the expulsion of the Jews from Stuttgart. Inevitably, the scene points forward, to later roundups of Jews for deportation: a stern warning to future German generations not to tolerate Jews in their midst, this accompanying Harlan's message that death is fair and legitimate deserts for "racial" and other Jewish crimes.[63]

By contrast with Harlan's *Jud Süß*, Fritz Hippler's film *Der ewige Jude* ("The Eternal Jew"; also 1940) claimed to be a documentary enlightening Germans about the manifold threats posed by the Jews—whether "visible Jews" rooted in tradition or their acculturated, "invisible" counterparts, poor or rich, socialist or capitalist, Jews as individuals and Jewry as a collective. Hippler, the head of the film division in Goebbels' Propaganda Ministry, used the opportunity to remind viewers of Jewry's vengeful character and present Jews as mass murderers. At one point, Hippler's film cited the Jewish holiday of Purim. (For context, Purim is a quasi-carnivalesque celebration of a mythic story, laid out in the Book of Esther. The story told is of Persian Jewry's rescue by Esther—a Jewish orphan who marries the Persian king—from a plot to annihilate all the Jews of Persia. At one point toward the end, the text references the aforementioned killing of 75,000 Persians[64]—as it were, an arbitrary revenge-fiction number—who were allied with the villain Haman plotting the annihilation. The story in any case has a happy ending: the Jews' deliverance through Esther's exposure of the wicked plot and the king's recognition of the Jews' right to protection and self-defense against those harming them.) The film commented as follows: "the ancient race of Israel is still rubbing its hands over its feast of revenge, even when dressed in west European garb, hiding its murderous nature."

In *Der ewige Jude*, Jews are equated with pests and rats—and ascribed with inhumane vengeful cruelty toward both human beings and animals. The film's narrative peak is a long scene grotesquely depicting the Jewish ritual slaughter of cattle and sheep, the implication here and throughout being that non-human Jewish violence has to be turned against the Jews: again the ubiquitous trope of legitimate and necessary self-defense. At the film's conclusion, viewers were presented with a contrast between the ritual-slaughter scene and Hitler's "prophesy" of the annihilation of the Jews of Europe.

Der ewige Jude was in any event far less popular than *Jud Süß*—but not because of its falsity and defamation. Rather, viewers were repelled, despite initial enthusiasm, by the ugly scenes they had to endure, the sight of rats and dying animals.[65] Still, over a million viewers paid to see Hippler's film; its message was also disseminated through non-commercial distribution among Hitler Youth and Wehrmacht.[66] It thus did manage to help shape public perception, including soldiers involved in the genocide being carried out in occupied eastern Europe.

Revenge Motives in the Killing Fields of Occupied Eastern Europe

Hitler's January 1939 speech became a frame of reference for later genocidal actions, as well as for rationalizing by the perpetrators. Key figures in the regime, including Goebbels and Hitler himself looking back, referred to the speech as a "prophecy"; in this way they reflected the quasi-religious nature of the "redemptive path" Hitler was seen as taking to settle the "Jewish question" once and for all.[67] Goebbels thus noted in a diary entry for June 20, 1941—that is, two days before the German attack on the Soviet Union marking the start of systematic mass murder—that "Jewry in Poland is gradually going to the dogs. A just punishment for the way it has caused disruption among nations and has intrigued to unleash this war. The Führer, of course, prophesied this fate for the Jews";[68] he would use the same prophecy-trope to make the same basic point in two later entries.[69] Five months after the June 1941 entry, on November 16, 1941—by then preparations for the first death camp in occupied Poland were underway, mass shootings, of Soviet Jews and of Jews in the first transports from the Reich and Protectorate, had become a general practice and Goebbels knew of Hitler's and Himmler's plans to extend the mass murder to the Jews of Europe—in an article in *Das Reich* entitled "Die Juden sind schuld!" ("The Jews are guilty!") Goebbels accordingly proclaimed: "we are seeing the fulfillment of this prophecy. The fate that is befalling the Jews is certainly harsh but more than deserved."[70]

The article was distributed in Berlin as a leaflet.[71] It amounted to an implicit confirmation, lacking details of where and how, that the annihilation of the Jews was actually being carried out—and was also a declaration that the Jews were responsible for their own destruction:

> Every Jew is our enemy in this historic conflict, regardless of whether he sits vegetating in a Polish ghetto, or carries on his parasitic existence in Berlin or Hamburg, or blows the trumpets of war in New York or Washington. All Jews, by virtue of their birth and their race, are part of an international conspiracy against National Socialist Germany. They want its defeat and annihilation and do all in their power to bring it about. The fact that they can find little opportunity to do so within the Reich . . . results from the fact that we took the measures we deemed appropriate against them.[72]

The defensive measures vaunted by Goebbels included turning an alleged Jewish principle of vengeance against the Jews: "World Jewry erred completely in its calculation of the forces at its disposal for instigating this war and now is gradually experiencing the process of annihilation that it planned for us and would have carried out without a second thought if it had possessed the ability. It is perishing according to its own law: 'an eye for an eye, a tooth for a tooth.'"[73] Following this insidious logic, he could declare that "here pity or even regret is entirely unmerited,"[74] especially, as he laid out the genocidal syllogism, in face of Jewish *manipulation* of German compassion through images of women, children, and the elderly, in reality merely pretending to be harmless civilians. Here again, Goebbels proposed a radical and depraved reversal: "For their sake alone," he exclaimed, "we must win the war. If we lose it, these harmless-looking Jewish chaps would suddenly become raging wolves. They would attack our women and children to exact revenge."[75] Goebbels' conclusion: there was "no turning back in our battle against the Jews—even if we wanted to, which we do not. The Jews must be removed from the German community for they endanger our national unity."[76]

In arguing for utter mercilessness, Goebbels presented pseudo-historical examples of merciless Jewry in the Soviet Union: "There are enough examples in history. That is what they did in Bessarabia and the Baltic states when Bolsheviks marched in, though neither the people nor the governments had done anything to them."[77] Similar ideas had already been expressed by Engelbert Huber, among others, in a book he published in 1933 on the Nazi party's ideology and structure: blaming socialist revolutions on the Jews, he claimed that in Russia, "Jewish criminals . . . slaughtered all of the bourgeois intellectuals—nearly two million people—out of cruelty and revenge . . ."[78] Two weeks after his November 16 article, Goebbels gave a lecture at the University of Berlin to an audience representing party, Wehrmacht, industry, press, and academia; he explicitly stated that the Jews faced a "gradual process of extermination [*Vernichtungsprozeß*]," as payback for having caused this war: "historical guilt of world Jewry for the outbreak and expansion of this war has been so extensively demonstrated that there is no need to waste any more words about it. The Jews wanted their war, and now they have it." The annihilation, Goebbels stated, that the Jews had intended for the Germans was now turned on them; Jews were "now perishing as a result of Jewry's own law: 'An eye for an eye, a tooth for a tooth.'"[79] By late 1941, alongside Goebbels various other prominent Nazi party figures were now openly proclaiming the need to "defensively" exterminate the Jews. For instance, a few days after Goebbels' November 16 article, Nazi party propagandist Alfred Rosenberg, recently appointed Reich Minister for the Occupied Eastern Territories, echoed Goebbels' ideas: for Rosenberg, the failed German revolution of November 9, 1918 was proof that the Jews

> were focused on the destruction of Germany. That this did not succeed is due only to the Führer and the strength of character of the German nation; therefore we must prevent a romantic [future] generation in Europe from accommodating the Jews again. And for that purpose, it is necessary to push them across the Urals or to bring about in some other way their eradication [*zur Ausmerzung zu bringen*].[80]

At this point, German forces had already murdered 1.5 to 2 million Jews in Latvia, Lithuania, Belorussia, Ukraine, and other parts of the Soviet Union. Following Germany's invasion on June 22, 1941, SS-Einsatzgruppen squads, assisted by some Wehrmacht units and police battalions and local collaborators, killed unarmed Jewish civilians by shooting, initially targeting men and people with political functions. As German forces swept through the Soviet Union's northern, western, and southern areas, they increasingly targeted *all* Jews; this marked the beginning of systematic mass murder. In late September 1941, members of *Sonderkommando* (SK) 4a of Einsatzgruppe C, assisted by the 3rd Waffen SS Company, Police Battalions 45 and 303, and local volunteers shot 33,773 Kievan Jews at the Babi Yar ravine in twenty-four hours.[81] In their mass murders, the SS-Einsatzgruppen squads were guided by Nazism's ideological obsession with destroying the Soviet Union: this both as part of a German quest for *Lebensraum* and out of a belief in the nexus between Jews and communism. Since within the Nazi Weltanschauung Jews were collectively responsible for communism, destroying the Jewish population served, among other things, to destroy communism, thus assuring survival of the German nation and "Aryan" culture. Here as well, a basic conceptual structure of "defense"-centered role-reversal fulfilled a key function in the perpetrators' justification for their horrendous mass crimes.

Ten days after the Babi Yar massacre, in his infamous "orders for conduct in the East," Field Marshall Walter von Reichenau, commander of the 6th Army of Army Group South, a close confidant of Hitler, told his men that they were exacting a "just revenge on subhuman Jewry." Moreover, he indicated, they were waging a "war against the Jewish-Bolshevistic system," with the aim of the "complete destruction of [Jews' and Bolsheviks'] means of power and the elimination of Asiatic influence from the European culture." For Reichenau, German soldiers were meant to "fulfill our historic task to liberate the German people once and for all from the Asiatic-Jewish danger." This, according to Reichenau, required a type of warfare exceeding "the one-sided routine of soldiering." Soldiers in the eastern occupied territories were not fighters "according to the rules of the art of war but also a bearer of ruthless national ideology and the avenger of bestialities which have been inflicted upon Germany and racially related nations." Moreover, the army sought "the annihilation of revolts in the hinterland, which, as experience proves, have always been caused by Jews."[82] Reichenau's rhetoric militarized unarmed Jewish civilians, holding them collectively responsible for anti-German resistance and for the Soviet system that the Germans set out to destroy. Here again, we find moral inhibitions against killing women, children, the elderly, and civilians in general evaporating through recourse to Nazism's ideological argument that destroying the Jews as a group was a necessary measure of self-defense. For Reichenau as for the party propagandists, German troops who murdered unarmed Jews were avengers of Jewish anti-German aggression.[83]

Such antisemitic fixations were not limited to German perpetrators. Collaboration in the mass murder took place in all of Europe's German-allied and occupied countries, but especially in areas previously under Soviet occupation, where some residents had greeted the Germans as liberators; at times the local murders were a communal initiative, with no or little German participation, the concept of Judeo-Bolshevism motivating and justifying these actions. For example, revenge on Jews for perceived collusion with the Soviets[84] was a central motivation for a pogrom in the town of Jedwabne, in eastern Poland, where, on July 10, 1941, Catholic Poles rounded up and forced their Jewish neighbors into a barn, which they set on fire.[85] The motive was also manifest in other

Figure 4 Men reading *Der Stürmer* at a display box, Worms, 1935; display boxes typically featured the slogan "The Jews are our misfortune" and this one also says "With the *Stürmer* against Juda [i.e. the Jews]"; Bundesarchiv 133-075; courtesy of Bundesarchiv.

pogroms, neighbors murdering their Jewish compatriots in broad daylight on their own behest, with participation by civilian men and women of all ages—for example in Kovno and Lvov in late June and early July 1941.[86] The idea of taking revenge on Jews was also one factor for local participation by collaborators in roundups and mass shootings; other factors were political (the killings seen as part of the fight against the Soviet Union and a national struggle for independence), personal (opportunism; careerism; the simple assertion of power), and material (the chance to steal Jewish property; other possibilities for personal enrichment).[87] In the summer of 1941, the willingness of local non-Jews to initiate and participate in pogroms, and to enlist as helpers and executioners for the SS-Einsatzgruppen squads, the Wehrmacht, and German police battalions, contributed to the loss of inhibitions and radicalization of German forces in territory conquered from the Soviet Union, so that what initially was the killing of Soviet functionaries and male Jews became the indiscriminate mass murder of all Jewish civilians.[88]

A top-secret, detailed, Einsatzgruppen "operational situation" report dated October 12, 1941 indicated that the shooting of over 51,000 mostly Jewish civilians at the hands of the members of *Einsatzkommando* (EK) 4a of Einsatzgruppe C—it swept through northern Ukraine from Sokal over Kiev to Kharkov—was motivated by the wish to eliminate "political officials, looters and saboteurs, active Communists and political representatives ... undesirable elements, partisans ... dangers of plague and epidemics ... rebels and agitators, drifting juveniles, Jews in general." The report also mentioned "Jewish sadism and revengefulness" as one source for the Einsatzkommando's mass murder.[89] The complete irrationality and radically ideological nature of that argument becomes particularly obvious in the context of the shooting to death of Jewish children. Some killing-squad members found this harder to stomach than killing adults—the children could, after all, hardly be accused of anti-German resistance or of building the Soviet system. SS leaders, concerned about the mental health of the men in their firing squads, then argued that shooting children to death alongside adults was a pre-emptive measure, taken to ward off potential future revenge acts by Jews.[90] For example, during the 1947 trial of SS-Einsatzgruppen leaders at Nuremberg, one of the American prosecutors, James Heath, asked defendant Otto Ohlendorf, the former head of Einsatzgruppe D, whether he agreed that there was "absolutely no rational basis for killing children except genocide and the killing of races." Ohlendorf disagreed: the murder of children, he replied, was "very simple to explain," considering that German forces sought to achieve "permanent security." Children were murdered because otherwise they "would grow up and surely, being the children of parents who had been killed, they would constitute a danger no smaller than that of the parents."[91]

The same rationale was offered by some of the defendants in the Einsatzgruppen trial of 1958 in Ulm, one of the ten defendants explaining that children had to be killed "so that they would not make difficulties later for our grandchildren."[92] Some killing-squad members traced this rationale back to Heinrich Himmler himself. Defendant Erwin Schulz, SS-Brigadeführer and commanding officer of EK 5 of Einsatzgruppe C, thus recalled that from August 1941 his unit had been instructed—through the command chain of Himmler, Higher SS and Police Leader Friedrich Jeckeln, and the commander of Einsatzgruppe C, Otto Rasch—to shoot and kill entire populations of Jews: "Only in cases where Jews were required for purposes of labor, consideration as to their executions should be given. Jewish women and children were, if necessary, to be shot as well, in order to prevent acts of revenge."[93] Himmler, concerned with the psychological toll that the shooting of women and children took on the shooters, emphasized the revenge-prevention argument during his visits to execution sites on conquered Soviet territory, as in mid-August 1941 when he visited Belorussia and attended a mass shooting of partisans and Jews near Minsk.[94] He returned to the theme when addressing senior SS members and other Nazi luminaries in two notorious speeches delivered in Posen on October 4 and 6, 1943. Germans murdered Jews, he declared, to protect their own people from Jewish aggression, committing those murders "in the spirit of love for our people"[95]; since it was a legitimate act of self-defense, they had not compromised their moral integrity: "our men and leaders suffered no harm to spirit and soul," he stated.[96] Himmler here specifically addressed the ongoing slaughter of Jewish children, again using the prospect of future Jewish revenge to justify a total genocide: "I did not feel that I had the right to exterminate the men—that is to murder them, or have them murdered—and then allow their children to grow into avengers [*die Rächer in Gestalt der Kinder*], threatening our sons and grandsons. The hard decision had to be made: to let this people vanish from the earth."[97]

In this manner, Himmler, Ohlendorf, and other mass murderers interpreted their own participation in horrific crimes—and the overriding mass crime of the "final solution"—as legitimate, within the framework of their own, ideologically constructed worldview; in doing so, they defined their criminal actions as a moral endeavor. They thus applied, on the ground, a trope that had become well-established in the Nazi propaganda effort since the party's inception, the aggressor-victim role-reversal that justified, from the start, plunder and murder of Jews as a patriotic duty. With an argument of Jewish aggression in the present more difficult to make in the case of children, prevention of future revenge served a crucial purpose.

Walter Mattner, a police secretary from Vienna, can serve as one example located on a lower level than Himmler or Ohlendorf. Mattner wrote to his wife Elisabeth about his participation in the shooting of over 2,208 Jews from Mogilev on October 2 and 3, 1941 by members of EK 8 of Einsatzgruppe B led by Otto Bradfisch and Arthur Nebe respectively, SS and police personnel (like Mattner) in the employ of Higher SS and Police Leader Erich von dem Bach-Zelewski, Police Battalion 322 and Ukrainian auxiliary police.[98] Initially, he recounted, his "hand was slightly trembling, but one gets used to this." After shooting nine truckloads of Jews, he continued, "I was already aiming more calmly and shot securely at the many women, children, and infants." Mattner, a thirty-six-year-old father of two, then explained to his wife that he was only protecting their own two children, "to whom these hordes would do the same, if not ten times worse."[99] Perhaps surfacing in Mattner's case was the ancient Christian ritual-murder fantasy of Jews murdering Christian children, absorbed with other such tropes into the Nazi antisemitic imagination.[100] Sharing his experience with his wife, seeking her approval, Mattner revealed no qualms whatsoever regarding any lost moral integrity—but rather, like Himmler, the opposite: the mass murder was *more* ethical than what his victims would have perpetrated, had the power relation been reversed.[101] For Mattner, his participation in the killing of Jewish children was nothing less than a heroic act, paternal protection of his own offspring from vengeful future slaughter by his Jewish victims.

This points to the immense concrete power of the propagandistic role-reversing defense trope that had been circulating over years, so it became a self-evident justification for monstrosity. Using a self-confirming logic and accompanying rhetoric, perpetrators such as Mattner disconnected themselves from the moral reality of their actions. Much of the self-confirmation centered on the need to be emotionless, unsentimental, and manly. It was accompanied by self-praise—for courage and bravery—and self-pity—for *having* to perpetrate a genocide, for the sake of national self-defense and the greater good of humanity. For example, in March 1942, after the United States had entered the war, the conditions for a world war thus being fulfilled, and after the mass murder of Jews had been extended to a global policy, Goebbels noted in his diary: "A judgment is being visited upon the Jews that, while barbaric, is fully deserved by them. The prophesy which the Fuehrer made about them for having brought on a new world war is beginning to come true in a most terrible manner." As if he still needed to convince himself, he continued as follows: "One must not be sentimental in these matters. If we did not fight the Jews, they would destroy us. It's a life-and-death struggle between the Aryan race and the Jewish bacillus." Then came the self-praise, tinged with self-pity: "No other government and no other regime would have the strength for such a global solution of this question." World Jewry had instigated the war, he added; this had to be "paid for dearly" by its European representatives, "and that's only right."[102]

In a pair of diary entries written nearly nine months later, Goebbels again took up both sides, German and Jewish, of the vengeance trope: "[T]he Jewish race has prepared this war," he ranted, "it is the spiritual originator of the whole misfortune that has overtaken humanity. Jewry must pay for its crime just as our Fuehrer prophesied in his speech in the Reichstag; namely, by the wiping out of the Jewish race in Europe and possibly in the entire world."[103] A few days later he continued in a second entry, "The Jews of Jerusalem have held noisy demonstrations of protest against us. They had a day of fasting. At the Wailing Wall they invoked the Old Testament Jewish curse against the Fuehrer, Goering, Himmler, and me." But he noted, "[u]ntil now I haven't noticed any effect on me."[104]

When the war—proclaimed by the Nazi leadership to have been caused by the Jews, for which they were now paying with their destruction—became more difficult for German forces, the Nazi propaganda machinery resorted to three tactics closely connected to fantasies of revenge. For one, it militarized the Jews, turning unarmed Jewish civilians into combatants collectively responsible for partisan and other anti-German resistance. In a diary entry of March 16, 1942, Goebbels noted that according to a report of the SD (i.e., the Security Service, the intelligence branch of the SS) about the situation in the occupied parts of the Soviet Union, partisan resistance had increased, and the partisans were "conducting a well-organized guerrilla war. It is very difficult to get at them because they are using such terrorist methods in the areas occupied by us that the population is afraid of collaborating with us loyally any longer." For Goebbels both the source of the situation and its solution was clear: "The spearheads of this whole Partisan activity are the political commissars and especially the Jews. It has therefore proven necessary once again to shoot more Jews. There won't be any peace in these areas as long as any Jews are active there." He added "Sentimentality is out of place here. Either we must renounce the lives of our own soldiers, or we must uncompromisingly prevent further propaganda by criminal and chaotic elements in the hinterland."[105] Often, German forces retaliated for sabotage acts and partisan killings of German soldiers with revenge murder of civilians at a ratio of 1:50 or 1:100.[106] By the end of 1941, German forces had murdered 100,000 civilians, including many Jews, in anti-partisan reprisal acts across German-occupied territory, but particularly in Serbia, Belorussia, and central Russia. Moreover, they had murdered 2 million Soviet POWs and 900,000 Soviet Jews in mass shootings.[107] At this point in the war and going forward, revenge murder of unarmed civilians became an integral part of Germany's brutal warfare and relentless response to anti-German resistance.[108] The June 10, 1942 razing to the ground of the Czech village of Lidice as revenge for the May 27, 1942 assassination attempt and subsequent death of SS-Obergruppenführer Reinhard Heydrich—head of the SS and police administration Reich Security Main Office (RSHA), the SD, the Security Police, and the SS-Einsatzgruppen and thus a central decision-maker in the planning and implementation of the Holocaust, and also Reich Protector of Bohemia and Moravia—became a symbol of this practice. On direct orders of Hitler, the men among Lidice's 503 inhabitants were executed; women were deported to the Ravensbrück concentration camp and some onward to Auschwitz; and less than 20 children considered "racially valuable" were forced into "Germanization" through adoption by German families, while over 80 children were murdered at the Chelmno death camp. A similar reprisal action took place two weeks later, at the end of June 1942, in the village of Ležáky, in addition to a brutal crack-down on the Czech resistance throughout the Protectorate.[109] Heinrich Himmler, who ultimately blamed the Jews for the attack on Heydrich, also secretly vowed to avenge Heydrich's death with amping up deportations of Jews from across the Reich and German-occupied Europe to death camps. Belzec, Sobibor, and Treblinka, the "Operation Reinhard" camps where some 2 million Jews would be murdered between summer 1942 and fall 1943 were named in Heydrich's memory.[110]

A second propagandistic tactic was to reenforce the longstanding projection onto the Jews of German genocidal violence: the trope of Jews as mass murderers of men, women, and children was now underpinned with forensic evidence. In spring and summer 1943 German forces uncovered, investigated, and made public the mass graves of over 20,000 Poles massacred by the NKVD at Katyn in 1940 and 9,400 Ukrainians executed at Vinnitsa in 1937 and 1938 as part of Stalin's "great purge." Building on the fantasy of the Judeo-Bolshevik nexus, Nazi propaganda exploited the mass graves as tangible proof of *Jewish* aggression. In addition, in line with the propagandistic logic that "international Jewry" ruled Britain and the United States, the intensifying Allied air war on the German civilian population was presented as proof of Jewish atrocity and mass murder. Although the Nazi leadership tried to keep its concrete mass murder operations and facilities secret, knowledge of the Holocaust among the German population, both at home and on the fronts, became ever more widespread.[111] In response, Nazi propagandists worked to pre-empt and suppress any popular feelings of compassion or identification with the Jews by portraying Jews as perpetrators of mass violence, Germans as their present and future victims. Focusing on the false claim that Jews were bombing "Aryan" Germans and massacring eastern European Slavs was a way to deflect public attention from the ongoing systematic German genocide.[112] "'These shots are truly gruesome,'" Goebbels remarked in his diary after seeing photos of the mass graves at Katyn, photos presented for widespread viewing in the *Wochenschau*, the weekly German newsreel. "One hardly dares to imagine what would happen to Germany and Europe if this Asiatic-Jewish flood were to inundate our country and continent."[113] In his own diary, Alfred Rosenberg expressed the same view concerning what he termed the "Jewish killing spree" at Vinnitsa: if it were not for Germany's defense of Europe's eastern borders, he opined, "hundreds of thousands would take the same path to the mass graves as the victims of Vinnitsa."[114]

In this role-reversal and genocide inversion logic, the claim that Jews were mass murderers served, in turn, as a necessary basis for vengeance against the Jews. According to Nazi architect Albert Speer—Hitler's close confidant and minister of armament and munition—that logic was maintained as something akin to a belief principle by Hitler himself: it seems that after 1942, Hitler often spoke of the annihilation of Europe's Jews as necessary revenge for the death of German women and children in Allied bombings.[115] It was in any case a core element of the most virulent antisemitic propaganda. On August 12, 1943, writing in *Der Stürmer*, Martin Froehling appealed to that publication's many readers as follows: "Let us remember that all the victims of Jewish hatred in German towns, in the graves of Katyn and Vinniza and all those mass graves which are still unknown today, the victims of the world war launched by the Jews, are crying out for revenge. When the hour of revenge strikes," Froehling continued, "we shall not let ourselves be softened by sentimentality! ... our hearts must be and remain hard and must know no other sentiment and no other emotion." And he explained why this was so by echoing the tropes of Jewish vengefulness as racial trait and historical fact necessitating Germans' revenge on the Jews:

> Let us not forget that the Jew has to pay for all the misdeeds he has committed against humanity during thousands of years! Let us remember that the Jew himself has passed sentence upon himself in his own laws: An eye for an eye, a tooth for a tooth! Let us oppose his criminal hatred with our great, sacred hatred! ... Juda must feel and realize that the hour of retribution and settlement has come, and that nothing will be forgotten and forgiven. Juda will then reap the hatred it has sown for centuries. Through this hatred Juda must perish.[116]

Painting Jews as mass murderers not only served to legitimize the mass murder of Jews; it was also a way—and this was the third propagandistic tactic—to mobilize the increasingly war-weary German population for the war effort. In the last two years of the war, much of Nazi propaganda thus focused on painting a picture of Jewish aggression and revenge, fostering a sense of forthcoming German annihilation *unless* Germany should win the war. Following the German defeat at Stalingrad in February 1943, the staggering German military losses at the eastern front began to affect every family; along with civilian losses due to Allied bombings of German cities, they created a sense of doom among the population and a loss of confidence in the "final victory."[117] Accordingly, starting with his call for "total war" in February 1943, Goebbels, together with other Nazi leaders, worked to kindle fears of that loss and bolster a sense of victimhood, for the sake of prompting Germans to fight with all means and at all costs.[118] The regime also ramped up its antisemitic messaging,[119] hammering home to every German: the Jews caused this war; the Jews are guilty of German suffering and loss; unless the Jews are punished with annihilation and this war fought by any means necessary, the German nation faces annihilation, Katyn and Vinnitsa style. Thus, again, the propagandistic leitmotiv was: annihilating the Jews was self-defense; but now it also deflected the responsibility that it succeed away from the regime's leaders onto the *Volksgemeinschaft*, the "people's community," planting the seeds of a sense of collective guilt.[120] Already earlier, in a Thanksgiving speech delivered on October 4, 1942, at the Berlin Sportpalast (an indoor arena that accommodated an audience of 14,000), Hermann Göring had urged his listeners to "engrave it in their hearts" that if the war is lost you are exterminated. The Jew with his unvanquished hatred stands behind these ideas of extermination. . . . Let no one deceive himself with the belief that he can come and say 'I was always a good democrat under the vulgar Nazis.' The Jew will give them the same answer whether you say you were the greatest Jew-lover or Jew-hater. He will treat both equally because his vengeance is for the entire German people.[121]

No matter how individual Germans felt regarding events "in the east," Göring's October message went, all Germans were in this together, and were collectively responsible for winning that war or be destroyed. Starting with Hitler, the Nazi leadership was well aware that provided the perception of doom and looming annihilation by Jewish avengers could be kept alive and nurtured, the more desperate the German population became over military setbacks and losses, and the more traumatic the bombings, the more staunchly the populace would back a fight to win the war. But with the war situation worsening, Nazi leaders also feared that despite the relentlessly messaged role-reversal trope the populace would see a correlation between German atrocities against the Jews and Jewish revenge upon the Germans. On September 30, 1944, seven months before Germany's surrender, Otto Dietrich, head of the press office at the Propaganda Ministry, therefore instructed the journalists and editorial staff of thousands of newspapers across the country in a secret directive: "when emphasizing Jewry's past or present revenge plots, those who are less grounded in ideology, might get the impression that we provoked that 'revenge' through our, as the enemy claims, gruesome behavior toward the Jews. As is widely known, revenge requires a previous injustice." Dietrich thus advised journalists to "only speak of the Jewish plans for annihilation [*Vernichtungsplänen*] and keep emphasizing again and again that Jewry has always been the aggressive part and we found ourselves on a vital defensive with our measures."[122] Emerging here is a concern on the Nazi leadership's part with deflecting responsibility and stifling any sense among the population that Jewish revenge might not be a racial trait and historical behavior of the Jews but rather a relatable Jewish reaction to the reality of ongoing German crimes against Europe's Jews; therefore government messages kept emphasizing: the war had always been strictly one of self-defense; whatever the means resorted to in defense against the Jews, the Germans were collectively implicated; and they had collective responsibility for winning that fight—or being annihilated.[123]

Revenge Fantasies on the Fronts and at Home

Did these propagandistic arguments made by central figures and functionaries of the Nazi state resonate with the wider German population? Did ordinary Germans see Jews as vengeful and fear Jewish vengeance? Ego-documents and public-opinion reports from the last two war years suggest ideological indoctrination had indeed borne fruit over time and that many Germans firmly believed the regime's antisemitic propaganda.

However, they also suggest that toward the end of the war, many Germans had a genuine sense of guilt and shame for the persecution and mass murder of the Jews, although they did not necessarily empathize with Jews or directly question the persecution as such. For many, fear of Jewish revenge, together with a general sense of victimhood, stemmed from frustration, anxiety, and a real sense of disaster in realization that the war was lost—and that they had believed in and acted on behalf of the wrong kind of political regime.

Letters from soldiers and civilians representing all walks of German society, and secret public opinion reports show that average Germans internalized the antisemitic imagery that Nazi propaganda had been disseminating for years. For example, in letters to *Der Stürmer*,[124] the revenge topos makes many appearances; it is useful to take a closer look at the way it was articulated on this popular level. We find widespread, firm belief that the war that Germany was fighting, and which had become increasingly desperate, had been instigated by Jews; that Jews were responsible for communism; that Jews ruled both the Soviet Union and the other Allied nations;[125] that Jews were responsible for anti-German resistance and the partisan fight in the Soviet Union;[126] and that interethnic violence by local non-Jews against Jews, for instance in Romania, was payback for crimes the Jews had committed against these nations.[127] There was also widespread internalizing of the fundamental assumption that Jews were intent on destroying Germany—and that for just that reason, destroying the Jews through systematic mass murder was the only option.[128] In this respect, there was some referencing of Hitler's "prophesy."[129]

Writing to *Der Stürmer*, soldiers on the eastern front indicated that their experiences in the war in Poland, Ukraine, Belorussia, and Russia had proven everything that the Nazi government had ever told the German population about the Jews to be correct; some thanked *Der Stürmer* for its "educational work" and for having taught its readers to see "the world with different eyes."[130] In one reader's letter to that pornographically antisemitic, highly popular publication, Ernst Dreilich, an SA man, party member, and father of seven children from Bunzlau in Silesia, writing from Ukraine in September 1941, related that encountering Jews when fighting in Poland, France, and Russia was far worse than what he expected, making him realize that "there is no greater and holier task for us than the complete annihilation of Jewry." He believed that "in everything the German Wehrmacht will mete out a just punishment" upon the Jews. "Wherever this pest has been done away with," he summarized his observations from the field, "the [local] population breathes a sigh of relief."[131] A private writing from Ukraine reached the same conclusion: "I did not believe it until I came here. But now I understand and find it appropriate. There is only one option for Jewry here: annihilation." He believed that the Jews, through introducing communist rule, had destroyed the country and thrust it into chaos, backwardness, and a low standard of living. In his view, Jewry's guilt was "enormous, the suffering they caused inconceivable and their murdering devilish. It can only be expiated through their annihilation." He further indicated that until his experiences in the Soviet Union he had rejected the annihilation of the Jews as immoral but now he understood that there was no other way, "among this *Ostjudentum* [Eastern Jewry] lives the scum of all criminality and I am fully aware of the uniqueness of our mission . . ."[132]

Such letters reflect the above-outlined, broader framework of indoctrinated beliefs and assumptions. The fantasy of Germans as victims of Jewish genocide is directly expressed in another soldier's letter, written in May 1943, an Obergefreiter (senior lance corporal) of the 12th Panzer Division at the eastern front: the world, he indicated, was witnessing "the war of Jewry against the Aryan man, against everything that is, cleaner, more diligent, and more capable than the Jew. In Germany he found his fiercest opponent, whom he seeks to annihilate with the help of other Aryans [i.e., the Allies]." For this German soldier as for countless compatriots on the fronts and at home, the Jew did not "act as a fighter himself, instead he operates and incites in the background and is pulling the strings . . . He is using all means and all nations."[133]

The case of a schoolboy living in Chemnitz, nine-year-old Horst Schlegel, offers a rather dramatic example of the fact that the revenge topos was by no means limited to soldiers at the front. In April 1943, Horst wrote *Der Stürmer* to call for a fight against "world Jewry," as he explained it—for the sake of following their own principle of "an eye for an eye." In the neat handwriting of a middle-schooler, he thanked the paper for teaching him to see the Jews as his "mortal enemy," elaborating that "I am unable to muster more hatred and contempt against anyone than against that devilish Hebrew riffraff [*Hebräergesindel*] that has once again brought so much misfortune over our part of the world.[. . .] Give it to world Jewry, those devils in human appearance, tear the mask of falsehood off their ugly faces, expose them and their criminal book of laws, the Talmud! [. . .] At the end of this fight will and must be our victory over world Jewry [*Alljuda*]."[134] In June, another, adult reader, Johannes Gläser from Leipzig, wrote that with all Jews being criminals, "there can only be one answer": their "radical annihilation!" But Gläser believed that the Germans needed to postpone the annihilation until after the war had been won—this because currently there were too many German soldiers and civilians in Allied custody, and the Jews would avenge themselves if the annihilation were implemented in the here and now. Meanwhile, it was best for the Germans to make do and remove all Jews from their Lebensraum, interning them in camps. He advised that those who would need to fulfil this important task had to be "pitiless individuals acquainted with the Jewish question and the Jewish thirst for revenge [*Rachsucht*]."[135]

Another reader, an SA man from Gelsenkirchen and coal miner by profession, calling himself a "fanatical opponent of the Jews," suggested the opposite: namely to urgently carry out annihilation of the Jews before the end of the war, because there could be no "peace among nations," no *Völkerfrieden*, until all of Europe's Jews of had been "exterminated," *vernichtet*.[136] This view, conjuring future peaceful coexistence predicated on Jewish *Vernichtung*, was carried to a revenge-centered climax of hate in an anonymous letter by an ethnic German from Goldap, northeastern Poland, written to *Der Stürmer* on May 1, 1943. The Jews, he indicated, were responsible for the war; they had been waging it against the Germans using other nations as their tools. "Day after day," he spewed out, "it must be driven home to the world that the Jew is the world's corrupter, waging the war . . ." However: "this eternal criminal will finally be taken to task in the severest manner and eradicated root and branch!" The war, he continued, had only taken

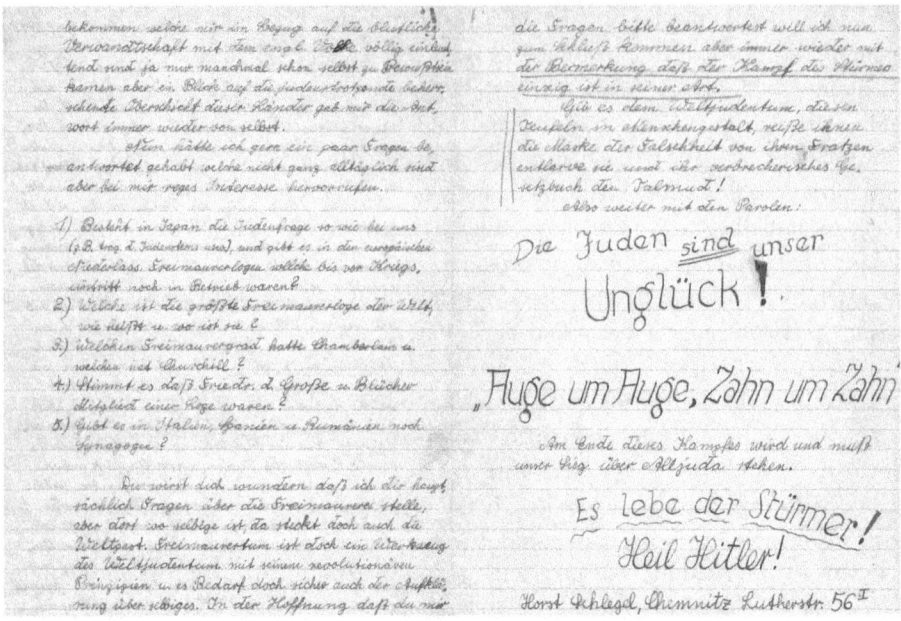

Figure 5 A page from nine-year-old Horst Schlegel's letter to the editor of *Der Stürmer*, April 9, 1943, Leo Baeck Institute Archives, New York, Bernhard Kolb Collection AR 360, series V, Stürmer Files; courtesy of Leo Baeck Institute.

"inhuman forms," with "women and children being butchered," because of the Jews; and further: "where the Jew cannot commit these murders himself, he is their instigator." As this letter-writer saw it, Jewish culture and Jewish law *demanded* that Jews murdered gentiles, a conclusion prompting his cry for vengeance: "Do we have to tolerate this people of murderers and criminals in Europe any longer? It is in our hands to give these criminals payback they have long deserved! Put them up against a wall and finish them off! For murderous arson and barbarism can only be fought measure for measure." And further, reading the Allied air war on German cities as a Jewish revenge plot against Germany: "the Jew will think ten times whether it is worth sending his arsonist pilots to Germany to murder women and children in peaceful places, if he has to fear that one Jew will be killed for every German murdered or wounded!!!" Finally, the writer referred to Katyn as an example of Jewish aggression, demonstrating that if Jews won the war, they would "perpetrate a bloodbath that the world has not yet seen! Hence away with them!" In light of Katyn, then, "every Jew, no matter where he is, has long deserved death!"[137]

Other letter-writers to *Der Stürmer* also referred to Katyn to explain why the Jews should be indiscriminately murdered, their children not spared.[138] At the time the letters were being written, in the summer of 1943, the Germans with the help of local collaborators had murdered around 4 million Jews from across the European continent. The consensus, expressed in letters by ordinary Germans to a widely circulating and widely read Nazi propaganda organ, that European and world Jewry necessarily had to be exterminated because of criminal plans to destroy the Germans reflected deep indoctrination into the ideological structure of role-reversal: the projection of German intent and action onto millions of their slaughtered victims.

Many, perhaps most, Germans saw a direct connection between annihilating the Jews and winning the war. Even some relatively moderate voices, critical of the war and aware of German responsibility, drew a connection to future accountability and revenge. For example, writing his brother from a camp for Soviet POWs on September 13, 1941, Dr. Konrad Jarausch, a high school teacher in Magdeburg before the war, exclaimed "[h]ow lovely it would be if this war could be followed by decades of peace for all of Europe. What we have seen here makes us wish even more fervently than before that the European peoples should have a time to heal their deep wounds and take on the tasks of peace," he continued. But for Jarausch, who had not been a member of any Nazi party organization, these hopes were clouded: "Sometimes I'm terrified by the thought that all these people whom we had to hurt and humble deeply, might at some time band together for revenge. My comrades usually say that when the Jews are gone, other forces will be able to determine things. But history . . . tells a different story."[139] Jarausch had already served in World War I; he was a Prussian patriot and committed Protestant. He had an anti-communist stance and prejudice against eastern European Jews, and against "the East" more generally, as was common among the educated Protestant middle class. He nevertheless did not lose his empathy for those victimized by the German campaign.[140] He learned Russian to converse with POWs he fed and whom he saw perish from malnutrition and disease by the thousands, until he himself died of typhoid fever in January 1942.

With Goebbels' "total war" propaganda and the growing military setbacks and losses the Germans faced from spring 1943 onward, fear of losing the war and suffering Jewish revenge and retribution—and such revenge and retribution from nations believed to be ruled by the Jews—intensified within the German army. Under the impact of the extended, brutal Battle of Stalingrad—it had cost some 1.8 million Axis and Soviet lives—in mid-February 1943 a Wehrmacht captain wrote as follows: "May God allow the German people to find . . . the peace of mind and strength" to be the "instrument needed by the Fuehrer to protect the West from ruin," because, he added, "what the Asiatic hordes will not destroy, will be annihilated by Jewish hatred and revenge."[141] The fear—as we have seen, already pervasive—that Germany *had* to win the war to prevent Jewish vengeance and destruction of the German nation, and Jewish rule over the world, now seems to have intensified.[142] Writing from Lyon, one soldier thus remarks that "it must in fact be the case that the Jew is behind everything, seeking to annihilate us and afterwards rule the world on its rubble. And this must not happen, come what may . . ."[143] A number of other soldiers' letters expressing the same basic, intense anxiety are extant; these certainly stand for the deep fear of Jewish revenge, and of the world succumbing to "Juda," felt by countless soldiers in the war's closing period.[144] Some soldiers expressed direct fear of becoming victims of what we now term genocide, a Wehrmacht private thus writing, in August 1944, that a lost war would mean that "we Germans will be irretrievably lost. The Jews are going to attack us and will exterminate everything that is German, it would be a horrific and cruel butchering [*Hinmorden*]."[145] Or, as one soldier succinctly put it on September 29, 1944, "The Jews will certainly seek retribution [and] they will recognize their enemies. . . . God's judgement is not yet over".[146]

The same fears were being expressed by German POWs in British and American custody, in conversations being carefully listened in on by their captors. Along with the depth of internalization of the vicious revenge-focused antisemitic propaganda, these conversations themselves reveal a strong element of self-pity—again showing the role-reversal trope in play. If the Nazi mass murder was criticized in these conversations, it was not because the genocide was morally wrong; rather, it was because of the unpleasant methods of killing, or else because of the consequences, now, for Germans—and the toll that future revenge would take on German lives. For example, an army lieutenant by the name of Priebe, conversing with his cell mate about the slave labor and mass shooting to death of Jews in Eastern Galicia in October 1943, remarked that "I don't believe anyone could hate or oppose Jews more than my father did, but he also said that the methods they used were horrible. . . . My god, if we ever have those people on top of us again!"[147] When conversing with a fellow POW in March 1945, captured Wehrmacht general Edwin Graf von Rothkirch und Trach confirmed his knowledge of the gassing of Jews and that he had personally seen mass shootings around Lemberg and Kutno; he again did not seem to question the mass-murder as such, but rather to abhor the practice of documenting the crimes—and then of not being more careful in whose hands the evidence would end up:

> Just think of it, some of these Jews got away and will keep on talking about it. And the craziest thing of all: how is it possible for pictures to get into the press? . . . They even filmed it, and the films, of course, have got abroad; it always leaks out somehow. . . . At some time the world will take revenge for that. If those people, the Jews, come to the helm and take revenge, it will of course be terrible.[148]

Von Rothkirch had a deep belief in the peril of Judeo-Bolshevism; the postwar future of the Germans, he felt, depended on whether they would be trusted by the Western Allies and seen as partners in the fight against the Soviet Union. Similarly with Wehrmacht Colonel Erwin Jösting. In a recorded conversation with another POW in April 1945, Jösting agreed that "Jews had to be turned out, that was obvious, but the manner in which it was done was absolutely wrong, and the present hatred is the result . . . I'd be first to agree to getting rid of the Jews; I'd show them the way – out of GERMANY! But massacre them?" He then clarified what he meant, to avoid misunderstanding: massacres could indeed take place "after the war, when we can say 'We have the power, we have the might; we've won the war; we can afford to do it!'"[149] For Jösting, then, it was all a question of manner and timing; things being what they were, the mistakes having been made, once the war was over, the Germans were bound to become victims of the Jews.

With Goebbels mobilizing the home front for what he declared, in a speech at the Berlin Sportpalast on February 18, 1943, to be "total war," Nazi propagandists intensified their attribution of German suffering and potential total defeat to the "Jewish war" against Germany.[150] Goebbels made clear once again, that there was a nexus between the struggle for survival of the Germans and elimination of the Jews.[151] Precisely because of that nexus and the looming worst case scenario that total war would lead to total defeat, many Germans—even some critical of the regime—understood the Allied bombing and Germany's increasingly alarming military situation to reflect, in one way or another, revenge by the Jews for the German persecution and mass murder. On March 3, 1943, after a heavy bombardment leaving "1,700 fires," the Berlin diarist Ursula von Kardorff noted that "[t]hroughout Berlin, the rumor spread that this attack was in retaliation for the roundup of Jews."[152] In this respect, an April 1944 public opinion report of the SD District Office in Bad Brückenau, Bavaria, remarked that many Germans expressed "the view that terror attacks," meaning the bombing of German cities, "especially on Frankfurt, are retaliation many times over for the 1938 Jewish action," that is the November pogrom. "Some say," the report further noted ". . . that our whole position on the Jewish Question, but especially its solution, was totally wrong, and the German people today has had to suffer the consequences. If they had let the Jews stay in the country, they say, no bombs would have fallen on Frankfurt."[153] Arguably, what we find here is an implicit acknowledgment of German guilt for the mass crime perpetrated on European Jewry; but any such acknowledgment was intertwined with the deeply internalized antisemitic stereotypes of Jewish power, revenge, and hostility toward Germany, together with the intensifying associated fears. In August 1944, a Nazi party report about the public mood in the area of Franconian Jura underscored these fears: if Germany were to lose the war, "Jewry will pounce on the German volk-body and realize all its devilish and bestial plans, as described in our press. Which is why we have the slogan: Death and destruction to the Jews – the future and life are ours!"[154] Also in August, a Wehrmacht private wrote his mother as follows:

> The war's approaching its end, but I don't think so for us. You know of course that the Jew is going to take his blood revenge, mainly against the Party people. Unfortunately, I was also one of those who wore the Party uniform. Matter of fact, I have already regretted it. Please get rid of that uniform, put it somewhere, anywhere, even if you burn all the stuff. I can no longer sleep well because of all this.[155]

Regret at party membership was not because of anything wrong with the party but because of looming Jewish revenge. In September, the Field Post Inspection Office intercepted a letter written to a gendarmerie police sergeant at the western front by his family in Germany: "Hitler has now been left in the lurch by many countries. He is surrounded by betrayal, and if the enemy continues in this way, we can almost predict what horrors shall befall us. If a miracle does not come to pass at the last minute, we are lost. Then probably the Jew will come in and in his manner, clean up and triumph in Germany."[156]

In this period, the Nazi regime was recruiting German civilians for the *Endkampf,* the final fight of the "people's community" against Allied troops closing in on Germany. Young boys and elderly men were being recruited for the *Volkssturm,* a militia under Nazi party auspices. From September 24, 1944 to the final days of the Nazi regime, a million older men and boys, insufficiently trained, poorly equipped, and often lacking coordination with Wehrmacht units, engaged in the German fight to ward off the Allied invasion.[157] Individuals signed up for the Volkssturm out of fear of social ostracization and communal punishment as well as of the approaching enemy armies; out of loyalty to Hitler; and out of belief in Nazi ideology. With German military losses in the war's last fifteen months (January 1944 through May 1945) higher than in the previous war years taken together—3.3 million out of a total of 5.3 million military deaths, and 1.5 million of them dying between January and May 1945 alone[158]—vengeance and accompanying atrocities were integral to the Endkampf. German civilians, including women and youths, were now committing brutal crimes at the home front—later to be labelled *Endphaseverbrechen*—motivated by a desire to settle scores with both perceived enemies from within and external enemies: foreign laborers; camp inmates;[159] downed British and American airmen, as many as 1,000 to 1,500 of whom were lynched, particularly in the war's final months.[160] Injured, isolated, and helpless airmen were targeted as Allied representatives, much of the violence explained by its perpetrators as revenge for the Allied air war on German civilians.[161] The internecine violence unfolding during the Endkampf was on an even wider scale: the period was marked by severe rifts in the "people's community," Germans turning on Germans over disloyalty to the collapsing regime, a pillorying of suspected defeatists, and lynchings, public hangings, and executions of both German civilians and Wehrmacht deserters.[162] Between January and May 1945, Wehrmacht courts sentenced circa 11,000 Wehrmacht deserters to death.[163] Of the 15,000 men executed for desertion during the war years, most were executed in the last eighteen months of the war, with an average of over 500 execution per month.[164] An even larger number of "defeatist" Germans were murdered by fanatic compatriots in extra-legal courts marshal, the ensuing public executions meant to intimidate the population into not surrendering to Allied forces.[165] In addition, civilians in rural areas violated emaciated concentration camp inmates as they were being moved away from the advancing Allied armies and marched westward into the German heartland on so-called death marches. Often SS guards relied on civilians to guard the prisoners and prevent escapes. On April 13, 1945, one day before the arrival of the US army, residents of Gardelegen in Saxony-Anhalt alongside SS guards massacred 1,016 prisoners of various nationalities evacuated from subcamps of Dora-Mittelbau and Neuengamme, locking them in a barn and setting it on fire.[166] Much of this violence accompanying the fierce final military confrontations inside Germany was motivated by either "active" or "passive" ideas of revenge: on the one hand, exacting vengeance on those seen as guilty of betraying the "people's community" in its final struggle, blurring the lines between different kinds of "enemies," Jewish as well as non-Jewish, German as well as foreign nationals; on the other hand the conspiratorial view of Jews as responsible for all and any harm, hardship and misfortune alongside the phantasmic fear, which we have seen as so pervasive throughout the Nazi years but now intensified to fever pitch, of "Jewish revenge" and its annihilation of Germany and the Germans.

At different stages in the persecution and mass murder of European Jewry, ideas of revenge served different sorts of enablers and perpetrators in both inciting violence against Jews and justifying it to themselves and others. Revenge rhetoric helped identify Jews as a threat to Germans and Germans as victims of the Jews; it served to legitimize persecution and dehumanization as both payback and self-defense.

As the revenge rhetoric unfolded through an enormous propaganda effort, Germans, with help from collaborators all over Europe, were murdering what turned out to be two-thirds of the European Jewish population, extinguishing the Jewish presence in parts of Europe where Jews had lived for centuries. In the Nazi killing fields and death camps, the rhetoric resonated with the perpetrators, helping in the rationalization of their horrendous crimes. The rhetoric also resonated at home, among the civilian population, and toward the end of the war even among Germans who did not consider themselves committed Nazis: after all, not only true believers in the Nazi cause suffered from fear of retribution. A capacity to acknowledge German agency and German crimes and feeling a certain amount of guilt did not necessarily mean absence of antisemitic stereotypes. The general sentiment was increasingly self-pity—a self-pitying anxiousness at perhaps now having to suffer repercussions for German deeds, *because* of the Jews. In this manner, the fears of suffering revenge felt by German soldiers and civilians alike, reveal the extent to which conspiracy-centered antisemitism had been internalized within broad strata of the population—so that, at the moment of collapse and defeat, the nation was united in belief in what had become, over the past twelve years, its own mendacious propaganda.

The Early Postwar Aftermath: "Jewish Revenge" in the Courtroom

Starting with the Nuremberg trials and continuing throughout the postwar decades, virtually no accused Nazi perpetrators took criminal responsibility in courts.[167] For its part, the early postwar German public by and large did not accept responsibility for the Nazi regime's crimes, blaming Nazi leaders, the SS, or select sadistic outliers; adults in defeated Germany tended to cultivate a sense of being victims, deserving to be left in peace after what they had endured. With little emotional capacity to confront themselves with the suffering they had caused across the European continent, Germans broadly rejected the Nuremberg and the other Nazi war crimes trials as "victors' justice"—and "revenge."

Although the defendants in the International Military Tribunal (IMT) trial at Nuremberg—twenty-two of the highest ranking Nazi leaders still alive and in Allied hands—were certainly aware that they might incriminate themselves if they voiced antisemitic sentiments too openly, they left no doubt they saw the trial as part of a "Jewish plot" against Germany.[168] This idea resulted from the Nazi axiom that the Allied powers were ruled by Jews. Accordingly, in the Nuremberg trial account of American court psychologist Gustave M. Gilbert (who himself was of Jewish background), we read that speaking with Gilbert, Julius Streicher declared the trial "a triumph of world Jewry."[169] Once the trial opened, Streicher complained to Gilbert that "they are crucifying me now ... I can tell. Three of the judges are Jews ... I can recognize blood."[170] When Gilbert visited defendant Robert Ley in his cell, before he committed suicide, Ley addressed him as follows: "If after all the bloodshed of this war some more s-sacrifices are needed to satisfy the v-vengeance of the victors, all well and good." Ley, we read, "now ... placed himself against the wall, crucifix-like" declaiming: "'Stand us against a wall and shoot us! – All well and good, you are the victors. But why should I be brought before a Tribunal like a c—, c—, like a c—, c—?'" (the word Ley could not bring himself to say would have been a "criminal").[171] Foreign minister Joachim von Ribbentrop himself believed the trial was controlled by Jews; "You have the power," he explained to Gilbert,

> and we cannot do anything about it—but it is so unwise to judge us in the midst of a war psychosis. It is not even wise for the Jews to express their hatred thus. I don't blame them a bit, you understand, but it is unwise—[...] Why can't the victors accept this as a historical tragedy that was inevitable, and try to work toward a peaceful solution?[...] It is no use heaping hatred upon hatred. It will hurt you in the end, I assure you.[172]

Other German observers complained about a large Jewish presence in the trial audience.[173] That was, in fact, not the case—neither at the court nor in the audience.[174]

While they had long considered summary executions, by spring 1945 the Allies had concluded that the enormity of the crimes required not just punishing those responsible but also offering a more public message concerning the nature and extent of crimes humanity could not afford to repeat. The Allied prosecutors built their cases carefully, based on millions of pages of documents produced mainly by the Nazi regime and bearing signatures of the defendants themselves; they also mainly used witnesses who were themselves committed Nazis, thus allowing the facts to speak for themselves. Aware that the defendants and the German public would reject their efforts as, precisely, victors' justice, the prosecutors and judges emphasized that the trial was not guided by vengeance but by fairness and due process. In his opening address on November 21, 1945, US Chief Justice Robert H. Jackson stated that the Allies "stay the hand of vengeance";[175] the British chief prosecutor Sir Hartley Shawcross spoke of victims "in their graves, crying out, not for vengeance but that this shall not happen again: 10 million who might be living in peace and happiness at this hour, soldiers, sailors, airmen, and civilians killed in battles that ought never to have been."[176] And similarly French chief prosecutor Auguste Champetier de Ribes:

> All the facts have been presented with strict objectivity, leaving no room for passion nor even for sensibility. The Tribunal have excluded from the proceedings

everything that, in their opinion, seemed insufficiently proved, everything that might have appeared to be dictated by a spirit of vengeance. For the chief concern of this Trial is above all that of historical truth. Thanks to it, the historian of the future, as well as the chronicler of today, will know the truth of the political, diplomatic, and military events of the most tragic period of our history; he will know the crimes of Nazism as well as the irresolution, the weaknesses, the omissions of the peace-loving democracies.[177]

The case against Julius Streicher was built on the claim that he, as editor of the widely-read *Der Stürmer*, had committed crimes against humanity by preparing the ideological grounds for the mass murder of the Jews and inciting Germans to participate in it. On January 10, 1946, British prosecutor Mervyn Griffith-Jones presented the evidence against Streicher; the presentation constituted a tour de force based on Streicher's own writings and speeches together with his weekly's violently antisemitic content. Griffith-Jones showed that the newspaper had used a wide spectrum of racial and religious antisemitic stereotypes, making use of a distinct genre of antisemitic caricature to transmit a specific the message: the Jews as functionally equivalent to everything evil, hence an exterminatory menace to the Germans. In his presentation, Griffith-Jones pointed to the use of revenge rhetoric in *Der Stürmer* as a tool for incitement—for example in the phrase "Revenge will break loose one day and will exterminate Jewry from the face of the earth."[178] Turning to the presiding judge Sir Geoffrey Lawrence, he argued as follows: "My Lord, it is my submission that that document is nothing but an incitement to the people of Germany who read it, an incitement to murder. It is filled with pictures of murder, murder alleged to be against the German people, and is an encouragement to all who read it to revenge themselves, and to revenge themselves in the same way."[179] Building on such dramatic evidence, later in the trial Griffith-Jones showed that Streicher had openly called for the extermination of all Jews while this was in fact taking place.[180]

Streicher and his defense attorney Hans Marx strenuously denied that Streicher had incited the German nation to mass murder: sharp language, the use of such vengeance-rhetoric, Marx argued, was only a way of speaking, not reflecting Streicher's real views.[181] Marx brought in Ernst Hiemer as a key defense witness. Hiemer himself had been the editor of *Der Stürmer*; he had authored some of its most venomous articles. He had also written the violently antisemitic children's book *Der Giftpilz*, conveying a range of vicious stereotypes of Jews to the youngest Germans, explaining to them that the Jews were "children of the devil" and that the world would find no peace until they had been annihilated. Hiemer defended Streicher's publication of *Der Stürmer* as merely having sought "to convey to every man and every woman of the German nation knowledge about the Jews. Streicher wanted the entire German people to realize that the Jew was a stranger among them."[182] Although the newspaper had indeed openly advocated the extermination of the Jews, Streicher, he claimed, had personally opposed it and thus had no role in the genocide. Streicher, Hiemer told the judges, had not known about the death camps until mid-1944—and then from the Swiss press. He had at first refused to believe it, rejecting it as a way to besmirch the good name of the German Volk; but then, he explained, Streicher had undergone a change of heart and opposed the mass murder. Streicher had "definitely deprecated what was done in the concentration camps. It did happen that Streicher, in anger—if he had been especially upset by political events—often or at times, asserted that Jews, as an enemy of the German people, should be exterminated. However, Streicher talked in that way only in the first phase of excitement. When he was calmed, he always opposed the extermination of the Jews."[183]

In this manner, Hans Marx tried to separate the objective facts of the crimes being adjudicated from subjective facts involving the defendant's relationship to the crimes. Publication of a widely circulating newspaper dehumanizing the Jews and propagating for their annihilation, and even Streicher's calling for such extermination in bursts of anger, did not, Marx argued, mean that Streicher had any resentment of Jews or condoned their mass murder. In his concluding plea for Streicher's innocence, Marx stated that the evidence "has shown nothing to the effect that already at that time there existed a plan for a war of revenge or aggression connected with the previous or simultaneous extermination of the Jews." He went on "If, nevertheless, a conspiracy should have existed, the latter would have confined itself to the restricted circle which revolved exclusively around Hitler. But the Defendant Streicher did not belong to that circle."[184] Hence, he had no active role and no responsibility for the mass murder of the Jews. Marx's defense of Streicher ultimately failed; he would be the only IMT defendant sentenced to death for, specifically, crimes against humanity, namely for his role inciting the mass murder of the Jews and shaping a genocidal mindset through propaganda.[185]

Defense lawyers for other Nuremberg defendants also downplayed the possibility of their clients harboring any hatred toward Jews, let alone feelings of revenge. At the same time, defense lawyers reminded the Allied prosecutors and judges that civilized nations ought not to be driven by vengeance and that the Nuremberg trial thus put the Allies to the test whether they were, in fact, as humane, ethical, and civilized as they themselves claimed to be in judging what they deemed Nazi barbarism. For instance, Otto Freiherr von Ludighausen, defense counsel for Hitler's early foreign policy organizer and nominally the Protector of Bohemia and Moravia Konstantin von Neurath, insisted that Germany had never been a nation guided by such feelings, but rather, often, a victim of vengeful campaigns by its neighbors, for example France. Von Ludighausen also reminded the Allies that the trial was only justified if not driven by vengeance.[186] A basic postulate of von Ludighausen and the other defense counsels was that the prosecutors were prejudiced; in their concluding pleas they consistently argued that their clients had not been guided by vengeance and should not suffer it either. Kurt Kaufmann, defense counsel for Holocaust-organizer Ernst Kaltenbrunner, asked the court if it was not altogether too early to hold a trial; his approach was empathy: "Could human beings, torn between love and hate, justice and revenge, conduct a trial immediately after the greatest catastrophe humanity has ever known—and constantly harassed by the statutory demands for rapid and time-saving proceedings—in such a way as to earn the thanks of mankind when the waters of this second deluge have withdrawn into their old bed?"[187]

At this moment in time, Kaufmann surmised, the Allied prosecutors might not have the required universalist love for all human beings, even for the men in the dock, for justice to be justice, not revenge—this, the implication went, despite the claims to rejecting vengeance.[188] Horst Pelckmann, defense counsel for the SS, echoed such concerns:

> I venture to hope that you, High Tribunal, will succeed in this titanic undertaking in being free of feelings of revenge, and will seek justice and nothing but justice. Will you, as non-Germans, who have not yourselves lived through the unique historic phenomenon of a mass psychosis and a tyranny of continental proportions—will you indeed be able to grasp and to picture to yourselves how such things could happen? Can you conceive that crimes were not committed by the bulk of the members, that they were not consciously organized by them, that they were not even known to them?[189]

Pelckmann's defense of the SS was based on the claim that Nazi antisemitic policy was not driven by hatred but rather was an attempt to resolve a "race problem" through rational, legal means; since sanctioned by the state, these means were not a crime.[190] In Pelckmann's view, the death camps "were established after 1942, after Hitler had declared war on the United States and now wanted to take his most bloody revenge for this development of the war, for which he held the Jews throughout the world responsible"; the camps were thus personal revenge on the Führer's part for which other Germans bore no responsibility.[191] Pelckmann further argued that not everyone in the SS was criminal, not everything the SS did a crime. "We therefore have to deal with the details of those matters," was his conclusion, "even though millions of people mourn the victims of the concentration camps, hundreds of thousands of the surviving inmates suffer from the aftermath, and even though the world accuses the SS in one single outcry of revenge."[192]

In turn, Hans Laternser, defense counsel for the German general staff and high command, appealed to the court to render a verdict "uninfluenced by the passions of everyday life, far removed from blind hatred and vengeance and the petty instincts of retaliation and which, standing out pure and unfalsified in the face of eternity and of a better future of the nations, is nothing but just!"[193] Robert Servatius, defending Thuringian Gauleiter and slave labor plenipotentiary Fritz Sauckel, likewise implored that "the punishment must not become a revenge. The measure of punishment must not be based on the theory that millions of victims necessarily imply the guilt of millions to be brought to punishment."[194] He suggested that whether there would be future peace and freedom depended on the court's ruling; for a "glance through the annals of European history in recent decades and centuries" demonstrated "again and again how might conquered right among the nations, and how the spirit of revenge beclouded the perceptions of mankind."[195] Peace and stability, Servatius argued, could only be achieved if this court reached its verdict not "merely with the cold logic of your keen mind, but also with the warm love of a seeing heart." Passing collective punishment on the German nation and "extend[ing] the consequences of a judgment to a large guiltless section of the German people would be to work against world peace." Any form of collective punishment, he instructed the court, would "mutatis mutandis repeat Hitler's idea of punishing a people—the Jewish people—collectively, and of exterminating them."[196] Servatius's concluding plea was as follows: "From the history of the Jews in the Old Testament we know that God would not have destroyed the city of Sodom, had but one just man lived there. Is not God's truth contained in these words—that a group may not be punished if even one member of the group is not deserving of punishment?"[197] In effect, collective punishment was not the Allies' goal at the IMT as they were seeking to punish individual crimes; Servatius basic argument was a postwar echo of the Nazi claim that Germans were victimized by a Jewish quest for vengeance.

Gustav Steinbauer, defense counsel for Artur Seyss-Inquart, former Reichskommissar of the occupied Netherlands, responsible for the deportation of Dutch Jewry to the death camps, voiced empathy for the Jewish victims by picturing their situation—as well as imagining their desire for vengeance. In the process, he confirmed, doubtless inadvertently, a linkage between Jews and revenge. "I visualize the march of the Jews from Dubno which slowly approaches the place of execution," he empathically proclaimed,

> how the individual victims help each other to undress, how the little boy persuades his parents to die bravely, and how they carry an old woman whose lameness prevents her from taking the few steps to the pit where the deadly bullet from the submachine gun awaits her. I once more hear the testimony of the French journalist, Marie Claude Vaillant-Couturier, who describes in deeply touching words how the sacred experiences of maternity and female honor were shamelessly trampled underfoot in the extermination camp.

Steinbauer acknowledged that "Auschwitz alone has swallowed up 3 1/2 million people—men, women, and children. That is really the most terrible weapon of the Indictment, that the spirits of all these innocent victims stand beside the prosecutor, admonishing and demanding revenge." To be sure, Steinbauer's figure for the mass murder in Auschwitz was too high, but consistent with what victims and perpetrators believed at the time. Noteworthy here is a parallel between Steinbauer's figurative language and prosecutor Gideon Hausner's claim, in his opening address in the 1961 Eichmann trial in Jerusalem, that he was not standing along but with him were six million dead. Upon acknowledging that death camp's victims, Steinbauer proceeded to equate their suffering to that of the Germans through Allied bombings and the war:

> But I do not stand alone, either. The many innocent war victims on the German side, women and children who have fallen victim to the terror attacks which violated international law, in Freiburg, in Cologne, in Dresden, in Hamburg, Berlin, and Vienna, and in almost all other German cities, stand beside me. My comrades from the Armed Forces, who, as honest and decent soldiers, have sacrificed their lives for the fatherland by the hundred thousand, young and old, faithful to their Oath of allegiance, also stand by my side.[198]

Paranoia and Elimination

Having established an equality in suffering between the Germans and their victims, Steinbauer made the case that Seyss-Inquart had not acted out of hate and revenge[199]—and appealed to the court to "not judge in wrath."[200]

Casting perpetrators as innocent, Germans as victims, downplaying antisemitism and claiming unfair anti-German prejudice also characterized the far more numerous war crimes trials before German courts, trials conducted on the basis of German law. From 1945 to the present, 95,000 Germans and Austrians have been convicted of Nazi crimes, mostly outside Germany, in eastern Europe. In Germany, in their different occupation zones the Allies convicted 8,812 Germans and Austrians; Germans courts convicted some 20,000 individuals, 12,776 of these in the Soviet Zone and then in East Germany. In the Western zones and then in West Germany, 36,393 people were investigated, 16,724 indicted, 6,656 convicted.[201] Throughout the postwar period, to distinguish perpetrators from mere accessories, West German criminal law placed considerable emphasis on the emotional state of participants in a killing. Accessories thus faced relatively lenient sentences (up to fifteen years in prison); this also meant that a person responsible for singlehanded murder could be classified as an accessory if the deed was not perpetrated out of "base motives"—for instance hatred or revenge—but on behest of someone else. Stemming from nineteenth-century criminal law, this approach made prosecution of state-sponsored mass atrocities especially difficult—the chances of convictions being all the slimmer due to the prevailing resentment-laden national mentality reluctant to acknowledge criminal responsibility of ordinary citizens who had just done what they perceived as their patriotic duty, together with a legal apparatus, from judges downward, filled with former officials in the Nazi state. In trial after trial, Nazi perpetrators minimized their emotional investment in murdering Jews and other victims, denied ever having had a Nazi Weltanschauung, and insisted they had merely caried out orders and duties. It is, in fact, only recently that German courts began confronting the matter of agency in choosing such duties—for example, in voluntarily engaging in mass shootings or working as a death camp guard.[202] The consistent legal defense here, frequently accepted, was a lie: fear, in difficult circumstances, of punishment for disobedience, the same as a denial of such agency, in essence a plea of self-defense.[203] In West German investigations and in courtrooms, perpetrators presented themselves as victims: of a rigid political regime, of thankless tasks involving killing, of those now trying to hold them accountable, for actions not judged criminal under Nazi law.[204]

For many such defendants, the survivors who offered incriminating evidence, cooperbated with prosecutors, and took the witness stand, were only seeking revenge. The defendant in one criminal proceedings before the Bremen District Court in 1953, a former kapo at Auschwitz and other camps put it succinctly: he was innocent; his trial reflected "the revenge of world Jewry on the German human being!"[205] In general, survivor-witnesses were met with suspicion that they exaggerated, invented, told lies to harm accused Germans; inaccuracy in dates, SS and military ranks, uniform insignia, were taken as proof that witnesses lacked credibility and were lying, fabricating stories to harm the defendants, out of a desire for vengeance. In this respect, a pattern emerges with close look at the verdict-record: an emphasis on no revenge and hatred being present in a survivor-witness—an emphasis indicating that precisely the contrary was, in fact, the court's and public's general expectation.²⁰⁶

A variation of this perception resurfaced at the trial of Adolf Eichmann in Jerusalem in 1961. Eichmann—a mid-level SS official in the SD and RSHA who had worked out the logistics of mass deportations of Europe's Jews to death camps—had once prided himself to have escaped the "*Rachejustiz*"²⁰⁷ of Nuremberg to Argentina. In May 1960 Israeli secret agents kidnapped him outside Buenos Aires and brought him to Israel to stand trial. Robert Servatius served as Eichmann's defense attorney. Although Servatius did not try to doubt or diminish the crimes of the Holocaust and rarely challenged survivor-witnesses in cross-examination, he nevertheless tried to save his client's skin by minimizing his power and personal responsibility. Upon the opening of the trial before the Jerusalem District Court, Servatius presented several objections, not just the unlawfulness of the abduction (which to many contemporary observers appeared as an act of vengeance), but rather that the judges of this Jewish court were biased. He implied that they were guided by vengeance because of their personal and emotional entanglement with the Holocaust. Accordingly, Servatius asked that any of the judges recuse himself in case he "or any near relative of his was harmed by the acts brought forward in the charges. An assumption like this is quite possible," he went on to elaborate. "It arises from the fact that the entire Jewish people were drawn into the holocaust of extermination. . . . The fear of prejudice exists, therefore, against all the judges in equal measure."²⁰⁸ The court rejected Servatius' objection arguing that it abided by the same professional ethics as "any judicial system worthy of the name". It further stated that "while in the bench a judge does not cease to be flesh and blood, possessed of emotions and impulses," he was nevertheless

> required by law to subdue these emotions and impulses for otherwise a judge will never be fit to consider a criminal charge which arouses feelings of revulsion, such as treason, murder or any other grave crime. It is true that the memory of the Holocaust shocks every Jew to the depth of his being, but when this case is brought before us we are obliged to overcome these emotions while sitting in judgment. This duty we shall fulfil.²⁰⁹

Servatius would probably not have had the same objections against a Dutch, Polish or any other national court adjudicating Nazi crimes committed against their nationals; yet with regard to Jews he echoed conspiratorial views and fears that had a long history and afterlife.

Notes

1. Karl Holz, editorial, *Der Stürmer*, no. 28, July 1938, in Office of United States Chief of Counsel for Prosecution of Axis Criminality (ed.), *Nazi Conspiracy and Aggression* (Washington, DC: United States Government Printing Office, 1946–1948), vol. 8, 24–5.

2. On the power of Nazi propaganda, especially in framing genocidal violence as defensive measures, see for example Susan D. Bachrach, Edward J. Phillips, and Steven Luckert, *State of Deception: The Power of Nazi Propaganda* (Washington, D.C: United States Holocaust Memorial Museum, 2009); Aristotle A. Kallis, *Nazi Propaganda and the Second World War* (Basingstoke: Palgrave Macmillan, 2005); David Welch, *The Third Reich: Politics and Propaganda* (London: Routledge, 1993). See especially also Nira Feldman, *Der Stürmer: The Power of a Hate Magazine* (Jerusalem: Carmel, 2023), Hebrew.

3. Jacoby, *Wild Justice*, 172.

4. Ibid., 172–3. In fact avenging imaginary or ideologically construed grievances allegedly caused by different kinds of people deemed "enemies" is a common feature of authoritarian regimes, from fascism through communism to religious fundamentalism. In fact vengeance then becomes a central component of the claim to power and the justification of the use of violence.

5. See, for example, Doris L. Bergen, *War and Genocide: A Concise History of the Holocaust* (Lanham: Rowman & Littlefield, 2016), 13–43; Eberhard Jäckel, *Hitler's World View: A Blueprint for Power* (Cambridge, Mass: Harvard University Press, 1981); Christian Gerlach, *The Extermination of the European Jews* (Cambridge: Cambridge University Press, 2016), 143–83; Eric D. Weitz, *A Century of Genocide: Utopias of Race and Nation* (Princeton: Princeton University Press, 2003), 102–43.

6. Richard S. Levy, "Antisemitism in Germany 1890-1933: How Popular was it?," in *The Germans and the Holocaust: Popular Responses to the Persecution and Murder of the Jews*, ed. Susanna Schrafstetter and Alan E. Steinweis (New York: Berghahn, 2016), 17–40, esp. 31–34.

7. For example in the Nazi party program (1920), published in *Documents on the Holocaust: Selected Sources on the Destruction of the Jews of Germany and Austria, Poland, and the Soviet Union*, ed. Yitzhak Arad, Israel Gutman, and Avraham Margaliyot (Jerusalem: Yad Vashem, 1987), 15–18. For a local history of how the Nazi party gained following, see William Sheridan Allen, *The Nazi Seizure of Power: The Experience of a Single German Town, 1922-1945*, revised edition (Brattleboro: Echo Point Books & Media, 2014).

8. Shulamit Volkov observes that Nazi antisemitic agitation was a matter of the "spoken word" in addition to periodicals, wall newspapers, books for adults and children. See Shulamit Volkov, "The Written Matter and the Spoken Words: On the Gap between Pre-1914 and Nazi Antisemitism," in *Unanswered questions: Nazi Germany and the Genocide of the Jews* ed. François Furet (New York: Schocken Books, 1989), 33–53.

9. See most importantly, Jeffrey Herf, *The Jewish Enemy: Nazi Propaganda During World War II and the Holocaust* (Cambridge: Harvard University Press, 2006); and Philippe Burrin, *Nazi Anti-Semitism: From Prejudice to the Holocaust* (New York: New Press, 2005).

10. Jeffrey Herf speaks of several antisemitic "campaigns" between 1933 and 1945, analyzing the principal party organ, *Völkischer Beobachter*; these intensified after 1941: "Four periods accounted for most of the front-page stories: July– August 1941 (seven), April–July 1943 (twenty-six), October–November 1943 (thirteen), and May–June 1944 (nine)." See Herf, *The Jewish Enemy*, 281.

11. The meaning of these terms was fluid and changed over time, moving from abstract ideas and figures of speech to concrete plans and policies only slowly; the Nazification of language however was an important precondition for the ultimate path to genocide. See Beth A. Griech-Polelle, *Anti-Semitism and the Holocaust: Language, Rhetoric, and the Traditions of Hatred* (London: Bloomsbury Academic, 2017) and Thomas Pegelow, *The Language of Nazi Genocide: Linguistic Violence and the Struggle of Germans of Jewish Ancestry* (New York: Cambridge University Press, 2009); Jeffrey Herf, *Three Faces of Antisemitism* (London: Routledge, 2024), 20–41, here 23.

12. See Peter Longerich, *Holocaust: The Nazi Persecution and Murder of the Jews* (Oxford: Oxford University Press, 2010), 29–130.

13. Herf, *The Jewish Enemy*, 50–91; the Nazi regime built on a long history of dehumanizing the Jews, see, David Livingstone Smith, *Making Monsters: The Uncanny Power of Dehumanization* (Cambridge: Harvard University Press, 2021), esp. 178–205.

14. See Paul A. Hanebrink, *A Specter Haunting Europe: The Myth of Judeo-Bolshevism* (Cambridge: Harvard University Press, 2018), esp. 83–162.

15. See, Adolf Hitler, *Mein Kampf*, transl. Ralph Manheim (New York: Houghton Mifflin, 1943), chapter 11 on "Nation and Race," 284–329; see the German critical edition, *Mein Kampf: Eine kritische Edition*, ed. by Christian Hartmann, Thomas Vordermayer, Othmar Plöckinger, Roman Töppel, and Edith Raim (Munich: Institut für Zeitgeschichte, 2016); and Ernst Hiemer's *Der Giftpilz* (Nuremberg: Der Stürmer, 1938), a children's book, laid out all the anti-Jewish tropes central to Nazi antisemitism for young readers, while openly calling for the annihilation of the Jews.

16. See, for example, Alfred Rosenberg, *Die Spur des Juden im Wandel der Zeiten* (1920) which claimed that Germany was ruled by Jews and "the Jew has hated the German people from time immemorial." Alfred Rosenberg, *The Political Diary of Alfred Rosenberg and the Onset of the Holocaust*, ed. Jürgen Matthäus and Frank Bajohr (Lanham, Maryland: Rowman & Littlefield, 2015), 356; see also Randall L. Bytwerk, "The Argument for Genocide in Nazi Propaganda," *The Quarterly Journal of Speech* 91, no. 1 (2005): 37–62.

17. Herf, *The Jewish Enemy*, 183–230; John J. Michalczyk, Michael Bryant, and Susan A. Michalczyk (eds.), *Hitler's "Mein Kampf" and the Holocaust: A Prelude to Genocide* (London: Bloomsbury, 2022), esp. 131–45.

18. See the written transcript of Raul Hilberg's interview with Claude Lanzmann in the film-documentary *Shoah* (1985): Claude Lanzmann, *Shoah: An Oral History of the Holocaust. The Complete Text of the Film;* preface by Simone de Beauvoir (New York: Pantheon Books, 1985), 71.

19. Ibid., 71.

20. Ibid., 72. Similarly also in Hilberg, *The Destruction of the European Jews*, 1–17; see also Peter Hayes, *Why? Explaining the Holocaust* (New York: W.W. Norton and Company, 2017), 3–35, here 8.

21. They literally envisioned a "world without Jews," as Alon Confino has argued in his, *A World Without Jews: The Nazi Imagination from Persecution to Genocide* (New Haven: Yale University Press, 2014).

22. Hitler, *Mein Kampf*, 65.

23. Saul Friedländer, *Nazi Germany and the Jews* (New York: HarperCollins, 1997), 73–112.

24. Karl A. Schleunes, *The Twisted Road to Auschwitz: Nazi Policy Toward German Jews, 1933-1939* (Urbana: Univ. of Illinois Press, 1970).

25. David Bankier, *The Germans and the Final Solution: Public Opinion under Nazism* (Oxford: B. Blackwell, 1992), 67–88.

26. This term, coined by Orlando Patterson with regard to slavery, was applied to Holocaust research by Marion Kaplan in her *Between Dignity and Despair: Jewish Life in Nazi Germany* (New York: Oxford University Press, 1998), 5.

27. The decision-making had two separate phases, first the decision to murder Soviet Jews taken in spring 1941 with the preparation of Operation Barbarossa; and second in early fall 1941 the decision to murder also Jews outside of Soviet territory; see and Christopher R. Browning

and Jürgen Matthäus, *The Origins of the Final Solution: The Evolution of Nazi Jewish Policy, September 1939-March 1942* (Lincoln: University of Nebraska Press, 2004).

28. See Ian Kershaw, "'Working towards the Führer': Reflections on the Nature of the Hitler Dictatorship," in idem, *Hitler, the Germans, and the Final Solution* (New Haven: Yale University Press, 2008), 29–48.

29. Browning and Matthäus, *The Origins of the Final Solution*, 268-277 and Waitman Wade Beorn, *The Holocaust in Eastern Europe: At the Epicentre of the Final Solution* (London: Bloomsbury Academic, 2018), 119–49; for a wider perspective on non-German perpetrators across Europe see Gerlach, *The Extermination of the European Jews*, 336–403.

30. Alex J. Kay, *Empire of Destruction: A History of Nazi Mass Killing* (New Haven: Yale University Press, 2021), 57–98; Patrick Desbois, *The Holocaust by Bullets: A Priest's Journey to Uncover the Truth behind the Murder of 1.5 Million Jews* (New York: Palgrave Macmillan, 2008); Dan Stone, *The Holocaust: An Unfinished History* (New York: Mariner Books, 2024), 103–221.

31. David Bankier, "The Germans and the Holocaust: What did they know?," *Yad Vashem Studies* 20 (1990): 69–98.

32. Bankier, *The Germans and the Final Solution*, 116–56; Longerich, *"Davon haben wir nichts gewusst!"*, 201–62; Peter Fritzsche, "Babi Yar, but Not Auschwitz: What Did Germans Know about the Final Solution?" *The Germans and the Holocaust*, 85–106.

33. As Thomas Kühne has argued, there was a distinct sense of communal bonding and comradeship through complicity in mass murder; the communal fear of revenge kept alive the memory of the collective crime; see Thomas Kühne, *Belonging and Genocide: Hitler's Community, 1918-1945* (New Haven: Yale University Press, 2010), 6–7, 177.

34. Longerich, *"Davon haben wir nichts gewusst!"*, 304–10; Frank Bajohr and Dieter Pohl, *Der Holocaust als offenes Geheimnis: Die Deutschen, die NS-Führung und die Alliierten* (Munich: C.H. Beck, 2006), 65–79.

35. Speech of Adolf Hitler, Sept. 18, 1922, in Office of United States Chief of Counsel for Prosecution of Axis Criminality (ed.), *Nazi Conspiracy and Aggression*, vol. 5 (United States Government Printing Office, Washington, DC, 1946), 80.

36. See, for example, also Goebbels campaign speech for the July 1932 Reichstag election, "The Storm is Coming" (July 9, 1932), calling upon Germans to "wake up!" and join the "army of revenge" to liberate Germany from oppression, hardship and betrayal; published in *Landmark Speeches of National Socialism*, ed. Randall L. Bytwerk (College Station: Texas A&M University Press, 2008), 32–9.

37. For the original German text, see Alfred Rosenberg's *Dietrich Eckart: Ein Vermächtnis* (Munich: Zentralverlag der NSDAP 1935 (originally published in 1928), 66. This English translation follows Michael Meyer, *The Politics of Music in the Third Reich* (Peter Lang 1991), 69–70. On the significance of the song and its wide usage at party rallies and in song books, see Günter Hartung, *Deutschfaschistische Literatur und Ästhetik: Gesammelte Studien* (Leipziger Universitätsverlag, 2001), 165–81, esp. 167–8. For slightly different versions of the text see *Liederbuch der Nationalsozialistischen Deutschen Arbeiter-Partei* (Munich: Zentralverlag der NSDAP, 1938), 12–13 and Michael Jung, *Liederbücher im Nationalsozialismus Band 2: Dokumente* (PhD thesis, Univ. of Frankfurt, 1989), 722.

38. Both songs are presently prohibited in Germany, but its motifs are used by neo-Nazis across the world. The text of Eckart's *Sturmlied* was published in the *Völkischer Beobachter* in Jan. 1923.

39. German text in *Liederbuch der Nationalsozialistischen Deutschen Arbeiter-Partei* (Munich: Zentralverlag der NSDAP, 1938), 7.

40. Hitler Youth song, "Unfurl the Blood-Soaked Banners," Office of United States US Chief of Counsel for Prosecution of Axis Criminality (ed.), *Nazi Conspiracy and Aggression, Supplement A*, 547; originally published in *Uns geht die Sonne nicht unter: Lieder der Hitler-Jugend*, ed. Hugo Wolfram Schmidt (Cologne: P. J. Tonger, 1934), 24. Other songs in the book sang of conquest of Europe and the world, war, and death to Jewry, as for example A. Pardun's song "Can You See the Dawn in the East?" which included a line saying: "Whether a townsman, a farmer or a worker, they will wield the sword and hammer for Hitler, for freedom, for work and bread. Germany awake, death to Jewry, People to arms" (translation in *Nazi Conspiracy and Aggression, Supplement A*, 546).

41. See "Hitler's Party Prepares Boycott in Revenge for 'Atrocity Tales,'" *The New York Times*, March 28, 1933, 1.

42. From the *Münchener Beobachter*, daily supplement to the *Völkischer Beobachter*, issue nos. 91/92 (April 1–2, 1933), "100,000 Demonstrate in Koenigsplatz against the Jewish Incitements to Cruelty," in Office of United States Chief of Counsel for Prosecution of Axis Criminality (ed.), *Nazi Conspiracy and Aggression*, vol. 8, 20–3, here 21.

43. See Streicher's account at the IMT trial, questioned by his defense counsel Hanns Marx, April 29, 1946, International Military Tribunal Nuremberg, *IMT*, vol. 12, 327.

44. Wolf Gruner, "'Worse Than Vandals': The Mass Destruction of Jewish Homes and Jewish Responses during the 1938 Pogrom," *New Perspectives on Kristallnacht: After 80 Years, the Nazi Pogrom in Global Comparison*, ed. Wolf Gruner et al. (West Lafayette: Purdue University Press, 2019), 25–50.

45. Ruth Andreas-Friedrich, *Der Schattenmann. Tagebuchaufzeichnungen: 1938-1945* (Berlin: Suhrkamp Verlag, 1947), entry for Nov. 8, 1938, 26.

46. Ibid., entry for Nov. 9, 1938, 28.

47. Report of the U.S. Consul General in Bremen, Edwin C. Kemp, Nov. 10, 1938, Office of United States Chief of Counsel for Prosecution of Axis Criminality (ed.), *Nazi Conspiracy and Aggression*, vol. 5, 312.

48. National Socialist German Labor Party Supreme Party Court, "Secret Report about the events and judicial proceedings in connection with the anti-semitic demonstrations of 9 November 1938" (13 February 1939), in *Nazi Conspiracy and Aggression*, vol. 5, 868–76.

49. Ibid., 873.

50. Ibid., 874.

51. "Juden, was nun?," *Das Schwarze Korps*, November 24, 1938, 1, translated in Anson Rabinbach and Sander Gilman (eds.), *The Third Reich Sourcebook* (Berkeley: University of California Press, 2013), 236–8, here 238.

52. Bytwerk, *Landmark Speeches of National Socialism*, 86.

53. International Military Tribunal, *IMT*, Jan. 10, 1946, vol. 5, 105–6.

54. USHMM Photo Archives # 31520.

55. Ernst Hiemer, "The Jewish Cry for Vengeance," *Der Stürmer*, no. 4, Jan. 1939, Office of United States US Chief of Counsel for Prosecution of Axis Criminality, *Nazi Conspiracy And Aggression, Supplement A*, 957.

56. Circulation had grown rapidly from 25,000 in 1933 to 113,800 in 1934 to 486,000 and between 800,000 and 1 million in the following years; special issues ran 1 million copies; see Fred Hahn and Günther Wagenlehner, *Lieber Stürmer: Leserbriefe an das NS-Kampfblatt 1924 bis 1945: eine Dokumentation aus dem Leo-Baeck-Institut, New York* (Stuttgart: Seewald, 1978), 8, 149 and Randall L. Bytwerk, *Julius Streicher* (New York: Stein and Day, 1982), 57.

See also Leo Baeck Institute New York, Bernhard Kolb Collection AR 360 / MF 1021, series V, Stürmer Files.

57. Although Nazi rhetoric was explicit in addressing annihilation of the Jews, it did not give factual information on the mass murder operations on the ground; see David Bankier, "The Use of Antisemitism in Nazi Wartime Propaganda," in *The Holocaust and History: The Known, the Unknown, the Disputed, and the Reexamined*, ed. Michael Berenbaum and Abraham J. Peck (Bloomington: Indiana University Press, 1998), 41–55; Randall L. Bytwerk, "The Argument for Genocide in Nazi Propaganda," *The Quarterly Journal of Speech* 91, 1 (2005): 37–62.

58. Speech of Adolf Hitler before the Reichstag, Jan. 30, 1939, cited in Rabinbach and Gilman, *The Third Reich Sourcebook*, 723–4, here 724. Other central figure also made use of the stereotype of Jewish "old testament vengeance," for example, Goebbels and Göring; see Herf, *The Jewish Enemy*, 127, 210–11, and Kühne, *Belonging and Genocide*, 131.

59. "... die Vernichtung der jüdischen Rasse in Europa." See speech of Adolf Hitler before the Reichstag, Jan. 30, 1939, cited in Rabinbach and Gilman, *The Third Reich Sourcebook*, 724.

60. See, for example, "Secret Report of the Security Service of the Reichsführer SS, The Popularity of *Jew Süss*," Nov. 28, 1940, in Rabinbach and Gilman, *The Third Reich Sourcebook*, 599; Gerhard Starke, "Review of *Jew Süß*," Sept. 26, 1940, ibid., 597–9.

See also the public opinion reports of Nov. 28, 1940, *The Jews in the Secret Nazi Reports on Popular Opinion in Germany, 1933-1945*, ed. Otto Dov Kulka and Eberhard Jäckel (New Haven: Yale University Press, 2010), 511–12.

61. Joseph Goebbels, *The Goebbels diaries, 1939-1941*, ed. Fred Taylor (New York: Putnam, 1983), entry of Aug. 18, 1940.

62. Susan Tegel, *Jew Süss: Life, Legend, Fiction, Film*, (London: Continuum, 2011), 182; during the Frankfurt Auschwitz trial one of the defendants, SS-Rottenführer Stefan Baretzki related that this film and other propaganda films had been shown to Auschwitz guards like him as a form of antisemitic incitement to do their job (187). On the film's impact, see Saul Friedländer, *The Years of Extermination: Nazi Germany and the Jews, 1939-1945* (New York: HarperCollins Publishers, 2007), 20–4 and Susan Tegel, *Nazis and the Cinema* (London: Hambledon Continuum, 2007), 190–208.

63. On the historical figure and its distortion by Harlan, see Yair Mintzker, *The Many Deaths of Jew Süss: The Notorious Trial and Execution of an Eighteenth-Century Court Jew* (Princeton, New Jersey: Princeton University Press, 2017) and Alexandra Przyrembel and Jörg Schönert (eds.), "Jud Süß": Hofjude, literarische Figur, antisemitisches Zerrbild, (Frankfurt am Main: Campus, 2006). After the war, Veit Harlan was tried twice for crimes against humanity; but he was acquitted in both trials on grounds of no demonstrable connection between the film and the murder of European Jews that followed. See the documentary film *Harlan—In the Shadow of Jud Suess* (dir. Felix Moeller, 2008).

64. Esther 9:16.

65. See the public opinion reports of Jan. 20, 1941, *The Jews in the Secret Nazi Reports*, 516–17.

66. See Jennifer Hansen, "The Art and Science of Reading Faces: Strategy of Racist Cinema in the Third Reich," *Shofar* 28, 1 (2009), 80–103, here 102; Stig Hornshøj-Møller and David Culbert, "'Der Ewige Jude' (1940): Joseph Goebbels' Unequaled Monument to Anti-Semitism," *Historical Journal of Film, Radio, and Television* 12, 1 (1992): 41–67, here 49. Although there are no comprehensive statistics about how many Hitler Youth and Wehrmacht soldiers were shown the film, some recall the impact of seeing the film. As a former member of the Hitler Youth who had seen *Jud Süß* at age thirteen to fourteen recalled when interviewed shortly after the war at age twenty-three: "If one saw this ... one could

really become involuntarily enraged and one got the impression that they [the Jews] must have been bad people." See Theodor W. Adorno, "Schuld und Abwehr," *Soziologische Schriften II*, in idem, *Gesammelte Schriften*, vol. 9, no. 2 (Frankfurt am Main: Suhrkamp 1997), 209. Both films were also shown to SS and police units before deportation and round up actions; Stefan Mannes, *Antisemitismus im nationalsozialistischen Propagandafilm: Jud Süss und Der ewige Jude* (Cologne: Teiresias, 1999), 114–15.

67. Hitler returned to his "prophesy" in three widely publicized speeches that featured in the *Völkischer Beobachter*, Jan. 30, 1941, Sept. 30, 1942, and Nov. 8, 1942, shifting the tone from probable condition to certain consequence; Robert Ley also referenced Hitler's "prophesy" in the same sense in speeches in December 1939 and May 10, 1942; see Herf, *Three Faces of Antisemitism*, 23–4.

68. Goebbels, *The Goebbels Diaries, 1939-1941*, 420.

69. On March 27 and Dec. 14, 1942; ibid., 148, 243.

70. Joseph Goebbels, "The Jews are Guilty," Nov. 16, 1941, in Rabinbach and Gilman, *The Third Reich Sourcebook*, 737–40, here 737; Joseph Goebbels, "Die Juden Sind Schuld!" in idem, *Das eherne Herz: Reden und Aufsätze aus den Jahren 1941/42* (Munich: F. Eher, 1943), 85–91.

71. Leaflet "Die Juden sind schuld," 1941, Deutsches Historisches Museum, Berlin, Do 70/190.1 II.

72. Goebbels, "The Jews are Guilty," 737.

73. Ibid., 737.

74. Ibid., 737.

75. Ibid., 738.

76. Ibid., 738.

77. Ibid., 738.

78. See Engelbert Huber, "The Antisemitism of the NSDAP" (1933), in Rabinbach and Gilman, *The Third Reich Sourcebook*, 192–4, here 192.

79. The speech was published as Joseph Goebbels, *Das eherne Herz: Rede vor der Deutschen Akademie* (Munich: Zentralverlag der NSDAP, 1942), here 34–5. See Herf, *The Jewish Enemy*, 125.

80. See Alfred Rosenberg "Speech by Reich Minister Rosenberg at the Press Reception on Tuesday, November 18, 1941," in Rosenberg, *The Political Diary*, 388.

81. Martin Dean, *Investigating Babyn Yar: Shadows from the Valley of Death* (Lanham: Lexington Books, 2024), 145; Dean estimates that 1,000 men perpetrated the Babi Yar massacre, 100 of them active shooters, the rest cordoned off the site, deceiving and escorting the victims, forcing them to strip and preventing their escape; handling clothing and mass graves.

82. Walter von Reichenau, "Orders for Conduct in the East: Crushing the Jewish-Bolshevist System," Oct. 10, 1941, Office of U.S. Chief of Counsel for the Prosecution of Axis Criminality (ed.), *Nazi Conspiracy and Aggression*, vol. 8, 585–7, here 585.

83. Ibid., 585.

84. Some Jews, especially the younger generation took prominent positions in local administrations out of conviction that the new rulers brought Jews equality and opportunity, but they were a small minority. In absolute numbers far more non-Jews served the Soviets than Jews, but Catholics and Protestants were not blamed for the political repression of the Soviet rulers against the local population, as arrests and deportations in the interior of the SU; Jews also suffered from that repression, far more than they benefitted. The perception that they were all in favor of the Soviets and collectively benefited was the result of old

traditions of seeing Jews as alien and disloyal and using them as scapegoats in times of crisis, blaming them for Soviet rule and repression. On the stereotype of the Jewish-Soviet alliance during the Soviet occupation of Poland, see Joanna B. Michlic, "The Soviet Occupation of Poland, 1939–41, and the Stereotype of the Anti-Polish and Pro-Soviet Jew," *Jewish Social Studies* 13, 3 (2007): 135–76; and Anna M. Cienciala, "Poles and Jews under German and Soviet Occupation, September 1, 1939–June 22 1941," *The Polish Review* 46, 4 (2001): 391–402. The stereotype of the Jewish-communist alliance predated World War II and survived it; see Joanna B. Michlic, *Poland's Threatening Other: The Image of the Jew from 1880 to the Present* (Lincoln: University of Nebraska Press, 2006).

85. On Jedwabne and revenge motives there, see Anna Bikont, *The Crime and the Silence: Confronting the Massacre of Jews in Wartime Jedwabne* (New York: Farrar, Straus and Giroux, 2015), 56, 118–19, 123–4, 448; Jan Tomasz Gross, *Neighbors: The Destruction of the Jewish Community in Jedwabne, Poland* (Princeton University Press, 2000), 246.

86. See Waitman Wade Beorn, "All the Other Neighbors," in *A Companion to the Holocaust*, ed. Earl and Gigliotti, 153–72; John-Paul Himka, "The Lviv Pogrom of 1941: The Germans, Ukrainian Nationalists, and the Carnival Crowd," *Canadian Slavonic Papers* 53, 2–4 (2011): 209–43; Wendy Lower, "Pogroms, Mob Violence and Genocide in Western Ukraine, Summer 1941: Varied Histories, Explanations and Comparisons," *Journal of Genocide Research* 13,3 (2011): 217–46; Tomasz Szarota, *On the Threshold of the Holocaust: Anti-Jewish Riots and Pogroms in Occupied Europe. Warsaw – Paris – The Hague – Amsterdam – Antwerp – Kaunas* (Frankfurt: Peter Lang, 2015); Grzegorz Rossoliński-Liebe, "Der Verlauf und die Täter des Lemberger Pogroms vom Sommer, 1941: Zum aktuellen Stand der Forschung," *Jahrbuch für Antisemitismusforschung* 22 (2013): 207–43. Testimony from Jews and non-Jews at early postwar trials against participants in local pogroms—in Brańsk, Goniądz, Jasionówka, Kolno, Radziłów, Rajgród, Suchowola, Szczuczyn, Wąsosz—indicates that revenge on Jews was a widespread motive for violence, see Mirosław Tryczyk and Frank Szmulowicz, *The Towns of Death: Pogroms Against Jews by Their Neighbors* (Lanham: Lexington Books, 2021).

87. On these motives see Kopstein and Wittenberg, *Intimate Violence*, 3–17.

88. See, among other, Martin Dean, "Local Collaboration in the Holocaust in Eastern Europe," *The Historiography of the Holocaust*, ed. Dan Stone (Houndmills, Basingstoke, Hampshire: Palgrave Macmillan, 2004), 120–40 and idem, *Collaboration in the Holocaust: Crimes of the Local Police in Belorussia and Ukraine, 1941-44* (New York: St. Martin's Press, 2000); Gabriel Finder and Alexander Prusin, "Collaboration in Eastern Galicia: The Ukrainian Police and the Holocaust," *East European Jewish Affairs* 34, 2 (2004): 95–118; Leonid Rein, "Local Collaboration in the Execution of the 'Final Solution' in Nazi-Occupied Belorussia," *Holocaust and Genocide Studies* 20, 3 (2006): 381–409.

89. Extracts from operational situation report U.S.S.R. no.111, Oct. 12, 1941, in Nuremberg Military Tribunals (eds.), *Trials of War Criminals before the Nuremberg Military Tribunals under Control Council Law No. 10* [hereafter *NMT*](Washington, DC: U.S. Government Printing Office 1946-1949), vol. 4, 145.

90. In addition to a revenge rhetoric, perpetrators used pseudo-humanitarian arguments to justify the murder of children, namely, that children would not survive without their parents who had already been shot, as for example in Byelaya Tserkov in late August 1941. See Browning and Matthäus, *The Origins of the Final Solution*, 291 and Ernst Klee, Willi Dressen, and Volker Riess (eds.), *"The Good Old Days": The Holocaust as Seen by Its Perpetrators and Bystanders* (New York: Free Press, 1991), 138–54. It was Reichenau who gave the order to shoot the children.

91. Cross examination of Otto Ohlendorf by James Heath, Oct. 15, 1947, in Nuremberg Military Tribunals, *NMT*, vol. 4, 356.

92. See Michael Bazyler, *Holocaust, Genocide, and the Law: A Quest for Justice in a Post-Holocaust World* (New York: Oxford University Press, 2016), 118.

93. Affidavit of Erwin Schulz in SS-Einsatzgruppen trial, Nuremberg, May 26, 1947, in Nuremberg Military Tribunals, *NMT*, vol. 4, 135–8, here 138.

94. See Browning and Matthäus, *Origins of the Final Solution*, 312. According to Robert Gerwarth, Reinhard Heydrich, head of the Einsatzgruppen, who had ordered shootings of women and children shared Himmler's "inverted logic" that their victims would turn into avengers if they survived, see Robert Gerwarth, *Hitler's Hangman: The Life of Heydrich* (New Haven: Yale University Press, 2011), 198.

95. "From a Speech by Himmler before Senior SS Officers in Poznan, October 4, 1943," in *Documents on the Holocaust*, ed. Arad, Gutman, and Margaliyot, 344–5, here 345. Himmler gave the same speech two days later, Oct. 6, 1943, before Gau-leaders, there are slight discrepancies in the wording but the same basic ideas. The Oct. 4 version was used as evidence at the IMT trial as PS-1919.

96. Heinrich Himmler, "Rede vor Reichs- und Gauleitern in Posen am 6.10.1943," in Bradley F. Smith and Agnes F. Peterson (eds.), *Heinrich Himmler: Geheimreden, 1933 bis 1945, und andere Ansprachen* (Frankfurt/M: Propylaen 1974), 162–82, here 169–70; translation LJ.

97. Ibid., 169; translation LJ.

98. Yitzhak Arad, *The Holocaust in the Soviet Union* (Lincoln: University of Nebraska Press, 2009), 188.

99. Mattner's letter to his wife, Oct. 5, 1941, cited in Browning and Matthäus, *The Origins of the Final Solution*, 298. The original letter is in Bundesarchiv Berlin-Lichterfelde Dok. Slg. Verschiedenes 301 v (048), Bl. 260–5 and published in *Deutscher Osten 1939-1945. Der Weltanschauungskrieg in Photos und Texten*, ed. Klaus-Michael Mallmann, Volker Rieß and Wolfram Pyta (Darmstadt: Wissenschaftliche Buchgesellschaft 2003), 27–8, 65.

100. See for example, Hiemer, *Der Giftpilz*: "Have you heard about ritual murders? In their course, the Jews kill boys and girls, women and men. The Jews are murderers from the start, the devil in human form" (50).

101. Himmler must have offered this justification for mass murder to different people on different occasions: In his essay, "The Final Solution of the Jewish question in Auschwitz Concentration Camp" (published in his memoir), Rudolf Höss quoted Himmler from memory as having said: "The Jews are the sworn enemies of the German people and must be eradicated. Every Jew that we can lay our hands on is to be destroyed now during the war, without exception. If we cannot now obliterate the biological basis of Jewry, the Jews will one day destroy the German people." See Rudolf Höss, *Commandant of Auschwitz: The Autobiography of Rudolf Hoess* (London: Weidenfeld and Nicolson, 1959), 183.

102. Goebbels, *The Goebbels Diaries 1942-1943* ed. and transl. Louis P. Lochner (Garden City, New York: Doubleday & Company, Inc., 1948), March 27, 1942, 148.

103. Ibid., Dec. 14, 1942, 243–4.

104. Ibid., Dec. 18, 1942, 250.

105. Ibid., March 16, 1942, 126.

106. This ratio was both the result of improvised army practice on the ground (which often even exceeded it) as well as central army directives; most notably, on Sept. 16, 1941, the head of the armed forces, Field Marshal Wilhelm Keitel, decreed that the death of 50–100 "communists" were a "suitable atonement" for every German life lost; see Wilhelm Keitel "Communist Insurrection in occupied territories," *Nazi Conspiracy and Aggression*, vol. 6, 961–2, here 961. A few days earlier, another Keitel order stipulated that killing Jews was an

essential component of fighting communism, "The fight against Bolshevism necessitates indiscriminate and energetic accomplishment of this task, especially also against the Jews, the main carriers of Bolshevism." (Keitel "Jews in the newly occupied Eastern territories," *Nazi Conspiracy and Aggression*, vol. 3, 636).

107. Kay, *Empire of Destruction*, 191; see also Timothy Snyder, *Bloodlands: Europe between Hitler and Stalin* (New York: Basic Books, 2010), 225–52.

108. Individual soldiers who engaged in reprisal actions experienced an urge to avenge their mutilated and murdered comrades; violating local Jewish and non-Jewish civilians in return for partisan attacks constituted a sense of comradeship and built a distinctly genocidal combat culture; see Kühne, *Belonging and Genocide*, 97, 101, 108–9, 117.

109. The massacre was widely seen among the western Allies as a symbol of German barbarism and mobilized anti-German resistance, see Jackson Bowman, "Turning a War Crime into a Weapon," *Central Europe* 5 (2024): 27–38.

110. See Gerwarth, *Hitler's Hangman*, 278–94, here 286.

111. Bankier, *The Germans and the Final Solution*, 100–15.

112. This had limited success, as some Germans took this as a reminder of their own atrocities and only added to fears of future revenge, Bankier, *The Germans and the Final Solution*, 105–6.

113. Goebbels, *The Goebbels Diaries 1942-1943*, 331, entry of April 16, 1943.

114. Rosenberg, *Political Diary*, 317, entry of July 31, 1943. Four days later he remarked, in reference to the severe British bombings of Hamburg in late July and early August that killed about 30,000 Hamburg residents: "But the morale [Haltung] of the population is exemplary. One cry: Vengeance! governs most of them." Ibid., Aug. 4, 1943, 318.

115. See Marcel Ophuls, *The Memory of Justice* (documentary film, 1976); in his interview with Ophuls, Speer refers to both private conversations and official briefings with army officers.

116. Martin Froehling in *Der Stürmer*, no. 33. Aug. 12, 1943, Office of United States US Chief of Counsel (ed.), *Nazi Conspiracy And Aggression, Supplement A*, 1213–14.

117. German combat fatalities in 1943 alone amounted to 812,000, almost as many as in the previous two years (929,000); in 1944 the number of fatalities doubled with 1.8 million; see Rüdiger Overmans, *Deutsche militärische Verluste im Zweiten Weltkrieg* (Munich: Oldenbourg, 1999), 266. For a nuanced analysis of how Germans both grew skeptical of the "final victory" and kept fighting, hoping that they "would see a future in which they would be both compensated for their own sacrifices and be shielded from the consequences of their crimes," see Alexandra Lohse, *Prevail until the Bitter End: Germans in the Waning Years of World War II* (Ithaka: Cornell University Press, 2021), here 158.

118. USHMM, RG Number: RG-60.4866, film ID: 2866. See the critical edition and commentary by Peter Longerich, *Die Sportpalastrede 1943: Goebbels und der "totale Krieg"* (Munich: Siedler, 2023).

119. For example in the Propaganda Ministry's directives to newspaper editors and journalists what themes to emphasize and how to talk about them as well as the actual number of prominent articles in party outlets, most prominently the *Völkischer Beobachter*, covering the Jews; see Herf, *Three Faces of Antisemitism*, 24–7.

120. That was clearly the message of Goebbels "total war" speech of Feb. 18, 1943; and of his essay "Der Krieg und die Juden" (The Jews and the War) May 9, 1943, in idem, *Der steile Aufstieg: Reden und Aufsätze aus den Jahren 1942/43* (Munich: F. Eher, 1944), 263–70.

121. Hermann Göring, "*Rede zum Erntedankfest im Berliner Sportpalast, 4. Oktober 1942*," cited in Bankier, "The Use of Antisemitism in Nazi Wartime Propaganda," 51.

122. "Vertrauliche Informationen, Nr. 215/44" (September 30, 1944), Bundesarchiv Koblenz, ZSg. 109 (Theo Oberheitmann Collection), file 51, 149, translation LJ.

123. Herf, *The Jewish Enemy*, 252.

124. Fred Hahn and Günther Wagenlehner, *Lieber Stürmer! Leserbriefe an das NS-Kampfblatt 1924 bis 1945: Eine Dokumentation aus dem Leo-Baeck-Institut, New York* (Stuttgart: Seewald 1978), 8, 149; Walter Manoschek (ed.), *Es gibt nur eines für das Judentum: Vernichtung. Das Judenbild in deutschen Soldatenbriefen 1939-1944* (Hamburg: Hamburger Edition, 1995); all translations are mine.

125. Manoschek (ed.), *Es gibt nur eines für das Judentum*, 50, 51, 61, 67.

126. Ibid., 45, 54, 59.

127. Ibid., 36, 51, 59.

128. Ibid., 65, 67.

129. Ibid., 43, 53, 59, 61.

130. Hahn and Wagenlehner, *Lieber Stürmer! Leserbriefe an das NS-Kampfblatt*, 167; Manoschek, *Es gibt nur eines für das Judentum*, 51, 62.

131. Ernst Dreilich, Sept. 21, 1941, LBI Archives, AR 360, box 2, folder 8, 315-16.

132. Manoschek, *Es gibt nur eines für das Judentum*, 65, Dec. 18, 1942.

133. Ibid., 67, May 9, 1943.

134. Horst Schlegel, Chemnitz, April 9, 1943, LBI Archives, AR 360, box 2, folder 5, 125-6.

135. Johannes Gläser, Leipzig, May 19, 1943, LBI Archives, AR 360, box 2, folder 5, 90-1. Gläser suggested how Jews should be murdered after the war: "in big halls with carbon monoxide gas for a humane and painless death, which they don't even deserve." He went on to state a fantasy of a genocide of the Germans if the annihilation of the Jews was not complete: "Annihilate the Jews, annihilate the devil. If that does not happen completely, every drop of German blood has been spilled in vain because then the time will come when this drama will repeat itself."

136. Emil Schurkopf [?], Gelsenkirchen, May 28, 1942, LBI Archives, AR 360, box 2, folder 4, 921.

137. Anonymous, Goldap, May 1, 1943, LBI Archives, AR 360, box 2, folder 5, 129-30.

138. For example, Hahn and Wagenlehner, *Lieber Stürmer*, 188, July 12, 1943. As Michaela Kipp has shown, soldiers' field post letters show a general justification of violence against Jews as "military necessity"; soldiers accepted the Jewish-Bolshevist nexus and held Jews collectively accountable for partisan activity. See Michaela Kipp, "The Holocaust in the Letters of German Soldiers on the Eastern Front (1939-44)," *Journal of Genocide Research* 9, 4 (2007): 601-15, and her *Großreinemachen im Osten: Feindbilder in deutschen Feldpostbriefen im Zweiten Weltkrieg* (Frankfurt am Main: Campus 2014). See also Klaus Latzel, *Deutsche Soldaten—nationalsozialistischer Krieg? Kriegserlebnis—Kriegserfahrung 1939-1945* (Munich: Schöningh, 1998); Martin Humburg, *Das Gesicht des Krieges. Feldpostbriefe von Wehrmachtssoldaten aus der Sowjetunion 1941-1944* (Wiesbaden and Opladen: Westdeutscher Verlag, 1998) and the collection of field post letters at the Museum für Telekommunikation, Berlin, https://www.briefsammlung.de/feldpost-zweiter-weltkrieg/ (accessed Feb. 24, 2025).

139. Konrad H. Jarausch (ed.), *Reluctant Accomplice. A Wehrmacht Soldier's Letters from the Eastern Front* (Princeton: Princeton University Press, 2011), 283.

140. See Konrad H. Jarausch, "In search of a Father: Dealing with the Legacy of Nazi Complicity," in idem (ed.), *Reluctant Accomplice*, 1-44, here 33.

141. Cited in Omer Bartov, *Hitler's Army: Soldiers, Nazis, and War in the Third Reich* (New York: Oxford University Press, 1991), 169.

142. This is reflected in, for example, the statement of a German soldier about mass shootings of Jews at Ponary, in Klee, Dressen, and Riess,*"The Good Old Days"*, 43; see Bartov, *Hitler's Army*, 170.

143. Manoschek, *Es gibt nur eines für das Judentum*, 68, May 15, 1943.

144. Ibid., 69, May 29, 1943; 69, June 12, 1943; 71, Dec. 22, 1943; 74, Aug. 16, 1944. For a sober assessment of German crimes and the dark future that will follow: ibid., 70, June 27, 1943.

145. Ibid., 74, Aug. 11, 1944.

146. Ibid., 78, Sep. 29, 1944. In his classic *If This is a Man*, Primo Levi observes the same fears emerging at the IG Farben factory in Buna—he had been transferred there from Auschwitz because of his knowledge as a chemist—among the SS and even German political prisoners, in response to the summer 1944 bombardments of Upper Silesia. Here Levi does not directly tie these fears to fear of "Jewish revenge": "At Buna the German civilians raged with the fury of the secure man who wakes up from a long dream of domination and sees his own ruin and is unable to understand it. The *Reichsdeutsche* of the Lager as well, political included, felt the ties of blood and soil in the hour of danger. This new fact reduced the complications of hatred and incomprehension to their elementary terms and redivided the camp: the politicals, together with the green triangles and the SS, saw, or thought they saw, in all our faces the mockery of revenge and the vicious joy of the vendetta. They found themselves in unanimous agreement on this, and their ferocity redoubled. No German could now forget that we were on the other side: on the side of the terrible sowers who furrowed the German sky as masters, high above every defense, and twisted the living metal of their constructions, carrying slaughter every day into their very homes, into the hitherto unviolated homes of the German people." See Primo Levi, *If this is a Man / The Truce*, transl. Stuart Woolf (London: Abacus, 2013), 111–12.

147. Cited in Sönke Neitzel and Harald Welzer (eds.), *Soldaten on Fighting, Killing, and Dying. The Secret World War II Transcripts of German POWs* (New York: Alfred A. Knopf, 2012), 121–2.

148. Cited in ibid., 129–30.

149. Cited in ibid., 125–6, emphasis in original.

150. Jeffrey Herf, "The 'Jewish War': Goebbels and the Antisemitic Campaigns of the Nazi Propaganda Ministry," *Holocaust and Genocide Studies* 19, 1 (2005): 51–80, here 69.

151. See Longerich, *Die Sportpalastrede 1943*, esp. 90–2.

152. Ursula von Kardorff, *Berliner Aufzeichnungen: 1942 bis 1945* (Munich: DTV, 1997), 72.

153. Kulka and Jäckel, *The Jews in the Secret Nazi Reports*, 647.

154. Ibid., 651–2.

155. Ibid., 653.

156. Ibid., 653.

157. Perry Biddiscombe, *Werwolf! The History of the National Socialist Guerrilla Movement, 1944-1946* (Toronto: University of Toronto Press 1998); David K. Yelton, *Hitler's Volkssturm: The Nazi Militia and the Fall of Germany, 1944-1946* (Lawrence: University Press of Kansas, 2002).

158. Of 18.2 million combatants of Wehrmacht and SS, 5.3 million were killed in action between 1939 and 1945; the vast majority died in 1944 (1.8 million) and 1945 (1.5 million); see Overmans, *Deutsche militärische Verluste im Zweiten Weltkrieg*, 266.

159. Sven Keller, *Volksgemeinschaft am Ende: Gesellschaft und Gewalt 1944/45* (Berlin: De Gruyter, 2013); Daniel Blatman, *The Death Marches: The Final Phase of Nazi Genocide* (Cambridge: Harvard University Press, 2011), 272–342. Thomas Kühne, *The Rise and Fall of Comradeship: Hitler's Soldiers, Male Bonding and Mass Violence in the Twentieth Century* (Cambridge: Cambridge University Press, 2017), 160–211.

160. Kevin T. Hall, *Terror Flyers: The Lynching of American Airmen in Nazi Germany* (Bloomington: Indiana University Press, 2021), 5; Claire Andrieu, *When Men Fell from the Sky: Civilians and Downed Airmen in Second World War Europe* (New York: Cambridge University Press, 2023), 198.

161. See Adorno, "Schuld und Abwehr," 273–4.

162. Stephen G. Fritz, *Endkampf: Soldiers, Civilians, and the Death of the Third Reich* (Lexington: University Press of Kentucky, 2004). On internecine brutality in Berlin sparked by conflict over regime loyalty, see Andreas-Friedrich, *Der Schattenmann*, 268–91.

163. Norbert Haase, "Justizterror in der Wehrmacht am Ende des Zweiten Weltkrieges," in *Terror nach Innen: Verbrechen am Ende des Zweiten Weltkrieges*, ed. Cord Arendes, Edgar Wolfrum, and Jörg Zedler (Göttingen: Wallstein, 2006), 85. Douglas Carl Peifer speaks of 25,000–30,000 death sentences for various offenses, and 18,000–22,000 executions; see Douglas Carl Peifer, *Hitler's Deserters Breaking Ranks with the Wehrmacht* (New York: Oxford University Press, 2025), 4, 34, 38.

164. Haase, "Justizterror in der Wehrmacht am Ende des Zweiten Weltkrieges," 84.

165. Richard Bessel, "Murder amidst Collapse: Explaining the Violence of the Last Months of the Third Reich," *Years of Persecution, Years of Extermination: Saul Friedlander and the Future of Holocaust Studies*, ed. Christian Wiese and Paul Betts (London: Bloomsbury, 2010), 255–68, here 262; Michael Geyer, "Endkampf 1918 and 1945. German Nationalism, Annihilation and Self-Destruction," in *No man's Land of Violence: Extreme Wars in the 20th Century*, ed. Alf Lüdke and Bernd Weisbrod (Göttingen: Wallstein 2006), 36–67, here 61.

166. Blatman, *The Death Marches*, 272–342.

167. Perhaps the sole exception: Oskar Gröning, an SS-Unterscharführer who worked as a bookkeeper at Auschwitz, mainly accounting the valuables confiscated from the victims at the ramp. In 2015 the District Court in Lüneburg sentenced Groening (then aged 96) to 4 years in prison for being an accessory to 300,000 counts of murder. During his trial, Gröning spoke openly about Auschwitz, expressed personal regrets, accepted moral responsibility. He also sought direct contact with the survivors who testified at his trial. See Peter Huth (ed.), *Die letzten Zeugen: Der Auschwitz-Prozess von Lüneburg 2015; eine Dokumentation* (Stuttgart: Reclam, 2015).

168. Biess, *German Angst*, 25–65; Ulrike Weckel, "'Jüdische Rache'?: Wahrnehmungen des Nürnberger Hauptkriegsverbrecherprozesses durch Angeklagte, Verteidiger und die deutsche Bevölkerung 1945/46," *Jahrbuch für Antisemitismusforschung* 22 (2013): 57–78.

169. Gustave M. Gilbert, *Nuremberg Diary* (New York: Farrar, Straus 1947), 6.

170. Ibid., 41.

171. Ibid., 8.

172. Ibid., 88.

173. Weckel, "Jüdische Rache"?, 70.

174. See Laura Jockusch, "Justice at Nuremberg? Jewish Responses to Nazi War-Crime Trials in Allied-Occupied Germany," *Jewish Social Studies* 19, no. 1 (2012): 107–47.
175. International Military Tribunal, *IMT*, Nov. 21, 1945, vol. 2, 98.
176. Ibid., vol. 19, July 26, 1946, 433.
177. Ibid., July 29, 1946, 530.
178. Ibid., vol. 5, Jan. 10, 1946, 104; see also *Nazi Conspiracy and Aggression*, vol. 2, 699.
179. Ibid., 102.
180. Ibid., vol. 12, April 26, 1946, 306–16; April 29, 1946, 317–78.
181. Marx' defense of Streicher: ibid., April 30, 1946, 403.
182. Hiemer's testimony in defense of Streicher: ibid., 406.
183. Ibid., 408–9.
184. Marx' concluding plea for Streicher: Ibid., vol. 18, July 12, 1946, 192–4.
185. See the judgment against Streicher, ibid., vol.22, October 1, 1946, 547–9.
186. Ibid., vol. 19, July 23, 1946, 217, 231; July 24, 1946, 276.
187. Ibid., vol. 18, July 9, 1946, 40.
188. Ibid., 50.
189. Ibid., vol. 21, Aug. 26, 1946, 566.
190. Ibid., 569–70.
191. Ibid., 609.
192. Ibid., 604.
193. Ibid., vol. 22, Aug. 27, 1946, 90.
194. Ibid., vol. 21, Aug. 23, 1946, 492.
195. Ibid., 544.
196. Ibid., 544–5.
197. Ibid., 545.
198. International Military Tribunal, *IMT*, vol. 19, July 19, 1946, 48.
199. Ibid., 50.
200. Ibid., 48.
201. Devin Pendas, "Perpetrators on Trial," in *Cambridge History of the Holocaust*, ed. Laura Jockusch and Devin Pendas (Cambridge: Cambridge University Press, 2025), vol. 4, 125.
202. See Frank Luettig and Jens Lehmann (eds.) *Die Letzten NS- Verfahren* (Baden-Baden: Nomos 2017) and Lawrence Douglas, *The Right Wrong Man: John Demjanjuk and the Last Great Nazi War Crimes Trial* (Princeton: Princeton University Press, 2016); Mary Fullbrook, *Reckonings: Legacies of Nazi Persecution and the Quest for Justice* (New York: Oxford University Press, 2018); Hans-Christian Jasch and Wolf Kaiser, *Der Holocaust vor deutschen Gerichten: Amnestieren, Verdraengen, Bestrafen* (Stuttgart: Reclam, 2017).
203. Christopher Browning has shown, for example, that men engaged in police-battalion mass shootings had the choice of not participating; only a minority refused, and only a minority showed real enthusiasm, the rest complying from peer pressure and masculinity-performance. Those who refused and those who eventually broke down faced no punishment. See Christopher R. Browning, *Ordinary Men: Reserve Police Battalion 101 and the Final Solution in Poland* (New York: HarperCollins, 1992). There was a similar lack of

sanctions for SS shooters, although here there was generally no reluctance, as these men were ideologically committed; see Hilary Earl, *The Nuremberg SS-Einsatzgruppen Trial, 1945–1958: Atrocity, Law, and History* (New York: Cambridge University Press, 2009).

204. Lawrence Douglas, "Was Damals Recht War: Nulla Poena and the Prosecution of Crimes against Humanity in Occupied Germany," *Jus Post Bellum and Transitional Justice*, ed. Larry May and Elizabeth Edenberg (Cambridge University Press 2013), 44–73.

205. Verdict of case no. 379, LG Bremen, Nov. 27, 1953, in C.F. Rüter and D.W. de Mildt (eds.), *Justiz und NS-Verbrechen* (Amsterdam: Amsterdam University Press, 2010), vol. 11, 587.

206. See for example case no. 400a, LG Bochum, May 22, 1954, ibid., vol. 12, 433, 438; case no. 473, LG Bonn, Feb. 6, 1959, ibid., vol. 15, 149; case no. 811, LG Mannheim, July 5, 1974, ibid., vol. 39, 771; case no. 812, LG Hamburg, July 25, 1974, ibid., vol. 39, 865; case no. 815, LG Freiburg, Oct. 31, 1974, ibid., vol. 40, 237-238; case no. 835b, LG Kleve, Nov. 5, 1975, ibid., vol. 42, 48; case no. 885, LG Frankfurt, July 8, 1977, ibid., vol. 45, 687. The accusation that survivor witnesses were seeking revenge through false testimony was also used by some of the defense lawyers at the Auschwitz trial in Frankfurt 1963-1965, as for example by Hermann Stolting II; see Rebecca Wittmann, *Beyond Justice: The Auschwitz Trial* (Cambridge: Harvard University Press, 2005), 206-208 and Devin Pendas, *The Frankfurt Auschwitz Trial, 1963-1965: Genocide, History, and the Limits of the Law* (Cambridge: Cambridge University Press, 2006), 106, 193, 216.

207. Adolf Eichmann, *Ich, Adolf Eichmann: ein historischer Zeugenbericht*, ed. by Rudolf Aschenauer (Leoni am Starnberger See, Germany: Druffel Verlag, 1980), 496.

208. The State of Israel, Ministry of Justice, *The Trial of Adolf Eichmann*, vol. 1, 8; April 11, 1961.

209. Ibid., 60; April 17, 1961.

CHAPTER 2
RESPONDING TO THE APOCALYPSE: JEWISH REVENGE DURING THE HOLOCAUST

On February 4, 1936, the twenty-six-year-old medical student David Frankfurter wrote his father, brother, and sister: "I can no longer bear the sufferings of the Jewish people; my joy in living has been destroyed. May God avenge all the wrong that has been inflicted upon us Jews. I myself hope to be an insignificant tool in His hand."[1] Hours later in Davos, Frankfurter shot and killed Wilhelm Gustloff, the German leader of the Swiss branch of the Nazi party. Born in 1909 in the Croatian town of Daruvar, then part of the Austro-Hungarian Empire, Frankfurter had studied in Leipzig and Frankfurt since 1929. He had witnessed the rise of the Nazi movement, which had a stronghold in the German academic world, leading him to transfer to the University of Bern in 1933. His close contact with relatives in Germany had made him keenly aware of the defamation, ostracization, and victimization of German Jews. This injustice had recently been furnished with legal backing through the Nuremberg Laws, which relegated German Jewry to a lower category of citizenship and banned marriage and sexual relations between Jews and non-Jews, for the sake of protecting "German blood and honor." Three years into Nazi rule, Frankfurter was desperate to avenge the injustice—by murdering the Nazi party's representative in Switzerland.

Two and a half years later, on November 7, 1938, seventeen-year-old Herschel Grynszpan, another young Jewish student, shot the diplomat Ernst vom Rath, third secretary at the German embassy in Paris, who died two days later. Twelve days beforehand, the German government had expelled 17,000 Jews with Polish citizenship from Germany, after Poland had threatened to revoke their citizenship. Poland refused to allow them back into the country; as a result, Jewish individuals and families were stranded in a no-man's-land between the two states. Before shooting vom Rath, Grynszpan wrote to his parents and sister, who were among the expellees, that "I could not do otherwise. May God forgive me. My heart bleeds at the news of twelve thousand Jews' suffering. I must protest in such a way that the world will hear me."[2]

Contrary to Nazi propaganda which portrayed vengefulness as a racial trait of the Jews and claimed that Jews had always harmed Germans irrespective of how Germans had treated the Jews, revenge acts by Jews were in fact reactions to their victimization by the Nazi regime. Frankfurter and Grynszpan were responding to a reality of persecution that had now reached an unprecedented extreme. Both had a sense that since the justice system was failing Germany's Jews—allowing the German state to remove their rights and turn them into outlaws who could be humiliated, mistreated, and dehumanized with impunity—they had no choice but to take matters in their own hands. Both students committed an illegal act—a murder—for the sake of swaying public opinion by shedding light on the injustices that had motivated the deed.[3] An extreme situation, they believed, necessitated an extreme act.[4] While still in Germany, Frankfurter had already played with the idea of shooting a major Nazi figure—he once missed an opportunity to shoot Hermann Göring;[5] in spring 1933, he had acquired a revolver from a Jewish World War I veteran. In his 1946 memoir, Frankfurter recalled a picture of Adolf Hitler in the room where he shot Gustloff with the words "Blood and Honor" written underneath. He also recalled the popular *Sturmlied* of the SA which in one of its numerous antisemitic variations predicted that "when Jewish blood splatters from the knife, all will be well again." Using violence, Frankfurter indicated, amounted to speaking to Gustloff, the "representative of the biggest gang of murderers in his own language, the only language he understood."[6] For Frankfurter, this was a matter of *Jewish* blood and *Jewish* honor.[7]

The Nazi regime would use both instances to fuel its victimization of Jews and to turn Gustloff and vom Rath—who had not been a Nazi—into martyrs for the Nazi cause. In both cases, the regime presented these acts of Jewish vengeance as perpetrated by agents of a Jewish anti-German conspiracy, of a Jewish collective that had been intent all along on victimizing Germans. The idea was propagated, for example, in Hitler's speech at Gustloff's funeral in Schwerin on February 12, 1936; and Wolfgang Diewerge, a member of Goebbels' propaganda ministry, made the case that a vengeful individual was acting on behalf of "international Jewry" in his 1936 book *Der Fall Gustloff*.[8] Initially, retaliation on German Jews for Gustloff's death was mitigated by the regime's concern about its international image on the world stage: Germany was the host of the Winter Olympics, which opened in Garmisch-Partenkirchen on February 6, 1936, two days after the assassination. But Jewish observers—for instance literary scholar Victor Klemperer in his famous diary[9]—knew that the payback was simply being postponed. In the case of the attack on vom Rath in November 1938, the situation was different. As we have seen, the killing would serve as a pretext for the November Pogrom—and the destruction of any hope for Jews that normal life in Germany was going to be possible.[10]

While at the time, most Jews living within the borders of the German Reich will have shared the sense of powerlessness, humiliation, anger, despair, and betrayal that had triggered the actions of both Frankfurter and Grynszpan, by and large they did not view violent revenge acts as a cure for their misery. In fact, most German Jews tacitly ostracized Frankfurter and Grynszpan; some Jews vehemently rejected their recourse to deadly violence as foolish, dangerous, irresponsible, and wrong: the Nazi leadership was, after all, only looking for excuses to victimize Jews even more while blaming Jews for their own victimization. Among the many letters that Frankfurter received in custody, one Jewish writer pointed out that he had both violated Judaism's ethical principles and endangered his coreligionists with his deed.[11] Hours after the news of vom Rath's death, the Reich Association of German Jews sent Hitler a telegram with condolences, asserting that "the German Jews, as all civilized human beings, detest political murder and the bloody deed of Paris."[12] In their acute awareness that the Nazi government was waiting for this opportunity to lash out against German Jewry and force "compensation" for "damage" supposedly caused Germany, the leaders of the Reich Association hoped that the foreign press would pick up on the condolence-letter, making such retaliation more difficult.[13]

Figure 6 A Nazi propaganda poster depicting a photograph of Herschel Grynszpan, Berlin, 1938; USHMM Photo Archives # 32663; courtesy of United States Holocaust Memorial Museum.

To be sure, Jews only rarely openly showed their anger at burning synagogues, ransacked shops, plundered apartments, violated bodies and arrests—not to speak of invoking revenge. One exception in Frankfurt am Main: on the morning after the pogrom, Henriette Schäfer (née Neu, born in 1882 in Odernheim am Glan), retorted when her local grocer justified the anti-Jewish violence as an expression of legitimate German rage over Grynszpan's deed. (Being her customer, tenant, and neighbor, Schäfer knew the grocer well.) Schäfer, who lived in a "privileged mixed marriage" with a non-Jewish man, begged to differ. However, the German people were not to blame, she also insisted, but rather the "blackguards, scamps, and criminals" of the Nazi government. "Hitler is the biggest bandit," she exclaimed, adding "If I could, I would poison them all." Schäfer went on to announce that "our people, the Jews, will eventually take revenge."[14] Either the grocer or another customer then denounced Schäfer to the authorities. She was tried and punished with a six-month jail sentence; eventually she was deported to Theresienstadt.[15] To be sure, although Schäfer had released her anger and despair over the pogrom night's events by voicing an abstract revenge fantasy, she had not actually endorsed Grynszpan's act. Frankfurter and Grynszpan remain exceptions to the general rule that in the 1930s under the Nazi regime, Jews considered violent revenge a societal and moral transgression.

Revenge is a deeply human response to injustice and trauma. Yet modern states and civil societies imposed strict boundaries on it. They developed ethical and legal norms confining revenge—both in terms of negative emotions as well as negative social behaviors—to a realm of moral and societal stigma, meant to be subsumed by a civilian ethos of a search for justice. In modern states, revenge acts by citizens have been criminalized; laws and legal institutions have emerged as the proper instruments for addressing harm and injustice; the state's institutions have held a monopoly on violence. Negative emotions accompanying revenge acts—anger, rage, resentment, hatred—are likewise branded as uncivilized, consequently inappropriate. The German criminal code of 1871 counted revenge as a "base motive" making homicide into murder, hence subject to severe punishment. Killing someone as an act of hate- or passion-grounded vengeance was, in other words, thought a graver crime than killing someone in the absence of such emotions, for example on orders of someone else. Whatever the motivating factors for violent personal vigilantism, it was a taboo for most ordinary, law-abiding, self-respecting citizens of the state. Refraining from revenge was moral common sense.

German Jews shared this ethos with other Europeans; as the 1930s progressed, revenge continued to seem an improper means to address the ostracization and persecution they faced on a daily basis. For as long as possible, the incremental radicalization of Nazi policies and actions could be perceived as conveying contradictory messages about what the regime held in store for German Jewry—which faced an acute identity crisis, that of being victimized in a country it had called its own, sharing its

Figure 7 A defaced *Der Stürmer* display box in Sankt Peter, Baden-Württemberg, *c.*1933; the slogan "the Jews are our misfortune" was manipulated to read "the Jews are our fortune"; USHMM Photo Archives # 18523; United States Holocaust Memorial Museum, courtesy of Miriamne Fields.

language, its culture, and, increasingly, its everyday habits. In the face of a gradually accelerating pace of persecution, German Jews initially relied on non-violent forms of advocacy and self-help, in the hope that the government of brown shirts, viewed as not representative of the true Germany, would pass into history quickly.

In the early years of Nazi rule some German Jews had recourse to self-defense through legal action, bolstered by rational arguments exposing and decrying Nazi atrocities; others petitioned the Nazi authorities and even the League of Nations, seeking to hold on to shrinking civil and minority rights.[16] Jews engaged in acts of defiance such as defacing Nazi symbols, verbal and written protest, disobeying Nazi laws and regulations, photo-documenting discrimination and abuse, responding to physical violence with physical self-defense.[17] In an ever more brutal and violent environment, with a regime taking ever more radical antisemitic measures—these tested on Jewish populations now under German control through annexation and conquest—Jews adopted a wide range of survival strategies, based on assessment of where Nazi policies might be headed and what options for self-preservation remained for Jews. In this increasingly nightmarish existential situation, most Jews chose a combination of forms of compliance with Nazi policies—in the hope of forestalling even worse measures—evasion, and resistance.[18] Revenge only gradually entered this reactive spectrum, once the measures had become indiscriminately lethal.

The anti-Jewish policies that had outraged Frankfurter and Grynszpan and had triggered their responses three and five and a half years into the Nazi regime only marked a beginning; they paled by comparison to what followed, eventually the systematic, continent-wide genocide of 5.8 million Jews. The more aware Jews in Germany and throughout Europe became that the Germans were targeting them for murder and cynically deceiving them about their fate, the more likely Jews were to abandon a civilian humanitarian ethos rejecting vengeance. Jewish vengeance in response to Nazi oppression and mass murder was fundamentally different from the putative "Jewish revenge" of Nazi perpetrators: as we have seen, a purely ideological construct nurtured by the inverted genocidal fantasy that Jews and "world Jewry"—in reality facing German extermination—were intent on destroying the German nation, and by extension "humanity" or "civilization" in general. Jewish revenge, by contrast, was a despairing response, an emotional coping reaction to the reality of Nazi genocide. The growing pace of Jewish revenge was directly aligned with the intensity of Nazi German mass murder: with the extent to which the genocide had been executed and remaining Jews had become aware of the systematic nature and massive scale of the loss of lives.

In March 1942, 75 to 80 percent of the Jews who would be murdered in the Holocaust were alive; by February 1943, only 20 to 25 percent were still living.[19] That means that 60 percent of the victims of the Holocaust died in that eleven-month period. Jewish revenge on Nazis and their collaborators correspondingly intensified during that year, its expressions becoming more furious and desperate, the moral stigma tied to it dissipating in line with the German violation of all socio-cultural conventions and ethical bounds. The agents of Jewish revenge were predominantly (albeit not exclusively) younger Jews, above the age of fifteen but below the age of forty, which is to say persons born after 1905 and before 1930. Jews in that cohort were more likely to still be alive and have some physical strength, and to have been selected for forced labor toward the end of the war. Such younger Jews were also less likely to be inhibited by norms harkening back to prewar normalcy than their older counterparts: they had, after all, lived for less time with such pre-"final solution" conventions. Nevertheless, the engagement with revenge emotions and behaviors was no general pattern but an individual response in extremis.

Whether or not individuals who suffer traumatisation turn to revenge as a coping mechanism and if and how revenge feelings lead to revenge behaviors depends on a complex set of interrelated factors: the severity and nature of the traumatizing event and the victims' cognitive appraisal processes assessing it and identifying those responsible; the victims' individual motivations (feelings of pain, anger, hate) and goals for revenge (the desire to restore self-efficacy, self-esteem, and a sense of security, establish deterrence, and seek justice); and the victims' individual attitudes toward revenge (as they depend on worldview, political orientation, religious ethics, value orientation, conceptions of justice, personhood, and autonomy), in addition to other factors such as age and gender.[20]

European Jews under Nazi rule had diverse social, educational, professional, economic, cultural, and national backgrounds; their religious and political views and wartime experiences and responses also varied. Their approaches to revenge were correspondingly diverse. Jews who engaged with revenge—as emotions, fantasies, or actions—were both secular and religiously observant. Political outlook played a role in the approach they took, together with combat experience—Jews with Zionist leanings and such experience were more likely to relate to revenge as a way of restoring a sense of Jewish national honor. In general, young people who fought in resistance movements—Zionist, socialist, Bundist, communist—and partisan units were more prone to revenge-taking (i.e., acting out their emotions by violent means), having some access to weapons and opportunity to openly express a fury considered legitimate. But revenge was not just a national project, and it was not limited to Jews with combat experience. Both male and female Jewish individuals took different forms of revenge; it served various functions at different points as the war and Holocaust unfolded. Furthermore, revenge was not a stand-alone response to the Nazi genocidal campaign, rather complementing other responses, survival strategies, and coping mechanisms. It was a particularly crucial coping reaction for individuals who realized that their murder was inevitable and who saw it as the only alternative to accepting utter powerlessness.

The case of Meier Berliner can here serve as an example. An Argentinian Jew of Polish background, Berliner had returned to Warsaw with his wife and daughter for a family visit in 1939; after Germany occupied Poland in September 1939, he was unable to return to Argentina. Starting in November 1940, Berliner and his family were trapped in the Warsaw ghetto together with over 400,000 other Jews. When the Nazi authorities deported over a quarter of a million Warsaw Jews to Treblinka in just seven weeks in summer 1942, the Berliners were among the deportees. Upon arrival at Treblinka in early September, Berliner's wife and daughter were murdered; he was selected to work in the death camp. On September 11, 1942, Berliner stabbed and killed SS-Oberscharführer Max Biala, one of the SS guards involved in herding Jewish men to their deaths in the gas chambers. Another SS guard immediately killed Berliner, the SS then retaliating upon the 600 Jews temporarily being kept alive for work in operating the camp by shooting and killing every tenth of them.[21] Similar revenge acts were committed by women, for instance the aforementioned Franceska Mann, who shot and killed an SS guard with his own weapon on the way to the gas chamber at Auschwitz-Birkenau. One observer of this was Zalmen Gradowski (born 1908 or 1909 in Suwałki), a member of the so-called *Sonderkommando* at Auschwitz-Birkenau—a group of Jewish prisoners temporarily kept alive to handle the remains of the murdered—whose secretly buried testimony, discovered shortly after the war, will be returned to later. Mann's act, Gradowski observes in this account, "inspired courage in other brave women, who slapped the faces of the enraged, savage beasts, the uniformed SS, and pelted them with bottles and other such objects."[22] But were Mann's and Berliner's courageous acts of suicidal defiance, and the acts they inspired, acts of revenge or acts of resistance? Where those who engaged in anti-Nazi resistance also engaging in revenge, and vice versa? What are the conceptual differences between revenge and resistance in the context of the Holocaust?

Revenge or Resistance? Differences and Entanglements

In a context marked by a complete absence of justice, its replacement by radical and all-encompassing injustice, both revenge and resistance constitute a response to oppression; both aim to affect the state of oppression, altering the victim-perpetrator power-relation. Yet the two responses differ. Resistance emerges from a sense of agency and optimism, revenge from a sense of despair, powerlessness, and pessimism.

Resisters act in the belief that they can intervene to mitigate, avert, or end a state of oppression. Resistance during the Holocaust—broadly defined as "any individual or group action in opposition to known laws, actions, or intentions of the Nazis and their collaborators"[23]—itself took many forms; but its entire range of actions stemmed from a belief, however tenuous, that the terrible events that were unfolding could be affected to the victims' advantage. It is the case that Jewish armed resistance, whether collective or individual, was less centered on hurting the Germans militarily than on a longer-term goal: sustaining Jewish society in the face of the genocide, even if in the interim the armed confrontation would cost many Jewish lives.[24] Through the combination of armed combat, mass breakouts, and escapes, underground groups in ghettos and camps aimed to break the perpetrators' otherwise absolute power and place victims in a better position to survive. Jewish partisan groups fought and sabotaged the German military apparatus in order to weaken and help defeat it, while also helping Jews survive until that point. Even if individual resisters anticipated not surviving this process, they saw what they did in terms of a broad strategic goal: saving what could be saved of the Jewish collective and liberation from Nazi rule.

The ways that goal was honored extended from providing medical aid to hiding Jewish births, smuggling food, non-compliance with German orders, and various forms of evasion and concealment of Jewish identity for the sake of sustaining lives. There was cultural resistance as well, often referred to by the Hebrew term *amidah* (i.e., "standing up"): taking the form of various cultural activities, religious observance, education, the salvaging of Jewish cultural objects and artefacts, the aim here continued to be the strategic aim of survival. Amidah reflected recognition that sustaining a sociocultural sphere, at least in some form, was a key component of the morale required for long-term defiance of Nazi German genocidal intent.[25]

Jews engaged in different forms of resistance simultaneously. For example, in the Vilna ghetto, members of the so-called Paper Brigade, whom the SS had conscripted to destroy Jewish cultural treasures, secretly salvaged many of these treasures. The same individuals, among them the Yiddish-language poets Abraham Sutzkever and Szmerke Kaczerginski, also documented and hid evidence of Nazi atrocities, found hiding places for Jews, smuggled weapons for armed resistance, and fought in partisan units while seeking to survive in the forests until the end of the war.[26]

In the contrasting case of revenge, the only option victims feel they have is attaching a price to the perpetrators' deeds by inflicting physical and emotional harm on them, or else doing moral damage in return for their acts. While that payback cannot undo the initial atrocity, it supplies a sense of empowerment. The avengers seek to express their pain and sense of loss and humiliation by inflicting the same, or at least a portion of that traumatic complex, so that the perpetrators can *feel* what they did to the victims. Even if the revenge act is not commensurate with the original injustice, avengers thus draw immediate emotional satisfaction by exacting a toll on the perpetrators—through executing a temporary, if partial, role reversal.

Both in the context of the Holocaust and in general, the distinctions between revenge and resistance are not always clear-cut; the two phenomena are often intertwined.[27] In fact, revenge and resistance are mutually complementary in complex ways: revenge acts can serve as tools of resistance; inflicting harm on the perpetrators as payback for the harm they did to the victims can be part of a larger resistance plot. In other words, the emotional benefits drawn from revenge might serve resistance that builds not just on combatting the perpetrators but also on sustaining the lives of the victims—boosting their morale and maintaining resilience. And the reverse can also be the case: acts of resistance against oppression can serve as a means of revenge on the perpetrators, exact a toll on them as payback for the harm they have inflicted. In general, defining which of the two phenomena is in play and how it interacts with its counterpart depends as much on the historical context as on the intent of the historical actors involved.

During the Holocaust, resistance and revenge often converged in armed resistance in ghettos and death camps. While armed uprisings mainly followed strategic goals centered on disrupting the deportation and killing process and enabling victims to flee and hide, resisting individuals also clearly often had vengeful impulses. Some of this has come down to us in revenge rhetoric, serving to motivate and morally justify the killing of Nazi perpetrators in a resistance plot. This is the case of Chaim Engel, one of the participants in the Sobibor uprising on October 14, 1943. Born in 1916 in Brudzew, Poland, Engel had arrived at Sobibor in September 1942 and was selected for labor in the camp, sorting the clothes of the murdered victims. Engel did not belong to the inner circle of prisoners who had been assigned roles in the plot to assassinate the SS guards, one after the other, as they came for fittings in the various tailor, shoemaker, and goldsmith workshops run by prisoners temporarily spared from murder. But he knew of the plan to kill SS personnel so that the death camp's 600–700 prisoners could escape. When one of the prisoners assigned to assassinate an SS officer panicked and was unable to perform, Engel felt forced to step in, knowing that the escape plot, and thus the lives of the prisoners, depended on this murder. While Engel saw the plot as necessary resistance, he nevertheless had moral qualms to singlehandedly kill a human being, even if that human being was an SS man operating a camp whose sole purpose was mass murder of human beings. Ultimately, thoughts of his murdered family gave him moral justification and resolve: "With every jab, I said, 'This is for my father, for my mother, for all these people, all the Jews you killed.'"[28] Other participants in the Sobibor uprising also invoked avenging murdered family members when killing the SS guards.[29]

In joint testimony furnished in 1998, Chaim and Selma Engel (the couple had met as prisoners and escaped Sobibor together) emphasized the collective responsibility to help the murders of SS personnel—and hence the uprising—succeed.[30] For Chaim, killing an SS officer was not an end in itself; it served to enable resistance aimed at saving a death camp's Jewish lives. Most of the prisoners involved would be killed by machine gun fire from Ukrainian guards, from landmines planted around the camp, and in the course of searches that Germans and Ukrainians conducted around the camp over the following days; perhaps fifty individuals, less than 10 percent of the prisoners who participated in the uprising, managed to survive the war. But if it had not been for these survivors, posterity likely would not have known about the horrors of Sobibor, with its 250,000 dead, and there would have been no witnesses for the postwar legal proceedings.[31] As Chaim Engel's example suggests, collective responsibility and coordinated action to render the camp dysfunctional, allowing an escape from certain death, not vengeance, was the ultimate motivation for the Sobibor uprising. But it appears that personal feelings of vengeance did spur individuals to participate in the resistance plot. The intertwining of revenge and resistance—an emotional thirst for revenge driving individuals to participate in an uprising they would likely not survive and which had the strategic goal of rendering the killing process dysfunctional, enhancing chances for some prisoners to escape the camp—also served as emotional ballast for other Jews participating in armed death-camp revolts, at Treblinka on August 2, 1943 and at Auschwitz-Birkenau on October 7, 1944.[32]

Resisters also had recourse to revenge rhetoric when their larger strategic goals became clearly unattainable. Participants in the 1943 Warsaw ghetto uprising conflated resistance with revenge as it became increasingly clear that beyond the symbolism of the uprising—it lasted nearly a month, from April 19 to May 16, 1943—the imbalance of power between the SS and the Jewish combatants made it impossible to alter the situation of the ghetto population, slated for mass murder. Revenge rhetoric gave purpose to the fighting and individuals—both the 700 sparsely armed youthful members of the Jewish underground and the larger ghetto population of approximately 56,000 Jews who were unarmed but large numbers were prepared to hide in bunkers—drew emotional satisfaction from the fact that, finally, the murder of Jews came at the cost of German lives. Why, wondered Zivia Lubetkin, one of the founding members of the Jewish Fighting Organization (Żydowska Organizacja Bojowa, ŻOB), were the young women and men who entered the fight on April 19, 1943 so "joyful and merry" despite knowing they were unable to match the SS in military strength? "We knew that our end had come. We knew beforehand that they would defeat us, but we also knew that they would pay a heavy price for our lives."[33] While revenge had not been the uprising's main objective, the temporary role reversal at work here imparted meaning as the uprising was beaten down and the Jewish death toll came to outnumber the German toll by the thousands. "It is difficult to describe," said Lubetkin, "that when . . . we saw German blood pouring in the streets of Warsaw, after so much Jewish blood and tears had previously flowed in the streets of Warsaw—we felt within us, great rejoicing and it was of no importance what would happen the following day." She further described the mood among the ghetto population at the beginning of the uprising: "Jews embraced and kissed each other; although it was clear to every single one that . . . it was almost certain that he would not survive, nevertheless . . . he had reached the day of our taking revenge . . ."[34]

Other members of the fighting organization basically echoed Lubetkin.[35] In testimony furnished in 1993 and 1994, a former Bund member of the ŻOB, Masha P. (born in 1924 in Warsaw), recalled that between the time of the "great deportation" in the summer of 1942 and the ghetto uprising, the desire for revenge built up, serving as an organizational motor. When the uprising itself got underway, it was clear that it was akin to "ants fighting elephants"; and yet there was hope that it would allow some Jews to escape the ghetto and serve a larger strategic goal of survival. The individual desire for revenge thus helped give fighters the emotional wherewithal to join a doomed fight.[36]

Revenge was consequently not the ultimate goal of the Warsaw ghetto uprising; but the emotional satisfaction it offered complemented the fighters' strategic purpose: to forestall liquidation of the ghetto in the hope that a portion of its population would be able to survive in subterranean bunkers, especially women, children and the elderly, or else by escaping the ghetto entirely through sewers.[37] For the combatants, however, that mission became increasingly suicidal. "Our last days are growing nearer," wrote twenty-four-year-old Mordechai Anielewicz, the commander of ŻOB, to Yitzhak Zuckerman on April 26, 1943, eight days into the uprising, which he would not survive. "But so long as we have bullets we will continue to fight and defend ourselves. . . . The revenge for our holy spilled blood will come!" Anielewicz also expressed the hope that some Jews would be saved to continue the struggle for liberation from the Germans.[38] On April 23, he had already written Zuckerman as follows: "Peace go with you, my friend! Perhaps we may still meet again! The dream of my life has risen to become fact. Self-defense in the ghetto will have been a reality. Jewish armed resistance and revenge are facts. I have been a witness to the magnificent, heroic fighting of Jewish men in battle."[39] When the SS discovered ŻOB's command bunker at Mila 18, Anielewicz committed suicide before the Germans murdered the 120 fighters in the bunker by throwing in gas grenades. By the time that SS-Gruppenführer Jürgen Stroop, commander of SS and army forces dismantling the ghetto, declared the uprising and the ghetto obliterated—and with it

Europe's largest Jewish community—on May 16, 35,000 Jews had been deported, including 6,500 to Treblinka, 14,000 to Majdanek, 10,000 to Poniatowa, close to 5,000 to Trawniki, and 1,000 to Budzyń. An estimated 15,000-20,000 Jews had been murdered during the uprising or shortly thereafter, while thousands of Jews tried to survive hiding in the ghetto ruins after the revolt or on the "Aryan side" of the city.[40]

The interconnections between the personal, emotional need for vengeance and resistance centered on collective political-national goals was most obvious among Jewish partisans. Individual Jews often referred to the wish to avenge murdered loved ones as their motivation for joining combat against Nazi Germany. Faye Schulman (Faigel Lazebnik, born 1919), a young female Jewish photographer from the eastern Polish (today Belorussian) town of Lenin, joined the Molotov Brigade, a partisan unit of mostly male non-Jewish combatants, because she sought to avenge the murder of her parents, sisters, and brother, shot to death along with 1,800 other residents of the Lenin ghetto on August 14, 1942.[41] (She would only find out later that one of her brothers had survived.) "I wanted to revenge. I felt that since my family was killed and I was the only survivor . . . this is my responsibility to revenge." But here too, revenge was no end in itself. Schulman fought for her own survival; she entered the partisan fight to defeat the Germans; and fighting among non-Jewish partisans, who had only accepted her because she had enough medical knowledge to serve the unit as a nurse, she also sought "to show that Jews can fight . . . if they have an opportunity. That they are not cowards and that they are not going into that 'like sheep,' but if they have a chance . . ., if they have the rifle, they are willing to help to free the people, to free the world from those Nazis."[42] At the same time she sensed that she was "lifting the Jewish dignity . . . the pride of the Jewish people."[43]

A complex interplay of personal and collective factors, of motivations involving revenge, resistance, and survival, shaped the struggle of Jews in partisan units. According to Miriam Brysk (born in 1935 in Warsaw), whose father was a doctor in a Jewish partisan unit near Lida in the Grodno region (now in Belorussia), for Jews who had escaped the brutal ghetto roundups and mass shootings, fled to the forests, and joined the partisans, "it wasn't a question of survival only, it was a question of *nekomeh*, vengeance. They had to avenge the deaths of their families so brutally murdered in so many of the ghettos all around." Brysk recalled that one of the men in their unit, a "Jew who lost his entire family in the ghetto slaughters," tied a captured German soldier to a tree and "put something in his mouth so he wouldn't scream and he just, with a knife, he said: 'this slice is for my mother' 'this is for my father' and so enumerated all the people that the Germans had killed in his family."[44]

When it came to revenge acts, what mattered was individual confrontation with a perpetrator—either someone known, directly responsible for a concrete killing, or more often any captured German soldier; it was important to engage in a direct confrontation, with an announcement of who the avenger was and who was being avenged. This was, in a sense, a twofold highly tragic performance: a display of the pain of the loss being avenged—hence commemoration of those lost—and an enactment of role reversal. Jewish partisan Sidney Simon would thus commonly introduce himself to the Germans he would kill after capturing them in combat as a member of the "Jewish SS."[45] He took enjoyment in the role reversal and the sense of payback for the murder of his family members on any German he could get hold of. According to Miriam Brysk, what kept many Jews in partisan units "alive and working was to avenge their families. They were going to kill as many Germans as they could."[46] While this might have been the aspiration, it most likely did not happen for lack of opportunity and resources. Nevertheless, some partisan leaders also made conscious efforts to suppress and contain vengeful impulses, for fear it would divert energies and resources needed for self-defense and self-preservation. This was tied to a careful weighing of the costs and benefits of taking up arms, Jewish underground arsenals being understocked, Germans likely to retaliate on defenseless Jewish civilians. For example, the "Bielski Brothers" (Tuvia, Asael, and Zus Bielski), who led a Jewish partisan detachment in the forests of Western Belorussia, opposed using ammunition to kill Germans for the sake of revenge and connected emotional satisfaction; rather, it was meant to be used strictly to defend and rescue Jewish lives. The Bielskis, in short, prioritized resistance over revenge.[47] But other partisan units, for example, the all-Jewish Nekama ("Revenge") battalion operating in the Belorussian Narocz forest from July to September 1943, had a very different stance.[48] Still, even for them, revenge was no end in itself but rather one way to resist together with sabotage and combat.

At killing sites and in death camps, on the other hand, revenge did become an end in itself, for reasons suggested above: a loss of all hope of escaping death, advent of a state of rage, frustration, and an unbearable need to defy absolute powerlessness. Franceska Mann and Meier Berliner murdered SS guards as a last-resort action, in a situation where they grasped the reality of the Nazi mass murder enterprise and understood that they were about to be murdered too. They had no way of saving their own lives or the lives of those around them; but they sought to make sure that their deaths would come at a cost for the murderers. The act itself, subversion of the massive power-disparity, possibly held a kind of redemptive meaning for the avengers, even if only for an instant; we may assume it had a similar effect on at least some of the other, witnessing victims as well.

As the examples of Mann and Berliner show, the Nazi retaliation for such revenge acts was brutal. Sonderkommando member Zalmen Gradowski, referring to the Auschwitz inmates he has witnessed being beaten to death by the SS and Ukrainian guards, observes that in the extreme death camp situation, basic collective survival instincts and the desire for revenge were in conflict; and that more often than not that collective survival instinct suppressed revenge.[49] Leon Weliczker Wells was only seventeen when he was forced to work in the Janowska camp *Sonderkommando 1005* from June through November 1943. Under SS-Standardtenführer Paul Blobel, this commando of Jewish prisoners from the Janowska Street camp in Lvov was tasked with eliminating traces of mass murder by exhuming mass graves of Jews murdered in mass shootings in Eastern Galicia in 1941 and 1942, burning their bodies on pyres, sifting the ashes, and crushing the bones. In addition, the commando was also forced to watch mass shootings of the remaining local Jews in Eastern Galicia and subsequently eliminate the traces of these crimes as well. According to Wells, groups of 40 to 50 men, women, and children were brought in trucks to a ravine in a mountainous area fenced in and heavily guarded by members of the Security Service (the SD) and the German police. The victims were forced to take off eyeglasses, socks, and shoes—to hinder escapes—and to undress and line up to be machine-gunned close to a burning pit. "Once a mother came with her child, and when she undressed, she spat in the face of the SD guard." Her act of revenge in the moment when she realized that she and her child had nowhere to escape death, seeking to break the absolute power of the perpetrator by humiliating him in front of both his peers and the victims who were still alive, was punished by an even more brutal death for both: "[T]hey took the child by the legs, knocked its head against a tree and put it in the fire, and hanged her by the feet. . . . The other women seeing this, thought—'What's the use . . .' This happened quite a few times – especially for mothers not [i.e. who refused, LJ] to undress children."[50]

These courageous and desperate acts carried symbolic meaning for both the victims and mass murderers. But systematically, Germans randomly killed more Jews in retaliation—an obvious utilitarian aim of at times nigh-unfathomable cruelty and sadism being to deter other such revenge acts. The strategy was effective: Chaika Klinger, a young and leading member of the Hashomer Hatzair (labor Zionist) part of the ŻOB underground in the Będzin ghetto, thus related in her diary—written while hiding, with the help of two Polish families, in the nearby village of Dąbrowska between late August and mid-December 1943 before her escape to Slovakia and onward to Palestine—that she consciously even suppressed a strong impulse to scream revenge slurs when arrested because she did not want to risk hurting the other Jews rounded up with her.[51] And Joseph K., born in 1926 in Gorlice near Krakow—he survived forced labor at Mielec and Wieliczka, deportation to Auschwitz, and a death march to Flossenbürg—indicated the following in testimony given in 1979: "Assuming that a German was abusing my father . . . my anger could be vented by attacking this German, doing harm to him. . . . But, the punishment that would be meted out to me would be negligible compared to the consequences knowing that ten innocent men would be executed because of my foolish act."[52]

For Joseph K., then, the Nazi attachment of a communal price tag simply augmented the *absolute* nature of Jewish powerlessness in face of the planned mass murder. "It is very difficult to raise a finger against a machine gun," he commented. "It is also very difficult to live knowing that because of my foolish act, ten men have been executed and there are widows and orphans."[53] What is clear is that individuals came up with different answers in the struggle to balance personal emotion and a deep-seated sense of communal responsibility. That struggle, together with basic human nature, serves as a backdrop to the fact that non-violent forms of Jewish revenge—non-violent acts of both an individual and collective nature, aimed at generating role reversal through indirect, non-physical harm, psychological pressure, and degrading the murderers' social and moral status through insult, humiliation, and ridicule—were much more widespread than their violent counterpart in this horrific context. These acts—which themselves need to be distinguished from cultural or spiritual resistance—were often outward-facing, public, and confrontative, addressing either the perpetrators themselves or other Jews (and, sometimes, non-Jews), but they could also be private and inward-facing: including highly personal, quotidian acts not known or not recognizable to the Nazi perpetrators as, precisely, revenge—but understood as such by other Jews. Such inward-facing revenge acts could involve, for instance, defacing Nazi symbols or spitting at display boxes of *Der Stürmer*;[54] or they could involve placing a knife with the body of a murdered Jew at burial, as equipment for revenge in an apocalyptic future: custom of one Hassidic group in Kolbuszowa, in Galicia, south-eastern Poland.[55] Or again, it could involve inserting lice into the potatoes served to SS guards, as did Isaac Brecher (born in 1927 in Rozavlea, Rumania), according to his 1998 testimony, working in the kitchen of the Ellrich-Juliushütte subcamp of the Dora-Mittelbau concentration camp toward the end of the war, after he had been incarcerated in the Dragomiresti ghetto, in Auschwitz, and in Buchenwald.[56] Or it could involve excrement. Marie Jalowicz Simon, born in 1922, struggled to survive passing as an "Aryan" in Berlin between 1942 and 1945. While she was sheltered by non-Jewish Germans from all walks of life at night, she often had no place to stay during the day, which she spent roaming around the city's streets, and parks, with stops in cinemas, subway tunnels, and stairways. Homeless, displaced, in constant fear of discovery, arrest, and abduction to Auschwitz, she at times defecated on the doorsteps of Berliners she deemed ardent Nazis.[57] And eight-year-old Janet B. (born in 1935 in Berlin), while helping to clean out her family's Berlin apartment before deportation to Theresienstadt, both cut her interior swing so nobody else could use it and urinated in a pail, then placed in a dark room, so that whoever walked into the room next would trip over and capsize the pail.[58]

Other forms of non-violent revenge took place in ghettos and camps and were of a more collective nature in that they were shared with other victims—for example, through singing about revenge. In September 1943 at a musical performance by Jews in the Theresienstadt ghetto, a chorus and orchestra directed by Rafael Schächter (1905–1944) performed Verdi's Requiem. The prisoner-musicians drew emotional sustenance by singing the *Dies Ire* to the SS luminaries in front-row seats, imagining the gates of hell opening right in front of them:

> *Dies irae – Dies irae – Dies irae*
> *Quantus tremor est futurus*
> *Quando judex est venturus*
> *Cuncta stricte discussurus.*

> The day of wrath, the day of wrath, the day of wrath—
> How much trembling there will be
> When the judge comes
> And strictly examines all things.[59]

Edgar Krasa (1924–2017; born in Karlsbad, Czechoslovakia) shared a room with Schächter in Theresienstadt; in testimony offered in 2003, he recalled that for Schächter, performing the requiem was about "wanting to be able to sing to the Germans in Latin what he couldn't tell them in German to their face." Krasa was part of the chorus. He felt that—despite a great deal of fear that the Germans would retaliate upon Schächter and the singers—he was "part of a group that despises the Germans and the Nazis, and that this is the best we can do to get even with them within our capabilities." Veiled in Latin, the message being sent to the audience of SS, police, and Nazi party personnel was that final judgment would come; that days of rage were to be expected.[60] Before each performance, Schächter urged the singers and musicians to think of their murdered loved ones and to confront the perpetrators in the audience.[61] Singing about revenge offered some solace and sense of empowerment to both the performers and other Jews who understood the hidden meaning—until October 18, 1944, when Schächter and his singers and musicians were deported to Auschwitz and murdered.[62]

Sonderkommando members at Auschwitz-Birkenau described victims' singing on the way to and inside the gas chambers as a form of "revenge through song."[63] It was empowering for the singers in the face of death but it was also humiliating for the SS guards who saw their victims not demoralized but instead "bold and calm, singing.... practically carefree, laughing death in the face."[64] It was not just the fact that the victims had the audacity to sing at the penultimate moment of their lives; it was also what singing the "International" and "Hatikvah" represented: the nearing Russian victory and vengeance; Jewish resilience and continuity. Hearing these songs from victims inside the gas chamber, Zalmen Gradowski believed, reminded the SS guards of German failure: failure to win the war and failure to erase the Jewish presence in this world. And it put them on notice that along with this failure they would also suffer violent payback in the near future. The singing of the "Hatikvah" anthem reminded the SS guards they had been misled by the illusion "that 'no Jew will exist in the world except in a museum,' that no one will be left to demand revenge—or himself take revenge." Under the impression of hearing the singing, Gradowski entertained his own revenge fantasy: that after the war Jews would "come together here from all corners of the world and each will look for his mother, his sister and brother" and would "assemble huge armies whose sole aim will be revenge. They will exact payment for all the victims, for the innocent blood that you are about to spill and for the blood that you have already spilled. The Hatikvah will not let them rest . . ."[65] In this way the singing was not only a coping reaction of men and women who knew they were about to meet their deaths, but also offered sustenance to a man who was being temporarily kept alive to handle the remains of the murdered—and was able to leave behind a record of the horrors he witnessed.

Revenge could take the form of ridicule, through songs, poems, jokes, idiomatic ghetto and camp expressions. Unbeknownst to the Nazi perpetrators, such expressions made use of irony and sarcasm, combined with fantasies of altered power relations centered on humiliation and status-degradation.[66] Jokes, poems, and songs proclaimed the defeat of the Germans long before it seemed likely—the jokes encapsulated the message that the murderers were not as powerful as they believed, suffered from self-delusion, were akin to animals, were morally deficient.[67] Many testimonies attested to the importance of mocking Nazi laws and measures as a way of coping.[68] Even if such verbal enactment of revenge and defiance remained counter-factual, theoretical, aspirational, phantasmagoric—it had a positive, empowering effect on the victims. Some ritualized forms of perpetrator behavior meant to express unlimited German power and cultural superiority were likewise

Jewish Revenge and the Holocaust

responded to with mockery and sarcasm. For example, educator, journalist, and Warsaw ghetto diarist Chaim Aron Kaplan (born 1880 in Gorodishche, Belorussia; murdered in 1942 or 43 in Treblinka) describes a ceremony in which Jewish passersby were forced to remove their hats and bow in front of a Nazi luminary visiting the ghetto; this was duly executed by Jewish children and young people—but in an exaggerated and clownish manner, to the amusement of the onlooking ghetto dwellers.[69] Similarly, Jewish descriptions of German atrocities referred to the mass murderers as "beasts," "animals," and "barbarians" and took up Nazi self-descriptions as "cultured," "heroic," "superior," and "of the master race" to mockingly indicate that the opposite was in fact true.[70] And traditional expressions that Jews had always used for perpetrators of anti-Jewish laws and violence—"will his/their name and memory be blotted out," invoking biblical references to Amalek and Haman, found a revival applied to Nazi murderers.

Expressions of Jewish revenge during the Holocaust were thus manifest in a wide range of forms, violent and non-violent, overt and hidden, directly confronting the perpetrators and addressing other Jews, real and imagined or hypothetical. The varieties of Jewish revenge reflected diverse outlooks, experiences, and cultural contexts. Under what circumstances did individuals choose one mode of revenge over another? What functions did the different modes have?

Confronting Nazi Perpetrators with Screams, Slaps, and Spit

Some non-violent forms of revenge involved face-to-face confrontation with the Nazi perpetrators using acoustic expression. When realizing that they had been deceived and that they were about to be murdered and had no way of escape, Jews being driven into the firing pits and gas chambers commonly articulated fear, despair, and rage by screaming, yelling, and singing revenge slurs at the perpetrators. Hardly any of these victims survived, but these acoustic expressions of revenge were transmitted by those who did, by local non-Jews, and by Nazi perpetrators themselves. Kazimierz Sakowicz (1894–1944), a non-Jewish Pole who was trained as a lawyer and worked as a journalist in Vilna, witnessed and chronicled the mass shootings of thousands of Vilna Jews at Ponary, watching from an attic window of a cottage in the woods near the shooting pits and from other proximate vantage points. During the Soviet occupation of eastern Poland between September 1939 and June 1941, Soviet forces had used the forest at Ponary to build a fuel storage facility; they had dug several pits for fuel tanks connected by trenches, but never completed the project. When the Germans occupied the area on June 24, 1941, they used the unfinished pits and ditches as a shooting and burial site for around 80,000 people, mostly Jews from Vilna and also Soviet POWs. Starting in July 1941, Sakowicz kept a meticulous diary of mass shootings. On October 1, 1943, one week after the SS and Order Police destroyed the Vilna ghetto with the help of Lithuanian and Ukrainian auxiliary forces, in the process shooting some 3,000 Jews and deporting 1,600 Jewish men to Estonia, 1,400–1,700 Jewish women to the Kaiserwald concentration camp outside of Riga,[71] he recorded hearing a woman scream at the shooters "'Don't shoot us, because there will be revenge.'"⁷² Standing inside the pit, naked, knowing that the Lithuanian and German gunmen would shoot down from the pit's edge and that the bodies of those who were shot would fall on top of each other, she must have hoped in this way to save her life and the lives of the Jews who were with her. Sakowicz relates that her intervention raised suspicions among the shooters that Jews were hiding in the forest nearby to take revenge, so that the next group of Jews to be shot were falsely told they could save their lives by giving up hiding places.⁷³ Although the woman was unable to change her situation, her incursion had some effect on the perpetrators.

Kurt Gerstein was an SS officer with training in medicine and engineering who worked for the Hygiene Institute of the Waffen SS in Berlin; he later claimed that he grew critical of the regime's "final solution" for religious reasons and had tried to pass information on the mass murder of Jews to two Swiss diplomats and the Vatican during the war. After being present at gassings of Jews at Belzec on August 18, 1942, he noted the following: "A Jewess of about 40, with eyes like torches, calls down the blood of her children on the heads of their murderers."⁷⁴ The woman had just arrived with a transport of 6,700 Jews from the Lvov ghetto. By then the deportees had lived through extreme violence, humiliation, and the destruction of their community of 150,000. Upon the German occupation of Lvov on June 30, 1941, SS-Einsatzgruppe C and local Ukrainian militias, together with local mobs, had murdered between 3,000 and 6,000 Jews in two violent pogroms on July 1 and 25.⁷⁵ An additional 3,000 Jewish men had been murdered in mass shootings following the first pogrom in early July. By the time the deportees arrived at Belzec, they had lived in an overcrowded ghetto for over eight months (80,000 Jews had been moved into a space where 25,000 Jews had already been living in November and December 1941), and they had lived through the first *Aktion* (violent round-up) in March 1942, when 15,000 Jews had been sent to their deaths at Belzec. Now, in August 1942, German Security Police had rounded them up and deported to Belzec; this second major *Aktion* lasted for two weeks, claiming the lives of 42,000 Jews, murdered in the ghetto or sent to their deaths at Belzec.⁷⁶ Of the transport whose gassing Gerstein described, over 20 percent—1,400 people—had died on the way to Belzec in overcrowded cattle cars packed with 150 people per car, with no food or water or sanitary conditions. Upon arrival at Belzec, armed Ukrainian guards and SS men forced those who were still alive out of the train and into the killing facilities. The SS deceived the victims, welcoming them and informing them by loudspeaker that they were now going to wash themselves, women receiving haircuts before being sent onward to work; clothes, glasses and artificial limbs should be removed, shoes tied together with string handed out by a small Jewish boy. "In one corner," Gerstein wrote

> a strong SS man tells the poor devils in a strong deep voice, 'Nothing at all will happen to you. All you have to do is to breathe deeply, it strengthens the lungs; this inhalation is a necessary measure against contagious diseases; it is a very good disinfectant!' Asked what was to become of them, he answered: 'Well of course the men will have to work, building streets and houses. But the women will not have to work. If they wish to, they can help in house or kitchen.'⁷⁷

Through this deception, and by systematically exploiting the deeply human impulse to hope, the SS forced the naked women, men, and children into the gas chambers. Those who hesitated were pushed by the mass of bodies behind them and the whiplashes and rifle butts of the Ukrainian and German guards. Once they arrived at the gas chamber, Gerstein related, "most of them, though, know everything, the odor has given them a clear indication of their fate!"[78] It was at that moment, trapped, that the anonymous mother expressed her fury over being misled, her fear of death, her helplessness at being unable to escape by screaming, yelling, hurling a revenge slur at the surrounding SS personnel and Ukrainian guards. Gerstein added that SS-Sturmbannführer Christian Wirth, the first commandant of Belzec, who was showing off his camp to the SS delegation and had just been promoted to inspector of the SS-Sonderkommandos of the "Operation Reinhard" camps—he would soon move on to organize the Treblinka death camp, using his skills as a mass murderer—was provoked by the woman's words. "Five lashes into her face, dealt by the whip of Police Captain Wirth himself, chase her into the gas chamber."[79] The woman was of course powerless. But we can assume that her verbal expression of rage, together with facial expression and body language, offered a way to confront an impossible situation. She may have imagined that the murderers would ultimately pay for all they were doing, even if at a point past her own lifetime. But Wirth's violent response showed that her words had already giving him pain, humiliating him through a prediction that his power was not unlimited and the elimination of her, her community and her offspring—she mentioned the blood of her already dead children—would fail in its broader genocidal ambition.[80]

We have other attestations of incidents of this sort. One such was related by Jewish witnesses at the 1966 trial in Bochum, Germany, of several massacre-perpetrators at Nowy Sącz and other locations: on April 28, 1942, as a Jewish woman was about to be murdered in Nowy Sącz's Jewish cemetery—the town was then part of the so-called *Generalgouvernement*—she yelled at firing SS men and policemen right before she was herself gunned down: "With this blood you're not going to win this war, this blood will not remain silent, the *nekama* will come!"[81] A similar case, that of Moses Silbermann, was related in a trial in Hannover in 1981. Silbermann was murdered by the SS during a death march from the Hannover-Mühlenberg concentration camp to Bergen-Belsen in March-April 1945. After pleading for his life and realizing that he was going to nevertheless be shot, he called out "revenge me!" to the other Jewish prisoners.[82] Other Jews, mostly Sonderkommando members who left secret notes or managed to survive, offered detailed descriptions of such acoustic evocations of revenge. Filip Müller (born in 1922 in Sered, Czechoslovakia), a Sonderkommando member at Auschwitz-Birkenau, recalled that when the prisoners in Auschwitz's "family camp" were murdered between July 10 and 12, 1944, "curses sounded in the gas chamber. 'You have cheated us! But your Hitler will lose the war! There will come the hour of revenge. Then you will have to pay for everything, murderers.'"[83] Hidden notes of other Sonderkommando members, most of whom would not survive, included many references to such outbursts of rage and pain. In most cases we do not know who the victims were and what they had endured.[84] Zalmen Gradowski's account mentions one "attractive young blond girl" yelling at the SS and Ukrainian guards as they were forcing a new transport of naked women and their children into the gas chamber: "You black criminals!," referring to their uniforms, "You look at me with your thirsting animal eyes. You feast on the nakedness of my shapely body." She sought to humiliate them by calling out their depravity and signaling that their sense of superiority and power was an illusion about to end. "Yes, it's your time now. In your civilian lives you could not even dream of such a sight. You criminals of the underworld, here you've found the perfect place to satisfy your sadistic eyes. But this pleasure won't last long." Not only was their power outdated, their enterprise failing, but they would suffer in return for the suffering they had caused: "Your game is over, you'll never be able to murder all the Jews. And you'll pay heavily for all of this." Gradowski noted that she jumped at SS-Oberscharführer Peter Voss, the commander of the crematoria IV and V, and slapped him three times. Voss and other guards beat her severely on head and shoulders so that she "entered the bunker with a broken head, from which warm blood flows." And yet, Gradowski believed that at this moment of seeming absolute powerlessness and terror, he could observe the impact of what we can understand as a powerful coping mechanism: "The warm blood caresses her body, her face glows with joy. She is happy and content, feeling in her hand the pleasure of slapping the face of the notorious murderer and bandit. She has reached her final goal. And walks serenely to her death."[85] (One wonders of course whether Gradowski's words didn't also convey his own projection so that he could remain sane, write, and go on living.)

What becomes obvious from Gradowski's account is that victims who expressed their desire for revenge in the last moments of their lives often had recourse to antisemitic stereotypes to instil fear in the perpetrators. They insinuated that Jews were indeed everything that Nazi propaganda portrayed them to be—omnipotent, world-ruling Judeo-Bolshevists, warmongers and child-murderers, aggressive and vengeful, posing a threat to the German existence—and that their war against the Jews would fail. Gradowski mentions a woman and her daughter, "a pretty nine-year-old with long blond, neatly plaited braids, hanging down her childish back like golden straps," who, together with her mother, stopped the file of naked women on the way to the gas chamber and confronted the SS men standing nearby. "Murderers, bandits, shameless criminals!" the mother addressed them, "Yes, today you will murder us, innocent women and children. On us, unarmed and unprotected, you cast the blame for this war, on me and on my child, it is we who brought the war on you. Remember, bandits," she continued, "with our blood you hope to cover your own defeats on the front. You have lost the war, it's certain now. You surely know of the huge setbacks you suffer daily on the eastern front." And then: "Remember, bandits, today you can do all you want, but a day will come, a day of vengeance. Great victorious Russia will avenge us and will cut your living bodies into pieces. Our brothers from the whole world will not rest until they have avenged our innocent blood."[86] She then addressed a female SS guard standing by to watch the Jewish women and children go to their deaths: "You bestial woman, you too came here to see our misfortune. Remember! You too have a child, a family, you will not enjoy them for long. Living chunks we will tear from your body, and your child, like mine, will not live much longer." Turning to the other guards, she announced "Remember, bandits! You will pay for it all – the whole world will wreak vengeance upon you." Spitting at nearby guards, she then ran into gas chamber with her child.[87]

The mother's words suggest that in the summer and fall of 1944, some Jews who were still alive in occupied Europe were well aware of how much Germans feared losing the war and being subject to vengeance from Soviets, Jews, and other perceived and real enemies of the Reich. Gradowski believed that because the mother's words confirmed German propagandistic stereotypes about Jews and verbalized German existential fears, she had made an impact on the SS guards, humiliating them by tearing "the mask from their faces" and showing them "what the future, the very near future, held in store for them. They all thought of this more than once, more than one black thought had clouded their minds, and now this Jewish woman had told them the truth."[88] For Gradowski, observing and transmitting, this incident was empowering. It bolstered his own desire for revenge, helping him cope with his own situation, being forced to watch the mass murder machinery proceed unimpeded. But Gradowski also used the incident as an opportunity to understand the SS guards' mentality and rationalization. He sensed that the woman had touched deep existential fears: "The Führer, their god, has explained . . . that victory is not on the battlefields of the east and west, but . . . here in this bunker, here is victory." For these SS men, the Jews they were murdering were, Gradowski wrote, "the mighty enemy" for whom German blood was "being shed now on all the fields of Europe" and "for whose sake the English planes are dropping bombs day and night and killing young and old" back home in Germany. Gradowski imagined the innermost thoughts of one of the SS men: "Because of them, because of these naked women here, he has to be far from his home, and his child has to give his life there on the eastern front. No, the Führer, got it right. We must eradicate, exterminate them. When naked women with their children are lying dead, that will be the decisive, the certain victory."[89] The faster and the more thoroughly the Jews were eliminated, the faster there would be peace: "The cannons would stop their awful roar—the planes would no longer drop their bombs—and the war would come to an end. All would be peaceful in the world. The children would come home from far away and a new, happy life would begin for them."[90] In short, in Gradowski's view, the angry and indignant cries of revenge from unarmed, naked Jewish women facing their and their children's death agony touched on the SS guards' deepest anxieties, in turn prompting recourse to a murderous ideological construction as they carried out mass murder.

Such verbal confrontations with the perpetrators were not limited to mothers and daughters; Jewish boys yelled revenge slurs at their murderers,[91] while fathers also spat and slapped to avenge the mistreatment of their children. Diarist Cypora "Cypa" Zonszajn (née Jabłoń, 1915–1942), noted a scene she observed from her hiding place during a brutal roundup action of Jews in the Siedlce ghetto in the Generalgouvernement, eastern Poland, in August 1942. A Lithuanian or Ukrainian auxiliary policeman had rounded up a couple with their toddler, kicking and beating the child with the butt of his rifle for not being able to walk faster. "Then the heartbroken father lunges at his child's torturer with his last effort and slaps him twice. In the blink of a second three shots and three corpses are lying on the street, and the torturer goes away whistling cheerfully." Like Gradowski, albeit in a different context, Zonszajn is both horrified by the scene and derives some gratification from seeing the father's defiant attempt at reversing the power relations for a fleeting moment in time. "I stand at my vantage point, frozen in terror, but I am glad that the 'pure Aryan' felt the dirty hand of a lousy, heartbroken Jew. May there be as many such accidents as possible."[92]

There is, in any case, an interesting gender component to the verbal evocations of revenge aimed at SS guards which seem to have been a predominantly, yet not exclusively female response. While women's confrontations with SS guards also had some physical components—namely, the fiercely indignant gesture of slapping and spitting aimed at humiliating the heavily armed male guard and reclaiming the unarmed female victim's sense of dignity—their principle tool however was the power of eloquent, extensive speech. The simple fact that these female victims were able to *talk* for several minutes before being murdered, thus silenced, and the perpetrators were forced to listen had more than symbolic import; the outward impact of the verbal response was both social and emotional: it lowered the SS guards' social status in front of their peers and caused distress, undermining their sense of power and superiority by speaking to their fears. The power of speech-acts lies in their performative component—in this case the victims' standing up and raising their voices in favor of a larger group of victims while forcing the SS guards to listen. The empowerment involved here, grasped at on the edge of a death-agony, was meant to have communal benefit: in the cited case, for the speaker herself, wielding the power of words; for her child; for a larger group of Jewish victims who had arrived on the same transport and were all seeking to cope with imminent inescapable death; and probably unbeknownst to the victim, even for the Sonderkommando members observing these scenes and transmitting them to posterity through written notes and postwar testimony.

Transmitting Revenge Imperatives for Jews in Inscriptions, Testaments, and last Letters

Other forms of outward-facing non-violent revenge did not involve any direct confrontation with the perpetrators but turned to other Jews. At deportation sites, in killing fields, and in death camps, Jews who knew that they were going to die very soon called on other Jews, who they hoped would survive, to take future revenge. Such revenge imperatives were often transmitted orally. In the latter half of January 1942, 10,103 Jews from the Lodz ghetto were rounded up and deported to the Chelmno death camp, where they would be murdered in gas vans.[93] Seeking to protect the ghetto from destruction, its Jewish council had furnished the Germans with the number of Jews they wanted to deport. Facing a terrible and unprecedented dilemma, the council tried to mitigate the German brutality inflicted on the ghetto population by letting the Jewish police assist in the roundup and by choosing those who would be deported, and those who could stay behind for labor. For deportation, the council chose Jews who were poor, had a criminal record, or had come into the ghetto from elsewhere. "Most of them—poor, broken, naked and starved," commented Shlomo Frank, one ghetto dweller, in a January 1942 diary entry. "Their deportation was extraordinarily tragic. All of them cried mournfully." He noted that mothers embraced children and screamed: "If we will die, you at least stay alive in order to be able to get revenge on those who are banishing us."[94]

The deportees did not know where the transport was going and what awaited them at their destination; they also did not know what the larger significance of the roundup was at this point. But after enduring twenty-three months of life in the ghettos under extremely difficult conditions that included brutality, starvation, and forced labor, they had an intuition that in addition to being separated from loved ones, their living conditions would even be worse, that they would not come back and would likely be killed. They did not expect, as they had no way of knowing, even imagining the possibility, that all of the ghetto population would be targeted and that there would be indiscriminate killing in a facility especially designed for mass murder. At this moment, they seem to have believed that those who stayed behind, especially the young, would live—and if the deportees did indeed die, would be able to avenge their deaths. It is not entirely clear whether the revenge they called for was meant for the German occupiers actually responsible for the roundup, for the Jewish council and/or ghetto police complying with the Germans, or for both the Germans and the Jewish ghetto administrators. Most likely, in January 1942 these victims did not know themselves, the thing that mattered being, in any case, the transmission: simply a way of coping in a situation of mortal peril, the evocation of a warranty should their worst fears come true.

Over time, with the ever-growing volume and pace of roundups and deportations, victims became increasingly aware—even if more as intuition than knowledge—that the Nazi regime was murdering Jews in a systematic way. The method and scale remained opaque, clouded in rumors, with some pieces of factual information coming from Jewish fugitives and the local non-Jewish population living and working in the vicinity of death camps and execution sites. The reality of indiscriminate mass murder by mass shooting and gassing was unimaginable—not only because of its unprecedented nature but also because of its profound counter-rationality, its violation of both common sense and core human ethics. Beginning to grasp the truth, some Jews responded by rejecting the information as impossible; some sought to minimize an intuitive response of outrage mixed with a desperate sense of powerlessness through rational arguments—that it was unlikely the Germans would not even spare women and children; that it was implausible they would murder healthy people fit to work, or skilled laborers, or medical doctors. Even when the reality that all Jews were being targeted, irrespective of sex, age, health, skills, economic means, national background, was indeed assimilated, hope remained that one's own life, one's own family and community, would be spared. Perhaps the mass murder was local, not global, unfolding in neighboring communities but not one's own. And perhaps there were ways for Jews to hold out, to delay the mass murder, so that the Germans could be defeated in time.[95]

It was when such last hopes of being spared were shattered that some Jews resorted to passing on revenge imperatives addressed to fellow Jews who they hoped would somehow survive. But verbal appeals for revenge needed real-time listeners—which is why some

Jews being hanged in front of other camp prisoners at roll call as punishment for resistance or attempted escape used this forum to scream out such appeals. We thus have testimony of Róża Robota calling out "revenge!" in Polish or else, according to other accounts, "sisters, revenge!" when about to be hanged—after undergoing months of brutal torture—on January 6, 1945, together with Alla Gertner, Regina Sapir, and Esther Weisblum, for having procured the explosives for the October 7, 1944 Sonderkommando uprising at Auschwitz.[96] Similarly, Leon Shumer, an Auschwitz prisoner who tried to escape and was captured, is reported to have yelled "may the survivors take revenge against the Germans" before his hanging.[97] We likewise have testimony from 1995 that when Isaak Saleschuetz was about to be shot to death by firing-squad of German police officers together with twenty-one prominent Jews in the Kulboszowa ghetto in April 1942, he first recited the *Shema* prayer and then yelled in Yiddish "Nekome, nekome, nekome . . ." until his end, as encouragement to the other Jews, including his own son, who had to watch the gruesome scene.[98] As an anonymous survivor recalled, during a mass shooting of prisoners at the Budzyń forced labor camp in 1943, he and another Jewish boy had been selected to live, but were forced to cover the murder-victims with sand. The boy's younger brother had been shot but was still alive, shouting out from inside the mass grave at his older brother to take revenge; the boy shoveling next to the anonymous survivor began to panic and was shot too.[99] In addition to verbal appeals of this sort, such messages took written forms, including notes, postcards, letters, and wall and floor graffiti. In writing, the messages had longevity; they could address a period beyond a writer's own place, time, and fleeting lifespan.

In the summer of 1943, Chaim Engel was ordered to sort the blood-stained clothes of a new transport of Jews. They had been gunned down at the train station of the Sobibor death camp after they had, allegedly, attacked SS guards. In one pocket, Engel found a handwritten note in Yiddish saying "take revenge for us."[100] The new arrivals had been members of the Belzec death camp Sonderkommando. For over nine months the SS—at the behest of SS-Obergruppenführer Odilo Globocnik and in an effort to destroy the traces of mass murder of over 430,000 Jews—had forced the Sonderkommando members, together with Jewish forced laborers from the Lublin District, to open the mass graves, burn bodies, grind ash and bones. Once they had completed their task, the SS shot most of the prisoners, keeping a smaller group to destroy the camp and level the ground. These prisoners were not murdered on site but deported to Sobibor.[101] Upon arrival, the anonymous author of the note must have expected that he and his group were going to be murdered in what was another murder-camp similar to what they knew from Belzec. Like Chaim Engel, several Jewish women temporarily kept alive to perform "female" tasks at Sobibor, such as sorting through the clothes and toys of the dead and washing and mending them for redistribution among Germans, found similar Yiddish-language notes with calls for revenge. For example, in testimony given in the mid-1960s, Hella Weiss-Felenbaum (1924–1988), one of the surviving escapees from Sobibor and then a partisan, recounted that one day "prisoners arrived from Belzec and were shot immediately. In their pockets we found notes in Yiddish: 'We are told we are on our way to work. It is a lie. Avenge us.'" Weiss-Felenbaum added, "later when I joined the partisans after my escape and was fighting in Poland, in Germany and in Czechoslovakia, I remembered these words. They gave me courage to survive."[102] The choice of Yiddish indicates that the writers were addressing a Jewish audience; they also presumably felt that a written call for revenge hidden in clothing was likely to outlast their own death—and that some Jews, a portion of the Jewish nation, might survive to enact the revenge they prescribed for the future.

Such notes were also found outside of death camps, for example in killing fields after mass shootings. In his 1946 memoir, poet Abraham Sutzkever (1913–2010), himself from Lithuania, cites the account of Salomon Garbel to that effect (Garbel was a member of the ghetto police in Vilna forced in April 1943 to bury some 4,000 rural Jews murdered at Ponary and sort their clothes).[103] Written revenge imperatives served as a vehicle to record the fact of mass murder—against the Nazi German efforts to erase evidence of this crime—and register the memory of the victims for their loved ones, for their communities, and for the Jewish collective. For the messages' desperate authors, there was an intrinsic connection between revenge, knowledge of the crime, and its commemoration. They addressed both specific family members and unspecified groups of Jews, often an imagined community of "survivors" acting in the name of the dead, or else Jews in the "free world," in Palestine and among Allied nations, who would eventually arrive as liberators. The emotional ballast of the messages for their authors is apparent: they gave a sense of agency; a sense of having produced and passed on proof of the atrocities; recording victims' names, including their own and those of their murdered loved ones; confirming, for themselves, that Jewish life would continue and that those finding the messages would act upon the revenge imperatives they contained.

We see this in the wall and floor graffiti scribbled on synagogues, in prison cells, and at execution sites by Jews who were being rounded up, or who were incarcerated and awaiting murder. The walls and floors became message boards for articulating anger, despair, and the desire for vengeance. The writers bore witness to the murder of their families and townspeople, bid farewell to loved ones, and voiced their hope for revenge in the future. The inscriptions on the walls of the synagogue of Kovel (eastern Poland before the war, now western Ukraine), are a famous example. The German army had entered Kovel on June 28, 1941, after it had been under Soviet occupation since September 1939. When the German occupation began, Kovel had around 12,700 Jews, half of its overall population. In May 1942, the German civil administration of the Kovel region established two separate ghettos: a large one in the old city where most of the Jews lived, housing around 10,000 Jews, and a smaller one in the new city, housing some 3,500 Jews, mostly skilled laborers and their families. Between June 3 and 5, 1942, the Germans destroyed the old city ghetto. Members of the Security Police, SD, German gendarmerie, and Ukrainian police rounded up the ghetto population, shooting some 300 old, sick people and children on the spot; they gathered the rest at the local train station, transported them on freight trains to a sand pit seven kilometers north of Kovel and shot them to death. Over three days, 9,000 Jews were murdered this way. From then on shootings became a daily reality in the new city ghetto. On August 19, 1942, 6,500 Jews from that ghetto and the surrounding villages were shot and killed in the Jewish cemetery.

German and Ukrainian police hunted down 1,000 Jews who had initially managed to escape, locked them up in the Great Synagogue, where they were held for days without food or water, then also murdered them in the Jewish cemetery.[104] Close to 100 inscriptions in Yiddish, Polish, and Russian were found on the vandalized synagogue's walls after the Red Army entered the city on July 6, 1944. "I was filled with horror. The walls began to speak. . . . [They] were covered with writing in pencil," wrote S. N. Grutman, a Jewish Red Army sergeant, to the Jewish writer Ilya Ehrenburg on December 2, 1944. "There was not a single empty spot on the wall. These were the last words of the doomed, their farewell to this world."[105] The inscriptions were "packed so closely together that each writer had tried to draw a line around their own so as to make their cry for help, for vengeance, stand out all the more strongly. . . . In every inscription the words for revenge . . . were written clearly."[106]

Some of the inscriptions commemorated relatives and friends who had already been murdered, others recorded who was trapped in the synagogue and awaiting deaths; they implored readers to exact revenge for the lives of murdered children, parents, spouses, friends: "Tserum Leyzer with his daughters and Sroul Katz died at the hands of the German murderers. Avenge them!' 'Gitl Safran . . . Rina Safran had her throat cut on Thursday, August 19, 1942. Take revenge!' . . . 'August 20, 1942, Selik, Tamar, Yellah Kozen perished. Avenge us!'"[107] One inscription, written by Israel Vaynshteyn on August 23, 1942, read: "Let innocent Jewish blood pour down on all Germans. Revenge! Revenge! . . . May lightning strike them."[108] Trapped with her child, Gina Atlas called on her husband Reuven Atlas as follows: "you should know that your wife Gina and your son Imus were murdered. Our child wept bitterly. He did not want to die. Go to war and take revenge for the soul of your wife and your one and only son. They are taking us to die, and we are innocent."[109] Young people voiced their anger that they were not given the chance to live and grow up. Some messages, such as that of Tania Arbeyter, also written on August 23, both captured fear and agony at impending death with a vivid fantasy of revenge to occur: "God, take us to your eternity! But the murderers will surely pay with their blood! How will I be able to rejoice if I am already in the grave? But I wished that their every last child would be cut up into pieces while still alive . . . One more hour and one more moment . . . Farewell my beautiful world, the world that I did not have time to get to know."[110]

Or, as Yehuda Shekhter implored future readers of his message, seeking to cope with anticipating death: "You who come after us, remember! The innocent blood of our young people will be spilled here in an hour's time, blood clean as the waters of the Sea of Galilee. We demand vengeance! Cruel vengeance!"[111] While some of the messages called in this way on other human beings to take revenge—those who would survive; future generations—others called on God, as was the case with Bluma, Yaakov, David and Yehuda on the 14th of Elul (August 27), 1942, who wrote: "Earth, do not cover our blood. Heaven, avenge our death. We are going to a cruel death at the hands of the brutal murderers together with the whole community of Kovel."[112] In just over eighteen days, German forces, assisted by local Ukrainians, shot 18,000 Jews from Kovel and the neighboring villages, wiping out Jewish life there.[113] The wailing wall of inscriptions in the Kovel synagogue transmitted the voices of some of the murdered, conveying their revenge imperatives beyond their deaths; Jewish soldiers who arrived with the Red Army recorded and preserved them for posterity.[114]

Elsewhere, revenge imperatives jotted down on walls and floors were transmitted photographically. The Lithuanian Jewish photographer George Kadish (Zvi-Hirsh Kadushin; born in 1910 in Raseiniai, Lithuania) documented such graffiti in a series of photos taken during and after the war. Kadish had been a science teacher at a Hebrew school and an amateur photographer in Kovno before the German occupation of the city on June 24, 1941. During the occupation, he worked in the x-ray department of the Jewish hospital, a position that gave him access to film and photographic equipment and allowed him to smuggle films into the ghetto. He secretly captured life and death in the Kovno ghetto in over 1,000 photographs, hiding his camera inside his coat, photographing through sleeves and button holes, sometimes, at great personal risk, pretending to be a German. Kadish stowed his negatives inside crutches and buried his photos in milk jars under his house.

On March 31, 1944, when the Gestapo learned of his secret documentation and began searching for him, he escaped the ghetto, then surviving with his wife and three children in a shelter dug out of earth on the "Aryan side" of Kovno. Kadish documented how the

Figure 8 The words "Jews, revenge!," written in blood on the floor of an apartment belonging to one of the 800 Jews murdered by Lithuanian nationalists in Vilijampole (Slobodka) June 25–26, 1941; photographed by George Kadish; USHMM Photo Archives # 04640; courtesy of United States Memorial Museum, copyright George Kadish.

Germans deported some 2,500 Jews to Dachau and Stutthof, shooting to death a nearly equal number of Jews when they destroyed the ghetto on July 8, 1944. When the Red Army arrived three weeks later, he returned to the ghetto ruins, retrieving his buried archive. In testimony offered more than fifty years after what he had recorded, reflecting on photography taken from the victims' perspective during the German genocide, Kadish said that despite great personal risk and the corporal punishment he had suffered, he was "taking those pictures for eternity . . ., I was full of hope that I would save those pictures and . . . bring [them] to a new, to a better world."[115]

Asked if he was satisfied with what he did at the time, Kadish replied:

> I can never be satisfied if I lost so many friends, relatives, sisters, mothers and found out later how much loss we had in the provinces . . . the little towns. It's impossible to say I am satisfied. But I am happier now than I would be without my camera and if I wouldn't have taken all those pictures, documents – without a camera. . . . And I am glad that I could be one of the Jewish people who tried, who started to [take] revenge against the terrible evil that happened in that time and I am glad I did it.

Several of Kadish's photographs document inscriptions expressing desires for revenge. One such image was taken two days into the German occupation of Kovno, when in the night of June 25-26, 1941, Lithuanian nationalists launched a massive pogrom in the Kovno neighborhood of Vilijampole (Yidd. Slobodka), where most of the city's 35,000 Jews lived, murdering over 800 Jews in their homes.[116] The image shows the Yiddish words "Jews, revenge!" scrawled in blood on the floor of an apartment that belonged to a Jewish family.[117] Kadish recalled that after hearing relentless screaming in his building, he found his downstairs neighbor lying on the kitchen floor of his apartment, bleeding:

> Half a finger was reddish and around his chest was all blood. And I saw him again picking up some blood from his chest and . . . writing on the floor the word Nekamah—revenge. I had a feeling that he is writing and talking and telling me. Don't use a gun, though use revenge by helping people, advising people, and giving them help as much [as] you can. [interviewer: with your camera?] With my camera, by putting everything down because the biggest Nekamah was . . . when we took pictures. We left this . . . for [the] future to show the people, the world what the Germans did.[118]

Strikingly, it was in fact Lithuanians who perpetrated the pogrom Kadish was here describing—looking back at the image decades after, Kadish did not make this distinction. Another of his pictures captured a Yiddish inscription that Jews had scrawled on a wall of the Vilna prison, dated May 2, 1942: "For Ponary we'll take revenge!"[119] (Notably, the manifesto of the United Partisan Union FPO in the Vilna ghetto called upon the ghetto population to confront the German forces seeking to destroy the ghetto would state of September 1, 1943: "To avenge Ponary, hit the murderers!"[120]) More pictures, taken in

1944, show the walls of the Ninth Fort, an execution site on the outskirts of Kovno. Here, starting in July 1941, SS-Einsatzgruppen and German police assisted by Lithuanian auxiliary forces shot around 50,000 Jewish men, women, and children, the murder only stopping upon arrival of the Soviets on August 1, 1944.[121] A Yiddish inscription captured by Kadish notes that a certain Hirsh Bursteyn was brought to the fort on July 7, 1944: "We're burning bodies and awaiting death. Brothers, take revenge! We're dying courageously for the Jewish people." The inscription is adorned by three stars of David.[122] Another inscription reads, again in Yiddish: "On July 4th, 84 men were brought from Vilna; 62 were killed right away (shot) and burned, 22 were shot later."[123] In a different corner, Isaak Lidski notes "brothers – revenge . . . May 10, 44."[124]

During his testimony at Adolf Eichmann's trial, Aharon Beilin related that while a prisoner doctor at Auschwitz, he had discovered inscriptions in various languages on the walls of Auschwitz-Birkenau's so-called sauna, where Jews selected for work were tattooed, had their heads shaven, and received camp uniforms: "I remember a quotation from Dante 'Abandon hope –all ye who enter here.'[125] I remember the Hebrew sentence: 'Avenge ye the blood of your brothers that has been spilt.'[126] I remember a sentence in Yiddish: '*Yidden, fargest nisht – nekome*' (Jews, do not forget – revenge). I remember a phrase which must have been written either by an educated Polish Jew or by a Polish prisoner. It was a citation of [poet Adam] Mickiewicz from the 'Improvision.' There is a passage there: 'Vengeance, vengeance, vengeance on the enemy – with God, and even without God.'[127] I saw this in Polish; since I had graduated from a Polish gymnasium and university, this was close to my heart."[128] Written by multilingual writers at home in several cultural contexts, these inscriptions, while addressed to a Jewish audience in Yiddish and Hebrew, point to something inherent albeit less directly evident in all the written appeals: that along with addressing particular Jewish circumstances unprecedented in both horror and moral significance, they constituted an imperative for human action with universal meaning.

Yet who were the intended targets of revenge demanded in these inscriptions? Some imperatives specified that revenge should be directed at local non-Jews who acted against their Jewish compatriots; fellow prisoners who had mistreated others; and sometimes also at Jews, perceived as having betrayed other Jews. Most seem to have taken for granted that revenge targeted Germans, specific perpetrators or the members of the German nation as a whole, alongside their Axis allies.

Jews who had lost all hope and expected death also called for revenge in last letters to loved ones, many handed to non-Jewish acquaintances left behind as their writers were rounded up, others simply tossed out of deportation trains. In most cases, the fate of both letter writers and addressees, and how the letters were transmitted, remains unknown. Along with assurances of love, expressions of sorrow, grief, despair, and helplessness, fear of death, wishes for wellbeing and survival, hopes for a better world, and final words of farewell, these last letters described how communities were destroyed, their inhabitants massacred, loved ones murdered. Against a background of extreme violence and in anticipation of their own death, the writers voiced urges for revenge, formulated as an

Responding to the Apocalypse

Figure 9 Yiddish inscription on the walls of the Vilna prison: "For Ponary we will take revenge! May 2, 1943." In Ponary near Vilna German forces and Lithuanian auxiliaries murdered 80,000 people, mostly Jews, between 1941 and 1944; photographed by George Kadish, 1944–1945. USHMM Photo Archives # 29932; courtesy of United States Memorial Museum, copyright George Kadish.

obligation bequeathed by the dead upon the living. On June 2, 1943, in a letter from Bratislava to unknown recipients, Eliezer Unger thus confided that "I heard hundreds of times from the martyrs whom I saw . . . as their souls departed in holiness and purity and their last words were: Our brothers, remember, take revenge, avenge our blood." Unger assumed that he would be among the survivors: "Indeed we, my brothers," he exhorted, "are the ones assigned to a sacred duty, and this duty is—revenge."[129] We see here that for Unger, standing as well for other letter-writers who used similar rhetoric, acting on behalf of systematically murdered unarmed victims furnished full moral legitimacy for violent revenge.

Such moral justification seems one reason many letter-writers furnishing detailed accounts of what they and others had endured. At the same time, the writers often seem to have been processing their own helplessness and outrage over the atrocities through documentation. But the documenting was no end in itself; it had an ethical component, allowing the writers to explain, before themselves and their addressees, why revenge was not ethically compromising but a befitting response to the most depraved conceivable crimes.

Arguably, such a revenge ethic, adhered to in a context of absolute injustice, informs an excruciatingly detailed description of unfathomable cruelty in an undated letter, signed only with the last names Gorwicz and Asz but written in the name of 112 Jewish men, women, and children. This group had been hiding in the Rudniki forest some forty kilometers south of Vilna, having taken shelter in two separate hideouts connected by a tunnel. In return for clothes, money, and valuables, a Polish woman known only by her first name, Marysia, a widowed mother of three children, procured food for them purchased from peasants in the area around Širviai. After making increasingly greedy demands, she threatened, finally, to betray the hideouts to the Germans unless she received five kilos of gold. Unable to meet the extortionist demand, the group had sent an eight-year-old girl with some valuables to ask for an extension; the girl was murdered. Two days later, Germans and Lithuanians, apparently tipped off by Marysia, arrived at the hideouts. For five days, six Lithuanians and five Germans assaulted women and girls as young as eight, gang-raped a twelve-year-old girl, sexually mutilated and otherwise sadistically tortured the Jewish men, and murdered some of the victims before marching the rest to Ponary to be executed. The letter, written in Polish—for fear, as the writers indicated, that it would be less likely preserved in Yiddish—and dropped onto the road on the forced march to Ponary, called on "brothers and sisters" to take revenge. "With tears in our eyes we ask for revenge, revenge," wrote the two authors, asking the letter's readers to give Marysia and her children payback for her blackmailing and betrayal. They closed with the words "We say goodbye to you. Goodbye to the whole world." And then again, written words serving, it seems, as both a source of some kind of desperate empowerment and as an appeal for the only available justice: "We call for revenge."[130]

Many last letters that called for future revenge were written not in a state of imminent death agony but out of knowledge that capture and likely eventual murder would arrive for the writer and loved ones in the near future; here again the letters reveal an effort to confront a sense of utter powerlessness. On July 31, 1942, Zlatka Wishniatsky wrote her husband, Moyshe Wishniatsky [Wishner], then in the United States, about the obliteration of their community in the village of Byteń, eastern Poland. After the Wehrmacht had occupied Byteń in late June 1941, its 1,200 Jews had suffered ghettoization, forced labor, hunger, humiliation, and random violence. By the time Zlatka wrote her letter, the German SS and police, Baltic auxiliary forces, and Belorussian police had begun to destroy the ghetto, rounding up its Jews and shooting them in pits dug by local peasants a few kilometers away from Byteń.[131] "We experienced a dangerous massacre," wrote Zlatka. "On July 25, 1942, mass slaughters happened here, as in all other towns. Three-hundred-fifty people survived. Eight-hundred-fifty were murdered and died a horrific death at the hands of the criminals. They were thrown into latrines like dogs. Children were thrown into pits alive." After detailing the scope of the brutality and inhumanity involved in the atrocities she had survived, she reflected on her own situation: "For now we managed to save ourselves, but for how long? Every day we await death, and in the meantime we mourn our relatives and loved ones. Your family, Moshikele, is no more, no trace of them remains. But I envy them." She continued, "I won't write much. I believe that someone will recount our suffering and our bloodbath. [. . .] But I will close. It is impossible to write and to scream out our ordeal. [. . .] Be well you all and the only thing you can do for us is to take revenge on our murderers." But Zlatka Wishniatsky still seems to have retained feelings emerging from another, infinitely less cruel world where revenge seemed to be a moral transgression; for perhaps a bit uncomfortable with her own words, she added: "Will say, a little bit of revenge," before concluding "I kiss you strongly, strongly. I bid you all farewell before our death."[132] (Zlatka's ten-year-old daughter, Jute, added a note to her father saying, "I say goodbye to you before death. We so much want to live, but what can we do – one doesn't let us. I am so afraid of death, for little kids are thrown alive into the grave."[133]) Zlatka, Jute, and her little brother Gordi, along with other Jews who survived the massacre escaped the ghetto into the nearby forests to join Jewish partisan groups. Zlatka handed her letter to a Christian farmer, asking him to send it after the war; he handed it to her brother, who survived among partisans in the area around Byteń. Zlatka and her children were murdered in the woods on January 20, 1943.[134]

Another example of such anticipatory letters communicating revenge imperatives: nineteen-year-old Fania Barbakow, the sixth of seven children of Ze'ev and Zisele Barbakow, owners of a flour mill in Druja (a small town on the Lithuanian-Belorussian border), was hiding together with eight other family members, including her toddler niece Zeldale, in a secret bunker in the basement of a storage room on the property of the parental home in mid-June 1942. The Germans had occupied Druja in early July 1941, after it had been occupied by the Soviets since September 1939. Apart from subjecting Druja's 2,200 Jews to different kinds of forced labor, they established a short-lived ghetto in late April/early May 1942, which they destroyed with the help of local police in mid-June. After crushing Jewish resistance, they rounded up the ghetto's inhabitants, most of whom had been hiding like the Barbakow family. On June 16, 1942, at 4 a.m., grappling with the certainty of her own death and that of those with her, Fania wrote a seven-page letter in Russian to her brother Manos and sister Chaya, who were in the Soviet Union.[135] "All of our Jewish brothers and sisters were murdered and died a shameful death at the hand of the murderers," she reported. "I don't know who will remain alive from our family." She expressed the hope that Manos and Chaya would survive and read her "proud greeting before death" while expressing her wish that they "[l]ive happily and well." She voiced her own sense of self-esteem as a Jew, saying "We are all marching proudly toward death, for this is our fate," yet also conveyed the impossibility of her situation: "We are all lying in one bunker. I am absolutely sure that you will all know the location of our burial. Mother and Father are barely holding on. My hand trembles and it is hard for me to finish writing. I am proud to be a Jew. I am dying for the sake of my people." At nineteen, she also expressed her sorrow over her life taken before she could live it: "How I yearn to live and reach some good in life. But all is already lost . . ." On the back she added a note in Yiddish: "God is just and His Judgment is just. We have sinned. Our meager possessions are concealed at home. But we have lost our lives. It is all finished. Brothers from all countries, avenge us. We are being led like sheep to the slaughter."[136] German and local police forces then rounded up and shot 1,318 Jews, including Fania and her family, in a mass grave by the Drujka River, burying some of the victims in mass graves in the Jewish cemetery[137]—Fania's notes survived, preserved by a non-Jewish acquaintance.

A similar example was offered by Natke, a young woman processing her fear of coming murder in Dąbrowa Górnicza, a town nine miles northeast of Kattowitz in East Upper Silesia, in July 1943. Bidding farewell to her sister Andzha, she expressed hope that her young daughter would survive in the hands of a caring non-Jewish couple. "Now we are in immediate danger, Andzha," she said of her own situation. Having come under German occupation in September 1939, Dąbrowa Górnicza's over 5,000 Jews had been confined to an open ghetto in November 1940. It was sealed in early 1943. While the German authorities exploited Jewish labor, they also deported Jews to the Będzin and Sosnowiec ghettos, as well as to Auschwitz. The Dąbrowa Górnicza ghetto was destroyed in late July 1943.[138] "Stay strong, but there is no chance that we will survive all of this," Natke wrote as the destruction was taking place, days before the remaining 1,000-2,000 Jews would be deported to Auschwitz in early August. "Just remember to someday avenge us if you can. We have no course of action. We cannot save ourselves because there is nowhere to escape. We are trapped from all sides. I won't write anymore because I do not want to cause you any pain."[139] Most likely Natke was murdered just days later at Auschwitz-Birkenau.

For some letter writers, the essential purpose of revenge was deterrence. Massive violence against Jews, they believed while experiencing utter powerlessness and despair, could only be stopped if it was answered measure for measure, by the same kind of violence. In a letter written in June 1942, Moshe Wald and his son Binyamin informed an unknown recipient that "[o]ur lives are very bitter, but we wish to live after the war in order to take revenge against the Germans and also most of the Poles, for [the] fate of our people." If the Jews were to have a future, Wald noted, and wanted to prevent "what happened to us to happen a second time," the revenge had to be "very great."[140] He left unstated what form it was meant to take. Other writers evoked indiscriminate payback upon an indiscriminate group of "murderers," "perpetrators," or "Germans"— on any Germans, no matter what role they had played in the mass murder. In late January 1943, for example, young Asher Schwartz wrote his sister Rivka, living in British Mandatory Palestine, that fewer than 100 of the former 15,000 Jews from the district of Sanok, near Krakow, were still alive. She and her children, he prescribed, "should know to revenge the pure Jewish blood that was spilled. You must educate your children in the spirit of arms and hatred towards the German people." Turning to "all Jews," Schwartz wrote as follows: "Don't look for business or job advancement, just take up arms, murder everyone you come across (from the German nation), people, women and small children, because that's what they did to us. The greatest writer," he added, "is not talented enough to describe their cruelty towards your brothers. Therefore, you must be intent on revenge only! Revenge! Revenge!"[141]

Some Jews, anticipating their deaths and writing in this vein, also expressed fears that future avengers would not implement their task. In March 1943, Zipora Birman, a partisan and member of the Zionist youth group Dror, writing friends in mandatory

Palestine from the Bialystok ghetto to try to locate her sister, Shohana Fink, in Palestine and send her regards, thus warned future survivors as follows:

> On you rests the absolute obligation to exact out our revenge. Let no one of you sleep at night or rest during the day: as we find ourselves in the shadow of death, let it be the same for you in avenging the blood that has been spilt. Cursed be whoever reads these words for whom it suffices to sigh and to return to daily chores; cursed be he for whom cheap tears suffice, who in his crying would bewail our souls. We call you to avenge – avenge without pity, without feeling, without words about 'good' Germans. . . . This is our demand. The scattered ashes from the ovens will not rest until this revenge will have been exacted. Remember and fulfil our wish and your obligation.[142]

As Zipora Birman wrote earlier in her letter she had no news from her family. "Today they most certainly are no longer alive. I, too, shall not be. Another week, maybe another month. I really wanted to meet [my sister]. At least for a few minutes. Too bad. Goodbye to her."[143] Birman would be killed in the Bialystok ghetto uprising in mid-August 1943, when the Germans destroyed the ghetto and deported the remaining 25,000 of formerly 50,000 Bialystok Jews to Treblinka, Auschwitz, Stutthof, Majdanek and various labor camps.[144] Her letter would be buried with the so-called Mersik-Tennebaum archive documenting the history of the Bialystok ghetto and its resistance and unearthed after the war.

Revenge Fantasies in Diaries written in Ghettos, Camps, and Hiding

Diaries or memoir-like personal accounts written by Jews trapped in ghettos, hiding places, and camps offered their authors a space for introspection over an extended period of time as their world was collapsing, their communities were being destroyed, their families and acquaintances were being murdered, and they were struggling with the daily reality of dehumanization, powerlessness, forced labor, violence, hunger, and disease. In our context, the lines between diaries and memoirs are fluid: something mostly due to circumstances, as for lack of paper and pencil or other constraints, Jews facing incarceration and murder did not have the opportunity to write a standard diary with regular entries; they often summarized earlier events when they had the opportunity and resources to write. But many accounts are not memoirs either, strictly speaking, because the time span between the lived events and the time of the account was brief, the writing still taking place during the events—as opposed to after the fact, as is the case with postwar accounts. Consequently, there is fluidity both in addressing the real time events and in narrating and reflecting back on events that occurred before the account. In this discussion, I will thus understand "diary" in broad terms, including accounts not necessarily written on a daily basis but from "inside" the events, rather than from postwar chronological distance.[145]

Diary-writing during the Holocaust was a cultural phenomenon and a collective practice with multiple functions. It was both a pastime and a means of self-encounter; diarists recorded incidents they had witnessed and spoke to loved ones they had lost, processed trauma and tried to make sense of the unfolding genocide.[146] They probed human relations, life-cycle experiences, beliefs and world views, and indeed the human condition as such. The diarists also wrote about revenge. Unlike last letters, which were written as an ad-hoc response to imminent or approaching death, in diaries and notes, revenge was considered over longer periods of time; it served a longer-term strategy for coping with ever worsening conditions. In the private refuge of these intimate texts, writers explored vengeful impulses emerging in response to an unprecedented crime. *Imagining* revenge gave solace without further endangering oneself or others—and both the possibilities and limitations of enacted revenge could be explored. In January 1942, one young diarist, from Stanisławów in Eastern Galicia, noted that seeking payback for injustice and hardship was like "howling at the moon" but nevertheless it was "nice to think about revenge that may never take place."[147] Revenge that remained in the realm of imagination remained free of moral complications and societal stigmas; but the act of imagination and writing themselves furnished emotional ballast helping the diary writers to cope in extremis.

For some diarists, writing about revenge was a visceral response that allowed a processing of outrage at one or another facet of everyday atrocities by the German occupation regime. For example, teenager Dawid Sierakowiak—he would die in August 1943, at age nineteen, of typhus or another famine-related disease in the Lodz ghetto—processed his anger over how German soldiers and local ethnic Germans harassed and humiliated Jews shortly after the Wehrmacht occupied Lodz in September 1939; he noted that he could only think about revenge in response.[148] And Hillel Seidman (1907–1995), a Hassidic writer and political leader with a doctorate in history who commented extensively on daily life in the Warsaw ghetto in his Yiddish diary, giving vent to despair at seeing the daily brutalities accompanying the massive roundup of some 265,000 Jews—the majority of the ghetto population—for deportations to Treblinka between July and September 1942, noted that a "spirit of bitterness holds sway everywhere.... Revenge is all that can bring some comfort now."[149] Leaving completely open what form the revenge was meant to take, such a diary-entry suggests that writing and thinking about the simple possibility was in and of itself consequential in a desperate coping effort. Other diarists could be more vivid: On July 30, 1943, Margarete (Grete) Bolchower, keeping a German-language diary while hiding in Czortków, Eastern Galicia, noted, six weeks after German police and Ukrainian auxiliaries had combed and liquidated the local ghetto and shot to death its remaining 2,500 inhabitants in nearby ravines, that a response to the mass murder of Jews needed to be "revenge that shakes the world to its very foundations." By then most of the town's 8,000 Jews had been murdered in mass shootings, or deported to death at Belzec, or else sent, if fortunate, into slave labor. Bolchower, who was mourning the murder of her husband Marek, added that "[o]therwise those in mass graves will know no peace"; the main task for the "very few [Jews] who will be left" after the war was "to avenge their murdered brothers!"[150] Still, here too the lack of specificity suggests that the mere idea, the possibility of revenge had meaning for individuals coping with profound humiliation and despair.

In their daily struggle with the German mass murder campaign, some diarists drew strength from news suggesting harm or setbacks to Germans—for example as news concerning Allied air raids on German cities. In his Warsaw ghetto journal famously discovered after the war, among other archival material of his buried in milk cans and metal boxes, the famed historian Emanuel Ringelblum remarked on June 26, 1942, that hearing about British bombs on Cologne "soaked our thirst for revenge somewhat." He further elaborated that "Cologne was an advance payment on the vengeance that must and shall be taken on Hitler's Germany for the millions of Jews they have killed.... After Cologne I walked around in a good mood," he noted "... my death is prepaid."[151] (Ringelblum and his family would be murdered by the Gestapo in March 1944.) For his part Bezalel (Calel or Calek) Perechodnik, a young Jewish agronomist, born in 1916 in Otwock near Warsaw, considered the toll taken on German civilians, in particular, in the Allied air war as a form of revenge. Between May 7 and August 19, 1943, hiding in Warsaw's "Aryan side," Perechodnik wrote a "confessional diary,"[152] to which he added an epilogue dated October 19, 1943. In February 1941, Perechodnik had become a policeman in the Otwock ghetto, hoping that his position would allow him to protect his wife Anka (Anna, née Nosfeld) and infant daughter Athalie. But on August 19, 1942, they were deported to Treblinka. In the diary Perechodnik expresses his sense of shame, guilt, and pain over their fate, while also reflecting on his traumatic experiences and the struggle for survival in hiding. Vengeance for his wife and child, and tied to this, rectification for what Perechodnik saw as his failure as a husband and father, are recurring themes in his diary. "Know that you will be bloodily avenged," he wrote on August 19, 1943, addressing Anka, who had already been murdered in Treblinka: "Know that the revenge has already begun, that daily air raids on Germany bring with them deaths to numberless women and children. It is a drop in a sea of blood that will be spilled in order to avenge You and millions of innocent Jewish women and children who fell at the hand of the German barbarians."[153]

Processing the brutalization and loss through, in part, ideas of revenge took place incrementally. Individuals were more likely to formulate such ideas later in the mass-murder process: the more violence they had experienced, the more it had surpassed anything they had thought conceivable, the fewer inhibitions they appear to have had in that respect. Thoughts of revenge were intertwined with the struggle to survive. "For almost everyone there was a desire to endure and, as the time passed, the desire for revenge grew stronger,"[154] noted Stanislaw Adler (1901–1946), a Warsaw lawyer. Adler had served as an officer in the Warsaw ghetto police but had sought administrative tasks; highly critical of the police, he resigned in the face of mass deportations in the summer of 1942. Working for the housing office of the Jewish council, he became its director, escaping the ghetto in February 1943. Hiding with his lover Lola Zeldowicz, a neurologist, he wrote about his experiences in the ghetto; in "personal notes" on Adler accompanying his memoirs, Zeldowitz indicates that for Adler, with Warsaw's Jews—facing mass deportations to Treblinka; knowing they would be murdered by gas there—only able to survive in hiding, thinking about future revenge was crucial for psychological endurance.[155] (Adler survived the war; but he committed suicide in July 1946.) Also writing in hiding in spring 1944, after more than four years into the German occupation, Emanuel Ringelblum noted that everyone still alive was talking about revenge.[156]

A Divine or Human Task?

Diarists had markedly different ideas about what form the revenge should take. Many considered the question of whether revenge was a human task or was meant for God. Depending on religious observance, strength of Jewish consciousness, and political views, grappling with the intensity of destruction and loss differed when it came to the division of labor between God and human beings in exacting revenge. The educator and journalist Chaim Aron Kaplan had received a traditional Jewish education at the Mir Yeshiva and teacher-training at the Jewish Teachers' Seminary in Vilna; but accompanying a fascination with Zionism and the Hebrew language, he left religious observance behind. Having established a Hebrew-language elementary school in Warsaw and serving as its principal, he tried to immigrate to Palestine in 1936–1937; but failing to receive an immigration permit, he returned to Poland. A regular Hebrew-language diarist since 1933, Kaplan chronicled the life and death of Warsaw Jews before being deported to Treblinka in August 1942.[157] Kaplan agonized over God's inaction. "Is there no revenge in the world for the spilling of innocent blood?" he asked on April 12, 1940. "The abominations committed before our eyes cry out from the earth: 'Avenge me!' But there is no jealous avenger. Why has a 'day of vengeance and retribution' not yet come for the murderers? Do not answer me with idle talk—I won't listen to you. Give me a logical reply!"[158] While Kaplan was disenchanted with God for allowing the atrocities, and also for not avenging them, in his view the revenge remained a divine task; he saw his own, personal mission as being to describe the atrocities he witnessed and thus serve a larger, human and historical purpose.[159]

Abraham Lewin was born in Warsaw in 1893 to an orthodox family; like Kaplan he had turned to Zionism and the Hebrew language, working as a teacher before the German occupation. His Yiddish-language diary chronicles the horrors of mass deportations to Treblinka and the growing awareness, from reports of escapees who returned to the ghetto, of indiscriminate mass murder,[160] including that of Lewin's wife Luba: "Almighty God! Why did this happen?" wrote Lewin. "And why is the whole world deaf to our screams? Earth, earth, do not cover our blood, and let no place be free from our cries!"[161] A few weeks later, he implored: "Avenging God! Take vengeance for our blood that has been shed, and whatever may be, let them never be forgiven the blood of our innocent children, of our mothers and of our parents. May they reap their just reward!"[162] The exact circumstances of Lewin's death in 1943 remain unknown. Both he and Kaplan, having received a traditional Jewish upbringing and being deeply rooted in Jewish tradition but eventually having turned to secular Zionism, found strength in a Jewish consciousness grounded in Jewish history and culture; both saw revenge in terms of divine intervention—but their faith that it would ever ensue was evidently badly shaken.

Responding to the Apocalypse

Other Jewish diary-writers maintained such faith. Hillel Seidman, a Hassidic political leader who before the German occupation served as executive secretary of Agudath Israel, the political party of orthodox Judaism, in the Polish parliament, and in the Warsaw city council, remained deeply religious in his response to the ghetto's unfolding destruction.[163] Under the shock and horror of the mass deportations, Seidman acknowledged that "[f]inally we appreciate—today more than ever before—the potency of revenge,"[164] citing vengeance episodes found in the Hebrew Bible and taken up in Jewish liturgy.[165] Writing on Yom Kippur 1942, he cited the *Avinu Malkeinu* prayer recited on Yom Kippur and other fast days: a prayer beseeching God to act on behalf of His people, specifically also in response to suffering and death Jews endured from persecution. Seidman found new meaning and urgency in one particular line from the prayer, a line imploring God to avenge the "spilt blood of Your servants."[166] Like Seidman, Marcel Nadjari (1917–1971), a Greek Jewish member of the Auschwitz Sonderkommando, drew strength from faith. In his secret notebook, Nadjari confessed that "Almost every time they kill, I wonder if there is a God"—his estimate of the Germans' victims at Auschwitz was 1.4 million.[167] Yet although Nadjari spoke of being "condemned to death by the Germans because I'm of the Jewish faith,"[168] he also stated that "I have always believed in Him and still believe that God wants it, let His will be."[169] His secret notebook makes clear that not only faith but also a belief in future revenge—divine and human—remained an essential element of his quest for survival.[170] Similarly with Norman Salsitz (Naftali Saleschuetz, son of aforementioned Isaak Saleschuetz), born in 1920 to a wealthy orthodox family in Kolbuszowa. At age eighteen, Salsitz cut off his sidelocks and discarded his Hassidic garb, turning to religious Zionism, with aspirations to become a doctor. While Salsitz secularized his way of life, he remained deeply connected to his Judaism. As Salsitz indicated in both testimony and different memoirs, he decided to pursue vengeance after an SS officer insulted him by mocking Judaism: his response was to flee into the forest and, eventually, join the Polish underground Armia Krajowa. Salsitz would survive the war; the rest of his large family was murdered in Belzec in July 1942.[171]

Some Jews placed their faith in secular political ideas combined with hope for something like apocalyptic revenge ending the ongoing horror. This was the case with the librarian and Bundist activist Herman Kruk (1897–1944), who meticulously chronicled the destruction of Jewish Vilna, where he had fled from Warsaw upon that city's German occupation. In his *Chronicles from the Vilna Ghetto*, Kruk recounts the testimony of Peyse Schloss, a sixteen-year-old Jewish girl, and of other survivors of mass killings of Vina Jews at Ponary, including a twelve-year-old girl being treated at the Jewish hospital for gunshot wounds, in early September 1941. Trying to process the fact that Jewish men and women, the elderly and children were systematically stripped naked and shot in the back of the head, Kruk commented as follows: "Can the world not scream? Can history never take revenge? If the heavens can open up [to accept Jewish supplication], when should it happen if not today?"[172] He struggled to find words to describe "fields reek[ing] with the stench of the dead bodies" a few survivors managing to "crawl out of there, and a few drag[ging] themselves to the villages"—"[h]ow can you write about all this? How can you collect your thoughts?"[173]—Kruk saw his principle mission in transmitting the truth about the German crimes to posterity.[174] Yet his articulation of despair over the enormous loss of life led to an evocation of revenge that challenged the idea of divine intervention: "If heaven is heaven," he exclaimed, "it should start pouring down lava; let all that is still alive be washed away once and for all. Let a greater world destruction than this one come—let a new world rise on the ruins!"[175] Citing the first line of the "International," " 'Arise ye wretched of the earth . . .' "[176] Kruk, true to his Bundist ethos, expressed a faint hope that all the destruction would produce a better world in the future. (In this respect, let us note Emmanuel Ringelblum's reference—Ringelblum was affiliated with the Marxist-Zionist Poale Zion movement—to people in the ghetto who believed that a socialist restructuring of society would offer both the ultimate answer to the suffering they had endured and witnessed and the best "collective revenge"[177] in the future.) Kruk would be deported to the Klooga concentration camp in Estonia and murdered.

Other voices maintained faith in the Allied armies as agents of future vengeance. In that respect, it is worthwhile to take a closer look at Calel Perechodnik's diary, because of its embrace of revenge in straightforward form, tied to a direct confrontation with religious faith and a tormented awareness of all the ethical ambiguities related to vengeance. Perechodnik was a highly educated secular Jew with an orthodox background; in the diary he acknowledged his loss of belief in the existence of God; in His absence, revenge was the sole remaining option for Jews in their death agony: "If I believed in God, in heaven or hell, in some reward or punishment after death, I wouldn't have written this at all," he commented, referring to his diary. "It would be enough for me to know that all Germans will roast in hell after they die. Regrettably," he continued, "I don't know how to pray, and as for faith, I have none! That's why I ask the whole democratic world—Englishmen, Americans, Russians, Jews of Palestine—to avenge our women and children burned alive in Treblinkas."[178] While he doubted and rejected God, he nevertheless relied on God to give peace to the dead.[179] He mocked both those who had remained religiously observant Jews and those who chose recourse to the Zionist idea of sovereign statehood in Palestine. "Today we indeed have proof of how good it is to find oneself under the power of divine protection," he remarked sarcastically in late spring 1943 from his Warsaw hiding place, then continuing: "And a time will come when the democratic world will win, and fanfares will announce the freedom of peoples. Jews will then be able to live freely, go back to Palestine—although from the 3 million [Polish Jews] will remain perhaps twenty thousand, a tiny number. . . . After one thousand years there will be new millions of Jews. Let us praise the name of God!"[180] In Perechodnik's view, Jews needed to confront the fact that "[w]e have lost the war."[181] Along with religious faith and Zionism, Perechodnik equally rejected Bundism, socialism, and liberalism, political approaches that, he felt, had failed in the existential crisis that Jews were facing. What remained was revenge and, for him personally, closely connected with this, having lost the love of his life and his infant daughter, suicide. In view of Perechodnik's profound bitterness, anger, and despair, his acknowledgment that, in a context of absolute injustice defined by state-sanctioned murder of Jewish children, he broke with the ethical norms by which he used to abide, is remarkable. But his words also point to the emotional ballast offered by the sheer act of *imagining* an ultimate form of revenge on those who murdered his family and were intentionally exterminating his people: "My heart is already pounding with joy; my cheeks are glowing with the thought of the physical and psychological tortures I would inflict on the Germans before their final death. And then, saturated with blood and revenge I could perish together with my enemies."[182]

In this way, Perechodnik offered a bitter echo of Nazi depictions of Jews as "parasites" destroying their hosts and dying alongside it.[183] For Perechodnik, his life had in any event essentially reached the point of having no sense beyond thoughts of violent revenge connected to suicide as a meaningful autonomous death. In its utter bitterness, his stance may appear at a remove from that of, for instance, Emanuel Ringelblum or Hermann Kruk. But whatever the difference in that respect, and however varied the approaches of these different diarists to questions of religion, Zionism, Bundism and so forth, they shared an effort to process the atrocities being inflicted on them, their families, and their collective—the enormous destruction they were witnessing and experiencing—and all looked to ideas of revenge as a strategy to help them cope.

Revenge and the Struggle for Survival

For many diarists, imagining revenge, offering justification for continuing to live after seeing their loved ones murdered, was connected with concern that they would not live to see the revenge enacted. On August 26, 1942, the writer Rachel Auerbach (Rokhl Eiga Oyerbakh, 1903–1976), who worked in social welfare and clandestine documentation of conditions in the Warsaw ghetto for Ringelblum's Oyneg Shabbes underground archive, remarked in one of her notebooks: "I want to live, am ready to kiss the boots of the commonest boor just to live to see the moment of REVENGE."[184] When she wrote this, after twenty-two months of confinement in the ghetto, where 83,000 Jews had already died through starvation and disease, some 265,000 Jews were being deported to Treblinka. "Such atrocities may already have happened in Jewish history, but there has never been such disgrace. Jews as instruments,"[185] she observed, voicing her feelings about how the Nazi regime was rendering Jews complicit in their own destruction through the Jewish councils and Jewish police—and by destroying their physical and psychological resilience, their will to live. "REVENGE! REVENGE!" she noted, "Remember, all you who read this: REVENGE! Vengeance for the trembling of the children and the suffering of the elderly, vengeance for bringing people to a state of such resignation and determination that they go voluntarily. Like sheep to the slaughter. [. . .] For the terror of the old ones, for the suffering of the young, for the powerless despair of men and women in their prime."[186] Without going into detail of what she envisioned, Auerbach nevertheless elaborated: "A human being who has been brought to stop fearing death is even more dangerous. And it is this moment that I want to see in Poland. Maybe some other Jews will live to see it as well."[187] She closed saying: "Perhaps this is my last will – REVENGE!"[188] (Auerbach escaped from the ghetto in February 1943 and survived the war on the "Aryan side" of Warsaw; she would be instrumental in locating and saving much of the Ringelblum archive and became a central figure in the development of

Israel's Yad Vashem and in finding survivor witnesses for the Eichmann trial.) Another contributor to the underground archive, the communal activist and economist Shmuel Winter (born in 1891 in Włocławek), voiced similar feelings; in January 1943, he wrote: "I don't want to leave the world when we can see from afar . . . a possibility to live to see . . . revenge against the killers."[189] Winter, a father of three, was hiding in a bunker with two of his children after his wife and youngest son had been deported to Treblinka during the mass deportations of the previous summer. On May 3, 1943, during the ghetto uprising, his bunker was discovered and he was murdered.[190] In his diary, Calel Perechodnik noted that with growing awareness among the Jews in the Otwock ghetto that deportation to Treblinka meant death, there was also a growing wish to survive to see an execution of real revenge: "Everyone still wants to live, wants to survive the war, wants to see with his own eyes the end of the hated Germans, wants to lend a hand to the general acts of vengeance and punishment for German barbarity, and so all live on."[191]

Cypa Zonszajn expressed similar thoughts. "Who will avenge us?" she asked in her diary, written in Siedlce in fall 1942. She and her family had been subjected to slave labor and violence since the Germans had occupied the town in September 1939; she had been living in the Siedlce ghetto for over a year. Zonszajn's diary entries recounted her experiences during the ghetto's liquidation between August 22 and 24, 1942. During these few days, roughly 17,000 Jews from Siedlce and the surrounding villages were rounded up, around 10,000 of them being forced to crouch on the town square in the August heat for two days without food or water, leading to 2,000 being randomly shot for "disobeying." The surviving Jews were deported to Treblinka, including her parents and extended family. She evaded deportation with the help of her husband Jakub, a ghetto policeman. For three days, together with her eleven-month-old daughter Rachel she hid in an attic over a bathhouse next to the Jewish police station, along with dozens of other Jews. Suffering from excruciating thirst and heat, she would hear screams and gunshots while she struggled to calm her infant, breast-feeding and sedating her so that the baby's cries would not call attention to the hiding place. She was tormented with guilt feelings for not having also tried to save her parents from the roundup. By the time of her diary-writing, Zonszajn had placed Rachel with her non-Jewish friends on Siedlce's "Aryan side," but had returned to the ghetto to be united with her husband. By then she had had contact with an escapee who had reported where the deportation trains were going, Treblinka, and that people were being murdered there en masse with poison gas. "Who will avenge our suffering and this horrible cattle like death of thousands of bright, valuable intelligent young people, among them doctors, professors and other scholars who died as well?" she wrote. "Who will avenge the suffering of parents whose children have been taken from them, the children who lost their parents, and wives taken from husbands? Who will avenge the suffering of the mother who has seen her child killed in front of her? If I could live," she added, "I would want to witness revenge. The moment that I myself could exact and take revenge for the deaths of my parents, cousins and uncles. Unfortunately, this will not happen."[192] On November 25, 1942, the ghetto was liquidated and its remaining 1,500–2,000 inhabitants marched to the Gęsi Borek neighborhood, where they were held for three days awaiting deportation to Treblinka. In

Gęsi Borek, Cypa Zonszajn and her husband committed suicide by poison; in retrospect we can understand her diary entries as articulating a tension between the desire to live, and to see revenge enacted, and the fear of death at the hands of the Germans.[193] (The Zonszajns' daughter Rachel would survive the war with the help of non-Jewish Poles.)

In drawing some solace from ideas of revenge, many diarists made use of fire imagery and related language, capturing both the fierce meaning these ideas had for victims and the destructive force of the revenge wished on their persecutors. Such language, we should note, is also present in postwar survivor testimony, for instance that of Masha P., a Bundist member of the ŻOB who recalled that young men and women preparing for the Warsaw uprising shared revenge fantasies in their bunkers and hideouts, their hatred for Germans being "boiling and on fire."[194] In her above-mentioned diary, Chaika Klinger similarly noted, about herself and other members of the Hashomer Hatzair underground, that "[w]e were burning, seething. Hatred and desire for vengeance were blazing inside us like a red-hot iron."[195] Likewise Ben Zion Kalb (born in 1910 in Strzyżów, Poland), noted while hiding in Slovakia: "Our revenge is boiling in our bodies . . . the earth is getting hot for these murderers."[196] And the diary of teenage Tamara Lazerson (born in Kovno in 1929), contains a poem she wrote hiding on a farm near Kovno in January 1944: "It is cold, so cold./ It is white in the yard./ It is cold, so cold, in the room./ It is cold and gloomy in my breast./ It is cold and white in my heart./ The desire for revenge warms me up./ Revenge for innocent suffering and great injustices."[197] (Lazerson would survive the Holocaust in hiding.)

Writing in Auschwitz-Birkenau, Zalmen Gradowski addressed future readers of his notes, using imagery related to fire, heat, and forces of nature to express the emotional energy he was experiencing and hoped to transmit: "I want . . . to wake some feeling in you, to sow a spark of revenge, which will burst into flame and take every heart by storm."[198] And later: "Perhaps a spark of my inner fire will ignite in you, and you will fulfill just a small part of our will in life, and you will take revenge, revenge on the murderers!"[199] Elsewhere, he evokes a "desire for revenge" that "will erupt like lava that has so long been seething deep inside us, like a volcano," and to fire that will erupt or explode someday.[200] Although fearful that his writing would only do justice to a small fraction of the truth about the unfathomable crime he was being forced to endure and witness,[201] Gradowski nevertheless hoped that his testimony would convey knowledge of the mass murder to posterity—and ignite an emotional spark for vengeance in the finders of his text.

Finally, in his secret—Greek-language—account, hidden in a thermos bottle, discovered severely damaged decades after the war, in 1980, but deciphered with technological help, Marcel Nadjari, who had been deported from Salonika to Auschwitz in April 1944, offered his own, tragic twist on the fire-theme: many times, Nadjari indicates in his twelve-page text, he has contemplated jumping into Auschwitz's burning furnaces to end his life, consumed together with the bodies of the victims he is being forced to burn. But, he adds, the urge to avenge the death of his father, mother, and sister has kept him from ending his life in this way. At the same time, Najdari also expressed the fear that he will die before having the opportunity to "get the revenge I want"—and the revenge that, he indicates, he would know how to exact.²⁰² Nadjari and other Sonderkommando members who worked in crematorium III, did not participate in the October 7, 1944 revolt in crematorium IV, and survived. Two days before the arrival of the Red Army at Auschwitz Najdari was sent on a death march to Mauthausen; from there he was incarcerated at Gusen and Melk where he was liberated.²⁰³ As his and the various other cited accounts by Jews in ghettos, hiding places, and death camps show, writing itself was an existential necessity under constantly worsening conditions; and evoking the possibility and prospect of revenge had a vital impact in an enduring quest for simple self-preservation.

Urges and Unease: The Ambiguities of Vengeance

Despite such empowering effects, for Holocaust victims thoughts of revenge were often charged with ambivalence, grounded in a tension between the desire for vengeance on the one hand, either moral reluctance to exact it or an inability to do so—safely or at all—on the other hand. For example, in Abraham Sutzkever's memoir—written in Moscow in spring 1945, following escape from the Vilna ghetto to the forests, partisan activity, and airlifting into Russia—we read how one day in the ghetto, a Gestapo officer beat his mother bloody as punishment for using a sidewalk forbidden to Jews. Sutzkever, enraged by both his mother's humiliation and her physical injury, felt a desire to take revenge for the sake of her honor. Shortly after, a Lithuanian collaborator entered the family's apartment to catch Jews for a roundup and Sutzkever hid in a storage room. Out of fear of being discovered and anger at the intrusion, but also from abiding rage over his mother's humiliation, Sutzkever grabbed an axe, bent on splitting the man's head. But instead of doing so, Sutzkever held his breath in the darkness until the Lithuanian turned around and left. Intuitively, he had realized that he was better off—certainly physically, but we may assume morally as well—evading confrontation and trying to stay undiscovered.²⁰⁴

Even some individuals who frequently expressed thoughts of revenge in writing and addressed their own vengeful impulses refrained from carrying them out from awareness this would compromise their moral standing and sense of self. Calel Perechodnik's diary, stamped as it is with bitter anger, reveals such moral inhibitions. One day, seeing an "Aryan" woman with an infant girl the age of his deported daughter, he noted: "My legs buckled under me. I recognized my daughter's stroller. I looked at the child, the small, innocent child, and I had an irresistible urge to strangle it with my own hands. I couldn't get it through my head that an Aryan child had a right to be walked in a stolen carriage"—Perechodnik clearly meant a carriage once belonging to now ghettoized or murdered Jews—"and my Aluska, because she had been born of Jewish parents, not only had no right to ride in her stroller but had altogether no right to live. This scene haunted me for a long time," he noted, "and from that time on I avoided the Polish area as much as possible."²⁰⁵ It appears that this reluctance stemmed from the possibility he might murder a child as futile payback for the loss of his own.

The idea of violence in response to violence troubled various diary writers. Some expressed doubts that Jews were capable, morally, physically, or both, of inflicting deadly retaliation on Germans and their collaborators by killing them. In October 1942, Yekhiel Gorny (1908–1943), a member of Ringelblum's archival project and like Ringelblum part of the Poale Zion movement, thus noted in his diary that Jews were "not capable of taking revenge through murder, burning or extermination ... not even against our mortal enemies, the Germans. We would not be able to do it."[206] Although here Gorny did not elaborate on the source or basis of this incapacity, he did seem to believe that *some* strategy for vengeance, albeit a non-violent one, was at least a possibility.

Still other victims of the German mass murder campaign rejected revenge for moral reasons. We see this, for example, in Chajka Klinger's diary, which furnished an account of the Będzin ghetto's previous three years, and specifically the history of its underground, as well as of her time in hiding. Klinger had endured severe torture at the hands of the Gestapo, after her ghetto bunker was discovered and she was found with a weapon. Slated for Auschwitz, she nevertheless managed to escape the ghetto and hide. Born in 1917 to a Hassidic family but with an advanced secular education, her notes were critical of the Jewish leadership in the ghetto, Jews in Palestine and America, Poles, and of course Germans. Processing grief and anger, she frequently addressed the possibility of and desire for revenge: "I was raging with madness and vengeance, that bloody, merciless vengeance,"[207] she reflected, looking back on the previous weeks in hiding:

> I wanted revenge, revenge. For the millions of Jewish children suffocated, suffocated in wagons, thrown like balls into trains, for those strangled by their own parents, for those abandoned by their own mothers. For the millions of Jewish young people blossoming and tall like trees who were strangled and executed, tormented and tortured in prisons, who toiled like horses in labor camps. And for our fathers, slaving away and exhausted by the harsh, toilsome life. I was raging with desire for a brutal revenge, more terrible than the world has ever seen. I wanted to suffocate, kill them all; whoever came to hand – adults, men women, children, tiny little children. I wanted to strangle, kill.[208]

But then Klinger encountered an ethnic German woman, with a child, who took her in after her escape from the ghetto. "Could I do her any harm? Or harm her child?" she asked. The sight of the German child, was a painful reminder of all the murdered Jewish children, and especially her three-year-old niece. "My heart is aching so much, so much. But I wouldn't be able to hurt this child. I've even grown fond of her. She's not to blame that the world's so cruel, so unjust."[209] Klinger acknowledged to herself that through the relationship with the mother and child, her "hate has somehow subsided"[210]. She felt torn between the emotional urge for violent, indiscriminate revenge and a rational understanding that not all Germans were guilty—and that indeed the German nation should not be destroyed: "The mind says that it's true. But the heart is bleeding profusely and calling for revenge."[211]

Jewish Revenge and the Holocaust

Vengeance and combat could be closely related. Some Jews who fought in partisan units set clear ethical boundaries when it came to carrying out revenge. For example, Celia K. (born in Szarkowszczyzna, a small town near Vilna, in 1923) participated in the killings of Germans and their Ukrainian, Lithuanian, and Polish collaborators when it was part of combat and followed a larger self-defense rationale. But, as she indicated in testimony given in 1980, when her battalion captured a seventeen-year-old wounded and helpless Wehrmacht soldier, she refrained from revenge. Her commander had handed him over to her saying "Cecily, he's all yours. You could torture him. You could kill him." But: "I couldn't do it. . . . I couldn't. I bandaged his knee, I fed him, and I turned him over with all the captured. I couldn't do it. I shot a lot of Germans, a lot of Ukrainians, a lot of Lithuanians in the course of my work, but not point blank to take the 17-year-old and kill him. I couldn't do it. Maybe I was soft-hearted. Maybe I'm sorry, I don't know. I just couldn't do it."[212] A connection with gender roles seems a strong possibility here, Cecilia K., although assuming a masculine role of fierce and merciless combatant, also remained true to a compassionate female role of giving care to the wounded—even to an enemy.

For other Jews trying to survive outside the partisan setting, simply becoming violent posed a basic moral dilemma: even if this served a resistance plot geared toward ending the mass murder and enabling escape and survival; even if strong thoughts were present of murdered loved ones whose deaths, the feeling went, needed to be repaid.[213] The dilemma was that someone who had suffered from terrible violence would need to resort to violence—still a dilemma when it was the only way to survive. For some, grappling with the dilemma led to self-harm. This was the case with the aforementioned Chaim Engel, his reluctant participation in the killing of an SS officer during the Sobibor uprising—which in testimony offered in 1990, he saw as justified revenge for the murder of his family—resulted in accidental self-cutting leaving a permanent scar. (In later testimony—1992—he did not refer to revenge in recounting this episode; but the theme resurfaced in testimony of 1998.)[214]

The inhibition when it came to violence could come from a conscious fear of losing one's own humanity—thus succumbing to, precisely, the dehumanization that the Nazis were inflicting on their victims. Jews with such feelings could see vengeance in strictly negative terms; they could fear both their vengeful impulses and that life in extremis would not let them control them. In his diary entry of August 18, 1943, after learning about Allied bombings of Bonn, Raul Raymond Lambert (1894–1943)—head of the council of Jews in France (Union Générale des Israélites de France, UGIF) first in the "free zone" under the Vichy regime and later for all of occupied France—since wondered: "Shall I have the strength to preserve my humanity when the time comes to settle scores?"[215] Three days later, he was arrested and deported to Drancy, then, on December 7, 1943, to Auschwitz, where he was murdered a few days after arrival together with his wife and four children.[216] In his notebooks Emanuel Ringelblum wrote that Yitzhak Giterman (1889–1943), formerly the director of the American Jewish Distribution Committee in Poland and then, as head of the Jewish Self-help Society and a member of the Jewish Fighting Organization ŻOB, coordinator of relief in the Warsaw ghetto, rejected the idea of indiscriminate revenge on Germans after the war: both because he believed that not all Germans were the same, that some were still human, and because he feared that revenge would only beget more violence. Gitterman died on January 18, 1943, while fighting German deportation operations in the Warsaw ghetto.[217] A seemingly even stronger position of that sort was maintained by Max Michael Rothschild, a German Jew born in Gunzenhausen in 1921; hiding for two years in the attic of a farm in Almelo in eastern occupied Netherlands (where he had escaped after his release from Buchenwald in 1938), he wrote as follows:

> We must stand against the death penalty in any form, even for those subjects who do not deserve the name "person" anymore because they behaved in inhuman ways during and even before the war. . . . No one benefits from their death, and also from the perspective of punishment, nothing is accomplished with their death. [. . .] We must insist that even the greatest evildoer be employed for the benefit of mankind, so that they and their families can make up for those they have harmed.[218]

For Rothschild, this meant re-educating Germans in the values of socialism, and having them do "labor in the destroyed areas (cleaning up, construction and colonizing activities)" and seeing to it that they were "willing to serve as research subjects for medical and scientific purposes in hospitals, universities and research institutes. [. . .] We must be willing to take on the education of the German people."[219] Rothschild believed that "It will be necessary," through sustained mental effort,

> to replace the hate against Germany by an attitude that stems from relying on socialism to be the spirit for the reconstruction of the world. This is the only context in which I can see a positive approach to the problems of the future. Hate cannot be combined with blind destructive rage and revenge. We want to overcome what Hitler has wrought in the psyche. We want to overcome the atrocities of our time by the creation of a new, socialist world.[220]

Consequently for Rothschild only education of German youth in socialism, viewed as "a conviction suitable to confronting hate," would prevent repetition of violence: "We want to eradicate, at its root, German youth's resentment over a lost war and the covert desire for a repetition of the same."[221] Aside from his belief in socialism, Rothschild thus rejected revenge and hate from a genuinely universalistic concern that expunging Adolf Hitler's ideas could not be achieved with continued violence, mass killing of Jews answered through mass killing of Germans, rebuilding made possible through more destruction. Revenge feelings and anger were meant to be channelled into reconstruction and education.[222]

Other Jews questioned revenge not only because of its perpetuating a cycle of violence but because of its incapacity to soothe grief over the unfathomable loss of life. For example, in his diary entry of September 6, 1942, during the "second action" in the Lodz ghetto, when 15,682 Jews—mostly children and people deemed unfit for work—were deported to Chelmno—the group included his own mother—Dawid Sierakowiak noted:

After dinner rumors spread that the Germans are now accompanying the medical commissions, and that they decide who will be taken and who will not. There's been an order that all the children who were released be gathered in one of the hospitals, but although Rumkowski assures us that he guarantees "safe conduct" for these children, no one really believes him; even policemen, instructors, and managers are despairing now. Laments and shouts, cries and screams have become so commonplace that one pays almost no attention to them. What do I care about another mother's cry when my own mother has been taken from me!? I don't think there can be ample revenge for this.[223]

Similarly, Abraham Sutzkever remarked that Solomon Mikhoels, the chairman of the Jewish Antifascist Committee in Moscow had told him after his appearance before the Committee on April 2, 1944, "that my testimony was a great act of revenge. But what pleasure can I take in such revenge, when my mother is burnt at Ponary and the Jerusalem of Lithuania is without Jews?"[224]

Many Jews weighing the possibility of vengeance were very conscious of the dilemma that, in the words of Zivia Lubetkin at the Eichmann trial, "no vengeance could fit our suffering."[225] Trapped in the Warsaw ghetto, at the end of Yom Kippur on September 21, 1942, Hillel Seidman noted that "[i]n Poland now, every house, every brick, screams for revenge. All our own instincts in common with millions of our murdered brethren, the persecuted, the tortured, and the innocent children – all demand revenge. Even so, what possible vengeance can outweigh what we have suffered in its severity, in its barbarism, in its enormity?"[226] Seidman quoted Hebrew-language poet Chaim Nachman Bialik's famous poetic expression of the same dilemma, in the context of "a far smaller catastrophe than ours," the 1903 Kishinev pogrom: "'Satan has not yet devised the appropriate reprisal for the innocent blood of a child.'"[227] Seidman continued: "All of us want to live, to escape, to survive until the end, but not on the basis of such a mass slaughter. What adequate redress is there for this horrendous bloodbath?" he asked. "We know that good outweighs evil and Divine reward is far greater tha[n] Divine retribution, but what possible good can result from this raging calamity?"[228]

Abraham Lewin was troubled by the same question. He, too, looked to Bialik, wondering, "if Kishinev was able to evoke such anguished echoes in a Jewish heart, what will there be in our hearts after the greatest disaster that has ever befallen us?" For Lewin as well, the scope and nature of the crime made revenge impossible:

But perhaps because the disaster is so great there is nothing to be gained by expressing in words everything that we feel. Only if we were capable of tearing out by force of our pent-up anguish the greatest of all mountains, a Mount Everest, and with all our hatred and strength hurling it down on the heads of the German murderers of our young and old—this would be the only fitting reaction on our part.

Aware that this was unrealistic he felt he was left with nothing, no adequate forms of payback, and no words to properly express his feelings: "Words are beyond us now. Our hearts are empty and made of stone."[229]

Whatever shape or form revenge could take, whether executed by human agents or by God, whether realized or remaining confined to fantasy, embraced or rejected on moral or practical grounds or for being indiscriminate, objectively it would indeed be incommensurate with the scale, scope, and perfidy of the Nazi mass murder of European Jewry; it could never ameliorate the loss and suffering. But despite this dilemma, thinking about revenge, even if only to reject it, served as a meaningful coping strategy, as it allowed, in an impossible situation, the retention of some sense of agency and existential control.

Generational Imperatives and Gender Roles

Revenge was closely connected to intergenerational relations. The indiscriminate and systematic genocide wiped out multigenerational families, upending the natural succession of generations as children were murdered before and in front of their parents and parents before and in front of their children. All age groups were targeted, girls and boys, women and men, but the elderly and young children were the first to die in unliveable ghetto and camp conditions. The elderly, women with children, and pregnant women were indiscriminately selected for murder in the death camps. Children made up 1.5 million, around 25 percent, of the Holocaust's 5.8 million dead. The generational contract in which children are protected by parents, elderly cared for by the younger, was destroyed. Thinking about revenge and passing on revenge imperatives thus often involved generational bonds, parents called upon to avenge their murdered children, daughters and sons to avenge their parents. The agonizing realization that all Jews were targeted, whole families meant to be wiped out in a vast mass murder process, nurtured fears that no one would be left to take revenge.[230] Parents, and especially older Jews who knew their own death was imminent, clung to the hope that their children and grandchildren would survive and avenge them. When fourteen-year-old Kalman Eisenberg was selected for forced labor in his native Starachowice-Wierzbnik on October 26, 1942—his family along with some other 4,000 Jews would be rounded up for Treblinka the following day—his mother told him: "My child, go. Maybe you will remain alive. But we, we know for sure that we are going to death. And you should take revenge for our blood, innocent blood that is being spilled innocently by the barbaric, murderous hands." Eisenberg parted "with such an embittered heart"[231]—and survived the Starachowice labor camp, then sent to Auschwitz in the summer of 1944 and onward to Buchenwald, where he was eventually liberated.

Kalman Eisenberg's memory of a mother who bequeathed the duty to live and avenge the family had its counterpart in memories of other sons whose parents' voices would ring in their ears for the rest of their lives. In his testimony of 1986, for example, Allen S. (born in Mikołajów in 1929), recalled that "my mother came over to me, and she said to me, I want you to . . . survive. I [said], why me, Mom? She said because you are the only boy. You'll carry on the family name. And one thing you've got to promise me, that when you survive, if you do survive, the only thing should matter to you is *nekome—nekome*, in Yiddish, means revenge . . .—and you'll take revenge for what you have seen and what they are doing to us. She says, I don't want to live anyway. Your father is not here. I don't want to live anyway."[232] Later in the testimony, Allan S. would repeat the imperative. To fulfil it, he joined the partisans: "I had only one ambition. And my Bible was one word—revenge. And that's all I cared [about]. I didn't care about any[thing] else."[233] Similarly with Norman Salsitz, who in his testimony of 1995 recalled his father's final words to him as he was being shot by German police: "Take revenge. He's so loud that, [un]til today, fifty years later, I can hear . . . the voice. And he—it was not like a human voice. It was a voice like it came from heaven."[234]

These experiences and memories are mirrored in the case of an anonymous mother going to her death at Treblinka. In his testimony of 1988, Chil Rajchman, one of the Jewish barbers at the death camp responsible for cutting the hair of women and girls in the gas chamber's antechamber, recalled one of the older women grabbing his arm and asking if young people would stay alive. Not daring to destroy her last hope in her final moments, Rajchman lied and answered yes. "Now I can die assured that my son who . . . came with me will live and take revenge for our misfortunes," the woman responded.[235] Rajchman, barely thirty, lied out of compassion for someone who could have been his mother and who knew she was about to be killed, an act of murder that Rajchman had no power to prevent; all he could do was help her cope and protect his own life. The encounter reminded Rajchman of his own mother—whose premature death he had been mourning since the age of fifteen. Within Treblinka's horrific reality of mass killing, Rajchman had been "happy" that his mother "did not live to be tortured, to experience a ghetto, poverty, hunger and, at the end, Treblinka: to have her hair torn away, to be gassed, then tossed into a pit like tens of thousands of other dead people."[236] Rajchman had been torn by a sense of guilt for still living while his family was murdered; while sorting through the clothes of the dead, at a point where there was no new transport for hair cutting, he found his sister Anna's dress. He tore off a piece, then hiding it in his own clothes during all his time at the camp;[237] he never forgave himself for not having shared his food with her on the deportation train, thinking that this contributed to her being selected for death, although that was in fact the rule at Treblinka. That terrible emotional burden notwithstanding, in an effort to cope with an unbearable reality, Rajchman nurtured an anonymous woman's hope for her descendant's survival—and for his revenge.

Some children felt obliged to care for their parents and soothe their emotions as they were trying to cope. As Vassily Grossman noted in his report about Treblinka, a survivor told him of "a young boy shouting out at the entrance to the gas chamber. 'Don't cry Mama—the Russians will avenge us!'"[238] Children whose parents were murdered also processed their loss by thinking about revenge. For example, Michal (Michael) Kraus, born in Náchod, Czechoslovakia, in 1930 as the only child of Karel and Lotte Kraus, was deported with his parents to Theresienstadt in December 1942, then to the "family camp"

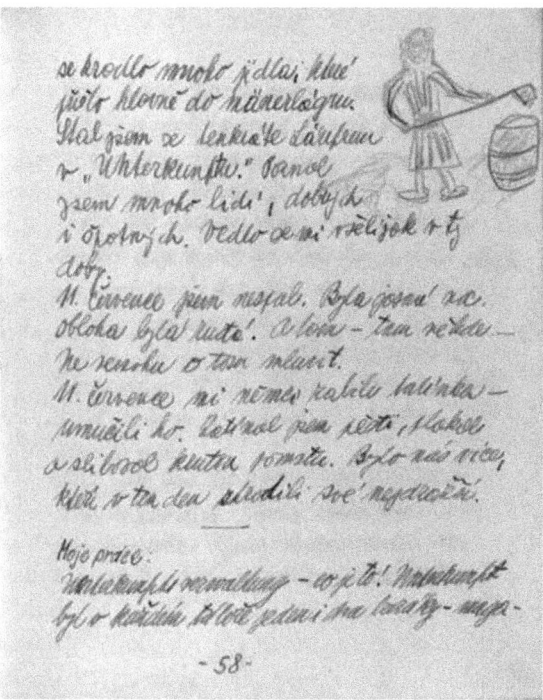

Figure 10 Diary of Michal Kraus; Michael J. Kraus Papers, USHMM Accession No. 1995.A.1067.1, file 5 Diary IIA 1945–1947; United States Holocaust Memorial Museum, courtesy of Ilana Kraus.

of Auschwitz-Birkenau in December 1943. In the summer of 1944, Lotte Kraus was deported to Stutthof, where she perished in January 1945; Karel Kraus was murdered in July 1944. Michal, along with other adolescent boys (the "Birkenau boys") was selected for work at the camp, before being driven on a death march to Mauthausen in January 1945. In the final months of the war, Michal Kraus was incarcerated at Mauthausen and several of its subcamps; he would be liberated at Melk. In his illustrated diary written shortly after liberation, Kraus wrote about the moment he was selected for work, as one of the "Birkenau boys," in early July 1944: "Leaving father was terrible. I see him in front of me, emaciated, sick, how he cried, he who had always been so good to everybody and now I left him, leaving him to die." Expressing profound guilt at leaving his father behind, Kraus added "I can't think about it because it was the most horrible moment in my life."[239] A few days later, Karel Kraus, along with 7,000 other prisoners in the "family camp," was gassed. "On July 11 I did not sleep. The night was bright, the sky red"—from the cremation of the bodies. "Of that—somewhere—I can't talk about it. On July 11 they killed my father. I balled my fists, I cried and promised to avenge him. Many lost their loved ones that day."[240]

In this way, bequeathal of a duty of vengeance followed an intergenerational logic, moving from the older to the younger generation, the younger generation in turn taking it upon itself to avenge the parents. Intergenerational revenge imperatives were often tied to distinct gender roles: sons being told by mothers to avenge them, or sons seeking to avenge their mothers and fathers, or mothers in particular seeking to avenge their children, using verbal means, as we have seen, screaming for revenge while spitting at or slapping guards, humiliating them in a desperate attempt at payback for the lives of their children. For Jewish observers, there was, in the words of Warsaw diarist Abraham Lewin, "no greater crime, no greater savagery than the murder of young and innocent children. The blood of our children will never be erased from the mark of Cain of the German people."[241] This was not merely because murdering the weakest and most vulnerable of unarmed civilians was a profound violation of all and any ethical boundaries—but because it intentionally eliminated even the possibility of future Jewish life.

Although, as Warsaw diarist Chaim Aron Kaplan keenly observed, Jewish women and men were equal in death, he also emphasized that murdering Jewish women had a different significance for the Nazi perpetrators. In this respect, Kaplan not only invoked the matrilineal transmission of the Jewish religion and identity, hence Jewish generational continuity. He also invoked Nazi German fears—as we have seen, rendered into a widespread popular belief through years of intensive propaganda—of future generations of avengers. Kaplan saw, acutely, that for the Nazis, as he put it in the wake of a German reprisal action in which 110 Jews, among them women, were shot to death, every Jewish woman murdered would "stop giving birth to children who would bring destruction upon the enemies of Israel."[242] There was thus, for Kaplan, a distinctly gendered dimension to the Nazi genocidal project itself. Venting his despair over the savagery shaking the Warsaw ghetto population in summer 1942, in the days leading up to the massive round-ups and deportations to Treblinka, he embraced a fantasy of payback for German crimes through a targeting of German women and children. "Daughter of Germany!" he exclaimed, "blessed is he who will seize your babes and smash them against the Rock!"[243] He here clearly assumed that the avengers would be men.

Jewish men tended to phrase their revenge imperatives around their roles as fathers, husbands, and sons. They experienced Nazi persecution as a form of emasculation, rendering them powerless to act "as men."[244] Some saw revenge as a way to rectify a perceived personal failure to have exercised the male role of protecting women and children. At the same time, some men saw revenge as a way to restore honor and self-respect—to their wives and children and to themselves. Calel Perechodnik was tormented, as mentioned, by his inability as a husband and father to save his wife and daughter from deportation to death at Treblinka. He extended that blame to Jewish men in general, both the reflection of a deep sense of powerlessness and emasculation and an internalizing of the antisemitic stereotype of Jewish men as weak and effeminate. "We Jewish men are not worthy of being avenged! We were killed through our own fault and not on a field of glory,"[245] he at one point exclaimed in his diary. But despite this expression of deepest self-despair, he also insisted that Jewish women and children were to be avenged; and as he articulated it, the revenge represented a distinctly male task—one through which, unmistakably, Jewish men could restore their honor and regain their agency. In passionate words, Perechodnik addressed first the women murdered at Treblinka, then his wife and daughter in particular, then the Jews being murdered in the death camp in general: "May God in the Highest grant your souls a deserving rest. We the sons, brothers, husbands of yours still living, we shall avenge you with blood, Amen. Ma femme bien aimée, tu seras vengée! Ma fille Athalie, tu seras vengée! Les cendres de trois millions hommes, femmes, enfants brulés à Treblinka, vous serez vengés!"[246]

Revenge, of course, was not solely a male domain. As we have seen, Jewish women found avenues to write, think about, consider and enact revenge alongside men. Some women saw themselves as having to take on what they viewed as male roles or act in "masculine" ways to avenge their loved ones, as partisan fighters. At the same time, women also chose distinctly "feminine" forms of revenge—forms underpinning "female" roles tied to care for others and motherhood. This is the framework in which we find the mentioned response to imminent death involving verbal attacks, spitting, and so forth, aimed at humiliating the murderers and making them afraid: feeding and reinforcing their fantasies about "vengeful Jews"; nurturing their anxieties about being weak and vulnerable and falling victim to a future reversal of power relations.

In the destruction of intergenerational continuity, there was now no assurance of anyone there, at all, to remember, mourn, and avenge the dead. With the loss of his child and sense of having failed as a protecting father being unbearable for Perechodnik, we can understand the vivid evocation of revenge in his diary, written in hiding, as—here as so often in the various written evocations of revenge—a desperate effort to cope. "In my whole life I never raised a hand against a fellow creature," he wrote, "but I feel that I would cease drinking, that my thirst would be quenched with German blood, especially that of small children. For my daughter, for all the Jewish children, I would take a hundredfold revenge."[247] Absent that generational continuity, he symbolically replaced his real, murdered daughter with his diary, using language suggesting that he saw himself in a feminine role, one stamped by gestation: "Once I wanted to have a child so that I would be remembered after death. Now, when I am completely alone, I cannot leave a creation that lives on after me; I had to beget a dead fetus into which I would breathe life. These diaries are that fetus."[248]

Beyond his own suffering, Perechodnik saw his manuscript as a monument to his wife and child, as well as to the destruction of Polish Jewry, a crime he hoped would spark revenge on the part of the victorious Allied forces. Memory and revenge were closely tied for him to a sense of virility, fertility, and continuity. "Now, when our daughter no longer lives, this second baby"—a reference to his diary—"must be nursed and protected until such time when no power can destroy it. Our second fetus may perish with me, and so I do not wish to keep it near me."[249] Anticipating his own death, Perechodnik gave his manuscript to a non-Jewish confidant, Władysław Błażewski, a lawyer from Otwock, for safekeeping, sometime in the fall of 1943. "I have lost You," he wrote, addressing his wife at the end of his manuscript, "but I will avenge You. Your second child, born in death pains, will avenge You." He added that by securing the survival of his manuscript, "my soul will regain its balance. Not only will I not fear death, but I also will not be afraid that I have remained alive, that I betrayed you so cravenly in the last moment. Now I feel an immortality in myself because I have created an immortal work. I have perpetuated you for the ages."[250] After transmitting his manuscript, Perechodnik joined the Armia Krajowa and took part in the Warsaw uprising in August 1944. He is said to have been murdered (or killed himself with cyanide) some time in October 1944, after his bunker was discovered by Poles and Germans.[251]

Thus, Jewish men processed shock and paralysis caused by the murder of their and other Jewish children with revenge fantasies of German children dying in return; they maintained some measure of hope that the Nazi mass murder would fail to create a world without Jews—and that there would thus be future avengers. In a Hebrew-language diary written between August and December 1943 during his internment in the Vittel concentration camp in France, Hebrew- and Yiddish-language poet Yitzhak Katzenelson addressed the German nation as follows:

> You killed them all, aged and young, women and children, even to the very last infant. [...] You ordered the annihilation so thoroughly that not a single one would remain in Europe to avenge us. Wicked and fiendishly foul that you are, you were afraid, lest someone should seek to redeem the blood of our whole people. [...] You feared that there would be a day of reckoning, so you murdered us all, to the very last one. But this will be of no avail. The hand of Israel will smite you.[252]

Katzenelson had lived in the Warsaw ghetto and had escaped to Warsaw's "Aryan side" after the Warsaw ghetto uprising. He mourned his wife Hannah and two of his three sons, Ben-Zion and Benjamin, who had been deported to Treblinka in August 1942. He was interned at Vittel with his third son, Zvi, because they held Honduran passports, a "privilege" that did not protect them from deportation in April 1944 to Drancy and Auschwitz-Birkenau, where they were murdered. "This loathsome nation, infected down to its very soul," Katzenelson predicted, "will soon surely perish. All its millions will perish, all—to the last of its killers. Old and young, women and children, all will die."[253] In Katzenelson's fantasy, then, the Germans would suffer the same indiscriminate destruction they had monstrously inflicted. Yet when was this revenge to come, and what would it really look like?

Anticipating the End: Signs and Scenarios of Vengeance

Signs of the decline of German power had an impact on Jews struggling to survive. News of German military losses and setbacks at the front lines and casualties from Allied bombing of German cities brought hope that the war would be over relatively soon. For example, in the Shavli ghetto, Aharon Pick (a medical doctor born in 1872 in Kėdainiai, Lithuania) closely followed news of German military defeats and civilian losses. Upon hearing of the German defeat at Stalingrad he noted in his Hebrew diary that despite German propagandistic efforts to cover it up, Stalingrad "will remain etched in world history in all ages to come ... The defeat has no precedent in the modern German history and has shocked the entire German nation like a lightning strike.... For the murdered Baltic Jews, this represents revenge, but for the more than six million Jews of Europe who have died, revenge has not yet come."[254] Likewise, some Jews hiding inside the Reich rejoiced at the devastation being wrought by the Allies—although they also feared for their lives, being unable to take cover in shelters because of the risk of identification, and agonized over the war's gigantic proportions of the destruction of human lives and culture.[255] The same basic emotional reaction and the frantic search for signs that the end of Nazi rule was nearing is manifest in testimony about deportation to camps. When Moishe Rutschaisky (Morris Rich), born in Kovno in 1924, was being deported in July/August 1944, he and his mother, along with other Jews from the Kovno ghetto (it had itself been turned into a concentration camp in September 1943[256]) witnessed a Russian air attack on Wehrmacht soldiers. In his testimony of 1996, Rutschaisky described hearing one of the German officers yell at a soldier lying on the ground, badly injured, "'Get up. Don't forget, you are a German soldier. Shame on you. Up!'" But the soldier could not do so, since "his legs were all blown up, torn. He didn't have boots even on his feet. And I said to my mother—and my mother start[ed] crying, too, we are all crying— 'We are seeing the end. We are seeing the revenge. We are seeing the downfall of the Third Reich'"[257] It gave satisfaction to Rutschaisky and the other Jews being marched to the train station to see that "the German army . . . was retreating too . . . the shiny German army who I thought were going to take the world . . . with the shiny boots"; that "same German army [was now] running without the boots, crawling, dirty, torn clothes. . . . laying by the sidewalks and on the streets."[258] But the Germans still continued their deportation of Kovno's Jews to Stutthof, Dachau, and Auschwitz.

With little access to writing material, Jews imprisoned in labor and concentration camps drew up imaginary revenge scenarios in anticipation of the change in power relations that would mark the end of the war. These often involved humor. In an interview with Claude Lanzmann, part of which would be incorporated into his documentary *Shoah*, Inge Deutschkron (1922–2022) pointed to humor and ridicule as offering emotional benefits helping her and her parents cope with daily Nazi discrimination and persecution.[259] Similarly, reflecting on his incarceration in Theresienstadt, Auschwitz, Dachau, and Türkheim, the Viennese psychologist Viktor Emil Frankl (1905–1997) noted, "Humor was another of the soul's weapons in the fight for self-preservation. It is well-known that humor, more than anything else in the human make-up, can afford an aloofness and an ability to rise above any situation, even if only for a few seconds."[260] Thus, there is an intrinsic connection with non-violent revenge because humor provided victims with a vehicle to perform a role reversal; through humor they empowered themselves and rose above the perpetrators. Jokes circulating among concentration camp prisoners served as vehicles for expressing hope for impending German defeat. For his part, Rudy P. (born in 1922 in Munkacs, Czechoslovakia, presently Ukraine), a forced laborer for the paramilitary engineering firm known as Organisation Todt and a prisoner at Gunskirchen, Mauthausen, Melk, and Birnbäumel, considered humor essential for survival; in testimony furnished in 1979, he related a joke about "two little Jewish guys who were supposed to be shot. And the Germans start lining up, ready to shoot them. And all of a sudden, the lieutenant comes. What? Waste on the Jews two bullets? We'll hang 'em. And one guy gives a nudge to the other. He says, 'Yankl, you hear? They're running out of ammunition.'"[261] Playing with the idea that the Germans were losing their power, and that the perpetrators' and victims' roles were facing reversal, strengthened resolve to carry on.

In an interview given in 2024, painter Yehuda Bacon—born in Moravska Ostrava, Czechoslovakia, in 1929; deported to Theresienstadt in 1942 and to the Auschwitz-Birkenau "family camp" the following year—notes that "everyone had their 'solution' [as to] what should happen to the Germans."²⁶² Often these "solutions" built on the idea of the German murder machinery being turned on the Germans. For Calel Perechodnik, surviving Jews "should deport the Germans to the same Treblinka—precisely there and not elsewhere."²⁶³ Emanuel Ringelblum ventured the idea that thousands of German nationals living in the United States be incarcerated in a concentration camp, "behind barbed wire, without food or water, and let them perish of hunger and need . . ."²⁶⁴ Mary Berg (Miriam Wattenberg, born in 1924 in Warsaw) noted "Germany must be wiped off the face of the earth. Such a people should not be allowed to exist."²⁶⁵ Yitzhak Katzenelson put it as follows: "The German nation, the vilest of all peoples, murdered the Jews of the whole of Europe, before the eyes of the world. . . . And now they will all perish! The day is close at hand when they will drown in an ocean of their *own* blood."²⁶⁶ And for Zalmen Gradowski, "those who made my people a sea of blood," will "drown in seas of blood."²⁶⁷ As he called out to those who would find his secret notes,

> You vast free world, will you ever notice that great flame? And you, man, will you one evening stop and stand where you are and raise your eyes to the deep blue heavens, masked with flames—know then, you free man, that these are the fires of Hell that burn here, endlessly fed with people. Perhaps your heart will one day be warmed by their fire, and your ice-cold hands will some day come here and put the fire out. And perhaps your heart will be infused with boldness and courage and you will change the victims of this fire . . . and may those who lit the fire [be] devoured in its flames.²⁶⁸

Ruth Klüger, born in Vienna in 1931 and imprisoned at the "family camp" at Auschwitz-Birkenau after being incarcerated at Theresienstadt, expressed the same idea in a poem she wrote as a fourteen-year-old. Entitled "chimney," Klüger let the chimney at Auschwitz-Birkenau speak for itself; having replaced the sun, it would swallow all life, including that of its builders: *Keiner ist mir noch entronnen,/ Keinen, keine werd ich schonen./ Und die mich gebaut als Grab/ Schling ich selbst zuletzt hinab./ Auschwitz liegt in meiner Hand,/ Alles, alles wird verbrannt.* (A rhymeless, literal version: "No one's escaped me,/ No one, I'll spare no one./ And those who've made me as a grave/ I'll finally gulp them down as well./ Now Auschwitz is in my hand,/All and everything will be burnt to ash.")²⁶⁹ Another Jewish child, Otto Dov Kulka (né Otto Deutelbaum), born in 1933 in Nový Hrozenkov, Czechoslovakia; in October 1942 imprisoned, like Klüger and Bacon, in the Theresienstadt ghetto and from there, eleven months later, deported to the Auschwitz "family camp," also sought to cope with the horrors inflicted on him by imagining revenge. In the camp infirmary, suffering from diphtheria, the ten-year-old befriended an older Jewish prisoner, Herbert, who involved him in a game: imagining, precisely, a "solution to the German question." Kulka, reflecting back on this idea, points out that in 1943 to 1944 he,

Herbert, and the other prisoners were not familiar with the term "final solution." They were, however, familiar with the long-standing "Jewish question" concept, as a euphemism for Jews as a problem needing to be solved. Prisoners did grasp the massive Auschwitz complex and the organized coercion, exploitation, and mass murder they were witnessing as central to Nazism's "solution" to its perceived question. At the time, Kulka did not fully grasp the meaning of Herbert's game. He does recall that prisoners were creative at imagining this "improvised reversal of fates";[270] but one thing above all remains etched in his memory: it was *not* the game's idea to simply incarcerate Germans at Auschwitz and kill them in gas chambers. Rather, it was to "load all women, children and elderly onto boats and sink them in the ocean," the men being "designated for some kind of slave labor."[271]

Looking back at the game, Kulka poses the question of why the prisoners were averse to the idea of Germans being forced into their own death machinery. His answer is that the prisoners held a deep "abhorrence at coming into contact with the act of murder, with the act of execution, the act of annihilation,"[272] although using the force of nature presumably also resulted in death. The game itself gave the prisoners "sarcastic amusement";[273] while involving an imaginative act, desire for revenge and the emotions behind it were very real.[274]

As Kulka indicates, Jews discussed revenge fantasies with each other, and sometimes did so using humor and sarcasm. Ridiculing the perpetrators and temporarily laughing off pain, anger, and fear of death were themselves empowering, helping individuals function under impossible circumstances. It becomes clear from survivors' testimony that fantasizing about basically every form of retaliatory bodily harm was treated as a legitimate expression of utopian wish-fulfilment.[275] In his Yiddish-language diary, written while hiding in a bunker in Kežmarok, eastern Slovakia in late 1944 and early 1945, Ben Zion Kalb, a Polish Jew who had escaped to Slovakia shortly after the German occupation began in 1939 and smuggled perhaps as many as 1,000 other Polish Jews into Slovakia, confirmed that he had discussed his fantasies of what he would do to the Germans once the war was over with the other Jews sharing his hiding place. This had resulted in such merriment that one of the women was temporarily unable to breathe from laughter, in a damp and stifling bunker only aired once daily. Kalb often returned to these revenge fantasies, as they were a crucial way of managing his worries about loved ones' fates, his own fears of death, and the boredom of waiting to see the end of the war in such confines.[276]

In the final months of the war mustering the strength to go living drew significantly from thoughts that revenge was near. "One reason to live still remains, which does not let me rest: to live, to live for revenge! And to perpetuate the names of my loved ones,"[277] noted Zalmen Gradowski shortly before his murder in the Auschwitz-Birkenau uprising on October 7, 1944.[278] At the Eichmann trial, Aharon Beilin, the above-mentioned Jewish physician at Auschwitz, testified that some prisoners were endowed with a "powerful will to live, and the motivation behind this will to live was to be able one day to take vengeance." (In this respect, Beilin suggested that revenge was also related to mentality, with west

European Jews more likely to give up and commit suicide, east European Jews to be driven onward by thoughts of revenge.)[279] Likewise another Eichmann trial witness, historian Israel Gutman (1923–2013), looking back on his survival of Auschwitz, Majdanek, and Mauthausen, indicated what kept prisoners alive "during the final and most arduous stages of camp life" was "desire and expectation of revenge."[280] József Debreczeni (1905–1978) recalled that as a forced laborer in the Gross-Rosen subcamp Eule in the fall of 1944, "A powerful resolve matures in me: I want to live, to live again.... I make a vow: no longer will I buy more tobacco in exchange for food. I want to live; I want to go home.... To run amok taking revenge, calling to account, and meeting out justice to those who dragged me here."[281] Victims' postwar testimony points to such desire sometimes serving as a check on contemplated suicide.[282] But often, revenge fantasies were themselves suicidal, individuals on the one hand imagining themselves as living to see revenge carried out on defeated Germans—while assuming on the other hand that they would die while enacting the vengeance, their lives having no purpose other than avenging everyone they had lost.[283] Some kept these fantasies to themselves as thought-play, indulged in during endless roll calls.[284] Others, as the Austrian-born Jewish psychologist Bruno Bettelheim (who had himself been interned at Dachau and Buchenwald) observed, literally dreamed of revenge: "Many dreams combined aggression and wish-fulfilment in such a way that the prisoner was able to avenge himself on the SS."[285] Still others verbalized the fantasies with prisoners they were close to. Eva L. born in Lodz in 1924, pledged with four other incarcerated girls she had known from childhood that they would get through the horror together; sharing their wildest, most uninhibited revenge fantasies was "what made us go on ... made us live.... And we said we're going to cut them into pieces. We're going put salt on them. We're going to tie them to two horses and let the horses run, the most horrible, horrible things that could come to a mind, we fed ourselves with hatred, and that made us go."[286] Notably, imagining such brutalities was closely connected to talk about the copious amounts of food they would share when it was all over.

We find the same basic function of revenge-fantasizing present in the so-called death marches marking the final months of the war: the forced move of 715,000 prisoners—emaciated, exhausted, lightly dressed in the depth of winter—into the Reich, one third of them dying along the way, either from SS bullets and clubs or from the exhaustion, disease, and cold.[287] In 1946, survivor Benjamin Piskorz recalled the march from Auschwitz-Monowitz to Dora-Mittelbau in January 1945. "[T]he people who did endure it," he indicated, "are to be marveled at, because one marched in hunger, in the frosts. And I don't know whether just the ... will to live ... whether also the ... will to take revenge, to remain alive and be united with ... families and with relatives, and marching together with friends with whom one had left one's home town ... kept ... a man alive."[288] For her part, Regina G., a survivor of Auschwitz-Birkenau and Ravensbrück, emphasized that what "kept us going" in the final weeks of the war was an all-consuming desire "to see the day ... [so much so] that it didn't matter for us if we were ever going to have a life, if we were ever going to be married, if we were ever going to have children, but to see them lose the war, to see them, that's what kept us." She further recalled that, barely twenty years old, she and other young women had given up on ever returning to peacetime civilian life:

We used to pray to live one hour to see them defeated, just one hour to see them defeated, and that was really the main thing. Not to eat, not to meet, not to dance, we didn't think about the lives, I think we had forgotten that there was such a thing as people actually walking in the streets or sitting at the tables, we were completely ... we [did not think of our] human needs. But the one thing was in me: hate and revenge.[289]

Regina G.'s candid and chilling assessment of her emotional state at war's end along with the multiplicity of voices from European Jews who contemplated revenge while the Holocaust was unfolding, suggest that in the face of systematic mass murder, many European Jews experienced the thought of reversing the victim-murderer power dynamic as the only trace of agency they had left. Engaging with emotions of vengeance and their possible translations into different kinds of revenge phenomena and behaviors—including the possibility of rejecting revenge—served as a coping reaction in the face of what was to them the European Jewish apocalypse; and it was a crucial factor for the relatively small number of Europe's Jews who managed to survive. Yet how did these desires for vengeance, revenge imperatives and scenarios develop once Nazi Germany surrendered and the war actually came to an end?

Notes

1. David Frankfurter, "I Kill a Nazi Gauleiter," *Commentary* 9 (1950): 133–41, here 136 (translation modified). Original document in his German memoir, written in 1946, published as David Frankfurter, *Ich tötete einen Nazi* ed. Sabina Bossert and Janis Lutz (Wiesbaden: S. Marix Verlag, 2022), 259.
2. Cited in Felix and Miyoko Imonti, *Violent Justice: How Three Assassins Fought to Free Europe's Jews* (Amherst: Prometheus Books, 1994), 218. See also Michael Marrus, "The Strange Story of Herschel Grynszpan," *The American Scholar* 57, no. 1 (Winter 1988), 69–79.
3. Frankfurter and Grynszpan both followed the models offered by the Armenian Soghomon Tehlirian and the Russian-French Jew Sholem Schwarzbard, self-declared avengers of their people's suffering. See Hannah Arendt, *Eichmann in Jerusalem: A Report on the Banality of Evil* (New York: Viking Press, 1963), 265–7.
4. Frankfurter, *Ich tötete einen Nazi*, 68.
5. Ibid., 67, 70.
6. Frankfurter, "I Kill a Nazi Gauleiter," 137.
7. Frankfurter, *Ich tötete einen Nazi*, 71.
8. Adolf Hitler's speech at Gustloff's funeral, February 12, 1936, Schwerin, Norman Hepburn Baynes, *The Speeches of Adolf Hitler, April 1922-August 1939* (London; Oxford University Press, 1942; Wolfgang Diewerge, *Der Fall Gustloff: Vorgeschichte und Hintergründe der Bluttat von Davos* (Munich: F. Eher 1936); see also Frankfurter, *Ich tötete einen Nazi*, 119, 149.
9. Klemperer, *I Will Bear Witness: A Diary of the Nazi Years, 1933-1941*, 153, entry of Feb. 11, 1936.
10. This sense is conveyed in many contemporary Jewish accounts, see, for example, Ruth Levitt (ed.), *Pogrom November 1938: Testimonies from "Kristallnacht"* (London: Souvenir Press, 2015).

11. Frankfurter, *Ich tötete einen Nazi*, 122.
12. Hans Reichmann, *Deutscher Bürger und verfolgter Jude: Novemberpogrom und KZ Sachsenhausen 1937 bis 1939* (Munich: R. Oldenbourg 1998), 111.
13. Ibid., 111.
14. Citation in Wolf Gruner, *Resisters: How Ordinary Jews Fought Persecution in Hitler's Germany* (New Haven: Yale University Press, 2023), 41.
15. Ibid., 47–8.
16. Avraham Barkai,*"Wehr dich!": Der Centralverein deutscher Staatsbürger jüdischen Glaubens (C.V.) 1893-1938* (Munich: Beck 2002); Philipp Graf, *Die Bernheim-Petition 1933: Jüdische Politik in der Zwischenkriegszeit* (Göttingen: Vandenhoeck & Ruprecht, 2008); Thomas Pegelow Kaplan and Wolf Gruner, *Resisting Persecution: Jews and their Petitions during the Holocaust* (New York: Berghahn Books, 2020); Douglas Morris, "The Lawyer Who Mocked Hitler, and Other Jewish Commentaries on the Nuremberg Laws," *Central European History* 49, no. 3/4 (2016): 383–408.
17. Gruner, *Resisters*.
18. Isaiah Trunk, *Jewish Responses to Nazi Persecution: Collective and Individual Behavior in Extremis* (New York: Stein and Day 1979); Jürgen Matthäus, Mark Roseman, Emil Kerenji, Alexandra Garbarini, Jan Lambertz, Avinoam J. Patt, and Leah Wolfson (eds.) *Jewish Responses to Persecution*, vols. 1–5 (Lanham: AltaMira Press, 2010–2015); Kaplan, *Between Dignity and Despair* and Finkel, *Ordinary Jews*.
19. See Browning, *Ordinary Men*, xv.
20. See Gäbler and Maercker, "Revenge and Trauma: Theoretical Outline," 43–4, 47–9.
21. See for example, Rachel Auerbach, "Oyf di felder fun treblinke," Supplement to *Dos naye lebn*, no. 52 (December 23, 1945), 1–4; see Laura Jockusch (ed.), *Khurbn-Forshung: Documents on Early Holocaust Research in Postwar Poland* (Göttingen: Vandenhoeck & Ruprecht, 2021), 642–95, here 681.
22. Gradowski, *The Last Consolation Vanished*, 116.
23. This definition comes from Wolf Gruner, based on Yehuda Bauer's earlier definition; see Gruner, *Resisters*, 2; and Yehuda Bauer, *Rethinking the Holocaust* (New Haven: Yale University Press, 2001), 119–20.
24. See David Engel, "A Sustained Civilian Struggle: Rethinking Jewish Responses to the Nazi Regime," in *A Companion to the Holocaust*, ed. Simone Gigliotti and Hilary Earl (Chichester, UK: John Wiley, 2020), 233–45, here 236.
25. Ibid., 237. For an overview of the changing perceptions of Jewish resistance, see Michael R. Marrus, "Jewish Resistance to the Holocaust," *Journal of Contemporary History* 30, no. 1 (1995): 83–110; Peter Hayes, *Why? Explaining the Holocaust* (New York: W.W. Norton & Company, 2017), 177–217.
26. David Fishman, *The Book Smugglers: Partisans, Poets, and the Race to Save Jewish Treasures from the Nazis* (Lebanon, NH: ForeEdge, 2017); see also Abraham Sutzkever's memoir, *From the Vilna Ghetto to Nuremberg: Memoir and Testimony*, ed. and transl. Justin D. Cammy (Montreal: McGill-Queen's University Press, 2021).
27. Therefore, some analyses have not made a distinction between revenge and resistance but subsumed revenge under resistance as Lerner, *National Vengeance* and Doerfer, *"Irgendjemand musste die Täter ja bestrafen"*. However, there is a need to distinguish between the two concepts.
28. Testimony of Chaim Engel, USHMM RG-50.030.0066, July 16, 1990, part 2, 6:58–8:44.

29. For example, Chaskiel Menche; see Jules Schelvis, *Sobibor: A History of a Nazi Death Camp* (London: Bloomsbury Academic 2014), 163.
30. See testimony of Chaim Engel and Selma Saartje Engel, March 30, 1998, USHMM, RG-50.549.02.0014, tape 1, 45:25–45:32 and 47:20–47:55.
31. See, for example, Schelvis, *Sobibor*, 231–42 and Chris Webb, *The Sobibor Death Camp: History, Biographies, Remembrance* (Stuttgart: Ibidem-Verlag, 2017).
32. See for example Samuel Willenberg, *Surviving Treblinka* (Oxford: Basil Blackwell, 1989), 178–82 and Gradowski, *The Last Consolation Vanished*, 73–4.
33. Zivia Lubetkin's testimony at the Eichmann trial, May 3, 1961, in *The Trial of Adolf Eichmann*, vol.1, 407.
34. Ibid., 407.
35. See Daniel Blatman, *For Our Freedom and Yours: The Jewish Labour Bund in Poland 1939–1949* (Portland: Valentine Mitchell, 2003), 117 and Avinoam J. Patt, *The Jewish Heroes of Warsaw: The Afterlife of the Revolt* (Detroit: Wayne State University Press, 2021), 324, 334, 338–9.
36. Testimony of Masha P., July 22 and 29, Oct. 29, Nov. 9 and 19, 1993, Feb. 1, 1994, HVT 3563, tape 7, seg. 22–3, tape 8, seg. 25, tape 10, seg. 31.
37. Zivia Lubetkin's testimony at the Eichmann trial, May 3, 1961, *The Trial of Adolf Eichmann*, vol.1, 406. See also Havi Dreifuss, *The People's Uprising and the Fall of the Warsaw Ghetto, April 1942-June 1943* (Waltham: Brandeis University Press, 2026).
38. Cited in Havi Dreifuss, "The Leadership of the Jewish Combat Organization during the Warsaw Ghetto Uprising: A Reassessment," *Holocaust and Genocide Studies* 31, no. 1 (2017): 24–60, 45. For the original Yiddish version, see "Anielewicz's Letters," GFHA 9523, letter 1.
39. Mordechai Anielewicz' letter to Yitzhak Zuckerman, April 23, 1943, in *Documents on the Holocaust*, ed. Yitzhak Arad, Israel Gutman, Abraham Margaliot (Jerusalem: Yad Vashem, 1981), 315–16.
40. Israel Gutman, *Resistance: The Warsaw Ghetto Uprising* (Boston: Houghton Mifflin 1994), 211; see Dreifuss, *The People's Uprising*, 323–5.
41. Faye Schulman, *A Partisan's Memoir: Woman of the Holocaust* (Toronto: Second Story Press 1995). There are other accounts of Jews from Lenin who joined the partisans to avenge their relatives; see *Kehilat Lenin: Sefer zikaron*, ed. Moshe Tamari (Tel Aviv: Va'ad yots'ey Lenin be-Yi´sra'el, 1956), 271–8.
42. On the distinct difficulties of Jewish women in non-Jewish partisan units see Anika Walke, *Pioneers and Partisans: An Oral History of Nazi Genocide in Belorussia* (New York: Oxford University Press, 2015).
43. Testimony of Faye Schulman, June 21, 1998, VHA 43411, seg. 47.
44. Testimony of Miriam Brysk, March 12, 2012, VHA 55650, seg. 105. Brysk also wrote a memoir, *Amidst the Shadows of Trees* (Ann Arbor: Yellow Star Press, 2007).
45. Testimony of Sidney Simon, July 31, 1994, USHMM RG-50.694.0151, tape 3; in their testimony of Nov. 22, 1997, Lisa Derman (née Nussbaum, born 1926 in Raczki) and Aron Derman (né Dereczynski, born 1922 in Slonim), USHHM RG-50.549.02.0009, tape 1, both tie personal feelings of revenge to collective military resistance.
46. Testimony of Miriam Brysk, March 12, 2012, VHA 55650, seg. 105.
47. See Nechama Tec, *Defiance* (Oxford: Oxford University Press, 2009), 112, 289–90.

48. Sara Bender, "Life Stories as Testament and Memorial: The Short Life of the Neqama Battalion, an Independent Jewish Partisan Unit Operating during the Second World War in the Narocz Forest, Belarus," *East European Jewish Affairs* 42, no. 1 (2012): 1–24.
49. Gradowski, *The Last Consolation Vanished*, 74–5.
50. Testimony of Leon Weliczker Wells at the Eichmann trial, May 2, 1961, in *The Trial of Adolf Eichmann*, vol. 1, 373.
51. See Avihu Ronen (ed.), Chaika Klinger, *I Am Writing These Words to You: The Original Diaries, Bedzin 1943*, transl. Anna Brzostowska and Jerzy Giebułtowski (Jerusalem: Yad Vashem 2017), 58–9.
52. Testimony of Joseph K., Dec. 2, 1979, HVT 61, tape 1, seg. 3.
53. Ibid.
54. See Gruner, *Resisters*, 22–38; Gruner categorizes such individual acts as resistance, not revenge, but as we will see, in these cases the distinction is not clear cut.
55. Testimony of Norman Salsitz (né Naftali Saleschuetz, born 1920 in Kolbuszowa), June 9, 1995, VHA 3331, tape 3, seg. 79.
56. Testimony of Isaac Brecher, Nov. 19, 1998, VHA 47399, seg. 87 (26:26–26:59).
57. Marie Jalowicz Simon, *Underground in Berlin: A Young Woman's Extraordinary Tale of Survival in the Heart of Nazi Germany* (New York: Little, Brown and Company 2015), 142.
58. Testimony of Janet B., Dec. 19, 1983, HVT 0227, tape 1, 16:53.
59. See Aaron Kramer, "Creative defiance in a death camp," *The Journal of Humanistic Psychology* 38, no. 1 (1998): 12–24.
60. Testimony of Edgar Krasa, Sept. 9, 2003, USHMM RG 50.030.0478, tapes 7 and 8; 80–4 of transcript.
61. Josef Bor, *The Terezín Requiem* (New York: Knopf 1963); Joža Karas, *Music in Terezín 1941-1945* (New York: Beaufort Books 1985). See the documentary film *Defiant Requiem* (dir. Doug Shultz and Peter Schnall), 2012.
62. Nick Strimple, "Music as Resistance," in *Jewish Resistance Against the Nazis*, ed. Patrick Henry (Washington: Catholic University of America Press, 2014), 319–38, 333–4.
63. Gradowski, *The Last Consolation Vanished*, 139.
64. Ibid., 139; more on singing: 140–1.
65. Ibid., 138 (translation modified).
66. Israel Kaplan, *The Jewish Voice in the Ghettos and Concentration Camps: Verbal Expression under Nazi Oppression*, ed. Zeev W. Mankowitz, trans. Jenny Bell and Dianne Levitin (Jerusalem: Yad Vashem, 2018); Perla Sneh "Khurbn Yiddish: An Absent Absence," *Lessons and Legacies XII* (2017), 215–31; Hannah Pollin-Galay, 'A Rubric of Pain Words': Mapping Atrocity with Holocaust Yiddish Glossaries," *Jewish Quarterly Review* 110, no. 1 (2020): 161–93.
67. Shirli Gilbert, *Music in the Holocaust: Confronting Life in the Nazi Ghettos and Camps* (Oxford: Oxford University Press, 2005), 70, 75.
68. See Eve F., Feb. 10, 1986, HVT 670, tape 1 (35:47–36:49); Erika J. and Marvina E., May 1, 1983, HVT 423, tape 1 (24:55); Rudy F., Aug. 7, 1979, HVT 22, tape 1 (46:46) and some Jews were denounced to Nazi authorities because of jokes, as in Dietrich G., Nov. 7, 1996, HVT 4085, tape 1, seg. 6; Manfred K., Nov. 10, 1987, HVT 1175, tape 2, 5:20.
69. See Chaim A. Kaplan *Scroll of Agony: The Warsaw Diary of Chaim A. Kaplan* (New York: Macmillan 1965), 153–4 (entry May 15, 1940).

70. See Victor Klemperer, *LTI; Notizbuch eines Philologen* (Berlin: Aufbau-Verlag 1947); after the war, working together Joseph Wulf and Leon Poliakov used a documentary technique that let Nazi documents "speak" for themselves, highlighting the mendacity of Nazi language by judicious use of quotation marks. Nicolas Berg, Elisabeth Gallas, Aurélia Kalisky, "'Unschuldige Wörter'? Jüdische Sprachkritik und historische Erkenntnis," *Zeithistorische Forschungen/Studies in Contemporary History* 20, no. 2 (2023): 187–203. There were also caricaturistic depictions of top Nazi leaders as animals published outside of Germany; see for example anti-Nazi zoo-animal caricatures printed in Palestine between 1940 and 1945, USHMM Accession no. 2019.7.5.1.

71. Elżbieta Rojowska, et al. "Wilno," *The United States Holocaust Memorial Museum Encyclopedia of Camps and Ghettos 1933-1945*, ed. Martin Dean and Mel Hecker, vol. 2 (Bloomington: Indiana University Press, 2012), 1148–52.

72. Kazimierz Sakowicz, *Ponary Diary 1941-1943: A Bystander's Account of a Mass Murder*, ed. Yitzhak Arad (New Haven: Yale University Press, 2005), 122.

73. Ibid., 122.

74. Report by Kurt Gerstein, April 26, 1945, English Evidence Code: PS-1553; Harvard Law School Library—Nuremberg Trials Project, HLSL item no. 4394, p. 6 (of the original report).

75. On the pogroms see John-Paul Himka, "The Lviv Pogrom of 1941: The Germans, Ukrainian Nationalists, and the Carnival Crowd," *Canadian Slavonic Papers* 53, nos. 2–4 (2011): 209–43; Wendy Lower, "Pogroms, Mob Violence and Genocide in Western Ukraine, Summer 1941: Varied Histories, Explanations and Comparisons," *Journal of Genocide Research* 13, no. 3 (2011): 217–46. The Ukrainian violence was given impetus by the idea of taking revenge on the Jews for alleged alliance with the preceding Soviet occupiers. The second pogrom, also known as the "Petlura Days," was most directly motivated by revenge for Sholem Schwarzbard's assassination of Ukrainian nationalist leader Simon Petlura in 1926: an act that itself was aimed at avenging the pogroms of Ukrainian Jews following World War I, some perpetrated by soldiers under Petlura's command. See also Edmund Kessler, Kaziemierz Kalwinski, and Lusia Sicher, *The Wartime Diary of Edmund Kessler: Lwow, Poland 1942-1944* (Boston: Academic Studies Press, 2010), 33–57.

76. Only about 1,500 of the 150,000 Jews living in Lvov on the eve of the German occupation would survive; see Christine Kulke, "Lwów," *The United States Holocaust Memorial Museum Encyclopedia of Camps and Ghettos 1933-1945*, vol. 2, 802–5.

77. Report by Kurt Gerstein, April 26, 1945, 6.

78. Ibid., 6.

79. Ibid.; Valerie Hebert, "Disguised Resistance? The Story of Kurt Gerstein," *Holocaust and Genocide Studies* 20, no. 1 (2006): 1–33; Saul Friedländer, *Kurt Gerstein: The Ambiguity of Good* (New York: Knopf, 1969).

80. "2,000,000 Murders by Nazis charged: Polish Paper in London says Jews are exterminated in Treblinska [sic] Death House," *The New York Times*, Aug. 8, 1943, 11. This newspaper article indicates that "some blaspheme" on the way to death before being silenced by death.

81. Case no. 635, LG Bochum, July 22, 1966; see *Justiz und NS-Verbrechen*, vol. 24, 353.

82. Case no. 873, LG Hannover, July 31, 1981, ibid., vol. 45, 105–6.

83. Müller, *Eyewitness Auschwitz*, 113.

84. Bernard Mark and Isaiah Avrech (eds.), *The Scrolls of Auschwitz* (Tel Aviv: Am Oved Pub. House 1985) and Pavel Polian (ed.), *Briefe aus der Asche: Die Aufzeichnungen des jüdischen Sonderkommandos Auschwitz* (Freiburg i. B.: WBG Theiss, 2024).

85. Gradowski, *The Last Consolation Vanished*, 135 (translation modified).
86. Ibid., 133.
87. Ibid., 134. On spitting as an expression of contempt and hatred, see Frank Gonzalez-Crussi, *The Body Fantastic* (Boston: MIT Press, 2021).
88. Gradowski, *The Last Consolation Vanished*, 134.
89. Ibid., 134.
90. Ibid., 134.
91. In his 1945 investigative report on Treblinka, Vassily Grossman mentions Max Levit (a survivor of the group-execution of boys who had been forced to participate in dismantling the Treblinka death camp) hearing—from underneath a pile of bodies—a boy cry out "Stalin will avenge us!" See Vassily Grossman, "The Hell of Treblinka," in Chil Rajchman, *Treblinka: A Survivor's Memory 1942-1943*, transl. Solon Beinfeld (London: MacleHose Press, 2011), 121.
92. See diary of Cypora Zonszajn, Rachel Zonszajn Benshaul Collection, USHMM, accession no. 2012.318.1 (English translation, p. 5).
93. As part of the "First Deportation Aktion" from Dec. 21 to May 15, 1942, 57,064 Jews and Roma were deported to Chelmno. See Laura Crago, "Łódź," *The United States Holocaust Memorial Museum Encyclopedia of Camps and Ghettos 1933-1945*, vol. 2, 75–82, here 80.
94. Isaiah Trunk, *Łódź; Ghetto: A History*, ed., trans., and annotated by Robert Moses Shapiro (Bloomington: Indiana University Press, 2006), cites the diary of Shlomo Frank, entry of Jan. 17, 1942, 230–1; see also Shlomo Frank, *Togbukh fun lodzher geto* (Buenos Aires, 1958), 230.
95. On knowledge and disbelief among Jews as the atrocities were unfolding, see Mark Dworzecki's testimony at the Eichmann trial, May 4, 1961, *The Trial of Adolf Eichmann*, vol.1, 448; see also Finkel, *Ordinary Jews*, 51–68; Amos Goldberg, "Rumor Culture among Warsaw Jews under Nazi Occupation: A World of Catastrophe Reenchanted," *Jewish Social Studies* 21, no. 3 (2016): 91–125 and idem, "Rumors in the Ghettos: A Case Study of Cultural History," *Lessons and Legacies* XII (2017), 67–86.
96. See Mark, *The Scrolls of Auschwitz*, 153; Gideon Greif, *We Wept without Tears: Testimonies of the Jewish Sonderkommando from Auschwitz* (New Haven: Yale University Press, 2005), 44; testimony of Lusia Haberfeld (born Lodz in 1931), Oct. 13, 1996, VHA 20848, tape 5, seg. 32, 34.
97. See Greif, *We Wept without Tears*, 315.
98. Testimony of Norman Salsitz, June 9, 1995, VHA 3331, tape 3, seg. 76–7.
99. Testimony of anonymous, HVT.
100. Testimony of Chaim Engel, USHMM, RG-50.030.0066, July 16, 1990, part 1, 40:41–42:20.
101. Yitzhak Arad, *The Operation Reinhard Death Camps: Belzec, Sobibor, Treblinka* (Bloomington: Indiana University Press, 2018), 427.
102. Testimony of Hella Weiss-Felenbaum, in *Sobibor: Martyrdom and Revolt*, ed. Miriam Novitch (New York: Holocaust Library 1980), 50. See also testimony of Esther Terner Raab, April 30, 1990, USHMM RG-50.030.0184, English transcript, p. 13.
103. See Sutzkever, *From the Vilna Ghetto to Nuremberg*, 73–5, here 74: Garbel found a note saying "Jews, we are being led to the slaughter! Avenge us!"
104. Alexander Kruglov and Samuel Schalkowsky, "Kowel," in *The United States Holocaust Memorial Museum Encyclopedia of Camps and Ghettos 1933-1945*, vol. 2, 1388–90.
105. Letter by S. N. Grutman to Ilya Ehrenburg, Dec. 2, 1944 in *The Unknown Black Book: The Holocaust in the German-Occupied Soviet Territories* Joshua Rubenstein and Ilya Altman, (Bloomington: Indiana University Press, 2008), 155.

106. Ibid., 156.
107. Ibid., 156.
108. Shloyme Perlmuter, "Haritot-kir—Graphita," *Kovel: Sefer ʿedut ye-zikaron le-kehilatenu she-ʿalah ʿaleha ha-koret*, ed. Eliezer Leoni (Tel Aviv: Irgun Yotsʾe Ḳovel be-Yiśraʾel 1957), 485–98, here 495, translation LJ.
109. Walter Zwi Bacharach (ed.), *Last Letters from the Shoah* (Jerusalem: Yad Vashem, 2013), 291.
110. Perlmuter, "Haritot-kir—Graphita," 496.
111. Ibid., 487.
112. Ibid., 487.
113. Kruglov and Schalkowsky, "Kowel," 1390.
114. See Perlmuter, "Haritot-kir—Graphita," 485.
115. Testimony of George Kadish, ca. 1997, USHMM RG-50.641.0001, part 1, 2:48–3:07; 27:48–29:05.
116. Stanislovas Stasiulis, "The Holocaust in Lithuania: The Key Characteristics of Its History, and the Key Issues in Historiography and Cultural Memory," *East European politics and societies* 34, 1 (2020): 261–79.
117. USHMM Photo Archives # 04640, Kovno, June 26, 1941, photographer George Kadish. Other Jewish sources also relate wounded people writing revenge imperatives in their blood; so, for example, in the Horodenka ghetto a dying Jewish teenager by the name of Nahman Schnapps wrote in his own blood on a gate after he was shot: "Here lies Nahman Schnapps. Don't forget to take revenge!" in Yiddish; see testimony of Brenda H., Oct. 13, 1991, HVT 877, seg. 7.
118. Testimony of George Kadish, part 1, 24:34–27:50.
119. USHMM Photo Archives # 29932, photographer George Kadish, 1944–1945.
120. Yitzhak Arad, *Ghetto in Flames: The Struggle and Destruction of the Jews in Vilna in the Holocaust* (Jerusalem: Yad Vashem, 1980), 412.
121. See Jürgen Matthäus, "Kaunas," *The United States Holocaust Memorial Museum: Encyclopedia of Camps and Ghettos 1933-1945*, vol. II, part B, 1066–9, here 1068.
122. USHMM Photo Archives # 81147, messages scrawled by Jewish prisoners on a wall inside Fort IX, shortly before their execution Aug. 1944, photographer George Kadish.
123. USHMM Photo Archives # 81150, messages scrawled by Jewish prisoners on a wall inside Fort IX, shortly before their execution, Aug. 1944, photographer George Kadish; see also # 81151 with similar inscriptions.
124. USHMM # 81146, messages scrawled by Jewish prisoners on a wall inside Fort IX, shortly before their execution, Aug. 1944, photographer George Kadish.
125. Dante Alighieri's *Divine Comedy*, Inferno, Canto III, translated by Henry Francis Cary, 1814. The original inscription was probably in Italian.
126. Probably a paraphrase of Genesis 4:10.
127. See Adam Mickiewicz, "Forefathers' Eve," *The Slavonic Review* 3, no. 9 (1925): 499–523, here 522. ("Then *vengeance, vengeance* on the foe / God upon our side or no!") The "Improvisation" is part III of that epic poem; that part was published in 1832.
128. Testimony of Aharon Beilin at the Eichmann trial, June 7, 1961, *The Trial of Adolf Eichmann*, vol. 3, 1258.
129. Bacharach, *Last Letters from the Shoah*, 288; original in Central Zionist Archives, S 26, 1419.

130. Yad Vashem Archives O.6/459; translation in Dafni and Kleiman, *Final Letters*, 123–6. Abraham Sutzkever notes in his 1946 memoir that he received a copy of this letter from a Polish woman in July 1944; see Sutzkever, *From the Vilna Ghetto to Nuremberg*, 215–16.

131. Andrew Koss, "Byteń," *The United States Holocaust Memorial Museum Encyclopedia of Camps and Ghettos 1933-1945*, vol. 2, 1172–4.

132. Dodl Abramaovitsh and Mordekhay V. Bernshtayn (eds.), *Pinkes Byten: Der Oyfkum un Untergang fun a yidisher kehile* (Buenos Aires: Bitener Landslayt in Argentine 1954), 551 (translation LJ); see also Bacharach, *Last Letters from the Shoah*, 106.

133. Abramaovitsh and Bernshtayn, *Pinkes Byten*, 551.

134. Ibid., 550.

135. Mordechai Neustadt, *Sefer Druyah u-ḳehilot Miyor, Droisḳ, ye-Leʼonpol* (Tel-Aviv? Be-hotsaʼat Yotsʼe Druyah yeha-sevivah be-Yiśraʼel 1973), 95–100; original letter is at Yad Vashem Archives, O.75/1303.

136. Translation from: https://www.yadvashem.org/yv/en/exhibitions/last-letters/1942/barbakow.asp (accessed Oct. 2, 2025).

137. Monika Tomkiewicz and Steven Seegel, "Druja," *The United States Holocaust Memorial Museum Encyclopedia of Camps and Ghettos 1933-1945*, vol. 2, 1180–2.

138. Aleksandra Namysło, "Dąbrowa Górnicza," ibid., 149–52.

139. Mendl Gelbart (ed.), *Sefer ḳehilat Yehude Dombrovah Gurnitsheh ye-ḥurbanah* (Tel Aviv: Irgun yotsʼe Dombrovah Gurnitsheh be-Yiśraʼel, 1971), 427.

140. Bacharach, *Last Letters from the Shoah*, 285. Original in YV O.48/44b-3, S.N. 6949.

141. Bacharach, *Last Letters from the Shoah*, 108–9; original Yiddish letter in Natan Mark and Shimon Friedlander (eds.), *Sefer yizkor; mukdash le-yehudei ha-ayarot she-nispu ba-shoa be-shanim 1939-44, Linsk, Istrik, Beligrod, Litovisk veha-sevivah* (Tel Aviv, 1964), 382–3.

142. Letter by Zipora Birman to her friends in Eretz Israel about life in the Bialystok Ghetto, March 1, 1943, Yad Vashem Archives, M.11, file 15; Yiddish original was buried in the Mersik-Tenenbaum archive in the Bialystok ghetto, citation is from pp. 20–1; translation LJ.

143. Letter of Zipora Birman, Feb. 4 1943, YVA, M.11, file 16, Hebrew.

144. Sara Bender, *The Jews of Białystok during World War II and the Holocaust* (Waltham: Brandeis University Press, 2008), 265–6.

145. For a discussion of the genre of Holocaust diaries and chronicles see Amos Goldberg, "Jews' Diaries and Chronicles," in *Oxford Handbook of Holocaust Studies*, ed. Peter Hayes and John K. Roth (New York: Oxford University Press, 2010), 397–413.

146. On the richness of diaries as sources for Holocaust studies see Alexandra Garbarini, *Numbered Days: Diaries and the Holocaust* (New Haven: Yale University Press, 2006) and Amos Goldberg, *Trauma in First Person: Diary Writing during the Holocaust* (Bloomington: Indiana University Press, 2017).

147. The diary of Eliszewa (Elsa) Binder (1920–1942), entry of Jan. 17, 1942, in *Salvaged Pages: Young Writers' Diaries of the Holocaust* ed. Alexandra Zapruder (New Haven: Yale University Press, 2002), 317.

148. Dawid Sierakowiak, *The Diary of Dawid Sierakowiak: Five Notebooks from the Łódź Ghetto* (New York: Oxford University Press, 1996), 38, 47; entries of Sept. 13 and Oct. 4, 1939.

149. Hillel Seidman, *The Warsaw Ghetto Diaries* (Southfield, MI: Targum Press, 1997), 130; entry of Sept. 21, 1942.

150. Quoted after Garbarini, *Numbered Days*, 146 (typed version of the diary, Yad Vashem Archives, O.33/774). Alexander Kruglov and Ray Brandon, "Czortków," *The United States Holocaust Memorial Museum Encyclopedia of Camps and Ghettos 1933-1945*, vol. 2, 770-2.

151. Emanuel Ringelblum, *Notes from the Warsaw Ghetto: The Journal of Emanuel Ringelblum* (New York: McGraw-Hill, 1958), 301. Victor Klemperer, on the other hand, noted in his diary that hearing about the British bombing of Lübeck "I felt sad for the beauty of Lübeck. [. . .] It appeared to be an English act of revenge—nothing but destruction of art." Klemperer, *I Will Bear Witness, 1942-1945*, 42; entry of April 19, 1942. His sadness over the destruction of culture also prevails in his description of the destruction of his hometown, Dresden, in February 1945; see entry Feb. 22-24, 1945, ibid., 406-13.

152. David Roskies and Naomi Diamant, *Holocaust Literature* (Waltham: Brandeis University Press, 2012), 69. Also David Engel, "On the Bowdlerization of a Holocaust Testimony: The War Time Journal of Calek Perechodnik," *Polin* 12 (1999): 316–29.

153. Calel Perechodnik, *Am I a Murderer?: Testament of a Jewish Ghetto Policeman*, ed. Frank Fox (Boulder, CO: Westview Press, 1996), 194.

154. Stanislaw Adler, *In the Warsaw Ghetto 1940 - 1943 an Account of a Witness the Memoirs of Stanislaw Adler* (Jerusalem: Yad Vashem, 1982), 282.

155. Ludmilla "Lola" Zeldowicz, "Personal Notes on Stanislaw Adler," in Adler, *In the Warsaw Ghetto*, xi–xviii.

156. Emanuel Ringelblum, *Ksovim fun geto* (Warsaw: Yidish bukh 1961), vol. 2, 140.

157. See Goldberg, *Trauma in First Person*, 175–89.

158. Kaplan, *Scroll of Agony*, 139. See also Garbarini, *Numbered Days*, 41–5.

159. Kaplan, *Scroll of Agony*, 323–5 (entry of July 26, 1942); also 101–2 (Jan. 16, 1940).

160. Abraham Lewin, *A Cup of Tears: A Diary of the Warsaw Ghetto*, ed. Antony Polonsky (Oxford: Basil Blackwell 1988), 185, entry of Sept. 25, 1942.

161. Ibid., 183, entry of Sept. 21, 1942.

162. Ibid., 226, entry of Dec. 21, 1942.

163. On Seidman, see Rebecca Berglas, *Hillel Seidmann: A reassessment* (MA Thesis, University of Haifa, 2012).

164. Seidman, *The Warsaw Ghetto Diaries*, 130.

165. Ibid., 130. (Deuteronomy 32:35, 32:43, Joel 4:21, and Job 16:18.)

166. Seidman, *The Warsaw Ghetto Diaries*, 130.

167. Witold Zbirohowski-Koscia (ed.), *Marcel Nadjari's Manuscript, November 3 1944: Conservation and Legibility Enhancement through Multispectral Imaging* (Auschwitz: Auschwitz-Birkenau State Museum 2020), facsimile of Nadjari's manuscript, 10 (11).

168. Ibid., 12 (13).

169. Ibid., 10 (11).

170. Ibid., 7–8.

171. Testimony of Norman Salsitz, VHA 3331, June 9, 1995, tape 4, seg. 111–12. See also Norman Salsitz and Richard Skolnik, *A Jewish Boyhood in Poland: Remembering Kolbuszowa* (Syracuse, NY: Syracruse University Press, 1992); Norman Salsitz and Amalie Petranker Salsitz, *Against All Odds: A Tale of Two Survivors* (New York: Holocaust Library, 1990); Norman Salsitz and Stanley Kaish, *Three Homelands: Memories of a Jewish Life in Poland, Israel, and America* (New York: Syracuse University Press, 2002).

172. Herman Kruk, *The Last Days of the Jerusalem of Lithuania: Chronicles from the Vilna Ghetto and the Camps 1939-1944*, ed. Benjamin Harshav (New Haven: Yale University Press, 2002), 91–2; entry of Sept. 4, 1941.
173. Ibid., 93.
174. Ibid., 91–2.
175. Ibid., 93.
176. Ibid., 93.
177. See Ringelblum, *Ksovim fun geto*, vol. 2, 140.
178. Perechodnik, *Am I a Murderer?*, xxi.
179. Ibid., xxxi, 51; 63, 74, 139.
180. Ibid., 172–3.
181. Ibid., 173.
182. Ibid., 173.
183. For example, Hitler noted in *Mein Kampf*: "The end is not only the end of the freedom of the peoples oppressed by the Jew, but also the end of the parasite upon the nations. After the death of his victim, the vampire sooner or later dies too." See Hitler, *Mein Kampf*, 327.
184. Rachel Auerbach, *Schriften aus dem Warschauer Ghetto*, ed. Karolina Szymaniak (Berlin: Metropol Verlag, 2022), 159; translation LJ.
185. Ibid., 159.
186. Ibid., 161, 163.
187. Ibid., 162.
188. Ibid., 162.
189. Cited in Samuel D. Kassow, *Who Will Write Our History? Emanuel Ringelblum, the Warsaw Ghetto, and the Oyneg Shabes Archive* (Bloomington: Indiana University Press, 2007), 157.
190. Ibid., 159.
191. Perechodnik, *Am I a Murderer?*, 106. Similarly, the urge to live through the war to defeat and revenge but also fearing to die before, see Aharon Pick, *Notes from the Valley of Slaughter: A Memoir from the Ghetto of Siauliai, Lithuania* (Bloomington: Indiana University Press, 2023), 264, 266; entry of Nov. 8, 1943.
192. Diary of Cypora "Cypa" Zonszajn, Rachel Zonszajn Benshaul collection USHMM RG 2012.318.1, p. 8 of the English translation.
193. Edward Kopówka and Laura Crago, "Siedlce," *The United States Holocaust Memorial Museum Encyclopedia of Camps and Ghettos 1933-1945*, vol. 2, 428–32.
194. Testimony of Masha P. (born in 1924 in Warsaw), July 22 and 29, Oct. 29, Nov. 9, 1993; Feb. 1, 1994, HVT 3563, tape 8, seg. 25.
195. Klinger, *I Am Writing these Words to You*, 118.
196. Diary of Ben Zion Kalb (Sept. 1944–Jan. 1945), USHMM, Ben Zion Kalb papers RG 2014.406.2; file 5; USHMM, p. 27 of the English translation.
197. Diary of Tamara Lazerson, entry of Jan. 11, 1944, USHMM Tamar Lazerson-Rostovsky's diaries RG 2017.103.1, file 3, p. 39 of the English translation.
198. Gradowski, *The Last Consolation Vanished*, 68.
199. Ibid., 101.

200. Ibid., 73–4.
201. For example, Gradowski, *The Last Consolation Vanished*, 82, 85.
202. See Nadjari's manuscript in Zbirohowski-Koscia, *Marcel Nadjari's Manuscript*, 10 (11).
203. Pavel Polian, "Das Ungelesene Lesen: Die Aufzeichnungen von Marcel Nadjari, Mitglied Des Jüdischen Sonderkommandos von Auschwitz-Birkenau, Und Ihre Erschließung," *Vierteljahrshefte Für Zeitgeschichte* 65, no. 4 (2017): 597–619, here 600.
204. Sutzkever, *From the Vilna ghetto to Nuremberg*, 15–16.
205. Perechodnik, *Am I a Murderer?*, 90.
206. Joseph Kermisz (ed.), *To Live with Honor and Die with Honor! Selected Documents from the Warsaw Ghetto Underground Archives "O.S."* (Jerusalem: Yad Vashem, 1986), 96 and 97.
207. Klinger, *I Am Writing these Words to You*, 46.
208. Ibid., 46–7.
209. Ibid., 47.
210. Ibid., 47.
211. Ibid., 47.
212. Testimony of Celia K., Feb. 25, 1980, HVT 36, tape 2, seg. 25.
213. See for example the accounts published in: *Jewish Partisans of the Soviet Union During World War II*, ed. Jack Nusan Porter (Brookline, MA: Academic Studies Press, 2021).
214. Testimony of Chaim Engel, July 16, 1990, USHMM RG Number: RG-50.030.0066, part 2, 6:58–8:44; Feb. 12, 1992, USHMM RG-50.042.0009, part 2, 5:25–6:40; testimony of Chaim Engel and Selma Saartje Engel, March 30, 1998, USHMM RG-50.549.02.0014, tape 1, 44:50–48:25.
215. Raymond-Raoul Lambert, *Diary of a Witness: 1940-1943* (Chicago: Ivan R. Dee 2007) 198; entry of Aug. 18, 1943.
216. Richard I. Cohen, preface to ibid., vii–viii.
217. See Ringelblum, *Ksovim fun geto*, vol. 2, 140. See also Kassow, *Who Will Write Our History?*, 347 and 468n.
218. Max Michael Rothschild, "War diary," 1942-44, pp. 12–13. Unpublished manuscript cited with permission of his daughter Shumalit Reinharz, who translated the ms from the German; I thank Shulamit Reinharz for allowing me to use her father's diary. See also Shulamit Reinharz, *Hiding in Holland: A Resistance Memoir* (Oegstgeest: Amsterdam Publishers, 2024).
219. Rothschild, "War diary," pp. 12–13.
220. Ibid., p. 59.
221. Ibid., p. 59.
222. https://jl-gunzenhausen.de/de/rothschild-karl.html (accessed March 4, 2025).
223. Sierakowiak, *The Diary of Dawid Sierakowiak*, 221.
224. Cited in Fishman, *The Book Smugglers*, 200.
225. Zivia Lubetkin's testimony at the Eichmann trial, May 3, 1961, *The Trial of Adolf Eichmann*, vol.1, 407. [In the Hebrew original she says "eyn nekamah," "there is no vengeance" clearly implying the meaning "that befits our suffering".
226. Seidman, *The Warsaw Ghetto Diaries*, 130. Similarly, Lewin, *A Cup of Tears*, 96, entry of May 25, 1942.

227. Seidman, *The Warsaw Ghetto Diaries*, 130, entry of Sept. 21, 1942. The original Hebrew line from Bialik's poem *Al Hashkhita* (1903) reads: "*Nikmant dam yeled katan od lo bara ha-satan*." Other diarists also invokes this line, as for example Aharon Pick after a violent Aktion on November 5, 1943, in the Siauliai ghetto, see Pick, *Notes from the Valley of Slaughter*, 263; entry of Nov. 8, 1943.

228. Seidman, *The Warsaw Ghetto Diaries*, 129–30.

229. Lewin, *A Cup of Tears*, 97, entry of May 25, 1942.

230. Wendy Lower, *The Ravine: A Family, a Photograph, a Holocaust Massacre Revealed* (Boston: Houghton Mifflin Harcourt, 2021), 97.

231. David P. Boder's interview with Kalman Eisenberg, July 31, 1946, Illinois Institute of Technology, Voices from the Holocaust, 22:31–23:55.

232. Testimony of Allen S., Dec. 14, 1986, HVT 833, tape 2 (19:58). He refers back to his mother's imperative in tape 3 (20:42).

233. Ibid., HVT 833, tape 4 (47:35).

234. Testimony of Norman Salsitz, June 9, 1995, VHA 3331, tape 3, seg. 77.

235. Testimony of Chil Rajchman (1914–2004), December 7, 1988, USHMM RG-50.030.0185, part 1, transcript p. 5. See also Chil Rajchman, *Treblinka: A Survivor's Memory 1942-1943*, transl. Solon Beinfeld (London: MacleHose Press, 2011), 23–4, 36.

236. Rajchman, *Treblinka*, 51. See testimony of Chil Rajchman (1914-2004), December 7, 1988, USHMM RG-50.030.0185, part 1, transcript p. 4.

237. Rajchman, *Treblinka*, 32f.

238. Grossman, "The Hell of Treblinka," 150.

239. Diary of Michal Kraus, Michael J. Kraus Papers, USHMM accession no. 1995.A.1067.1, file 5 Diary IIA 1945-1947, pp. 55–6.

240. Ibid., p. 58.

241. Lewin, *A Cup of Tears*, 96; entry of May 25, 1942.

242. Kaplan, *Scroll of Agony*, 313; entry of July 13, 1942.

243. Ibid., 313.

244. See for example, Maddy Carey, *Jewish Masculinity in the Holocaust: Between Destruction and Construction* (New York: Bloomsbury Academic, 2017); Carey's study does not explore the topic of revenge; the study by Florian Zabransky, *Jewish Men and the Holocaust: Sexuality, Emotions, Masculinity. An Intimate History* (Berlin/Boston: Walter de Gruyter GmbH, 2024), considers revenge in the context of men in partisan units.

245. Perechodnik, *Am I a Murderer?*, xxi

246. Ibid., 51.

247. Ibid., 173.

248. Ibid., 191.

249. Ibid., 192.

250. Ibid., 192.

251. See Perechodnik, *Am I a Murderer?*, 203–5; David Engel, "On the Bowdlerization of Holocaust Testimony: The Wartime Journal of Calek Perechodnik," *Polin* 12 (1999): 316–29.

252. Yitzhak Katznelson, *Vittel Diary (22.5.43-16.9.43)* transl. Myer Cohen (Lohame HaGeta'ot: Ghetto Fighters' House 1964), 188–9, entry of Aug. 28, 1943. As a poet, Katznelson also

wrote about revenge taken by the dead on the perpetrators in his poetry; see Sven-Erik Rose, *Making and Unmaking Literature in the Warsaw, Lodz and Vilna Ghettos* (Waltham: Brandeis University Press, 2025), ch. 3.

253. Katzenelson, *Vittel Diary*, 188; entry of Aug. 28, 1943.

254. Pick, *Notes from the Valley of Slaughter*, 243-4; entry of Feb. 5, 1943.

255. See Richard Lutjens, *Submerged on the Surface: The Not-So-Hidden Jews of Nazi Berlin 1941-1945* (New York: Berghahn Books, 2018), 78, 88-90.

256. Evelyn Zegenhagen and Christoph Dieckmann, "Kauen Main Camp," *The United States Holocaust Memorial Museum Encyclopedia of Camps and Ghettos 1933-1945*, vol. 1, 847-53.

257. Testimony of Morris Rich, Aug. 12, 1996, VHA 18626, tape 5, seg. 138.

258. Ibid., tape 5, seg. 137.

259. Claude Lanzmann Shoah Collection, USHMM RG-60.5044, Inge Deutschkron part 1, 22:13–25:40. See also Chaya Ostrower, *It Kept Us Alive: Humor in the Holocaust* (Jerusalem: Yad Vashem 2014). Mary Berg observed in her diary (Oct. 29, 1941): "The typhus epidemic itself if the subject of jokes. It is laughter through tears, but it is laughter. This is our only weapon in the ghetto—our people laugh at death and at the Nazi decrees. Humor is the only thing the Nazis cannot understand." Mary Berg, *The Diary of Mary Berg: Growing up in the Warsaw Ghetto* (London: Oneworld Publications, 2018), 104.

260. Viktor E. Frankl, *Man's Search for Meaning* (Boston: Beacon Press, 2006), 43.

261. Testimony of Rudy F., Aug. 7, 1979, HVT 22, tape 1, 46:42–47:13.

262. Interview with Yehuda Bacon in the documentary "Yehuda Bacon: Glück ist eine Möglichkeit" in the German TV series "Zeuge der Zeit," ARD Mediathek (April 8, 2024), https://www.ardmediathek.de/video/zeuge-der-zeit/yehuda-bacon-glueck-ist-eine-moeglichkeit/ard-alpha

263. Perechodnik, *Am I a Murderer?*, 173.

264. Emanuel Ringelblum, diary, June 10, 1942; Ringelblum, *Ksovim fun geto*, vol. 1, 372; cited in *Documents on the Holocaust*, ed. Arad, Gutman, and Margaliot, 240-1.

Victor Klemperer relates in his diary a debate with an acquaintance, also a German Jewish man—identified as Seliksohn—seeking to survive in Germany with the help of non-Jews; Klemperer identified the ambivalence in feeling, gratitude and dependence on help provided by individual Germans on the one and anger and resentment at the collective of Germans for having brought Jews in the position they tried to survive: "Yesterday Seliksohn spoke with gratitude of helpful Aryans, very ordinary people. [...] Immediately afterward he demanded with utter hatred that the whole German people be exterminated. I said, he himself acknowledged that the atrocities were by no means supported by everyone. He responded: One could not allow the criminal whole to exist for the sake of the few who were good." Klemperer, *I will Bear Witness: 1942-1945*, entry of July 27, 1942, 110-11.

265. Berg, *The Diary of Mary Berg*, 86; entry of Sept. 20, 1941.

266. Katzenelson, *Vittel Diary*, 126; entry of Aug. 15, 1943 [emphasis added].

267. Gradowski, *The Last Consolation Vanished*, 68.

268. Ibid., 150.

269. Ruth Klüger, "Der Kamin," *Zerreißproben. Kommentierte Gedichte* (Vienna: Zsolnay, 2013).

270. Otto Dov Kulka, *Landschaften der Metropole des Todes. Auschwitz und die Grenzen der Erinnerung und der Vorstellungskraft* (Berlin: DVA, 2013), 77.

271. Ibid., 77-8.

272. Ibid., 78.

273. Ibid., 78.

274. Ibid., 75–6.

275. See for example the testimony of Masha P. (born in 1924 in Warsaw), July 22, 29, Oct. 29, Nov. 9, 19, 1993, Feb. 1, 1994, HVT 3563, tape 8, seg. 25.

276. Diary of Ben Zion Kalb, Ben Zion Kalb papers, USHMM RG 2014.406.2; file 5; p. 5 of English translation.

277. Gradowski, *The Last Consolation Vanished*, 102.

278. Hermann Langbein cites other Sonderkommando members who linked their determination to survive after all loved one had been murdered to the prospect of taking revenge. One reportedly said: "Do you people think that I volunteered for this work? What was I to do? Sure, I could have gone into the wire, like so many comrades. But I want to survive. Maybe a miracle will happen! We could be liberated today or tomorrow. And then I want to take revenge as a direct witness of their crimes. . . . Believe me, I don't want to survive for the sake of living. I don't have anyone anymore because they have gassed my whole family. But I want to live so I can report about it and take revenge." Hermann Langbein, *People in Auschwitz*, ed. by Harry Zohn and Henry Friedlander (Chapel Hill, NC: University of North Carolina Press, 2004), 194.

279. Testimony of Aharon Beilin at the Eichmann trial, June 7, 1961, *The Trial of Adolf Eichmann*, vol. 3, 1258. The correlation between revenge and will to survive, or rather, between suicide and absence of feelings and acts of revenge was also observed by Bruno Bettelheim, *The Informed Heart: Autonomy in a Mass Age* (New York: Avon Books, 1971), 224.

280. See Israel Gutman's remark during the Fourth Yad Vashem International Historical Conference in Jerusalem in January 1980: Israel Gutman and Avital Saf (eds.), *The Nazi Concentration Camps: Structure and Aims, the Image of the Prisoner, the Jews in the Camps* (Jerusalem: Yad Vashem, 1984), 521.

281. József Debreczeni, *Cold Crematorium: Reporting from the Land of Auschwitz* (New York: St. Martin's Press, 2023), 141.

282. See testimony of Hillel K. (born in Krakow in 1923), May 3, 1980. HVT 69, tape 1, 26:39; and testimony of Larry K. (born Zhuprany, Poland in 1925 in in), Nov. 4, 1990, HVT 1734, tape 1, 36:42 and tape 2, 13:34.

283. See, for example, Gradowski, *The Last Consolation Vanished*, 75; Filip Müller, *Eyewitness Auschwitz*, 113–14; Zbirohowski-Koscia, *Marcel Nadjari's Manuscript*, 8.

284. Testimony of Emrich Gonczi (born in 1925 in Ivanka Pri Nitre, Czechoslovakia), Jan. 16, 1997, USHMM RG-50.120.0321, 4:21.

285. Bettelheim, *The Informed Heart*, 128 n 10.

286. Testimony of Eva L., May 12, 1982, HVT 71, tape 3, 4:35.

287. See Blatman, *The Death Marches*, 1–18, 407–32.

288. David P. Boder's interview with Benjamin Piskorz, Sept. 1, 1946, Illinois Institute of Technology, Voices of the Holocaust, here 00:31:52.

289. Testimony of Regina G. (born in Drobin, Poland, in 1925), HVT 1286, Nov. 13, 1989, tape 2, seg. 13.

CHAPTER 3
FROM WARTIME DESIRE TO POSTWAR FANTASY: JEWISH REVENGE AFTER THE HOLOCAUST

In his secret notes from Auschwitz-Birkenau, Sonderkommando member Zalmen Gradowski offered a prediction for the German nation: "That day, when the world celebrates universal freedom—will be the day of their enslavement. On that day of peace when on the streets of all of Europe, people will kiss and hug, on that day they, the criminals and murderers, will sit in hiding somewhere in fear and terror of the great day of Judgment—the day of reckoning with the world."[1] Gradowski was right about German postwar existential angst. At the war's end and in the immediate postwar years, many Germans phrased their experiences of defeat, powerlessness, and humiliation in terms of fears that "the Jews" were coming after them; many saw the collapse of the Nazi regime, the lost war, the military occupation, and the war crimes trials not as a consequence of unprecedented German crimes but as a manifestation of "Jewish revenge" on Germany.

German angst about "Jewish revenge" was an expression of a complex mixture of ideological biases and emotions that shaped Germans' perceptions of the postwar moment: conspiratorial views of Jews, hammered home in years of Nazi propaganda, reversing victim and aggressor roles, positing Germans as victims of Jews intent on annihilating Germany and in control of the Allied nations, especially the Soviet Union; emotional distress caused by the experiences, after six years of brutal war, of Germans' actual total national collapse, their subjugation by enemy armies and the physical destruction of their country; Germans' resentment at Nazi leaders for having led the nation into downfall and disaster—after years of preaching racial superiority, promising prosperity, power, and invincibility, Germans were now humiliated and shamed by their de facto impotence and meekness; and interlaced with all of this, a vague sense of collective guilt for Nazi crimes.[2]

Consequently, these anxious narratives of vengeful Jews seeking to mistreat Germans as payback for what they had done to the Jews were often also admissions, however indirect and involuntary, of German guilt. And often, they were articulated in terms of a resentment against Jews for reminding the Germans of their guilt. Paradoxically, however, for many Germans the collapse of the Nazi regime and growing public awareness of the scale and scope of its crimes did not prove Nazism wrong, but seemed to reaffirm some of its basic assumptions about Jews. Although power relations had changed and the Nazi regime had ceased to exist, the heritage of years of ideological indoctrination lived on, finding expression in both overt and covert forms. When Kurt G., born in Krefeld in 1927 to an old German Jewish family, returned to Germany in a British military uniform in 1947 to find out about the fate of his relatives in Mühlheim an der Ruhr—he had last seen them in 1939, when he and one of his two older brothers had escaped Germany on a Kindertransport to Britain—he encountered German fears and stereotypes of vengeful Jews. One day, Kurt G. walked around Mühlheim with his only remaining childhood friend, Werner. When Werner introduced Kurt to an acquaintance as an old Jewish friend and former compatriot, the man told Kurt G.: "Yes, it is terrible what was done to the Jews. Either *all* should have been murdered or none of them. Today those who are still alive are here to take revenge."[3] Survivors such as Kurt G., who found his former family home bombed away, none left from his family except for an uncle in Krefeld, his mother and brother murdered at Treblinka, encountered little empathy for their pain and loss; rather, they faced a general suspicion that they had only come back for revenge. For his part, Kurt G. did not hate the Germans, only despised specific Nazi perpetrators; he was actually empathic to the German population, whom he saw as having been seduced by the Nazi regime. When he was discharged from the British army, he returned to Germany permanently and for political reasons made East Germany his home.

Germans of all walks of society saw themselves as victims. Many indeed were victims, but their victimhood was a consequence of the regime's war and genocide. In their basic views of the world few Germans placed German suffering in a context of the suffering that Germans had caused across the European continent and beyond. Thus while German civilians embraced their own victimization by Allied bombings, they disconnected it from the Luftwaffe's massively destructive bombing of other countries.[4] Likewise popular campaigns for the release of German POWs in Allied custody dissociated these prisoners, especially those in Soviet hands, from the preceding military aggression and war crimes in Germany's war of conquest and genocide.[5] After years of propaganda casting the Allies as being ruled by "international Jewry," Germany's defeat and military occupation by the Allied armies only seemed to indicate a Jewish plot. As did the presence of large numbers of mostly eastern European Holocaust survivors who temporarily lived in Germany as Jewish Displaced Persons (DPs) under protection by the Western Allies in the first five postwar years; Germans could conveniently ignore that the Nazi "final solution" implemented by a wide range of perpetrators from all walks of German society had in fact murdered two-thirds of European Jews, in many locations across Europe permanently obliterating a Jewish presence that had gone back many centuries. If anything, then, a growing awareness of the full scope of the Nazi regime's mass murder through newspaper coverage, reeducation, and war crimes trials, an awareness penetrating widespread wilful ignorance and denial, reinvigorated preexisting stereotypes of Jewish revenge, stirring up the sediment left by years of Nazi propaganda defining the Jews as the ultimate threat to German wellbeing and world peace.

It seems to have mattered little to Germans fearful in this way that in Allied-occupied Germany and in the period that followed, people were not actually falling victim to massacres[6] or being subjected to forced labor, beyond cleaning up liberated concentration camps and burying the dead[7]—the new reality was viewed by many as a reflection of "Jewish vengeance."[8] In February 1947 in Polish custody, awaiting trial before the Polish Supreme National Tribunal, Auschwitz commandant Rudolf Höss wrote in his memoir: "I also now see that the extermination of the Jews was fundamentally wrong. Precisely because of these mass exterminations, Germany has drawn upon herself the hatred of the entire world. It in no way served the cause of anti-Semitism, but on the contrary brought the Jews far closer to their ultimate objective."[9] (The trial would be held in March; it ended with a sentence of death by hanging, carried out on April 16, 1947, on the grounds of Auschwitz I.) Clearly, more than a few Germans will not have adhered to Höss's brand of antisemitism, and certainly not as radically and openly. But while many will have felt guilt and shame, Germans continued to maintain anti-Jewish stereotypes that the Nazi regime had promoted for years; and they cultivated self-perceptions as victims. Yesterday's *Volksgemeinschaft*, united around Hitler as a "people's community," had become a *Schicksalsgemeinschaft*, a community of fated victims, bound by complicity in genocidal crimes and the hardships of rebuilding after total collapse.[10]

Saul K. Padover, an American intelligence officer of Viennese Jewish background who interviewed many different kinds of Germans in 1944 and 1945, observed that although people were generally keeping antisemitic feelings to themselves, some nevertheless indicated in his interviews that Adolf Hitler liberated Germany from the Jews. Many Germans, Padover noted, had a "strange sense of guilt about the Jews, an uneasy feeling." Although he frequently encountered "an open admission that a great wrong has been committed," most Germans denied any personal wrongdoing; they saw the mass murder of the Jews as "Hitlers 'greatest error'. All the blame is being put on the Fuehrer in an attempt to escape moral responsibility." Padover also observed "fear of revenge and a dread of hearing the worst about the horrors that have been inflicted on the Jews in Poland. The Germans simply dare not face the awful truth."[11]

Similarly, interviewing Germans from all walks of life and ages, women and men, for his sociological work on antisemitism in 1950 and 1951, Theodor W. Adorno observed that most Germans rejected any personal guilt for Nazi crimes, no matter how much they had been involved in them. Germans, he confirmed, had wrapped themselves in a sense of victimhood; his findings indicated they found it unnecessary to acknowledge any wrongdoing on Germany's part. Furthermore, Adorno observed, they delegitimized any emotions Jews held toward them as vengeance, while claiming they themselves had never harbored any feelings of vengeance toward or hatred of Jews. Instead of showing empathy and compassion, a recognition of Germany's grave injustice, they condemned what they perceived as a Jewish intent to harm Germans. One of Adorno's interviewees claimed that "Jews today assume that the injustice committed against them gives them the right to commit injustice in return and . . . therefore they are now doing the most impossible things . . ."[12] The interviewee left open what these "things" were, perhaps because he and other Germans believed that the Jews were behind everything happening to them in that postwar moment.[13] Adorno's interviews also showed views of Jewish DPs as criminal, violent, and intent on harming the Germans—old stereotypes adapted to new circumstances—that augmented the German sense of fearful defeat and humiliating victimhood.[14]

Germans had of course gravely suffered during the war, particularly after 1943, with massive loss of life and property. But, Adorno found, rather than acknowledging responsibility for following, collaborating with, and benefitting from the Nazi regime and at least acknowledging a role in its mass crimes, many Germans blamed the crimes on the Nazi regime's leading figures and its "criminal organizations." Adorno's interviewees criticized the Allies in the name of humanitarianism, despite showing no humanitarian concern for Nazism's victims just months earlier—and held the victorious Allies and Jewish DPs to a higher moral standard than themselves. To many, the mere fact that Allies held trials and were seeing through denazification and re-education was proof that they were in fact flouting human rights and international law—that they were acting out of revenge.[15] If the Allies were really concerned about justice and human rights, Adorno's interviewees argued, they would stop holding Germans accountable, allow them to live in freedom and peace and to forget the recent past.[16]

German fears of Jewish revenge were widespread and drastically disproportionate to the number of revenge acts committed by Jews against Germans. Few Germans seem to have understood that their fears of Jewish vengeance were irrational, a result of Nazi propaganda, the few remaining Jews hardly being in a position to take significant revenge on Germans. There was dramatic distortion of demographic reality at work here, itself the new form of an old antisemitic trope, Jews being posited as numerous and powerful, non-Jews as outnumbered and weak—this being integrated into a viewpoint denying the fact that massive murder operations had wiped out most Jewish families and communities in Europe. Speaking to Saul Padover, Bernhard Thal, a thirty-year-old businessman from Aachen who had been affiliated with Catholic youth movements in the 1920s and, after a brief flirtation with the Nazi youth movement, had become critical of the regime and retreated to his father's business, observed that the German nation "has been corrupted spiritually to a degree that is unprecedented. At least eighty percent of the Germans have sinned against the Jews," he continued. "They have robbed and murdered the Jews, not out of conviction, but for profit, the most heinous of sins. Now," he explained, "they are troubled in their consciences and a great fear is among them. They dread what Goebbels calls 'Jewish vengeance.'" For Thal, this was sheer projection. "What a lie!" he exclaimed. "As if Jews had the power to revenge themselves—as if Jews were Germans [. . . and] believe[d] in *Vergeltung* [retaliation]!"[17] Few Germans seem to have been aware of the projection. And few seem to have been aware that acts of vengeance and retribution Germans experienced at the war's end were in fact by and large not perpetrated by Jews but members of many other national groups.

Already during the war, some Jewish observers—who for the most part did not survive the war—anticipated that postwar vengeance on Germans would be a quest by many national groups, Roma, Poles, and Soviets, as central agents of revenge alongside Jews. In his evocation of Jewish revenge, for example, Chaim A. Kaplan insisted that Poles would also take revenge on Germans for the destruction and defeat they were experiencing.[18] Similarly, Abraham Lewin noted the following on May 28, 1942: "The Gypsies' blood, like our blood, will cry out forever from the earth and will cover with shame and contempt the faces of Hitler's blond beast. The 'voice of thy brother's blood that cries to me from the earth' will, I believe, never be stilled and will demand forever: 'Revenge!'" On June 7, 1942, he added: "Jewish and Polish blood is spilled, it mingles together and, crying to the heavens, it demands revenge!"[19] As German power crumbled in fall 1944 and through the final days of the war into its immediate wake, liberated concentration camp inmates, forced laborers, POWs, resistance fighters, and partisans, along with Allied soldiers, engaged in violence against German civilians and the surrendering German military.[20]

Indeed, in the violent and tumultuous postwar transition to peace, hatred of Germans was, some contemporary observers noted, universal among people from liberated countries the Nazis had occupied and victimized, across the continent;[21] there was a quest for vengeance among former slave laborers and concentration camp inmates. Many Germans, regardless of their roles under the Nazi regime, indeed became victims of violent payback. The depth of the feelings at work here are made clear in Padover's reference to his encounter with a non-Jewish Polish prisoner—a school teacher from Katowice who had been incarcerated at Auschwitz before being transferred to Buchenwald—shortly after the camp's liberation. The teacher told Padover: "'I saw them murder the Jews. God Almighty, do you know what it means to see human beings being burned to death? They were God's children, like us. God's children, like everybody, except the Germans.'" Speaking hysterically and in a breaking voice (so that Padover put his hand on his shoulder) the man then

> burst into such a flood of imprecations against the German race as I have never heard. He raised his arms and cried out to God to bring down His vengeance upon the German nation; to exterminate every German man, woman, and child; to strike to death every living German being; to cleanse the earth of all German blood unto eternity. I was tempted to say Amen, and I felt like crying.[22]

In Padover's assessment, while all liberated national groups felt hatred and rage, eastern Europeans, especially Russians and Poles who had suffered staggering death tolls, were more eager to "get even" with the Germans than western Europeans.[23] Similarly, American Jewish writer and journalist Meyer Levin, working as a war correspondent for the United States Office of War Information, reported that "Poles, it was said, were the most savagely vengeful" among the liberated.[24]

Early postwar violence against Germans occurred in a broader context of violence throughout continental Europe against purported collaborators with the Nazis among various national groups. In countries formerly under German occupation, the end of German rule was marked by violent retribution against compatriots accused of such collaboration.[25] In France, some 10,000 French people were executed in what is known as the "wild purge," the *épuration sauvage*.[26] Between 10,000 and 20,000 Italians deemed fascists were killed in retribution, mostly by Italian partisans.[27] Head shaving and other public shaming of thousands of women in Belgium, Denmark, France, the Netherlands, and Norway—women accused of sexual relations with German soldiers, often an unwarranted assumption—allowed their male and female compatriots to celebrate their own sense of innocence and build resistance myths foundational for the postwar future.[28] In the borderlands between Poland and Ukraine, as well as in the Balkans, end-of-war violent retribution was even more widespread, with 90,000 Poles murdered by Ukrainians, 20,000 Ukrainians murdered by Poles, and 70,000 Yugoslavians of different backgrounds murdered—both at the war's end and in its wake—by their compatriots.[29] According to some estimates, 2–3 percent of the populations formerly under German occupation was affected by immediate postwar violent retribution.[30] Revenge on Germans and perceived collaborators thus occurred within the broader context of normalized excessive violence, political disintegration, and moral collapse.

Violent revenge against Germans, in the form of both attacks on specific Nazi perpetrators as well as indiscriminate acts against civilians, were, in fact, a central element in the process of Allied liberation of German-occupied territory and the move into Germany proper. Retribution would become a matter of state policy, with some 12–14 million ethnic Germans,[31] mostly women, children, and elderly, suffering expulsion—12 million from Czechoslovakia and Poland[32] and 1.8 million from Hungary, Romania, and Yugoslavia.[33] Numbers of how many died in that process vary between 15,000–30,000 and 500,000–1.5 million.[34] At the same time, between 1944 and 1955, mainly in 1945, Red Army soldiers, and to a lesser degree members of the Western Allied armed forces, committed mass rape,[35] with at least 860,000 German and Austrian women as victims[36] (according to some estimates perhaps even 1.9–2 million women),[37] causing thousands of suicides.[38] According to some estimates, an additional 2–2.5 million women were raped by the local population in the context of the expulsions from eastern Europe.[39] Moreover, Allied troops, often under the impact of the atrocities they saw when liberating concentration camps, engaged in the summary executions of SS guards and Wehrmacht soldiers, rather than taking them captive; they often let liberated prisoners take revenge on their former tormenters. One—American Jewish—soldier wrote his parents that what he had seen at the liberation of Dachau on April 29, 1945, along with the stories the surviving prisoners told the American troops, made him want to "tear the eyes out"[40] of every German soldier he encountered. He noted that on the day his unit arrived at the camp, they did not take German POWs but shot all the guards they ran into.[41] Meyer Levin, having seen Ohrdruf, a subcamp of Buchenwald near Gotha, and the first Nazi camp to be liberated by American troops in early April 1945, noted that people came away "swearing the only thing to do was to throw them [the Germans] down, tear them apart."[42] Enraged over what they saw as the relative comfort and high standard of living of German civilians inside Germany proper, soldiers also engaged in looting, alongside the prisoners and forced laborers they had liberated. "In the soldiers there was a hatred bred of resentment at being dragged from home, turned into killing brutes, forced through discomfort and fear and loneliness to hate the bloody enemy that had brought all this upon a man," recalled Levin. "Added to this was the undeniable 'lust of conquest,'" he noted, emphasizing that it was fueled by the sense that on average the German population still enjoyed good clothes, bedlinens, and homes of a quality that the families of many Allied soldiers did not have.[43] In the eyes of the soldiers, Germans deserved to suffer in retaliation for their crimes. "But looting had another meaning, the ancient meaning of all war … the devouring of the enemy so that one might have his strength, and the symbolic way of devouring the enemy was through the fetish—carrying his weapons, wearing his scalp, taking his women. All this was a way of obliterating the enemy and at the same time absorbing his power, his strength."[44] To Levin, vengeance was "a normal complement of war."[45]

In Ohrdruf, the 4th Armored Division and 89th Infantry Division of the Third US Army found a harrowing site of mass murder, with bodies of prisoners burnt alive by the SS as the camp leadership escaped the US army's advances. A week later, on April 12, 1945, Generals Dwight D. Eisenhower, George S. Patton, and Omar Bradley visited the camp. After the tour Patton learned that a presumed surviving prisoner who had educated the three US generals about the practices of torture at the camp turned out to be a former SS guard: a Russian survivor had identified him and murdered him in revenge.[46]

Across continental Europe the end-of-war and immediate postwar moment had its distinct moral fabric, one markedly different from that stamping pre-war civil society; different kinds of actors operated with a basic sense of impunity. In the turmoil of liberating camps and taking control of Germany, the boundaries between revenge acts and combat were blurry.

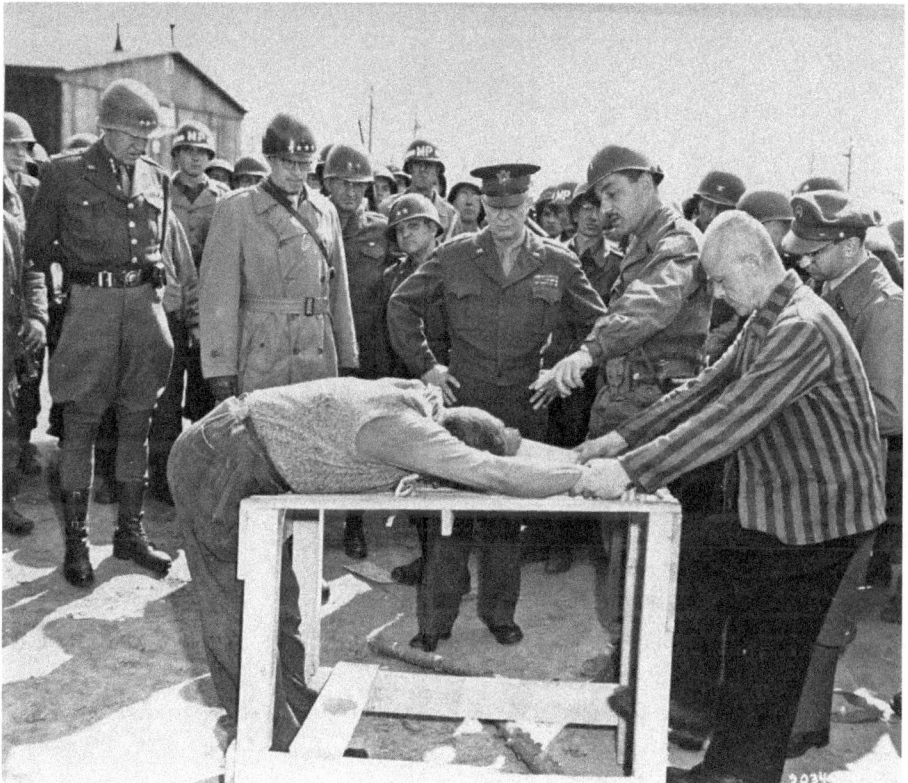

Figure 11 Ohrdruf survivors demonstrate torture methods to highest ranking American generals General Dwight Eisenhower (center), General Omar Bradley (second from the left), and General George S. Patton (left), April 12, 1945. As can be inferred from additional film footage, the man bending over the table (who later appears talking to the generals with the help of the mustached soldier-interpreter, Alois J. Liethen) seems to be the SS guard who posed as a liberated prisoner; compared to the other prisoners, he appeared to be in good physical condition with no prisoner garb and without a shaven head; USHMM Photo Archives # 63511; United States Holocaust Memorial Museum, courtesy of National Archives and Records Administration, College Park.

HEADQUARTERS
THIRD UNITED STATES ARMY
OFFICE OF THE COMMANDING GENERAL
APO 403

15 April, 1945

My dear Ike:

I wrote a personal letter in the enclosed wording to each Corps Commander and to the Chief of Staff, which I believe was in line with your idea.

It may interest you to know that the very talkative, alleged former member of the murder camp was recognized by a Russian prisoner as a former guard. The prisoner beat his brains out with a rock.

We have found at a place four miles north of WEIMAR a similar camp, only much worse. The normal population was 25,000, and they died at the rate of about a hundred a day. The burning arrangements, according to General Gay and Colonel Codman who visited it yesterday, were far superior to those which they had at OHRDRUF.

I told the press to go up there and see it, and then write as much about it as they could. I also called General Bradley last night and suggested that you send selected individuals from the upper strata of the press to look at it, so that you can build up another page of the necessary evidence as to the brutality of the Germans.

We all enjoyed your visit very much.

Most sincerely,

G. S. PATTON, JR.

General of the Army D. D. Eisenhower
Headquarters SHAEF
APO 757
U. S. Army

Incl.
    Copy, personal letter.

Figure 12 Letter from George Patton to Dwight D. Eisenhower, April 15, 1945, mentioning the revenge killing of a former SS guard who had posed as a prisoner when the US generals toured Ohrdruf three days earlier; Dwight D. Eisenhower Presidential Library, NAID #12007734; courtesy of Dwight D. Eisenhower Presidential Library.

Outrage and fury, frustration and helplessness over the previously unimagined horrors that liberating Allied troops were finding in the camps furnished a sense of legitimacy when it came to carrying out what were war crimes under international law.[47] Some soldiers did move to prevent prisoner violence on captured guards, in an effort to observe such law and uphold personal moral standards,[48] but few soldiers who engaged in vigilantism at liberation faced serious disciplinary consequences.[49] Even troops not actively participating in violence enabled it by turning a blind eye; there are many examples of Allied liberators who saw prisoner abuse SS guards, prisoner functionaries, and purported informers during or shortly after the liberation and did not intervene.[50] They tended to empathize with prisoner rage, especially against guards who pretended to be prisoners by wearing prisoner garb or who tried to blend in with civilians but were identified and killed by some of their victims.[51] Leon Bass, a black GI who had liberated Buchenwald and who himself suffered from prejudice and discrimination in the then segregated US Army, noted: "I saw some of the inmates who had been freed, they were surrounding a . . . a guard that they had captured. And they were beating him. And they wanted us to join, but we did not. They took him into a building, they beat him to death. I could understand their feelings. I don't condone what happened, but I certainly understand it."[52]

In many instances, Allied soldiers verbally encouraged the liberated prisoners to beat, even kill captured guards, often enabling vigilante justice by providing weapons—something frequently attested to in survivor testimony. While some Western Allied soldiers had a gendered perspective on the revenge acts, seeing them as normal behavior for liberated men but less so for women,[53] it seems that Soviet officers made no such distinctions, tolerating violent revenge by women as well as men. Knowing that their actions were sanctioned, even desired by their liberators, some prisoners acted out their anger. Although men were more likely than women to engage in such violence,[54] women often witnessed it, alongside men, as spectators and condoned it, perhaps even giving it impetus.[55] Voluntarily or involuntarily, these former prisoners were bystanders to the violent behavior of some of their peers alongside Allied soldiers.[56] Numerous post-liberation photographs of murdered SS guards, kapos and other prisoner functionaries suggest that acts of vigilante justice were an integral part of the transition from war to peace. The exact division of labor between soldiers and liberated prisoners in this violence cannot be determined; likewise with the rough number of Jewish prisoners involved—Jews were more likely to give testimony after the war, and this might present a misleading impression of their role in what transpired.[57]

In this postwar moment of vengeance, some Jewish actors did pursue revenge plots that seemed like realizations of Germans' worst anxieties. In spring 1945, sections of the Jewish Brigade—a division of 5,000 Jews from Mandatory Palestine who from fall 1944 fought in the British army—stationed in Northern Italy murdered between 50 and 150 former SS men across the border in Austria. In a secret operation, Jewish Brigade operatives targeted specific SS men, executing them after verifying their identity and conducting short "trials" in which the men were sentenced to death. Once this became known to superior officers in the British army, the operatives faced sanctions.[58] Beyond these secret executions, soldiers of the Jewish Brigade—and the survivors who

Figure 13 A group of survivors and two soldiers from the 11th Armored Division of the Third US Army view the corpse of a camp guard killed by survivors after liberation of Gusen, Upper Austria, May 12, 1945, photographed by Sam Gilbert. USHMM Photo Archives # 82868; United States Holocaust Memorial Museum, courtesy of Wilfred McCarty.

encountered them—drew much symbolic meaning from their presence in occupied and defeated Germany, playing on the suggestive power of military uniforms adorned with Stars of David and the fear it sparked in a German public that "the Jews" were "coming" for them.[59] In April 1946, the SS men in American custody in Stalag 13 outside Nuremberg suffered symptoms of food poisoning. The bread that the American military fed to them that day had been drenched in arsenic. But since the concentration of the poison was weak, it did not cause any deaths. A group of young Holocaust survivors, mostly from eastern Europe, who had gathered and formed a loose group of about fifty persons named Nakam (as noted earlier, "revenge"), led by the poet and partisan Abba Kovner and his future wife Vitka Kempner, were responsible for the bread poisoning.

It was the group's plan B. Plan A had been to poison the water supplies to four major German cities, in order to kill six million Germans as payback for the Holocaust. Only, the reasoning went, if the world understood that the murderers of Jews paid a price with their own lives would there be a chance to end murder of Jews in the postwar world. That payback for the genocide would also act as a deterrence. This plan grew out of what some Jews—Calel Perechodnik, Zalmen Gradowski, Otto Dov Kulka among others—had already contemplated during the war: a fantasy of meting out a "final solution" to the German perpetrators of *the* "final solution," translated into postwar reality. The members of the Nakam group, all of whom had known Kovner as a youth leader in Hashomer Hatsair before the war, as a wartime ghetto underground fighter, or as partisan leader, were grieving at the loss of their loved ones, the annihilation of their communities. Severely traumatized, many grappled with finding a purpose in having survived and in going on living. Some expected to die, during or as a result of the act of vengeance, or through suicide afterwards.[60]

Given the hostility and, sometimes, violence that returning Jews were encountering at, especially, the hands of Poles, Lithuanians, and Ukrainians, the sense Nakam members had of likely continued postwar murder of Jews was in itself not unrealistic.[61] The plotters of this mass poisoning saw no future in Europe; many feared new oppression and persecution, this time from the Soviet Union. As committed Zionists, the idea of vengeance on the Germans was understood in national terms: they saw themselves as representing the Jewish nation in wreaking vengeance on the German nation; this harmonized with engaging in the Bricha (Hebrew for "flight") movement bringing survivors out of eastern Europe to Mandatory Palestine. For the Nakam group, whose members came from diverse religious and educational backgrounds and had varied wartime experiences, the quest for vengeance in Europe, their engagement with aid and emigration, provided a community and social network, indeed something like a surrogate family. The group formed in Lublin in fall 1944 and spring 1945; it moved southwestward into Allied occupied Germany in the summer of 1945. Plan A then got underway, some members of the group taking jobs at water works in Nuremberg and Abba Kovner traveling to Palestine in fall 1945 to procure poison. He faced skepticism and even resistance from Yishuv leaders—including David Ben-Gurion and Chaim Weizmann—who thought that such a revenge act would be both inappropriate and harmful to the interests of Zionism and quest for sovereignty in Palestine. Apparently, Kovner managed to secure some poison from a chemist at the Weizmann Institute of Science without the knowledge of either Ben-Gurion or Weizmann. But on the way back from Palestine in December 1945, embarking from Egypt on a British ship and posing as a British soldier, Kovner was arrested—not because of the plot, of which the British were unaware, but because they suspected Kovner of belonging to Etzel or Irgun, the militant Jewish groups engaging in anti-British terror.[62]

Even if the British had not thwarted Kovner's plans, it is doubtful that Nakam's self-appointed avengers could have caused the deaths of even a fraction of the Germans whose deaths they had envisioned. Within the group, some members had moral qualms about the indiscriminate nature of Plan A, not only because not all Germans had been perpetrators in the same way, but also because the poisoned water was likely to kill Allied liberators and potentially even survivors. A more distinct targeting of German POWs, many of whom were former members of the SS, was not only more doable logistically but also more morally acceptable. But even Plan B was clumsily executed, and failed.[63] In testimony given in 1995, one former member of the Nakam group, Shlomo Kenet (né Kanterowitz, born in Vilna in 1921), described joining the group as the "natural thing" to do; at his interview's end he insisted he was not ashamed of the Nakam's plans but in fact felt some disappointment at not having "paid the dues toward the dead."[64] But he also noted that the group needed to be seen in the specific circumstances of the moment.

In any case, despite the presence of such Jewish revenge efforts which were not widely known but secret at the time, the role that Jews actually played in payback against Germans was vastly inflated in postwar Germany, more ideological fantasy than reality, informed by the years of relentless propaganda focused on Jewish evilness, and aggression, Judeo-Bolshevism, fantasies of Jews overtly and covertly ruling the world and of having always victimized the Germans.[65] Along with the projections of hatred, guilt, and victimhood onto the Jews, we here find a continuation of the victim-aggressor role-reversal that had been so central in Nazi antisemitism. In survivor testimony, we find fairly frequent assertions that compared to other national groups, especially the Russians, Jews actually played a minor role among Europe's postwar avengers[66]—as indicated, a more historically accurate assessment. Very likely, this was in part a result of simple demographics. Most Jews under Nazi rule did not survive long enough for liberation; they had been murdered in ghettos, killing fields, death camps, and concentration camps. By the end of 1943, 80 percent of the Holocaust's victims were dead.[67] Of the 715,000 prisoners registered in the German camp system in January 1945, perhaps 200,000, i.e., less than 30 percent, were Jews.[68] Over 465,000 (65 percent) of these prisoners died in the last four months of the war, in death marches, from violence, exhaustion, hunger, disease, and exposure to the elements. An estimated 250,000 camp prisoners were liberated from camps in Germany and Austria in April and May. Perhaps 90,000 of them were Jews, of whom 30,000 died in the days and weeks after liberation.[69] Jews were thus not the majority among the prisoners liberated from concentration camps; they were an even smaller minority among the eight million foreign nationals—mostly political prisoners, forced laborers, and POWs—on the move in Allied occupied Germany, some of them inclined to engage in vengeance in the days and weeks following the end of the war.

Revenge in the Twilight between War and Peace

What did revenge mean for surviving Jews? How did they handle their own desires for revenge and the revenge imperatives they had heard from others during the war, once warfare was over? What led some Jews to act out their desires but prevented most from exacting revenge? How did survivors' perspectives on revenge change over time as they rebuilt their lives?

For Jews who had been liberated from camps or emerged from hiding sometime between fall 1943 and spring 1945, the search for surviving family members, friends, and acquaintances was as urgent as procuring food, clothes, and shelter. Letters were a central avenue for that search—they were signs of life and served as first accounts of traumatic experiences, commemoration of loved ones, and information on how they had died. But letters were also spaces to express hopes for the present and future. Many letters included abstract motifs of vengeance that echoed the imagery and rhetoric resorted to during war. Far more urgent now than carrying out revenge, however, was rationalizing survival and learning who and what was irretrievably lost.

In these circumstances, revenge rhetoric was above all a means to express fathomless pain and grief. Some of the rhetoric conveyed a generational revenge imperative, a message from dead parents to surviving children, as did a letter written in August 1944 letter from Aba Tarlowski in Grodno, western Belorussia. Writing as a family friend to sisters Shulamit and Yudith Lipshitz, still in Tashkent (Uzbekistan) at the time, Tarlowski informed them about the fate of their parents Frida and Meir and Grodno's 25,000 other Jews after the town came under German occupation in June 1941: ghettoization followed by mass murder. It seems that the sisters escaped the Germans, fleeing east to the Soviet Union and surviving in Soviet Central Asia. Before their mother was deported from the Grodno ghetto to Treblinka in November 1943, Tarlowski relates, she told him "'. . . I am happy that my children are still alive and that they will take revenge on the fascists for having shed our innocent blood.'"[70] Thus Tarlowski, evidently a close family friend, provided vital information connecting the sisters to their mother and broader community; at the same time he sought to ease their pain and potential sense of guilt for having left their family and friends behind, letting them know that their mother had gone to her death finding solace in her daughters' survival. But with this, he also seems to have conveyed an intergenerational call for revenge—although we cannot know if these were indeed Frida's words, or rather an expression of Tarlowski's feelings.

In early September 1944, nearly a month after liberation by the Red Army, Grisha Birman wrote from Kovno to acquaintances in Palestine: "You surely know that we have been under Hitler's reign of terror. His victory over us is heart-rending. Wherever he set foot he pretty much crushed us completely. [. . .] Now, I am finally able to compose myself and write you a letter. We are totally devastated."[71] Birman estimated that of the 250,000 Jews of Kovno, Shavli, and Vilna, less than 40,000 had survived. This meant, for him, a need to "avenge our arch enemy according to the principle 'an eye for an eye and a tooth for a tooth.'"[72] Similarly Leib Shaus, taking stock of the Lithuanian Jewry's destruction after returning to Vilna from Alma-Ata, Kazakhstan, where he had taken shelter after escaping the Germans: "We walk among the graves with bleeding hearts and tightened fists. What else remains for us today, except the thirst for revenge?"[73] And again Azriel Tunik, referring to his hometown Stolpce, in the Nowogrodek region of Poland, in late August 1944: "Nothing is left here, neither people nor houses. Our one and only goal right now is: Revenge! Nothing else interests us. Our lives are broken forever. We are no longer normal human beings. It is impossible to remain a human being after experiencing hell."[74] His sister Hava, who had been a partisan, confirmed: "Now is the time for revenge. We must destroy the Germans to the last one."[75] Hava and Azriel Tunik were mourning the death of their parents and six of their eight siblings (two had emigrated to Palestine before the war) with their spouses and children. Azriel Tunik had lost his wife and son.

But while after the war as well, evoking revenge was, clearly, an effort to cope with pain at events that seemed beyond human comprehension, revenge was also impossible, and in any case futile. Azriel Tunik said as much, writing on November 7, 1944: "There are no words to describe what the Germans and their vassals did. No revenge will ever be big enough. We alone are incapable of carrying out such massive revenge; it is history that must help us. We are positive that Hitler's killers will get their due, but we'll never be satisfied. We have paid a heavy price."[76] It would appear that over a period of several weeks, Azriel processed his pain, initially measuring it in the currency of revenge, then realizing that any revenge doing justice to his loss would be so excessive as to be impracticable, thus delegating it to a realm of "history," perhaps invoking God. For Tunik and other survivors who spoke of revenge, ideas of what it meant, how it would be carried out and on whom, whether on specific murderers or Germans as a collective, or their collaborators among the nations, often remained vague, even phantasmagoric.

In the context of end-of-the-war turmoil and brutalization, some early postwar Jewish voices did offer explicit, even graphic descriptions of revenge acts against Germans. We find references to urges for revenge, to revenge acts, and revenge fantasies in a range of early postwar survivor accounts, for example those appearing in the Yiddish historical journal *Fun Letztn Khurbn* ("From the Last Annihilation"), published in ten issues between 1946 and 1948,[77] and in the aforementioned collection of 130 survivor interviews by psychologist David P. Boder, recorded on a wire recorder when he toured Germany, Italy, Switzerland, and France between July and September 1946: this earliest audio-recorded oral Holocaust-history project includes many expressions of raw emotion and unfiltered rage. This is the case with Boder's interview with Benjamin Piskorz, held on September 1, 1946. A native of Warsaw, Piskorz fought in the Warsaw ghetto uprising as a member of ŻOB and was deported to Treblinka. Selected for work, he was sent to Majdanek, Auschwitz-Monowitz, and Dora-Mittelbau. Toward the end of the war, he escaped from Dora-Mittelbau, eventually, ending up in the Tradate, Italy DP camp, the site of his interview with Boder. Piskorz openly acknowledged having engaged in acts of revenge:

> Benjamin Piskorz: Because I knew well, I understood and spoke German well, and so there I took a bit of revenge on the Germans, and later on I left.
>
> David Boder: What does it mean took revenge [*nekome*]?
>
> Benjamin Piskorz: What does 'took revenge' mean? I did the same thing as they did with us.
>
> David Boder: For instance?
>
> Benjamin Piskorz: For instance, I struck down a few people. I, too, tortured.
>
> David Boder: Killed dead?
>
> Benjamin Piskorz: Yes, killed dead. I, too, tortured a few people. And I also did the same things with the German children as the SS men did in Majdanek with the Po-. . .with the Jewish children.
>
> David Boder: For instance?

Benjamin Piskorz: For instance, they took small . . . small children by the little legs and beat the head against the wall so long until the head cracked and [the child] was killed.

David Boder: Did you do the same thing?

Benjamin Piskorz: I did the same to the German children, because the hate in me was so great, but only . . . maybe I would have in time forgotten all of this, if not [for the fact] that the Germans themselves had reminded me that when the Russians will enter they will be killed and they will be sent to Siberia and the same things will be done to them as [they did] to the Jews. And the Germans still worried at the same time why Hitler didn't exterminate all the Jews so there shouldn't be anybody left to take revenge on them.[78]

It is striking that Piskorz here explained his hatred and burning drive to seek revenge, perhaps bound to ebb over time, as having been rekindled toward the end of the war when learning of German fears of Jewish revenge, not simply fears of revenge from the approaching Soviet army. It is also striking that he seemed well aware that Germans justified the indiscriminate mass murder of Jews with the claim that future revenge from surviving Jews had to be prevented. It remains unclear, however, where Piskorz encountered the German objects of his vengeance—possibly this was after his escape from Dora-Mittelbau after which, disguised as a wounded SS man, he made his way to the Sudentenland where he worked as a farmhand. We learn in this interview that Piskorz did not hate Germans as a collective: he mentions a love-relationship with a German girl while working on the farm. It is in any case unclear if the revenge murder of German children, in his account carried out in the exact same manner as that used by the SS to murder Jewish children, actually happened—or whether it represented a post-traumatic fantasy, accompanying him as he tried to rebuild his life. We learn in the interview that Piskorz had just become a father; perhaps, in the wake of his horrific experiences, he was fantasizing about what he would do to whomever harmed his child.

When Jewish survivors did commit revenge acts, these were most likely to occur immediately after liberation, in the tumultuous and violent war-peace transition period. Liberated and liberators alike had a clear sense that there was a short window of opportunity for violent revenge; some recall a proverbial period of two to three days of mayhem marking the process of Allied takeover of control, a period in which violent revenge was deemed acceptable and committed with impunity.[79] Clearly, that temporal assessment may well have been entirely subjective, based on individual experience of the events; measured objectively the transitional phase may well have been longer, several days, perhaps even weeks, depending on the timing of liberation and end of warfare in a given location. Notable here is the fact that individuals had a sense that this window of opportunity and impunity would close once combat was over and Allied control had been consolidated, marking a path toward a normalcy and stability possessing different parameters for judging violent payback. In a documentary film of 2012 by Alexa

Karolinski entitled *Oma & Bella*, about two survivors—Regina Karolinski from Krakow and Bella Katz from Vilna—liberated by the Soviet army, Bella Katz describes this unwritten statute of limitations on revenge as follows: "You got two days and that was enough. A free hand. You were allowed to do whatever you wanted. [. . .] But then comes a normal life." Asked by her friend Regina's granddaughter whether she had killed anyone, Bella responds: "I saw how somebody was killed, yes. Well, I heard it happen. Afterwards one was trembling and confused for a couple of days, because we were not used to such things and we never did that ourselves, but. . . ." At this point, she is interrupted by Regina Karolinski: "People we were not quite normal back then. Life had not been normalized yet."[80]

From this and other testimony, it seems clear that along with others, survivors had a good sense that what was legitimate *now* would again become illegitimate *then*, in the fast-approaching future. And indeed, with the return of rule of law, vigilante justice again treated as a criminal act, the desire and incentive for revenge faced objective constraints. After having endured years of brutal persecution, the survival of camp imprisonment, why would anyone wish to risk another jail sentence for murdering a former SS guard? Survivors were not above the law—even if they felt rightfully entitled to enact violent payback for the trauma and loss they had endured. Risking a jail sentence was inopportune when trying to build a future.

But even within the available window of opportunity, not all acts thought of as revenge were aimed at murdering guards, or else Germans and their collaborators more broadly. There was a wide range of possibilities for action aimed at humiliation. Often one-time acts were involved here, serving as personal rites of passage allowing traumatized survivors to move on with their lives. Hanna F. (born in Czemierniki, near Lublin, in 1923), had survived Auschwitz, Majdanek, and Płaszów, had been evacuated to Germany, had escaped from a death march, and was then liberated by the Russians on the outskirts of Prague. So weak that she could barely stand, sitting in the gutter of a busy street, she saw Russian soldiers marching a train of German POWs. "They were coming closer. I got my full strength. I got up, and picked my right arm up and hit one in the face. He didn't know what hit him. The blood started running. I felt such a relief. I just sat down in the gutter and cried. Everybody was applauding, but I couldn't even get up." It is remarkable that F. remembered that it was her right arm. She might not have mentioned it had it merely been for the fact that she was right-handed. Rather, raising her right arm in her act of payback seems to have had distinct meaning for her because the right arm was typically used to perform the Hitler salute. "And you just hit him with your hand?" asked interviewer Lawrence Langer. "With all my might. That was the revenge I took," Hanna F. replied.[81]

In this way, Hanna F. made clear to Langer that she was able to let go of revenge. Her violent gesture, transforming a captured German soldier into a passive and emasculated object of her aggression, marked a reversal of gender roles with significance for the revenge act itself. The violence enacted against German bodies by other liberated individuals, especially women, was of a bloodless and often symbolic nature: it could be the violence of forcing guards to clean and work for the former prisoners; and it could be the violence of haircutting, enacted upon former female guards or forewomen. The spectacle, played out before liberated women, of cutting a female camp guard's hair was itself a mark of reversed power relations. Here cutting hair instead of killing amounted to symbolic mutilation; but there was a deeper meaning to this form of payback. Prisoners in Nazi concentration, labor, and death camps had themselves endured systematic haircutting. It was aimed at divesting individuality, turning individuals into objects and numbers, as well as, on a practical level, preventing escape attempts since the shorn bodies were then marked as prisoners. For both men and women but especially women, head-shavings obliterated gender- and sexual identity; it was meant to have, and had, a profoundly humiliating and dehumanizing impact. Consequently, the sheering of female camp guards' hair as vengeance involved a defeminizing and masculinizing of the guards, their sexual humiliation. (In one related vengeful gesture, liberated women at Bergen-Belsen humiliated a female guard by "washing" her hair in a latrine.)[82] Head shaving had a lasting effect—it took months for hair to grow back; consequently, the spectacle continued after a guard moved away from the space of the camp into Allied captivity.[83]

Women freed from the camps also degraded their former tormentors by stripping them off their uniform boots, which had once represented their power, and by making them clean floors under verbal assaults and kicks.[84] Another revenge rite was desecration of the corpses of specific guards killed by Allied soldiers: stepping on or beating the bodies,[85] both payback for the lack of dignity that had been accorded the victims and a confirmation, even celebration, over the guards' dead bodies, of the prisoners' own escape from the jaws of death. And again, some of these rites of payback and passage into the postwar world were not related to German bodies but to German property. This resulted from both years of deprivation and present material needs, as well as redress for enormous amounts of property stolen from Jewish households as a basic part of the Nazi German wartime economy. Liberated women and children ransacked and destroyed German homes, often stealing items with symbolic, personal meaning for the avengers.[86] Women here took revenge on women in the domestic sphere, destroying traditionally womanly things such as porcelain, emptying cupboards, taking soap and using the bath for hygiene, reappropriating clothes in the presence of German owners (who seem to have understood in the moment that they would be better off playing along, since power relations had changed).[87] Children and young teenagers participated in property destruction, theft, and some violence.[88] They also stole toys from the homes of German children as their revenge. One example in particular, from testimony given in 1995, encapsulates various activities of this sort: Flora Carasso Mihael (born in Salonica in 1935) had survived thirteen months in Bergen-Belsen together with her parents, in the "privileged" position of Greek Jews who also held Italian and French passports; shortly before the liberation they were transferred from Belsen in the direction of Brandenburg and, on April 13, 1945, liberated en route by American troops in Thuringia. Over the following days, Mihael and her parents looted and destroyed property at the home of an SS officer in Ellersleben. For Mihael, it was about "the pleasure of revenge, of giving back your feelings to the Germans," about wanting "to destroy as much as they destroyed you"; ten-year-old Mihael's particular revenge was stealing toys.[89]

Jewish Revenge and the Holocaust

Practical Impossibilities of Violent Revenge

Most Jews who had hoped for revenge—even intensely so—during and at the end of the war, did not exact it. There were various reasons for this, practical, psychological, and ethical. The most common reason was physical weakness and complete exhaustion. Although the opportunity for revenge was there—power relations had changed, Allied soldiers offered encouragement and impunity, weapons were readily available—the would-be avengers were too frail to do something: "years of oppression and calculated starvation had taken the fight out of the slaves," Saul K. Padover noted about liberated concentration camp prisoners he encountered; similarly Meyer Levin found many survivors were "too weak to carry or push even a little retribution."[90] Furthermore, a primordial search for food, shelter, clothing, and care had priority over the pursuit of revenge—the Austrian Jewish communist Otto Feuer noted just that about, in his estimate, 80 percent of the persons liberated from Buchenwald like him.[91] In his testimony, Moishe Rutschaisky (Morris Rich), a survivor of the Kovno ghetto and Dachau concentration camp, noted that at liberation, although the thought of taking revenge on a former SS guard occurred to him, this was only after he had secured food. Forced on a death march away from Dachau, Rutschaisky found himself somewhere between Greiling and Bad Tölz with American soldiers approaching. He escaped from the death march and a German girl hid him in a barn. Soon after, an SS guard from Dachau concealed himself on the upper floor of the same barn. When American soldiers arrived on May 2, 1945, "they loaded me up with food. I had so much I could not eat [any] more.... and I grabbed one soldier and I kissed him."[92] The soldier turned out to be Jewish; he conversed with Rutschaisky in Yiddish. Ravenous, grateful, and overjoyed, Rutschaisky ate and sent some of the soldiers in the direction of a valley where the other prisoners were being held by the SS. "And then: I forgot all about ... [pause] And I said to the soldier, there is [an] SS man hiding himself upstairs. I was so confused, I was so out of this world that my main enemy, my guard, the SS man is upstairs sitting there and hiding himself. He thinks he's going to get away with murder."[93] After the soldiers captured and disarmed the SS man, Rutschaisky continued, the Jewish soldier told him: "If you want to knock his face off, do it right now. Beat ... that SS man!" But:

> I was a skeleton. I weighed 60—about 68 pounds. —Almost like 33 kilos. That was my weight.... And I was about to give him that real punch in his face and tear him apart. But I gave him a little punch, a little thing, I thought I almost broke my wrist here. The man said, I know you couldn't beat him. We are going to do it for you. And he gave him a couple kicks and pushes.[94]

Soon after, Rutschaisky was reunited with his brother, and "here is all the food that the Americans gave me, sit down and eat! ... And we sat down in the stable booth and we start[ed] eating ... and we ate so much in that stable and we were liberated ... "[95] Rutschaisky's description of the abundance of food and the amounts of his consumption seems to reflect the intensity of his *experience* of food rather than of actual quantities;

eating large amounts would potentially have been life-threatening for his emaciated body. In any case, the basic, overriding urge for food was a dominant reality for camp and death-march survivors.[96] Along with food came medical care and recovery. Then, as they regained some strength and put on body weight, surrounding conditions changed, and with them their perspective on revenge. The period of impunity had passed; weapons were no longer easily found; their possession and usage became sanctioned under Allied military law: in September 1945, Proclamation No. 2 of the Allied Control Council banned possession of all weapons, munitions, and explosives.[97]

Elly Gotz (born in 1928 in Kovno) was an angry seventeen-year-old when liberated from Kaufering, a Dachau subcamp. As he recovered with his father, two of his uncles, and other survivors at the St. Ottilien monastery on the outskirts of Munich—Gotz weighed seventy pounds at liberation—conversations revolved around "how we all hated the Germans and the other nations amongst whom we lived for thousands of years and who often betrayed us in our hour of need,"[98] and around revenge. "We were so weak that getting out of bed was an effort," Gotz writes in his memoir, "but many people were nonetheless dreaming of revenge."[99] As he gained strength and volunteered to work as a locksmith for the monks, his "head was full of thoughts about exacting revenge on the Germans. Every German man of a certain age was a suspect in my mind, and I daydreamed about what I would do: Poison them in large numbers? Lay some explosives somewhere?"[100] Although a visit to Munich made him see "the immense destruction caused by Allied bombing," prompting his realization that "the Germans had also suffered in the war," Gotz nevertheless "did not think that was enough. I was full of hate, of anger. So many scenes of the Germans' brutality during the war years were spinning around in my memory."[101]

After six months in the hospital and a gain of fifty pounds he was determined to kill Germans. But he was unable to find a weapon.[102] While searching for a gun in the summer of 1945, he increasingly experienced a psychological obstacle: he enjoyed the idea of revenge in the abstract but was appalled by the concrete prospect of committing a murder. His thoughts circled around the question of "whom do you want to kill?" and in an internal monologue he kept questioning the legitimacy of the targets he picked: "You don't know whom to kill! For example, that woman standing there, you want to kill her? And I said to myself: I don't want to kill her. She has done nothing to me. So whom do you want to kill? That man? He looks like he could have been a guard in Dachau. Yeah, but you don't know. . . . You don't know whom to kill. You don't know who has done what."[103] Gotz gave up. Along with his revulsion at the prospect of committing a murder, his inability to find a target, and a weapon, he understood that "[y]ou can't kill people in peacetime."[104] With growing consolidation of the postwar order, acts of revenge would be judged ordinary crimes, no matter the emotion and experience behind them, their intuitive historical-moral justification.

Revenge no longer served survivors' political, social, and emotional needs. For many, revenge lost its validity once the power relations had changed. As the writer Jean Améry (born in 1912 in Vienna as Hanns Chaim Mayer) noted—Améry had escaped Vienna for Belgium, been active in the anti-Nazi resistance, and was then arrested, incarcerated, and tortured at Fort Breendonk before being deported to Auschwitz, Dora-Mittelbau, and Bergen-Belsen—revenge had an "existential value" for Jews if exacted against the "heavily armed oppressor."[105] From that perspective, there was nothing to be gained from taking revenge on Germans who were already weak. In the eyes of some survivors, focusing on the pursuit of revenge hindered rather than served their recovery and their ability to rebuild their lives and build a future. According to Otto Feuer, prisoners who had been affiliated with the Buchenwald underground—he had been one of them—came to realize that revenge "was not in our interest" in the early postwar period. Rather, the priority was now to build a political leadership, for the sake of seeing to present and future needs of the liberated prisoners. Feuer emphasized that Buchenwald prisoners had "dreamt of vengeance for years"[106]—that no roll call went by without this being talked about. While in general the prisoners doubted they would make it to the war's end, they were certain a German defeat was coming, and with it "eventual vengeance."[107] In the hours before the Americans arrived, prisoners went looking for SS guards—who had abandoned the camp—seeking not "to kill them at once" but to let them "have the same pain that we had."[108] But revenge would remain more theoretical than actual; the SS men whom the prisoners did manage to capture would be handed over to the American troops.[109] According to Feuer, when prisoners did, finally, have a chance for revenge, they realized that the violence would not serve them: "we don't think that this was the right way, to go and to . . . kill now German children or kill German women, because they have killed Jewish children and Jewish women."[110] In this way Feuer pointed to a self-conscious break between wartime desire and postwar behavior, emotional drive and rational decision-making. For Feuer, who had been persecuted as both a Jew and a communist, this meant building political representation and a new political order.

Similarly, Elly Gotz realized that thinking about how to pay back the Nazi perpetrators connected him to the traumatic past—at the cost of his present and future personal needs. "You're not thinking about yourself, what do you want to be when you . . . grow up and . . . get out of here. Don't think about them. Think about yourself."[111] As a result, Gotz changed his behavior: "I forced myself to give up hate and I did succeed after a while. I practiced stopping certain thoughts immediately after they started."[112] He did so by pushing his head sideways every time he felt hate and thought about revenge, possibly as a kind of symbolic slap,[113] then "refocusing on good thoughts"[114] aimed at building a future. It seems that in his own way, Gotz came to realize that hatred was a legacy of Nazi ideology itself; that seeking revenge would tie him to the horrific past and give Nazis enduring power over his life. "I am very conscious of that moment when I decided that hate was killing *me*, not killing anybody else,"[115] Gotz recalled. "When I freed myself from feelings of hate, I felt that I started living again."[116]

The Ethics of Non-Vengeance

Both Feuer and Gotz pointed to basic ethical obstacles that stood in the way to enacting revenge—Feuer feeling that murdering German women and children because Germans had murdered Jewish women and children was "not right," Gotz feeling unease at the idea of targeting random Germans whose guilt or innocence he could not know. The sense of such obstacles could in any case take different forms: in his testimony of 1983, for example, Martin L. (born in Lodz in 1916) first indicated that in the Lodz ghetto, at Auschwitz and in the Gross-Rosen subcamp Friedland, thoughts of revenge kept him and others alive, but that when the opportunity was there, real revenge was impossible because "a little bit of humanity was left in us."[117] Like Feuer and Gotz, then, for Martin L. and other survivors he knew, violent revenge would have meant a negation of moral status. Other testimony points in that same direction. For example, in 1991 Violet S. (born in Berehovo, Czechoslovakia, in 1928) recalled, exactly like Martin L., being kept alive during the war by the idea of vengeance after—but then dismissing the possibility because, as she saw it, violent vengeance would have made the Jews no better than those who had persecuted and murdered them.[118] And, from the different perspective of a Jewish GI, George Tievsky (born in New York in 1917) recalled the account of a liberated prisoner at the Allach concentration camp near Munich who set out with others to get payback on one of the most brutal SS guards there—the group then changing their plan after talking through its moral implications.[119]

Ethical concerns were, in fact, the strongest impediment to revenge. Some survivors rejected revenge out of hand, refusing to take the opportunity when it presented itself. Others struggled to define the revenge act's moral boundaries, for the sake of honoring vengeful emotions on the one hand, limiting them so that they were compatible with basic ethical values, on the other hand. Inherited from a civil world before the war, these values may have been shaken, even fundamentally so, by the horror of what followed. But now subjected to scrutiny and reassessment, they were still a presence; confronting them was an important element in survivors' postwar rebuilding of their lives. For some, at stake was preserving the essence of what it meant to be human—and creating essential distance from the fathomless inhumanity that had been witnessed, the dehumanization endured.

Disavowing revenge was both empowering and a sign of coming back to life. On May 27, 1945, in his formative speech addressing liberated Jews hospitalized in the St. Ottilien monastery the medical doctor, survivor of Kovno and Kaufering, and postwar Jewish leader Zalman Grinberg noted the following: "Hitler has lost every battle on every front except the battle against defenseless and unarmed men, women and children. He won the war against the Jews of Europe. He carried out this war with the help of the German nation. However, we do not want revenge. If we took this vengeance," he continued, "it would mean we would fall to the depths of ethics and morals the German nation has been in these past 10 years. We are not able to slaughter women and children! We are not able to burn millions of people! We are not able to starve hundreds of thousands!"[120] This ethical rationale also informed a refusal by a number of survivors—some of them still teenagers at liberation—to give in to an incitement to violence by Allied soldiers. According to Regina Spiegel (née Gutman, born in 1926 in Radom)—she had survived the Radom ghetto, Auschwitz, Bergen-Belsen, and the Elsnig labor camp, a subcamp of Buchenwald—upon liberation by Soviet soldiers in Elsnig, they encouraged her to shoot any German she came across. Spiegel recalled her response: "I didn't like what they were doing to us! So why would I go do that [to them]?"[121] Similarly, in testimony given in 1992, Siegfried Halbreich (born 1909 in Dziedzice, Upper Silesia) who fled Poland for Yugoslavia but was arrested and interned at Sachsenhausen, Gross-Rosen, Auschwitz, and Dora-Mittelbau, noted: "I had occasions to take revenge on the SS, on the Germans, but when I intend to hurt somebody ... my arm refused even to---. My God, why should I hit him? When I hit him am I no better than they? And I wanted to be a better human being."[122]

Accepting the presence of vengeful emotions but overcoming the impulse to act them out restored survivors' sense of dignity, humanity and self-efficacy. In testimony of 1984, Rose K. (born in Sosnowiec, Poland, c.1930) recalled how she and other liberated prisoners refused to take revenge on a guard at the forced labor camp in Oberaltstadt, Sudetenland (today Horní Staré Město in the Czech Republic), a subcamp of Gross-Rosen. In the presence of the captured *Kommandoführerin* Irma (Irmgard) Hoffmann, they were addressed by a Soviet officer as follows: "She is all yours. You take her to your camp, you can kill her with one bullet, you can kill her by cutting her to pieces and putting salt actually on her, punish her in whatever way you feel is suitable to you. So we could get our anger out," Rose K. commented. "And believe me there was still enough hate in our hearts towards that woman." Hoffmann was forced to sit on a chair in the center of the camp's parade-ground, in the presence of 2,000 liberated women and girls; her head was shaved. But aside from that humiliation, she was left unharmed. "[E]ven though we were suffering so, even though we were faced with so much inhumanity, we still had enough value in us for life, we valued life so dearly, it was so precious that we could not take a life. And today I am proud of it that there was still humanity left in us," was Rose K.'s retrospective assessment.[123] This reassertion of one's sense of humanity was connected to the ability to control emotional impulses and to make conscious ethical choices that were guided by empathy. Lothar (Larry) Orbach, who was born in Berlin in 1924 and had survived Auschwitz and Buchenwald, recalled that upon his return to bombed out Berlin, a desperate young German mother with a hungering one-year-old boy approached him begging for food. Although he was haunted by the memory of seeing a guard at Auschwitz "slam the head of a Jewish baby into the wall of a shower room. The baby had died instantly, his brain protruding and his blood spurting," Lothar shared his American ration. "I reached over and coaxed several bite-sized chunks of Spam directly into the child's mouth. He was innocent, this little boy, and I needed to do something to feel that I was still human."[124]

Together with regaining such sense of agency, by confronting the moral dilemma posed by revenge survivors could reaffirm their cultural and religious heritage; they could honor those who had taught and exemplified ethical values in their previous lives. While a teenage prisoner at Buchenwald, Blechhammer, and Flossenbürg, Kurt Klappholz (born in Bielsko-Biała, Poland, in 1927) dreamt about food and revenge. But as he indicated in testimony given in 1995, at liberation he told an American soldier encouraging him to beat up a captured SS man that "I haven't got the strength ... even if I wanted to"—and that in any case he "wouldn't beat anyone who lies defenseless on the ground." Klappholz, then eighteen-years old, had the impression that the soldier, who was probably not much older than Klappholz, ended up feeling "rather ashamed," realizing that he had encountered "an ex-concentration camp inmate who didn't seem to have lost his sense of morality completely."[125] As Klappholz explained this episode retrospectively, he had maintained moral principles his father had instilled in him as a child before the war: not only not to hurt those in a weaker, defenseless position, but also the "futility of revenge, that revenge leads to an endless circle, a never-ending circle." While rejecting the idea of collective responsibility in his testimony, Klappholz's rejection of vengeance was accompanied by sober assessment of the society from which his tormentors had stemmed: ". . . how often was it said about the Germans that having lived under Hitler since 1933, it was not surprising that they should have lost all sense of morality? Well, I think I was a counterexample to that theory of moral behavior. I had spent three years in circumstances that were somewhat worse than those of most Germans, but I hadn't lost all my sense of morality despite the fact that I remained an atheist."[126]

For his part, Norbert Wollheim (born in Berlin in 1913), who had survived both Auschwitz and the Heinkel subcamp of Sachsenhausen, recalled in testimony offered in

Figure 14 Survivors in Dachau berate an SS guard captured by US troops, April 29, 1945. USHMM Photo Archives # 82952; United States Holocaust Memorial Museum, courtesy of National Archives and Records Administration, College Park.

1992 that after escaping from a death march and reaching the US army near Schwerin on May 3, 1945, he and his friends had the opportunity to use weapons that the SS and Wehrmacht had left behind in flight from the Allies. "You could grab them, and you could start your own private war," he recalled. "And if we had ... just killed these ... criminals ... under the circumstances prevailing in these days, nobody would ... have had objections." However: "we didn't do it. It was not part of our education. It was not part of our value system.... we believed that one day there would be justice, and justice should be meted out by the proper authorities."[127] His value system, Wollheim explained, had been shaped by belief in liberal democracy and the rule of law. At Auschwitz, he had befriended a Jewish prisoner, Jakob, who was religiously observant. When Wollheim, whose background was secular, encountered Jacob praying during an hours-long rollcall in icy winds, he asked his friend in suffering how he could praise and thank God in "this hell." Jakob replied: "'I'm thanking God for the fact that he didn't make me like the murderers around us.'"[128] This answer struck a responsive chord with Wollheim, as he shared the same ethical self-understanding. For Wollheim, who had studied law in Germany before he was excluded from the educational system as a Jew, the ability to *not* take revenge on sadists and murderers, even when the opportunity presented itself, was "part ... of the heritage of which I am very, very proud."[129]

Other survivors echoed Wollheim's conviction that whether secular or observant, a rich and unbroken tradition of Jewish ethics offered a foundation for refraining from violent revenge. "Why do I have to have blood on my hands?" asked Abraham Malnik (born in Kovno in 1927) in his testimony of 1990, "Let God punish them."[130] Many other survivors rejected revenge without deferring to divine authority, pointing to an innate moral sense, or childhood socialization, or physical inability and revulsion instead. "I didn't have it in me,"[131] "I couldn't ... I didn't have the heart of revenge in me,"[132] "it's not in my blood,"[133] "we were not animals like ... the Germans were.... We were not cruel. We couldn't do it"[134] were typical explanations. At work here, it seems, was a fundamental humanism confronting the very values that Nazism had rejected and sought to destroy—and an expression of often very conscious strength and moral superiority.

For some Jews the basic ethical dilemma involved *indiscriminate* revenge. While to them revenge seemed legitimate when it came to specific perpetrators, it was morally objectionable if applied to just any German. That was the main issue for some of the most vocal critics of Abba Kovner's Nakam operation, including committed Zionists who had fought in the armed underground like Zivia Lubetkin and Yitzhak Zuckerman.[135] For Zuckerman (born in Vilna in 1915), as he explains in his Warsaw ghetto chronicle, Kovner's plan for indiscriminate revenge amounted to "perverse romanticism, which totally unhinged a few people."[136] Killing a few thousand Germans indiscriminately would not only have achieved nothing for Jewish survivors but would also have betrayed Jewish ethical principles. "I absolutely refused to support ... things like poisoning wells, rivers and such. Even after everything the Germans had done to us, Jewish humanism couldn't be destroyed. I wouldn't have taken part in 'blind' operations against masses, acts of collective revenge.[...] The mass activities that were prepared weren't a response; they were just stooping to the level of the enemy. That was craziness."[137] While Zuckerman grappled with how to deal with his anger, it was clear to him that "I'm not willing to kill every German indiscriminately. I don't hate every German; but I have to know who the person is."¹³⁸ Retribution was thus not out of the question; but it had to be individualized, based on knowledge of personal wrongdoing.

The idea of such limitation resonated with many survivors: "I think Moll—I would have liked—to—to kill," said Paul P. (born in Mikulov, Czechoslovakia in 1925) in his testimony. Paul P. was a survivor of Theresienstadt, Auschwitz, and its subcamp Gleiwitz I; he was referring to SS-Hauptscharführer Otto Moll (1915–1946), a notorious killer and torturer.¹³⁹ Paul P. was of course speaking in the abstract, looking back at his younger self's relationship to revenge—he was twenty-years old at the war's end. Moll had supervised the Jewish prisoner Sonderkommandos at the burning pits of Auschwitz-Birkenau (among other functions) and was later commandant of Gleiwitz I. "You know, the whole thing of revenge was very difficult for us, but Moll – it would have been a pleasure. He was extremely sadistic. He, he kicked people very, very hard. He beat people. He . . . I saw, I saw him shoot people and Moll, it would have been a pleasure. With other people, it was always problematic, you know. You [would] always at the last moments say, did he really do it?"¹⁴⁰ To be sure, Paul P.'s openness to vengeance in this particular case remained theoretical—Moll would be sentenced to death by an American military court at Dachau for his actions in Dachau's Kaufering subcamps and hanged at Landsberg in May 1946.¹⁴¹

As historian Yehuda Bauer observed, "the survivors had neither the tools to track down criminals nor to set up a clandestine judicial system and carry out judgments; at most, they could strike at groups of criminals, such as SS men in captivity. It seems in any case that would-be avengers were mainly deterred by the fact that they would be attacking individuals whose guilt was unproven."¹⁴² Jewish actors may have viewed Germans, as a collective, as morally deficient—as fully complicit in the destruction of their families and of the Jewish people; at the same time, they may have recognized that individuals within that collective needed to be treated as human beings, judged individually for guilt or innocence. From both an emotional and ethical standpoint, the dilemma this could pose was not easily resolvable. We see an extreme form of the dilemma in Meyer Levin's discussion of sexual assault on German women—and his personal confrontation with that possibility. For Levin, "in war there is a reversal of the general code of the community of men" as it is "right to kill, and with this sanction comes a compulsion to reverse all the other civilized injunctions: to steal, lie, blaspheme, and rape."¹⁴³ Levin consequently considered taking personal revenge on a German woman through rape. His descriptions of German women, in general, were full of contempt and resentment; they also reflected a male conqueror's patriarchal gaze. The contempt was grounded, for him, in what he saw as a "willingness to be violated"¹⁴⁴ by those who had taken power, as a "lustful eagerness of the German girls to fulfill their roles as conquered women."¹⁴⁵ This, Levin believed, "frustrated the victorious soldier's rage for vengeful release of all his guilts"; as a result, he wrote, "every man in the area felt within himself a kind of approbation for the tales of genuine rape." Although American GIs "outwardly expressed abhorrence" for the large-scale sexual assaults on German women by Red Army soldiers, they inwardly might have empathized, approved, and have wished to do the same—and many did.[146]

"We were no different from the others," Levin noted, referring to himself and his friend Erik: a French Jewish survivor and former member of the French resistance—with whom Levin pursued a plan of raping a random German woman. "Like all men, we wondered about ourselves—how far could we go, in war? of what were we capable? . . . Erik had infinitely greater motivation for revenge; my own bitterness was general—a bitterness for what the Germans had done to my people; Erik's was personal, for what they had done to himself and his family."[147] But once they pursued a young woman in April 1945, they were both unable to follow through with their plan:

> She was beginning to show her fright. This was in a sense exciting, and yet within ourselves we began to feel entirely false. We struggled with the moment. It was a sunny day, clear, warm. [. . .] All we did was to roar at her to get the hell back where she came from. She mounted her bike, turned, and wheeled off. When we drove away we could scarcely look at each other. The tension had been terrible. We realized we simply hadn't been able to do it. It wasn't in us.[148]

On a later occasion, this time without his friend Erik, Levin again could not act out his revenge fantasy—although the targeted woman in fact turned out to be a staunch Nazi.[149] For Levin, then, at this time, there was a struggle between wanting revenge and not wanting to be violent, on a concrete level between seeking revenge on a German woman, even a Nazi, and not wanting, in the end, to commit a rape.[150]

Levin's male gaze upon German women at the end of the war can be contrasted with the female gaze of Yaffa U. (born in 1927 in Švenčionys, Poland, presently Lithuania) in testimony given in 1995. Shortly after her liberation from a death march from Stutthof in March 1945, Yaffa U. and other Jewish women were taken in by a German family in a village near Landsberg (Prussia, today Górowo Iławeckie in Poland) where they were given food and a place to sleep. At night a group of roughly twenty inebriated Red Army soldiers entered the house and raped the women. Yaffa and the other Jews were spared because of their emaciation and their telling the soldiers they were persecuted Jews infected with typhus. But they witnessed the rape of the three German women in the house—two sisters and their elderly mother. Shocked, fearful, and helpless, Yaffa felt torn: between solidarity—as a woman—with the German women on the one hand, knowing that she and her companions were spared through sheer luck and could suffer the same fate any time; and, on the other hand, an inclination to see this as deserved payback, the Russians' expression of justified hatred, as a Jew who had barely escaped murder by the Germans: "It was very unpleasant," Yaffa U. recalled, "the German women – could not even stand on their feet afterwards – and for me that was something – I saw for the first time in my life, such, such – orgies or what we may call this. On the one hand, I thought 'this is the revenge!' but – [on the other hand] revenge should be taken on the SS men. But – on private individuals, it was – a bit – inappropriate . . ."[151] The fear of rape is a common theme in female survivor testimony.[152] Jewish women often convey a sense that gender-based violence of the postwar moment turned all women into spoils of war, whether they were Germans, Jews or female personnel of the Allied armed forces, at times leading to empathy and acts of solidarity among women.[153] For some women, like Jaffa U., it meant letting go of desires for revenge.

Other survivors overcame revenge for different reasons. After weeks of emotional limbo between the urge for violent vengeance and a reluctance to inflict it on a random German individual, Elly Gotz decided: "I could not hate a whole people – hating that way was what Hitler had taught!"[154] At age seventeen, he was well read in European and Jewish literature in German, Yiddish, Lithuanian, and Russian. As a younger teenager he had read Goethe, Schiller, Heine, Tolstoy, and Dostoyevsky in the Kovno ghetto library; this had in his view shaped his ethical thinking.[155] Looking back in 2023, at the age of ninety-five, Gotz put it as follows in an interview: "I don't think I could have really killed a person consciously, but I could have killed him when I was full of hate. So, thank God, I didn't find the gun. But there's no question in my mind that moral teaching does something to help you overcome hate."[156] For Gotz, then, that capacity emerged from a Jewish and broader European ethical tradition. At least implicitly, Primo Levi offered a similar explanation when asked in the 1980s if he hated the Germans: "I regard hatred as bestial and crude, and prefer that my actions and thoughts be the product, as far as possible, of reason. Much less do I accept hatred directed collectively at an ethnic group, for example at all the Germans. If I accepted it, I would feel that I was following the precepts of Nazism, which was founded precisely on national and racial hatred." Levi then added the following guarded caveat: "I must admit that if I had in front of me one of our persecutors of those days, certain known faces, certain old lies, I would be tempted to hate, and with violence too; but exactly because I am not a fascist or a Nazi, I refuse to give way to this temptation."[157]

Ultimately, letting go of revenge was itself a kind of liberation, allowing survivors to turn from the past toward the present and the future. In this respect, it is impossible to separate the sense of basic morality many of them articulated, looking back, from a sense of both dignity and triumph over their would-be murders. We see this, for instance, in a summing up offered by Aryeh Sandowski (Leibek) in a reminiscence appearing in 1991; Sandowski had escaped from Poland for Yishuv Palestine just before the war's outbreak, but returned to Europe as a Jewish Brigade volunteer to fight the Nazis—and avenge the murder of his family and European Jewry.[158] "We have not allowed Hitler to enjoy a posthumous victory over us," he stated. "We have shown that the misery, cruelty, despair and injustice that were inflicted on us did not break our indomitable spirit. We have not become consumed with hatred to the point of destroying our own and other people's lives. We did not become terrorists; we did not kill innocent people; we did not even pursue or kill our persecutors."[159] Some survivors directly tied such a second liberation to abandonment of a search for some form of direct payback: a decision that, for Eva Mozes Kor, itself constituted a form of revenge: Josef Mengele had subjected Kor and her twin sister to his sadistic medical experiments on Jewish twins in Auschwitz; she openly declared nothing less than forgiveness for such criminals—for the sake of, precisely, liberating herself from them.[160] This can be seen as an idiosyncratic form of a general

Jewish Revenge and the Holocaust

pattern, a reluctance of survivors to debase themselves by behaving—in any sense whatsoever—like their former Nazi persecutors. But for a considerable number of survivors, such conscious abnegation of *violent* revenge was accompanied by other modes of payback that were very much active, while, as concrete actions and gestures, also possessing symbolic import to varying degrees.

Realms of Non-Violent Vengeance

Some survivors channeled an enduring desire for vengeance into actions that did not inflict direct physical pain or bodily harm. Rather, the damage was meant to be psychological, a humiliation itself inverting the victim-perpetrator relationship through a diminishing of perpetrators' sense of power, moral status, and material and emotional well-being—as well as a negation of their ability to control both the victims' testimony about what had happened and tied to this, the truth about the crimes that had been committed. The actions involved here were profoundly personal, as was the degree of emotional benefit that the avengers would gain. These forms of non-violent action centered around a specific symbolic meaning: that Jewish survival and continuity were themselves revenge on those who had tried to totally destroy European Jewry.

Especially immediately after the war, Jewish survivors had conflicted emotions concerning their personal survival. Many had a severe sense of guilt for having survived while loved ones had not, and a sense that survival lacked meaning, that there was little purpose in staying alive after such destruction and loss. It would take decades for many survivors—and also those around them—to speak of survival in positive terms. Gradually, though, pride in survival surfaced, guilt, shame, and feelings of marginalization began to recede.[161] The pace of this change had much to do with both public interest in the Holocaust and personal biography. Many testimonies capture the subjects' changing relationship to survival from a sense of despair in the early postwar years to valuing survival itself in later decades.[162] But even early on, there was some solace in knowledge of continued existence of the Jewish collective and its culture—albeit largely outside of Europe, in Israel and the United States. Individual survival gained purpose when seen as part of a larger struggle for survival of the Jewish people. In this way, non-violent revenge constituted a symbolic expression of the power of life as payback for massive death—something that sometimes emerges in survivors' testimony on a level of more or less spontaneous assertion.[163] Acts of revenge of this sort were meant, on one level, to foreground a failure in the Nazi project of a "world without Jews"; they were meant to catalyze distress among Nazi perpetrators by signaling failure, powerlessness, and disgrace.[164]

Jewish Presence in the "judenfrei" German Living Space

Since the Nazi regime had sought to make the German Reich "Jew-free," *judenfrei*, marking a Jewish presence in a defeated Germany emerged as one avenue of revenge. On a basic level, there was certainly emotional satisfaction in having lived to see Nazi Germany defeated, Germany destroyed, the Germans weak, demoralized, and subservient under Allied occupation. But the encounter with Germans and Germany was in any case painful and charged with ambivalence—no vengeful glee could balance off grief and pain, and, for many, deep unease at simply having to *be* in that country. For the circa 300,000 Jewish DPs temporarily living in the western zones of occupation between 1945 and 1949, the reasons for being in Germany involved a mix of involuntary wartime displacement, postwar flight from antisemitic violence in eastern Europe to relative safety in this Allied-occupied country, political and economic restrictions in countries now under Soviet rule, and hope for eventual migration elsewhere: to America; to Yishuv Palestine until May 14, 1948, and Israel thereafter. Whatever the reasons for their presence in the land of the murderers, some Jews derived some satisfaction, a certain degree of Schadenfreude, from seeing that presence itself as a form of revenge.

In early 1946, poet, partisan, and Vilna ghetto survivor Abraham Sutzkever came to Germany from Moscow to testify as one of three Jewish witnesses at Nuremberg. Everything about the people and the landscape reminded him of the mass murder he, his family, community and people had witnessed and suffered. "We flew over Germany. Its villages—red-colored, two-story houses. The plane descends even further. In every village—a red-brick church in the style of the Middle Ages. Everything is red, saturated with our blood,"[165] he noted in his diary. He offered his impression of an inn-keeper and her child while having a meal at a beer house in Herzfelde, near Berlin, as follows: "A blond Germanic beast of a woman with an irritatingly ugly false smile brings us mugs of beer. Her name is Frau Schulze. A three-year-old child is playing with a doll nearby. The three-year-old is already a German girl down to the smallest detail. Her eyes cut through me as if they were a knife. How many Jewish children were incarcerated and strangled with a smile by such younger and older Schulzes!"[166] Both Sutzkever's newborn baby and wife had been murdered in the Vilna ghetto. Upon arrival in Berlin, Sutzkever observed: "It's not long ago that the brown plague frolicked here. In the ghetto it was hard for me to imagine myself ever setting foot here one day."[167] The inn where he was spending the night had a sign with the inscription *Die Sonne mit uns*, "may the sun be shining on us"; playing phonetically on German *Sonne* and English "Zone," he commented: "as if the Germans knew that there would be a zone—a Soviet zone, an American zone, and others."[168] But later, no irony: "I fall into bed. My tears are choking me."[169] Over the following days, Sutzkever recorded that he was finding some solace in seeing Berlin's destruction, especially: "The city center is a ruin. The American and British pilots were artists."[170] For Sutzkever, the poet, there was some beauty in the destruction:

> The paved streets are almost entirely intact – the brick buildings were reduced to rubble and lie agape on the side of the road. We come to the famous Brandenburg Gate. Hitler held his parades here. A vast emptiness all around. Amid the nothingness – ruins. Alexanderplatz still has something of its former grandeur and looks like an old, worn-out whore who is still trying to look young. The Tiergarten, Frankfurter Allee are a wreck, full of debris. Capsized boats obstruct the Spree.

But then: "A pleasant ruin has been made of you, Berlin! But it's not enough. May you be cursed for all eternity and never rise again! [...] I would not care at all if not a trace was left of this land and its people."[171]

In their everyday interactions with defeated and occupied Germans, some Jewish survivors gained a sense of revenge by observing them carry out quotidian cleaning and service chores, especially if these involved emasculation: for instance German men sweeping floors and cleaning latrines, but also digging graves for the corpses of Nazi victims.[172] In her testimony of May 1990, Susan F. (born in Berlin in 1919) put it as follows: "So they had to dig graves and carry them in their arms, the skeletons, and bury them. That was a wonderful view. Wonderful to look at. If I hate? Did I want revenge? Yes, I do."[173] Moishe Rutschaisky was very aware of and gratified by the humiliation involved in a former Dachau SS guard, now in American custody, cleaning the floors at the site of his previous reign of terror, chasing every cigarette butt that the GIs threw on the ground. Looking back, Rutschaisky expressed it bluntly: "The SS who used to be my guards now cleaned my room. So the satisfaction was so big."[174]

Some survivors effected the reversal of power-relations, exacted non-violent revenge, through open mockery; others by taking over—or taking back—pleasant, functional apartments inhabited by known Nazis. An episode recounted in the testimony of Julius O. (born in Schwarzenborn in 1923) combined both these things: After liberation from Theresienstadt, Julius O. returned to Kassel, where he had lived with his family before their deportation to the Riga ghetto in November 1941. One day, on encountering the German woman who had to vacate her apartment for him, he greeted her with "Heil Hitler"; when she reflexively responded by raising her arm, he laughed at her saying "you can't get rid of it, can you?" Julius O. also recalled mockingly confronting the officials in the local municipal administration who, having harassed him a few years earlier, now greeted him with servile friendliness.[175]

When it came to non-violent revenge, consensual sexual relationships with German women had deeply symbolic import, defying and mocking the anti-miscegenation ideology and practice embodied in the Nuremberg Laws and countless "race defilement" lawsuits, with its everyday expression, before the mass deportations to ghettos and death camps began, as public shaming. Now some young German women were entering into relations with Jewish men; for young male survivors, the sex involved served as a tool for regaining and expressing a sense of vitality, making up for years of deprived youth.[176] Mocking Nazi symbols had a similar life-affirming quality; such mockery could move from a realm of real revenge, in confrontation with living Germans, to its symbolic enactment for a Jewish audience. At the first postwar celebration of the Purim holiday (March 16-17, 1946), survivors in displaced persons camps across Germany dressing up as Adolf Hitler and Joseph Goebbels at public celebrations and Purim plays and marches. They prepared effigies, posters, and cartoons of Hitler behind prison bars or hanged and mock tombstones to mark his death and the collapse of the Nazi regime.[177] Hence on the occasion of a joyful holiday celebrating Jewish endurance in face of oppression and murderous threat, survivors aligned the ancient villain Haman

From Wartime Desire to Postwar Fantasy

Figure 15 Mock tombstone for Adolf Hitler, Landsberg, Purim 1946; Yad Vashem Archives # 1486/1431; courtesy of Yad Vashem Archives.

with Hitler.[178] Where back then, in the mythic account, mass killing had been averted with the help of Jewish heroine Esther, now at least a small portion of Europe's Jewish collective had survived an actual, transnational genocide. "Why didn't I remember the downfall of my grandfather Haman and not get involved with the Jews?" read a Purim poster with a caricature of Hitler. It also featured a short Yiddish rhyme echoing the words, from the German national anthem, "Deutschland, Deutschland über alles" as *"daytshland, daytshland iber ales, itst hob ikh di mapole mitn doles"* / "Germany, Germany above all, now there's downfall and destitution."

Purim celebrations at Landsberg—where one of the largest Jewish DP camps was located—also included a public burning of *Mein Kampf* and posters depicting it. This was a form of payback for the Nazi book burning of May 1933, when Nazi students burned, notoriously, works condemned by the regime or by authors considered its enemies, among them many Jews. But this symbolic gesture also derived force from the fact that twenty-two years earlier, Hitler had been confined in the nearby Landsberg prison, where he had written *Mein Kampf*. Now the prison held Nazi war criminals

Figure 16 Photograph of a banner in the Landsberg DP camp with a cartoon illustration of Hitler hung during a celebration of the Purim holiday, 1946–1948. Includes an acrostic to Haman's name, a caption about Hitler not remembering his grandfather Haman, and another mocking the German national anthem "Deutschland über alles." USHMM Photo Archives # 69498; United States Holocaust Memorial Museum, courtesy of Rita Friedman Hattem.

awaiting trial; soon it would serve as the execution site for those sentenced to death at the Nuremberg trials.[179]

Repurposing and reappropriation of property and institutions held great symbolic meaning for survivors as it meant retroactively negating the Nazi regime's ideological-political goals. In Munich survivors reappropriated the printing plant of the *Völkischer Beobachter*, the Nazi party organ; the plant was now responsible for producing Jewish DP newspapers.[180] Jewish DPs also came together in places in and around Munich holding symbolic meaning for Nazism, for example at the German Museum and the Bürgerbräukeller, the beer hall where Hitler initiated his failed putsch against the Weimar Republic in 1923.[181] A group of 150 young survivors—many of them orphans who had found surrogate families in peers and youth leaders—reappropriated the Pleikershof, Julius Streicher's 350-acre farm outside of Fürth, maintaining it as an agricultural training farm, now called Kibbutz Nili in preparation for—Bricha and Yishuv assisted, at the time illegal—emigration to Palestine and future farming there.[182] The young survivors on the kibbutz saw working Streicher's land as symbolic revenge; they used Hebrew words for the estate's buildings and named the guard dog "Julius".[183] Streicher was himself now sitting in the dock at Nuremberg, soon to be sentenced to death for incitement to crimes

From Wartime Desire to Postwar Fantasy

Figure 17 Jewish DPs dress up as Hitler and Goebbels for a Purim play at the Feldafing displaced persons camp, 1946–1948; USHMM Photo Archives # 39919; United States Holocaust Memorial Museum, courtesy of Allen Rezak.

against humanity in his *Stürmer*. Other survivors set up similar kibbutzim, for example Kibbutz Buchenwald, where former prisoners in that concentration camp trained as agricultural laborers on a farm in Egdorf, near Weimar. One of the motivations had been to channel the youths' desire for revenge on Germans into a symbolic realm and provide them with education, labor, and community.[184] Immediately before Thuringia became part of the Soviet zone of occupation, they moved to a farm in Gehringshof near Fulda, in the US Zone. Here too, staying on "blood-soaked" German soil had an intended symbolic dimension in preparing for life and sovereignty in Palestine.[185]

Figure 18 Poster displayed in the Landsberg DP camp, decorated with an image of two Jews throwing a copy of *Mein Kampf* into the fire after having painted a tombstone with the inscription, "Here is buried Adolf Hitler, may his name be blotted out." The caption on the bottom reads, "His legacy to the German People," Landsberg, 1946–1948; USHMM Photo Archives # 69492; United States Holocaust Memorial Museum, courtesy of Rita Friedman Hattem.

Survival and Nation-Building

For many Jewish DPs, who, wherever they ended up immigrating, overwhelmingly supported Zionism, the idea of statehood for Jews in Palestine contained an element of symbolic vengeance. In December 1945, Selimar Frenkel (aka Shlomo Shafir, born in Berlin in 1924), editor of the Zionist DP newspaper *Nitzotz*—a continuation of his underground paper that circulated in the Kovno ghetto and the Dachau subcamp Kaufering—summarized that particular symbolic dimension along with other forms of vengeance as follows: "Of course we were not considering revenge proper: an eye for an eye and a tooth for a tooth. We sought to take revenge on our enemies through disparagement, rejection, banning and keeping our distance rather than in acts of vengeance that could only bring gross instinctual satisfaction to the individual." Ultimately, Frenkel argued, only separating from the Nazi perpetrators and their collaborators among the European nations will "satisfy our desire for vengeance which in essence means: doing away with the European exile and building our homeland in the Land of Israel."[186] As forced laborers, POWs, concentration and labor camp prisoners of other nationalities returned to their home countries, repatriated by the Allies in the course of 1945, Jewish survivors, especially those from eastern Europe, often refused repatriation. They saw no possibility for homecoming. Their families had been murdered, their communities annihilated en masse; neighbors had taken over their apartments, stores, and possessions; although some compatriots had been helpers and rescuers of Jews, most had been indifferent or even complicit in Jewish suffering—or worse. Survivors who did return, looking for surviving relatives, hoping to rebuild where they once belonged, often decided to leave because of enduring antisemitism, economic hardship, and growing political repression from new communist regimes. Zionism had a distinct appeal to Jewish survivors on the move in postwar Europe because it provided a "usable past," a vision of the future, and a guideline for the present—one based on the principle that Jews could not live in the Diaspora unharmed and would only be safe through sovereignty over a piece of their historic land. Based on that principle, DPs and other survivors could join the Zionist movement, fight for political recognition of a sovereign state, and help in its construction.

The message at work here offered tremendous emotional and existential ballast, both the Yishuv and the project of a Jewish state providing a surrogate family for survivors orphaned in every possible way. Symbolic revenge was part of this equation. "The survival of many Holocaust victims had defeated the Nazi goal of blotting the Jewish people out of history; the renewal of Jewish life in Eretz Israel was emblematic of the true vengeance against the murderers," historian Hanna Yablonka has noted. "Thus, moving to Israel and achieving personal rehabilitation along with the national resurrection, provided therapeutic qualities that also had qualities of revenge—the revenge of resurrection."[187] Thus Jewish DP leaders urged the survivor population to channel their pain, grief, and anger, indeed their desire for revenge, into creative forces and toward productive ends and—through education and cultural and political activism—build a continued, life-affirming, self-sufficient existence in a sovereign state. Samuel Gringauz (1900–1975), chairman of the Landsberg displaced persons camp, himself a survivor of the Kovno ghetto and Dachau-Kaufering, urged young survivors on the occasion of the Yom Kippur holiday in September 1945, *not* to live in a state of "memory and sorrow" but rather to "live and build, work and liberate" themselves. Quoting a line from Chaim Nachman Bialik's famous 1903 poem—"Satan has not yet created a fitting revenge for the blood of a small child"[188]— Gringauz emphasized what he saw as a befitting revenge for the German attempt to wipe out Jewish existence altogether: living, and living a productive, self-determined life. "[Y]ou, our young people," he stated, "are the agents of our revenge which ought to be a proud assertion to continue life. You must readily show the world and all our enemies that despite everything we are here to stay. Your revenge must be in working and toiling for your own land. You must create and build, dance and sing, open yourselves to life, to living and labor."[189]

Many survivors felt that this affirmation of life on a personal and collective, national, level and with it their support for Zionist project of a sovereign state constituted an obligation toward the dead. In the words of Abraham Sutzkever, "It was the martyrs' dream that Jewish life be rebuilt in the land of Israel." Mourning the death of his mother and child and the destruction of Jewish Vilna, the "Jerusalem of the North," Sutzkever saw the only recompense for the enormous loss of life and culture in national rebuilding;

"the greatest revenge against the murderers of our people will be when we will secure our own free Jerusalem," he noted in May 1944.[190] In his Eichmann trial testimony, Aharon Beilin explained that before his mother was murdered in Auschwitz, she had made him promise that if he survived, he would go to Palestine. "And ... I kept my obligation ... And I think I owe [it] to all the mothers who were taken before their time, and to all the children who were snatched from their mothers for destruction, for annihilation."[191] Thus for Beilin, as for Sutzkever, Gringauz and many other survivors in the postwar moment, building the Jewish state proved that the Nazi project had failed. The practical reality of this quest for building however meant being thrust into yet another war which resulted in continued armed conflict.

In 1948, some survivors who had been members of ghetto undergrounds and partisan units saw a direct continuity between fighting to survive the Nazis and military action on behalf of the newly-proclaimed, UN-sanctioned state. Survivors who had recently come from Europe made up one fourth of Israel's troops during the 1948 War against Arab forces trying to destroy that state at the start.[192] Some soldiers with that traumatic

Figure 19 A survivor dressed up as Hitler in the Landsberg DP camp, Purim 1946; Yad Vashem Photo Archives # 1486/698; courtesy of Yad Vashem Archives.

background now transferred their negative emotions about Germans onto the Arab enemy combatants. Abba Kovner, who served as an education officer in the Givati Brigade in the Negev, stated that fighting the Egyptian army felt like fighting the Nazis.[193] Kovner's perspective changed in the course of the war, as he developed empathy for the Palestinian refugees uprooted by what Palestinians came to call the *Nakba*, "catastrophe," which as a result of both expulsion and flight permanently displaced some 750,000 Palestinians from the territory that would become the State of Israel. Within the Israeli public a widespread perception emerged that the Nazis of yesterday and Arab neighbors of today constituted a single, timeless "Amalek," not least because of the wartime connections between the Palestinian national leader and Mufti of Jerusalem Haj Amin al-Hussaini and Adolf Hitler.[194] That notwithstanding, understanding Israel's ensuing conflict with the Palestinians and the Arab world solely through the lens of "displaced revenge" for the *Holocaust*, or "redirected aggression"—from the Nazis onto the Jews and from the Jews onto the Palestinians—seems facile and misleading as it opens the door to "Holocaust inversion" which equates Israel with Nazi Germany.[195] It appears to reflect more a psychological explanation than a grounded historical judgment. Moreover a deterministic interpretation that would explain Israel's conflict with the Palestinians and the Arab world as "Holocaust revenge" ignores the real existential threats that the Jewish state has faced since its proclamation even as it has gained military power built on deterrence and has come to dominate and victimize Palestinians as an occupying force and settler society in the West Bank; it also ignores historical contingency and deprives the Palestinian side of all political agency in this conflict. While the complex history of the Israeli-Palestinian conflict and Israel's relations with the Arab world is beyond the scope of this book, what matters in our context is the shift, in the early postwar Zionist project, from revenge on "Amalek" in Germany to a symbolic form of revenge focused on Jewish continuity: through nation-building and—in both Israel and the diaspora—reproduction.[196]

Survival and Reproduction

Jewish demography became an avenue for symbolic revenge. The Nazi regime had targeted and murdered 1.5 million Jewish children, the aim being to assure that there would be no Jewish future. Heinrich Himmler, Otto Ohlendorf, and other mass murderers had explicitly rationalized the murder of children as a guarantee that no Jews would we left to take future revenge on Germans.

For many Jewish survivors, having children was integral to post-traumatic recovery. Children symbolized Jewish continuity and healing. Historian Atina Grossmann has tied the fact that during the Nazi genocide, pregnant Jewish women and mothers were murdered with their children upon arrival at the death camps, and that loss of menstruation among female camp inmates sparked fears of infertility, to the essential role played by motherhood and childbearing in survivors' recovery from trauma. Marriage and reproduction affirmed survival—but they also served as a personal, family-centered form of symbolic revenge.[197] "There was a kind of in-your-face quality to Jewish

Figure 20 Young mothers take their infants for a stroll in the Landsberg DP camp, *c.*1948; USHMM Photo Archives # 96460; United States Holocaust Memorial Museum, courtesy of Dorit Mandelbaum.

mothers brandishing their babies," Grossmann observes about Jewish DPs, "just as there was to the Zionist banners flying from former German official buildings or the posters carried in processions and parades through German towns."[198] There was a baby boom among Jewish DPs in postwar Germany; it mirrored the negative birth rate of non-Jewish Germans.[199] Here, we can consider reproduction, in its affirmation of life—in its move from harming perpetrators toward enriching the lives of surviving victims—as a distinctly female approach to vengeance. Among members of the Nakam group, women were the first to leave behind the idea of suicidal revenge—namely making the pursuit of a phantasmagoric revenge plot to rectify the traumatic past the center of life and accepting that one might die along the way—for the sake of focusing, instead, on the present and the future by establishing new families and building a nurturing environment for raising children in a Jewish state.[200]

Even past the immediate postwar years, some survivors continued to refer to their families, sometimes humorously, as a type of revenge.[201] In the presence of two sons, their wives, and eight grandchildren, Esther Raab (née Estera Terner, born in Chełm in 1922), a Sobibor survivor, put it as follows in testimony offered in 1997:

> When I look around and I think back what we both went through, it's unbelievable to me that we are here and that we have so much to show for all our misery and suffering that we went through. And I think this, that we both survived and built a

new family, and a new generation, is the biggest revenge that we could take on the Nazis, because they didn't kill us. We started—again. And we were strong and we felt that we wanted to prove to ourselves that we could make it if we are here. And we made it. And we are proud of it. I have a very nice husband. I have beautiful children every one of them. And we are very proud of them. And that's our biggest revenge.[202]

Esther's husband Irving Raab (Izaak, aka Yitzhak, born in 1918 in Wojslawice), who fled the German occupation of Poland into the interior of the Soviet Union, explained that he became "anxious to have the first child" when he understood, returning to Poland from the Soviet Union shortly after the war, that he was the sole survivor of his entire family. Knowing that he had "nobody" he felt the desire that "someone would *be*."[203]

In a PBS documentary broadcast in 2019, the writer and artist Samuel Willenberg (born in Częstochowa in 1923; died in 2016), the longest-living survivor of Treblinka, stated that the death camp never left him; it was with him wherever he went. But sitting alongside his wife Ada (née Lubelczyk, born in Warsaw in 1929, who survived by escaping the Warsaw ghetto and going into hiding) he expressed similar sentiments to those of Esther Raab: "We are alive. We are still alive. . . . My greatest revenge is that I created a beautiful loving family. The best revenge is to have a good life."[204]

Survival and Witnessing

Non-violent revenge also found expression in survivors' gathering of evidence of Nazi atrocities: for the historical record; for the courtroom; to publicly identify the murderers; and to preserve the memory of the victims from erasure.[205] The Holocaust was a crime meant to have no living witnesses among the victims and to leave no traces of evidence. Truth-telling and documentation thus had powerful meaning for survivors; it constituted a form of non-violent revenge that reconnected with earlier cultural traditions. The Russian Jewish historian Simon Dubnow noted, writing in Berlin in 1923 under the impression of the massive pogroms that had occurred in the Ukraine following World War I, that the "Jewish intellect cannot relate to the thought of the ancient Roman poet: 'May you arise an avenger from our bones!'[206] Our only revenge is – to eternalize the atrocities in history." For Dubnow, inscribing atrocities "on the black tablet of Jewish history is the severest moral punishment"[207] that Jews mete out against their oppressors. Dubnow himself remained true to this rationale until he was shot in the Riga ghetto in 1941 and this approach widely resonated among European Jews. In early 1942, an anonymous contributor to Emanuel Ringelblum's Oyneg Shabbes archive already noted that not only was writing a form of self-preservation in the face of persecution and mass murder, but the simple record of unimaginable atrocities, the compiled evidence, would "when the time comes—and it surely will—let the world read and know what the murderers have done." It would allow surviving Jews to mourn the dead and would serve as "the avenger's strongest substance when he comes to accounts" with the perpetrators. The anonymous writer believed that the "unswerving, stalwart avenger" would in the end arrive and that recording the truth was a way to "support him with all our might, help him even if it means paying with our own, today all too cheap, lives."[208]

After the war, survivors across Europe chronicled the atrocities they had endured and witnessed.[209] In April 1945, in an article published in Lodz, one of the pioneers of Jewish Holocaust documentation, the Polish Jewish historian Philip Friedman, called on the "surviving remnant," the She'erit Hapletah in postwar Poland to see to this task. Friedman empathized with the complex emotions that survivors were experiencing, in particular their pain, loss, and urge for revenge. Friedman made a strong case that documentation of Nazi crimes *was* in fact a form of revenge on the perpetrators, a way of avenging the dead. "Those future generations will at some point ask: What did they do, the Surviving Remnant, so as to renew the life of our Jewish people, to exact revenge for the suffering of their millions murdered?" Every survivor had the duty to write and "fulfill the commandment of 'tell thy son'"; this was "the demand of our dearest and closest when the bestial hangmen delivered them to bloody murder. Until today, their blood screams at us from under the earth: 'Do not remain silent! Take revenge!' And how do we take revenge?" To answer his question, Friedman urged survivors to prepare "a large accusation file" documenting the Nazi crimes. "The shadows of our murdered brothers, the ruins of our destroyed, burned down houses and ghettos demand and cry out: Take revenge! And you shall tell your son! Every Jew is obliged to fulfill his historic duty: one, by testifying; another, by bringing documents and photographs; a third, by showing where historical materials can be found, and on and on."[210] In various ways, other survivors as well conveyed a sense that confronting the Germans with the horrors they had inflicted, simultaneously a demonstration that despite Nazi intentions, there were indeed living witnesses, was a form of vengeance. One example is offered in the testimony of Norman Salsitz, whose above-mentioned defiant resistance during the war was spurred forward into postwar self-awareness by revenge imperatives from both his parents: by his father yelling 'revenge!' before he was shot; and by his mother writing him a letter before deportation, urging him to stay alive, in part to inform others—his brothers in the US and Palestine, the wider world—of the Nazi genocide. Salsitz foregrounded his mother's imperative, in particular, as the reason for testifying: "This is why I am sitting here and why I am going out and I talk and talk and talk. This is my mother's legacy. I have to tell and retell the stories. Because if we wouldn't tell the stories someone else would write it for us and it will be all wrong."[211]

Confronting Germans who claimed not to have known or seen, who viewed themselves as victims (of the Nazi regime; the war; the defeat and Allied occupation), not allowing them to focus on their own hardships—in oblivion of the horrors they had caused to others—and move on with their lives, was a mission for many survivors. In his 1963 account *La tregua* (published in English as *The Truce* in 1965), Primo Levi describes his odyssey, following liberation from Auschwitz, via Soviet-controlled Poland, Ukraine, Belorussia, Rumania, Slovakia, Hungary, Austria, and Germany, to his hometown Turin, an odyssey endured through most of 1945. He relates his emotion when passing through Germany in mid-October of that year as follows: "As I wandered around the streets of Munich, full of ruins, near the station where our train lay stranded once more, I felt I was moving among throngs of insolvent debtors, as if everybody owed me something, and refused to pay." Levi further comments,

> We felt we had something to say, enormous things to say, to every single German, and we felt that every German should have something to say to us; we felt an urgent need to settle our accounts, to ask, explain and comment, like chess players at the end of a game. Did "they" know about Auschwitz, about the silent daily massacre, a step away from their doors? If they did, how could they walk about, return home and look at their children, cross the threshold of a church? If they did not, they ought, as a sacred duty, to listen, to learn everything, immediately, from us, from me; I felt the tattooed number on my arm burning like a sore.

But in this respect, Levi had to grapple with disappointment. "The men," he indicates

> were few, many were mutilated, many dressed in rags like us. I felt that everybody should interrogate us, read in our faces who we were, and listen to our tale in humility. But no one looked us in the eyes, no one accepted the challenge; they were deaf, blind and dumb, imprisoned in their ruins, as in a fortress of willful ignorance, still strong, still capable of hatred and contempt, still prisoners of their old tangle of pride and guilt.[212]

The labor of vengeance or account-settling that Levi wished for, confronting Germans with their crimes through the spoken and written word, would be a very long-term, and to be sure incomplete project.

Survival and Justice-Seeking

For some European Jews who had managed to live through the war and then became active in identifying Nazi war criminals, bringing them to trial, and testifying against them was itself a form of revenge. Jean Améry explained how this process unfolded for him: he refused to use retaliatory violence against Nazi perpetrators who had abused him because he believed that torturing his former torturers would have made him complicit with them; but seeing them arrested, tried, sentenced, and locked away gave him considerable emotional satisfaction, without that complicity.[213] A conscious decision to abandon violent revenge for a non-violent, indirect counterpart that relied on the legal system is one distinct pattern emerging in postwar memoirs and testimony.[214] Although revenge and retributive justice are commonly understood as opposites, for survivors they were in fact intrinsically connected: helping to see Nazis brought to justice in national, international, and military tribunals and ultimately seeing them convicted, sentenced, and sometimes hanged *was* a form of revenge. Identifying suspects, collecting evidence, and testifying against murderers and torturers meant settling accounts on behalf of the dead.

On February 27, 1946, testifying for the Soviet prosecution at the IMT trial in Nuremberg, Abraham Sutzkever related how the Germans had murdered his infant child in the Vilna ghetto's hospital; he described the mass murder by shooting of some 80,000 Vilna Jews, among them his mother, at Ponary. Sutzkever struggled to decide on the most suitable method for accommodating his desire for revenge: should it be a violent act? Or rather, should it be such courtroom testimony, preventing perpetrators on the stand from successfully claiming non-involvement and ignorance and helping see to their punishment? Before travelling to Nuremberg, Sutzkever had planned to shoot Hermann Göring in the courtroom. But the writer Ilya Ehrenburg, whose journalistic oeuvre during the war had been essential in exposing the specific atrocities that the Germans directed against Soviet Jews and had at times included passionate vengeance rhetoric,[215] convinced Sutzkever that bearing witness was more powerful revenge. "I did not take my revolver and six bullets to the Nuremberg Trial," Sutzkever would later remark. "It was not destined that a Yiddish poet should execute vengeance on the German Marshal who instead took poison and died by his own hand."[216] Testifying at Nuremberg, detailing how his mother and child had been murdered together with nearly all other Lithuanian Jews, was the revenge of Sutzkever, the poet, through language. Sutzkever requested to testify in Yiddish, but was forced to use Russian.[217] In the eyes of the Soviet prosecution team, he was a successful witness. He covered mass shooting, ghettoization, plunder, cultural genocide, murder of Jewish children, Jewish resistance, names of German mass murderers. He was emotional but not overtaken by emotion. But although Sutzkever found his appearance in court meaningful, and his testimony to be a kind of kaddish, a Jewish prayer for the dead, he felt frustrated at not being allowed to bear witness for them in their own language. Sutzkever struggled with ambivalent feelings—and with enduring vengeful emotions. In his diary, he wondered: "what is stronger, my sorrow or my desire for revenge?"[218]

Although finding it hard to be among Germans on German soil, Sutzkever derived satisfaction from seeing Germany in ruins and occupied, some of the genocide's organizers and executors held accountable for their crimes. "The name Nuremberg will leave a mark on history for all eternity," he stated. "Nuremberg laws—Nuremberg trials. It is symbolic: there, where the battle cry for the destruction of the Jews was developed, the perpetrators are tried. And I, perhaps the only surviving Yiddish poet of occupied Europe, come to the trial at Nuremberg not only as a testifier but also as a living witness to the innocence of my people."[219] Other survivors as well, notably young men in their twenties who may well have decided otherwise, abandoned the option of violence in favor of testimony. Moishe Rutschaisky, having first been too frail, we will recall, to beat a captured Dachau guard when American soldiers gave him the chance, and having later punched a guard, then realizing that engaging in violence gave him no satisfaction, took his revenge by testifying in the investigations and trial of Dachau camp personnel. Recovering at the St. Ottilien hospital, he volunteered for this when American investigators came looking for potential witnesses. "I hate to say that word 'revenge,'" he said at one point in his 1996 testimony,

> and I must say that would be the best thing in my life, if I can meet eye-on-eye with the commandant from Dachau and look him in the eyes. That would be—[what]

people were wishing in the camps just to punch one of these guys in the nose and then die. That kind of wish they used to have in the camps. And I have opportunity like that, if I can, if I am going to be able to go through with the interview and be selected, I would thank God. I would fall on my knees.[220]

One night in the fall of 1945, an American colonel working on the trial allowed Rutschaisky to eavesdrop on the forty defendants—"big shots before," for whom "to kill a man, a human being . . . is like stepping on an ant"[221]—waiting in a room and arguing with each other:

And then I see them all of a sudden like babies they were fighting and I was standing there listening [to] everything and one was blaming the other. . . . I was, I was in heaven. That was for me a very powerful, you know, for my heart, you know, feeling, to see that. Because memories came to my mind. All the people that were killed and the wishes they had while they were dying and I . . . I am right here, I'm living. . . through that, you know. So it was for me, morally, such an accomplishment and such a . . . I must say again . . . that bad word 'revenge.'[222]

Like Moishe Rutschaisky, Roman Sompolenski exercised his vengeance through participation in a trial—in his case, it was the British "Belsen trial." Born in Zgierz, Poland, in 1923, Sompolenski survived forced labor at Auschwitz-Monowitz and a death march to Bergen-Belsen, where he was liberated. The trial gave him the opportunity to directly confront the principal defendant, Josef Kramer, former commandant of Auschwitz-Birkenau and Bergen-Belsen. Shortly before Bergen-Belsen's liberation on April 15, 1945, Kramer had caught Sompolenski and two other prisoners stealing rotten potatoes from the camp kitchen—prisoners were starving and deaths from starvation and disease were skyrocketing. Kramer shot and killed the other prisoners as punishment. Because Kramer remembered Sompolinski from Auschwitz—he had worked there in the Sonderkommando for four weeks before being sent to Monowitz[223]—he spared his life, simply shooting him in the hand.[224]

Sompolinski was being treated for the shot in the camp infirmary when the British arrived. With his health improved, he once encountered Kramer in the camp—the former commandant was now being forced by the British to work there: "The Germans were dragging the bodies cleaning up the camp, he went with two British MPs. And he passed by and I walked over and I smacked him in the face. I almost got hit from a British [soldier] with a carabine. He said 'Bend down!' . . . Maybe he wanted to hit me, maybe he had to do it . . . just that I took revenge I did smack him in the face."[225] Despite Sompolinski's urge for vigilante justice, British investigators saw him as a good potential trial witness: he could directly tie his wound to Kramer; and he was familiar with his brutality from both Auschwitz and Bergen-Belsen. Sompolinski would be convinced that his trial testimony helped get Kremer his death sentence. Although he found meaning in confronting the man in court, he refused to be present at Kramer's execution, of which he approved: "I was invited to the hanging. Just I didn't want to go . . . because I saw enough hangings in the camps. And I saw enough hangings in the towns in Poland and I said, I had enough."[226] It seems that in the end Sompolenski, like numerous other survivors, was satisfied by having contributed to a process of legal reckoning.

That was also the case with Michael (Micki) Goldman-Gilead. Born in Katowice in 1925, Goldman-Gilead was a survivor of the Przemysl ghetto, deportation to Auschwitz, and forced labor for I.G. Farben at Auschwitz-Monowitz. After escaping from a death march, he managed to hide with a non-Jewish family in Poland and eventually joined the Red Army. He immigrated to Israel, became a police officer, and worked as an investigator for Bureau 06, the investigative police unit that prepared the Eichmann trial. As prosecutor Gideon Hausner's assistant, Goldman-Gilead sought out witnesses and convinced them to testify at the trial. He observed how some survivors were torn between a sense of moral duty to testify and fear their testimony would not be believed, or else that testifying would reactivate trauma—often, witnesses had to be persuaded that appearing in the stand was indispensable. Seated at the prosecutor's table, Goldman-Gilead closely followed all the trial sessions. "It was a heavy emotional burden," he recounted in his testimony of 2015. "[F]rom time to time I had the feeling that the Holocaust happened to me personally again. It was a moral duty and we knew that . . . this trial was very important. . . . It was difficult, but I had the satisfaction that I made a contribution to this very important matter."[227] Goldman-Gilead did not take the witness stand himself; but one witness, Josef Buzminsky, a Jewish doctor who had treated Goldman-Gilead in the Przemysl ghetto after a brutal flogging—he was convinced the patient would not survive—identified him during his testimony.[228]

"I had no feeling of revenge," Goldman-Gilead insisted in his testimony. "Revenge, there is no revenge. There is no revenge, no human revenge for that what was done to us. There is no such thing. Even when I was standing in front of Eichmann before he was hanged, I had no feeling of revenge."[229] And again: "We did not look for vengeance. Eichmann just was the only one that we could put to trial. The others disappeared. Eichmann would not have been able to do by himself what he did. After all, there were thousands who cooperated in the Holocaust, in the killing of Jews. [. . .] We only could hang him once. This was no vengeance . . . it was our duty that he would be convicted."[230] The same upon hearing the verdict: there were "no feelings of vengeance. It was a satisfaction to me that he got his conviction. It also was no surprise to me that he was sentenced to death. It was the only possibility of the trial."[231] As a police officer, Goldman-Gilead was asked to serve as state witness during Eichmann's execution and cremation in the night from May 31 to June 1, 1962. When witnessing Eichmann's hanging and signing the protocol, he had "no feeling at that moment. No vengeance. Nothing. I was surprised that I was standing there without any feeling. That was the judgement only on one, it was not possible to hang him six million times. It was only the justice won at this moment, nothing more."[232] When he observed the body's transfer on a hearse to the cremation and the group walked through the fenced-in and torchlight-lit yard of the Ramle prison, Goldman-Gilead had a flashback to his own incarceration, "just like in Auschwitz. The lights and the fence. Like in Auschwitz. But now this was the Auschwitz for Eichmann and not for me."[233]

In any case, Goldman-Gilead clearly had a deep sense of process: of trying and sentencing Eichmann in Israel, and this as a reversal of power relations, hence as a form of just retribution, even if he insisted that it was removed from an emotional sensation of revenge and was ultimately incommensurate with the crime. That the revenge theme was repeatedly addressed indicates his paradoxical presence. And in the testimony, the theme was actually present through its bitter flip-side as well: Eichmann's ashes were now brought to the Jaffa port, from where the witnesses boarded a police boat and spread the ashes at sea, outside of Israel's territorial water. When Goldman-Gilead and police officer Arie Nir, the commander of Israeli prisons, opened the urn to disperse the ashes, the wind blew and a "little piece of the ash went into my eye and started to burn." As Goldman-Gilead rubbed his eye, Nir quipped, "'you see how he takes vengeance on you, even after his death.'"[234] At this point in the testimony, Goldman-Gilead grinned; but the emotional pain and physical discomfort, even revulsion, tied to presence at the execution, the cremation, the sea-dispersal of ashes, is palpable. The physical pain caused him to look away, cover and rub his eye, turn inward, attending to his pain for a moment rather than doing what he had been ordered to do. It is in any event clear that legal proceedings mattered greatly to Goldman-Gilead: that he considered the trial and sentencing something categorically different than any violent payback—and far more important than the violent act of the execution itself.

Following Eichmann's sentencing in mid-December 1961, a group of prominent Israeli intellectuals, among them Martin Buber, Shmuel Hugo Bergmann, Ernst Simon, Nathan Rotenstreich, Gershom Scholem, Lea Goldberg, along with the survivor and trial witness Yehudah Bacon pleaded with the Israeli government to commute Eichmann's death sentence to life imprisonment. They argued that they refused to let the hangman Eichmann force Israeli society to appoint a hangman from its midst. They feared the death sentence would make it seem as if Germany's debt toward the Jews was paid by Eichmann's blood. And after all, they found it to be a more severe sentence for Eichmann if he had to live with his deeds for the rest of his life. Israeli president Yitzhak Ben-Zvi rejected this plea (and Eichmann's own appeal) on May 31, 1962, and confirmed the death sentence, which was executed without delay.[235] Meanwhile a fierce debate over the matter had ensued in particular in the Yiddish-language survivor press in Israel, with many unabashedly embracing the idea of vengeance and seeing the death sentence as necessary and well-deserved revenge on Eichmann.[236]

Especially in the immediate postwar years, survivors were crucial in identifying suspects and bringing them to trial, not only in Allied military but, especially, in domestic German courts. Samuel Lerer (born in Żółkiewka in 1922)[237] was a Sobibor survivor living as a DP in Berlin after the war. On July 30, 1949, he encountered Erich Bauer at a fair in the Victoriapark, Berlin-Kreuzberg. Bauer, who was at the fair with his wife, had been an SS-Oberscharführer and so-called *Gasmeister* at Sobibor: between April 1942 and December 1943 he had operated the gassing facilities at the camp while killing individual Jewish deportees in other ways as well. Lerer immediately called nearby policemen over and managed to convince them to take Bauer into custody.[238]

To make sure Bauer was not immediately released, Lerer brought in an acquaintance and fellow Sobibor survivor, Esther Raab, also living in Berlin at the time, to confirm both Bauer's identity and Lerer's account. Lerer and Raab had been among the few hundred Jews temporarily kept alive to work at the camp, approximately 250,000 Jews from Poland and across Europe being murdered upon arrival over a seventeen-month period. Lerer was responsible for attending the SS horses; Raab sorted and mended the clothes of the murdered victims for redistribution among the German population. Both fought in the October 14, 1943, uprising which aimed to enable the escape of approximately 600 prisoners; some 300 were murdered by guards and killed in the surrounding mine belt, 300 others managing to escape, some 100 of whom were murdered outside the camp. Only around sixty managed to survive the war, most hiding with local peasants.[239] Such was the case with Raab and Lerer, who hid on a farm in an earthen hole until the Soviet arrival, together with Raab's brother Idel.[240] Both Raab and Lerer had intimate knowledge of Bauer's crimes. With the help of a bribe in the form of 3 pounds of coffee, they got the German policemen—who claimed they needed to set Bauer free unless there were three witnesses against him—to open an investigation. This led to a court case in May 1950, before the Berlin District Court in the West-Berlin borough of Moabit.[241]

Both Raab and Lerer were outspoken that at Sobibor, witnessing the daily mass murder of trainloads of Jews, the fathomless sadism of the SS and Ukrainian guards, constantly fearing for their own lives, they harbored strong wishes for revenge. Asked what kept him going in the camp, Lerer put it bluntly: it was the hope "that someday . . . I will [get] revenge. Someday I'll see these murderers, these animals get their . . . get their punishment. I wanted to see them suffer. I . . . wanted to live to see them suffer."[242] Watching the atrocities every day, knowing that all the prisoners kept alive for work "had a death sentence in their pocket. It just was a matter of time," they nevertheless never "gave up that hope . . . for revenge. And I think that kept us going."[243] Raab also recalled that the murder of twelve SS guards during the uprising brought some satisfaction. "I cannot explain . . . all my fear was gone," she recalled, "Just the joy. We killed a Nazi! The revenge for all those who are burning over there . . . that their death is not in vain."[244]

After the war, Raab, Lerer, and many other survivors of ghettos and death camps translated their thirst for violent revenge into another mode of vengeance: that centered on helping bring the torturers and murderers to justice, in the process exposing them through presentation of the facts that they sought to deny. Both Lerer and Raab testified at Bauer's trial, along with two other survivor witnesses. He would be sentenced to death for crimes against humanity; but because West Germany abolished the death sentence, the sentence was commuted to life imprisonment, which Bauer served until his death in 1980.[245] As it happens, Bauer incriminated his fellow SS men, many of whom were tried in subsequent proceedings.[246] Both Lerer and Raab testified in all Sobibor-related trials (and retrials).[247]

Taking the stand and confronting the defendants, exposing the mendacity of their denials, came with its own sense—however limited and muted—of satisfied vengeance. Raab was, for example, able to publicly convey the facts about Karl Frenzel, former commandant of camp I in Sobibor: his shooting twenty-four prisoners in the face to demonstrate what would await those trying to flee;[248] his grabbing a baby from the newly arrived deportation trains by the feet and "smash[ing] his skull against the box car."[249] Decades later, in her 1990 testimony, Raab recalled that "I was at his trial twice. And I brought it out. He got [a] life sentence, just for that one case. But he said I accused him falsely. But I told him in court, tell me that you didn't do it!' He didn't."[250] Although going to Germany and confronting the perpetrators was very difficult for her,[251] she saw this as her obligation toward the dead. "[T]here're thousands and thousands of stories like my story," stories of people "who fought, who died, just for that revenge, and just for . . . protecting that honor of those who didn't make it," but who were "not here to tell it . . . so I have to do as much as I can. It's not easy, but I won't give up as long as I live."[252]

Frenzel was, as it happens, the only defendant in the Hagen Sobibor trial to receive a life sentence, for the murder of six Jews, including the baby.[253] Although Raab drew satisfaction from the fact that the defendants "admitted Sobibor," and "admitted what happened there,"[254] she also emphasized that "they never took any personal responsibility and never said that the genocide was wrong."[255] For that basic reason, reading her later testimony, we see that in her case, the satisfaction was sharply limited. In the testimony, Raab focuses on the pathological violence inflicted by Sobibor's personnel as part of their daily routines, the forced exercise until inmates dropped dead or were beaten to death for collapsing, their experience of such cruelty as entertainment and pleasure, in a universe of unlimited power over life and death.[256] But at trial, these same criminals presented themselves as small cogs, ordinary, law-abiding citizens who had just done their professional duty: "when you talk to them today, everybody followed orders and whatever they did, wasn't wrong, even. Wasn't their fault. And that hurts. It hurts."[257]

In short, the satisfaction of confronting former torturers and murderers in a court of law, of forcing them to acknowledge their crimes in general terms, was significantly tempered by their total denial of agency, both individually and in respect to Sobibor as an institution, one devoted to torture and murder.[258] In general, Nazi defendants in German criminal trials had devoted defense lawyers, sympathetic jurists and spectators; the survivor-witnesses had none of this. In Germany unaccompanied, eye to eye with their former tormentors, they fended off attempts of the defense to confuse them and find minor inconsistencies in their testimonies, confronting them with petty details about insignia on uniforms, exact measurements of distances, dates, and times, making skilled use of disparaging language to generate witness discomfort and influence the judges—to discredit them and dismiss their testimony.[259]

None of the defendants in the many trials Raab attended showed any consciousness of wrongdoing, prompting a conclusion she voiced in the courtroom and recalled in her testimony: "If Frenzel would have a chance to wear a uniform, he would do it all over again; but maybe he would make sure now that we wouldn't escape to tell the story."[260] Survivors such as Raab were essential for criminal trials of Holocaust perpetrators being organized in Germany *at all*; only a fraction of Holocaust perpetrators were ever brought to trial. Most investigations did not end in trials.[261] And those who were tried by and large received lenient sentences, thanks to their denial of "base motives," of agency and

195

intent, and narrow rules for use of evidence unsuitable in the case of a mass crime meant to leave few or no witnesses: a legal framework within which higher ranking officers frequently received lower sentences than their subordinates. In this way, the survivor witnesses now had to witness something akin to a decriminalizing of mass murder as assembly-line routine within military hierarchies and in line with orders—and resulting acquittals and mitigations in sentencing. Furthermore, after the first five postwar years, they witnessed a lessening in the number of Allied and German trials in which they were invested: a development due to Cold War political alliances and resulting amnesties.[262]

This legal-political reality caused deep frustration to many survivors with a commitment to the courts for legal redress: in this respect, we can view Raab's voiced disappointment—a significant and gradually more forceful lessening of any satisfaction gained in the shift she had accepted and seen through from violent revenge to its legally framed non-violent counterpart—as emblematic. Survivors had a sense that prosecutors and judges did not understand the basic situation, with its distinct dilemmas, facing Jews during the Holocaust.[263] Chaim Brettler, a survivor from the western Ukrainian town of Skala-Podilska, reflected in a memoir on his experience as a prosecution witness—along with other survivors—at several trials of German officers who exploited, abused and murdered 1,600 of the town's 5,000 Jews between summer 1941 and spring 1944. In February 1970, he traveled to Hamburg from New Jersey to testify at the trial of Artur Engel, one of the officers being tried for the murder of eighteen-year-old Chone Schwartzbach on June 19, 1943. Brettler had mixed emotions. On the one hand, he felt considerable satisfaction at seeing a man who had humiliated and murdered fellow Jews in his hometown brought to trial.[264] On the other hand, testifying was painful, it made Brettler anxious, causing him to relive traumatic years.[265] Driving through Hamburg in a taxi, "looking at the newly built streets, the stores full of goods, I compared Hamburg to the Polish cities and towns the Germans had destroyed and emptied of their Jews. My heart clenched in pain. Nazi Germany had indeed been defeated, but for us, Hitler had won."[266] But confrontation with a once-powerful perpetrator like Engel gave Brettler a sense of pride and dignity; in a broader sense he saw confronting Engel's lies in court as "vengeance on the German murderers."[267] His view of Engel was as follows: "Sitting in the defendant's chair I saw a middle-aged, overweight, fat Gentile wearing a brown suit, having the face of a drunk, and whose blue, watery eyes looked like those of a pig. This creature could hardly answer the questions the court posed him. He burst into tears when he found it convenient to make that impression." Brettler asked himself whether this "bag of guts" could actually be Engel, "the cold-blooded murderer before whom an entire town trembled. . . . Seeing his pitiful state in that German court, among armed guards and facing a jury, I was proud of our martyrs, his victims. They were less decrepit than he was at the moment of their deaths."[268]

Brettler was dismayed at Engel's acquittal. Although Engel admitted to killing Schwartzbach, he was acquitted of the murder charges because of an absence of proof that Engel had killed out of Jew-hatred, hence out of "base motives," which would have qualified his deed as murder rather than manslaughter. As nothing more demonstrable than manslaughter, the deed fell under the prevailing statute of limitations.[269] "I realized how hard it is to be a witness thirty years after the events," Brettler recounts in his memoir. "In addition to the pain of reliving the Holocaust, the lawyers pepper a Jewish witness with questions from every angle, in hopes of unnerving him. If a shrewd lawyer succeeds in throwing a witness into a quandary, the witness is in embarrassed agony, while the murderer can go home if the witness testimony fails to persuade the court."[270]

Often, Brettler observed, West German newspaper articles spoke of "the Jewish trials"; in this way, he found himself confronting the topos of Jews as unwilling to forget or forgive, forever demanding, as Brettler put it, "their pound of flesh."[271] In the popular reception of the German court proceeding, just as, to a degree, in the trials themselves Germans had as it were become victims of the Jews. Survivor witnesses like Brettler were thus caught in a dilemma: was it better to see a few Nazi perpetrators held accountable, albeit given lenient sentences, or simply forego the entire process as unbearable—hence foregoing for those who saw it that way, the opportunity for gaining at least a limited sense of nonviolent post-Holocaust revenge?

Ultimately these witnesses were grappling with a problem of proportionality: what did justice writ large—and revenge—even mean with regard to a crime as global and enormous as the Holocaust? Would it not always be partial and disproportionate to the crime and deeply unsatisfactory? And ultimately, neither revenge nor justice would fill the void that the dead had left. Abraham Sutzkever captured these dilemmas in a poem he wrote in Nuremberg after his testimony before the International Military Tribunal, in February 1946. The two stanzas of *Farn Nirnberger Tribunal* ("Before the Nuremberg Tribunal") explore the tension between justice and revenge:

> They say I must demand justice in the name of millions
> That will last forever
> Yet the millions won't be coming back
> So what kind of justice can I demand?
>
> I must be a thousand Shylocks
> To cut evil from the earth.
> My people! You will forge such a sword,
> If God is too weak to demand retribution![272]

On the one hand, Sutzkever expresses gratification at having been able to demand justice for the millions of dead by testifying; but at the same time, this has failed to assuage the pain over massive and irretrievable loss. This leads him to question, in the poem's first stanza, whether any true justice is possible after the genocide—and what the concept of justice can even mean: can any legal institution do justice for millions of dead?

Leaving these questions unanswered, his second stanza refers to Shylock: if we really wanted to remove all evil from the world, we would need to be a thousand times more vengeful than Shakespeare's vengeful figure, possibly a reference to the idea, pursued by

Jewish Revenge and the Holocaust

Abba Kovner—Sutzkever had met him in Vilna after the war—that the Germans needed to pay for what they had done with their own flesh. Paid back in their own suffering, then no nation would again dare commit a *felkermord* of the Jews. But Sutzkever only raises the idea as an option. His thrust is to express disillusionment with God: if God is too weak to guarantee divine justice, then the Jewish people needs to take matters into their own hands, constructing a sword that can cut out evil from the world. Sutzkever leaves this idea, as well, in the conditional. And he leaves open what this "sword" would concretely be: a sovereign Jewish state with a court system to try mass murderers? Military strength and self-defense against enemies of the Jews? All vagueness notwithstanding, Sutzkever's poem highlights the tension between courtroom justice and vengeance; it suggests that if justice fails, both through an impossibility to bring back the murdered and through failure to serve as a deterrent, then the Jews needed to act on their own behalf. What the basic reality Sutzkever captured meant for individual survivors varied. Most lived with the tension: justice writ large was not, likely could not, be served; but that as individuals, bringing individual torturers and mass murderers to justice, having survived to provide evidence of their crimes, telling truth as a counternarrative to the mendacious and exculpatory narratives of the defendants, thwarting their wish to live on in the comfort of denial, was indeed a form, however fragile, of revenge.

Revenge as Timeless Fantasy and Utopia

As survivors sublimated their desire for revenge, the accompanying negative emotions waned over time.[273] What remained was engagement with revenge as a theoretical construct, a utopian goal, a fantasy that—as the survivors who entertained it knew very well—would never be implemented because it was both practically impossible and—were it ever to become reality—would be a moral transgression and criminal act. Thinking about revenge in this utopian framework offered some emotional compensation for lives stamped with past suffering. Creating a rhetoric centered on *wishing* calamities onto Germans, calamities that were too drastic to ever become reality, offered those harboring such wishes a valve—one defined by symbolic revenge.

One example of this is offered by one of the earliest memorials for murdered European Jews erected in postwar Germany, an obelisk that Jewish DPs in the US zone built in the Jewish section of the cemetery of Gauting, some ten miles southwest of Munich, on October 19, 1947. A group of 170 survivors who had died following liberation by the American army while being treated for tuberculosis in the local hospital were buried there.[274] The Hebrew inscription on the obelisk asked the Jewish people (*am olam*) to commemorate its 6,000,000 dead and expressed the following wish: "May the German nation drown in the blood of its victims."[275] This death wish—an evocation of the destruction Germans had inflicted on the Jews coming back as self-destruction—offered mourning Jews who read the inscription a possibility to engage with a revenge wish that itself remained, in its very terms, impossible, located in a realm of the unreal. Another example was offered by none other than Abba Kovner and Vitka Kempner, claiming in an interview decades after the war that the Nakam group had known its plot would not succeed—that it was in fact a utopian idea. The "most important thing" about Nakam, Kempner insisted, "was the idea. Like the uprisings in the ghetto. The effect was supposed to be symbolic."[276] He never meant to harm women and children, Kovner claimed; but he built on the possibility of revenge as a deterrent. The idea itself had the power to "show the nations of the world that Jewish blood could not be shed without reprisal."[277] The *idea* of Jewish revenge was the essential thing: "When I heard there was an atomic bomb I dreamed that if I could drop it on Germany," he recalled. "What I wanted to tell the world with the Nakam was that those who survived Auschwitz could destroy the world. Let them know that! That if it ever happens again, the world will be destroyed."[278] As Kovner now explained things, not only was the failure in plan-implementation calculated, but the implementation did not actually matter. What mattered was the theoretical possibility of the act and emotional satisfaction of engaging with its idea, at the same time a source of practical deterrence.

Yet other survivors chose imaginative literature and poetry to articulate fantasies and utopias of revenge; some wrote poems they continued to recite decades later while knowing that the revenge expressed there would never be realized. In his testimony of 1987, Victor S. (born in Kozienice, Poland, in 1910), for example, reads a Yiddish poem written during the war to commemorate the murder of his family, including his wife and child, in a mass shooting in Krasnik near Lublin, while he was imprisoned in a labor camp in Budzyn: "You hugged the child tightly and sang it a song, and the murderer shoots, and the blood burns. It burns. It calls, and it screams for revenge. My heart is aching. My blood drips."[279] Commemorative efforts of this sort were meant to serve as well as to transmit both the idea and its history to future generations.

As survivors let go of their rage and hatred of Germans as a collective, they nevertheless struggled over how to relate to them. Many set personal boundaries: some refused to hear or speak German; some to pass on the language to their descendants;[280] to consume German literature and music; buy German goods;[281] travel to or through Germany; and even accept compensation from the German state.[282] A certain sense of revenge could be woven into these personal decisions: in his testimony of 1988, Hans N. (born in Hannover in 1921), for example, notes that in refusing to speak German, his mother tongue and pass on the language to his children, "[i]t's probably, to some extent, displacement—displacing emotions about Germany. And one's rejection—one's rejection—all the emotions that were internalized, and they had no outlet. This was my revenge, or my getting even, or my memorial, my remembrance."[283] Others maintained personal rituals of return to specific sites of past suffering. Andrew S. (born in 1929 in Portrete, Hungary), a survivor of Auschwitz, Mauthausen, Melk, and Ebensee, would not only return to the concert hall in Salzburg but also the sidewalk café in Melk where the Melk camp commandant Julius Ludolph used to go after the daily business of executions. For Andrew S., going back there with his daughter for his "own satisfaction" was a personal ritual celebrating his survival, but also "as a [form of] revenge. To tell the world I'm here.

He is not any longer...."[284] (Ludolph was sentenced at the Dachau trials and executed in July 1947).

Whatever their particular nature, the boundaries at work here expressed emotional resistance to normalizing relations with Germans, show empathy or understanding for them; indeed, often, a wish to excise the German nation from a world of human interaction, as an expression of irretrievable loss and pain. This found expression in formulaic curses centered on Nazi perpetrators or even the German nation and meant for generations to come. "Murderers! bloodhounds! What have you done to us!" the Yizker (memorial) book of Dęblin called out. "Why did you murder our mothers and fathers! What had our little children done to you! As long as the sun rises, as long as just one human creature remains on this earth, your memory and the memory of your people will be forever damned!"[285] Elsewhere the book addressed the Earth directly: "Land, do not cover their blood! Damned be the German Nazis! May you remove their memory from Earth–and we say amen."[286] The murdered were also addressed directly: "Cursed should forever be the murderous German people, who cut off your life in the years when your life was flowering."[287] At times survivors vowed to avenge the Jews murdered in their communities while eulogizing them: in Rovno, surviving Jews held a memorial ceremony in October 1945 dedicating a memorial plaque in Yiddish, Hebrew, and Russian on the mass grave of 23,500 Jews shot in November 1941, stating that "Your innocent blood will forever be a mark of shame on Hitler's Germany. Rest peacefully where you lie. We, the Surviving Remnant, will avenge your blood – our blood."[288] (Survivors photographed themselves on the grave with the memorial plaque, turning the photographs into surrogate memorials as they emigrated.)[289] Yet it was more common to relegate the task of vengeance to God. A formulation widely used in Yizker books, on memorial stones, and at commemorative events was "may God avenge their blood"[290]—this after mention of dead relatives and friends.[291] In these cases, the revenge wish was delegated, in the Hebrew, to God, indicating that revenge was no longer a human task but only a human wish. It had, in other words, been transformed from human to divine action, and from an imperative to utopian desire. Those who used this formulation could, perhaps as part of a healthy process of post-traumatic recovery, absolve themselves of any sense of personal obligation and delegate ideas of revenge to a realm beyond human responsibility and control.

Moreover, the artistic expression, especially the literary genre, emerged as a central realm where non-violent, utopian forms of revenge could be imagined and "acted out" by survivors, their descendants (and others who identified with them). While the literary representations of revenge across different languages began, as indicated, during the war, they continued to flourish throughout the postwar decades, creatively blurring the lines between genres—poetry and prose, fiction and autobiographical writing, theater play and film script—and reaching across generational divides and into audiences from across the clearly conceived victim-perpetrator-bystander divides. While the much deserved exploration of "literary revenge" is beyond the scope of this study, it is important to note that such literary and artistic representations have remained a fruitful arena for setting and resetting boundaries and also enabling new dialogue, also with the perpetrator society, or rather their descendants.[292]

While the boundaries that survivors set for themselves in different ways could last for decades, they were also flexible, for instance individuals making distinctions between different generations of Germans, between those who lived in the Nazi era and those born after. Personal boundaries evolved and softened over time, often due to survivors' interactions with their descendants, especially grandchildren. (For example, the refusal of Treblinka survivor Samuel Willenberg to go to Germany lasted until 2001 when the Israeli embassy in Berlin opened a new building designed by Willenberg's daughter, the architect Orit Willenberg-Giladi.)[293] Some survivors, even those who traveled to Germany and interacted with Germans, retained a final emotional boundary in the form of *resentment*—a latent sense of bitterness, anger, and frustration grounded in a fathomless injustice that cannot be undone; a sense of powerlessness to openly articulate such feelings because doing so is deemed inappropriate. Often, in any case, survivors with such feelings made conscious decisions to not pass them on to their descendants.[294]

Jean Améry rejected notions of collective guilt, Germans having had many different roles, behaved in different ways, in the wartime years.[295] But in a somewhat countervailing way, he keenly analyzed the nature of his resentment toward Germany and Germans. Writing in the 1960s, he argued that it stemmed from disappointment over the countless continuities of careers from the Nazi regime into postwar West German society; from the acknowledgement of responsibility for historical wrongdoing in the abstract without deeper acknowledgment by individuals of their personal responsibility; from German eagerness to leave the "historical accident" of the past behind, following a certain due diligence in sentencing a minute portion of Nazi war criminals and the material sacrifice of compensation payments.[296] Améry accurately described the contemporary postwar context: West Germany's phenomenal rise from defeated pariah to Cold War ally; its rapid transformation into an economic superpower through industrial products conquering the world market.[297] This development was tied for Améry to a distinct mentality: a broad self-perception of Germans as victims, framed by the Cold War's tacit legitimation, in German eyes, of Nazi Germany's fight against the Soviet Union, in a way the postwar present was a continuation of a war that Hitler had begun.

"The Germans will never forgive the Jews for Auschwitz" is an observation ascribed to the Austrian-born Israeli psychologist Zvi (Franz) Rex: the encapsulation of a "secondary antisemitism" involving resentment of Jews *because* of the Holocaust; and accompanying denial, relativizing, and abasing the significance of the genocide itself.[298] In a random conversation with a German businessman, Améry was told that "the German people bear no grudge against the Jewish people"—a generosity-gesture masking the same victim-perpetrator role reversal that, we have seen, was a key leitmotif in Nazi propaganda.[299] Part of Améry's experience of his own resentment was grounded in an encounter with a specific societal premise: that his emotional state was groundless, out of place, even inappropriate in peacetime—which made Améry feel like, precisely, a Shylock.[300] At the same time Améry acknowledged that those like him who held the ensuing resentment could not just cast it aside: they were caught up in it, had a conflicted, ambivalent relationship with it. On the one hand it was cumbersome, coming at a price. "It nails every one of us to the cross of his ruined past," was the way Améry put it; it sought to achieve something that could never be achieved. "Absurdly," he observed, "it demands that the irreversible be turned around, that the event be undone. Resentment blocks the exit to the genuine human dimension, the future. I know that the time-sense of the person trapped in resentment is twisted around, dis-ordered, if you wish, for it desires two impossible things: regression into the past and nullification of what happened."[301]

On the other hand, the ressentiment, Améry argued, had positive qualities, being necessary to prevent perpetrators from moving on too easily; as unlike their victims they enjoyed freedom from lasting trauma, it was the only way to give them a glimpse of their terrible crimes: "But my resentments are there in order that the crime become a moral reality for the criminal, in order that he be swept into the truth of his atrocity."[302] For Améry, who would commit suicide in 1978, "[t]he experience of persecution was, at the very bottom, that of an extreme *loneliness*."[303] Perhaps, Améry, remarked, an individual murderer such as his torturer, the SS man Wajs, experienced such loneliness when about to be executed, together with a desire to turn back time, make the crime undone.[304] But most perpetrators of the genocide, he felt, would be free of that loneliness.[305] From that perspective, resentment was a way to force Germans to integrate rather than neutralize their past.[306]

A similar emotional state was also described by Edith P. (born in Michalovce, Czechoslovakia, in 1920) in her testimony of 1980:

> I have been liberated 35 years . . . and . . . as I get older, and my children . . . are all self-sufficient and are no longer at home and I am no longer busy being a mother and a wife . . . I have given a great deal of thought [to] how I should conduct myself with the Germans. How I should feel. Should I hate them? Should I despise them? Should I go out with a banner and say 'Do something against them!'? I don't know, I never found the answer in my own soul. And I have to go according to my own conscience. . . . And the only thing I can say is that up until now I ignored them. I don't hate them. I can't hate, I feel like I would waste a lot of time of my life. But sometimes I wish—in my darkest hours—that they would feel what we feel sometimes, when you are uprooted and bring up children. I am talking as a mother and a wife . . . when there is nobody to share your sorrow or your great happiness, when there is nobody to call to say something good happened to me today, I have given birth to a beautiful daughter. . . . I want to share it with somebody who knows me really. . . . There isn't even a grave to go and cry to. And I sometimes wish they would feel that. It is not easy to live this way . . . And ever-so-often, I cry because I am . . . I feel a human being. And I don't wish the German nation any harm . . . but I hope they'd . . . know what we have . . . the loss of identity, the loss of communication with people that you really trusted.[307]

Like Améry, Edith P. here acknowledged an ambivalence that only grew with age. Here as well, she acknowledges a—quasi-utopian—wish, in her case only surfacing sometimes, that Germans would experience the same loss and loneliness as her own. Some

Figure 21 The memorial at the Waldfriedhof Gauting, Germany, today; photographed by Tamar Aizenberg; courtesy of Tamar Aizenberg.

Jewish Revenge and the Holocaust

resentment, Edith P. suggests, is legitimate even necessary as an expression of lifelong aftereffects of loss and pain that will never go away, for which there is no remedy or compensation. Thus, there remains a utopian yearning: if only perpetrators could be made to suffer the same ever-present "afterdeath" (Lawrence Langer) for the rest if their lives. "Oh son of death, we do not wish you death," reads the last stanza of Primo Levi's poem "For Adolf Eichmann," written in July 1960, two months after Eichmann had been captured in Argentina and brought to Israel where he awaited trial:

> May you live longer than anyone ever lived.
> May you live sleepless five million nights,
> And may you be visited each night by the suffering of everyone who saw,
> Shutting behind him, the door that blocked the way back,
> Saw it grow dark around him, the air fill with death.[308]

The Gauting cemetery obelisk still stands; the survivors who erected it two years after the war are gone now, their descendants scattered. The public parks administration of Gauting keeps the memorial plaque neat. It is adorned with wreaths on the memorial days of January 27 and November 9. Yet most days, the only ones taking care of the obelisk are people who cannot read the stone's imperative and likely have little familiarity, if any, with the historical chapter it represents. The official German and English translation of the Hebrew text does not convey the vengeance fantasy on the plaque. Instead of the evocation of a German nation drowning in its victims' blood, it says that "the perpetrators shall receive their just punishment" for the murder of six million Jewish human beings.[309]

Notes

1. Gradowski, *The Last Consolation Vanished*, 139–40.
2. Frank Biess, "Feelings in the Aftermath: Toward a History of Postwar Emotions," in *Histories of the Aftermath: The Legacies of the Second World War in Europe*, ed. Frank Biess and Robert G. Moeller (New York: Berghahn Books, 2010), 30–48 and Anna M. Parkinson, *An Emotional State: The Politics of Emotion in Postwar West German Culture* (Ann Arbor: University of Michigan Press, 2015); see also Robert G. Moeller, *War Stories: The Search for a Usable Past in the Federal Republic of Germany* (Berkeley: University of California Press, 2001).
3. Testimony of Kurt G. (born in Krefeld in 1927), Sept. 10, 1996, HVT 3730, tape 2, seg. 20.
4. See Jörg Arnold, *The Allied Air War and Urban Memory: The Legacy of Strategic Bombing in Germany* (Cambridge: Cambridge University Press, 2011), esp. 711–40.
5. Frank Biess, *Homecomings: Returning POWs and the Legacies of Defeat in Postwar Germany* (Princeton: Princeton University Press, 2006). Closely connected was the myth of the "clean Wehrmacht."
6. There were some delusional claims that Jews as actually murdered masses of Germans in revenge, indeed, committed an inverted Holocaust, as for example, Martin Meyer, *Auge um Auge, Zahn um Zahn: der jüdische und der deutsche Holocaust* (Frankfurt am Main: Haag + Herchen, 1992) and some committed Nazis who were serving sentences perceived themselves

as haunted by Jews, as for example, Ilse Koch; see Tomaz Jardim, *Ilse Koch on Trial: Making the "Bitch of Buchenwald"* (Cambridge: Harvard University Press, 2023), 260–3.

7. See Christopher Mauriello, *Forced Confrontation: The Politics of Dead Bodies in Germany at the End of World War* II (Lanham: Lexington Books, 2017); in addition, German civilians were shown footage of concentration camp liberation which many experienced as intentional shaming rather than education to democracy, see Ulrike Weckel, *Beschämende Bilder: Deutsche Reaktionen auf alliierte Dokumentarfilme über befreite Konzentrationslager* (Stuttgart: Franz Steiner Verlag, 2012).

8. Biess, *German Angst*, 25–65 and Feinstein, *Holocaust Survivors*, 101.

9. Rudolf Höss, *Commandant of Auschwitz*, 178.

10. Richard Bessel, "The End of the Volksgemeinschaft," in *Visions of Community in Nazi Germany: Social Engineering and Private Lives*, ed. Martina Steber and Bernhard Gotto (Oxford: Oxford University Press, 2014), 281–94, here 292. Frank Bajohr uses the term "Schuldgemeinschaft," in Bajohr and Pohl, *Der Holocaust als offenes Geheimnis*, 73.

11. Padover, *Experiment in Germany*, 111. See also Saul K. Padover papers, Manuscripts and Archives Division, The New York Public Library MssCol 2325.

12. Adorno, "Schuld und Abwehr," 258–60.

13. In addition to military occupation, trials, and de-Nazification the putative "Morgenthau plan" drawn up by the US Secretary of the Treasury, Henry Morgenthau Jr. in September 1944 which sought to deindustrialize postwar Germany and turn it into a decentralized, divided agricultural state. The plan was eventually abandoned in 1947; before it was abandoned it was widely criticized by Germans, and propagandistically exploited by Nazi leaders; it was also criticized inside the Roosevelt administration, in particular by Secretary of State Henry L. Stimson, who attacking Morgenthau for his Jewish background, called the plan Morgenthau's "Semitism gone wild for vengeance". See Kochavi, Arieh J., *Prelude to Nuremberg: Allied War Crimes Policy and the Question of Punishment* (Chapel Hill: University of North Carolina Press, 1998), 87; John Dietrich, *The Morgenthau Plan: Soviet Influence on American Postwar Policy* (New York: Algora Pub., 2013), 68.

14. Adorno, "Schuld und Abwehr," 251–6.

15. Ibid., 207.

16. Ibid., 261–3.

17. Padover, *Experiment in Germany*, 71.

18. See Kaplan, *Scroll of Agony*, 20, 25.

19. See Lewin, *A Cup of Tears*, 103, 125.

20. During the war, the Office of Strategic Services already warned that because the Nazis used revenge as a tool to persecute their "enemies," the liberating Allied armies would need to be prepared to control the impulse among Nazi victims to pay back their tormentors; see Franz Neumann, Herbert Marcuse, Otto Kirchheimer, Raffaele Laudani, *Secret Reports on Nazi Germany: The Frankfurt School Contribution to the War Effort* (Princeton: Princeton University Press, 2013), 254, 257, 286.

    Similarly, in his 1946 study of the Nazi concentration camp system, Eugen Kogon (who survived six years at Buchenwald) observed that most concentration camp inmates—no matter what their background—were filled with a passionate thirst for revenge as a "psychological response to helplessness"; Eugen Kogon, *Der SS-Staat: Das System der deutschen Konzentrationslager* (Munich: Heyne, 1994), 399. Revenge is therefore also a topic in the diaries of non-Jewish prisoners, as for example the Norwegian resistance fighter Odd

Nansen who rejected revenge; Odd Nansen, *From Day to Day: One Man's Diary of Survival in Nazi Concentration Camps* (Nashville: Vanderbilt University Press, 2016).
21. See for instance Padover, *Experiment in Germany*, 343–4.
22. Ibid., 358.
23. Ibid., 346–7, 344.
24. Levin, *In Search*, 264.
25. In the early postwar period, reemerging Jewish communities were divided by accusations leveled against some survivors who had held held functions in ghettos and camps that involved supervising other prisoners—kapos or *Blockälteste*—in return for some "privileges," be it more food, a better sleeping place, warmer clothing, or less backbreaking work assignments. While in general kapos advocated for prisoners under their watch, some were cruel; for this reason many prisoners made no distinction between them and the SS. It is important to note that with kapos having all kinds of national backgrounds, going after them at liberation was a general phenomenon. This represents a contrast with the violent confrontations that sometimes broke out in reemerging Jewish communities across Europe that involved alleged collaboration of some Jews with the Nazi authorities. In fact, there was a widespread perception among survivors that both Jewish communal leaders and Jews forced to work for the Nazis in ghettos and camps had behaved inimically to their fellow Jews. Those cast under such a cloud included members of the Jewish councils and ghetto police, together with former Jewish kapos. The belief was that enjoying positions of privilege and power, these individuals were meant to save Jewish lives but had instead had been preoccupied with saving their own necks, and those of their families.

More than a few survivors believed that some of the Jewish councils supplying forced laborers and assembling transport lists were worse than the Nazi officials who put the mass murder machinery in action. One renowned German-Jewish intellectual, Hannah Arendt, went in the same direction. "To a Jew," she famously noted in her book on the Eichmann trial, "this role of the Jewish leaders in the destruction of their own people is undoubtedly the darkest chapter of the whole dark story." (Hannah Arendt, *Eichmann in Jerusalem: A Report on the Banality of Evil* (New York: Viking Press, 1963), 91 esp. 104, 111, 116; here 125, and 115.) For Arendt, there would have been fewer victims if Jews had been leaderless, disorganized, and unwilling to cooperate with the Nazis. But in fact, claims of this sort misrepresented the actual power-relation between the Germans and their Jewish victims. The Jewish councils had been deliberately forced to engage in a form of tragic triage: to try to save at least some people at the cost of others, and thus to become complicit, in a sense, in organizing their own communities' destruction. As for Jewish kapos, some were indeed cruel or abusive, but all faced a choice between carrying out their supervisory duties in the camps or being themselves murdered. The harsh judgement passed on surviving Jewish consul members and kapos by fellow survivors had at least as much to do with post-traumatic recovery, an effort to cope with an experience of total powerlessness, senseless destruction, and irretrievable loss as with objective facts concerning the persons involved. With anger against them sometimes extending from verbal to physical assaults, what remained of Jewish communities across Europe now established "honor courts" to try Jews accused of complicity with the Nazis. The hope was that in this way, the visceral response to alleged treachery to the Jewish people would be taken off the street, and channeled into a mediated, intramural setting. These courts had no relevance outside of the—drastically diminished—Jewish communities; their legal basis was improvised. But they did provide a space in which survivors could negotiate the painful issue of internal betrayal—by hearing witnesses, listening to the accused, and if warranted passing social punishment that ranged from moral rebuke to banning a survivor from holding public office or even membership in the Jewish community—this punishment intended as a communal-judicial annulment of any justification for violent and non-violent vengeful acts. See See Rivka Brot, *Be-ezor ha-afor: ha-kapo ha-Yehudi ba-mishpat: mishpatim shel Yehudim meshatfe pe'ulah 'im ha-Germanim* (Ra'ananah: Lamda, 2019); Laura Jockusch and Gabriel Finder (eds.), *Jewish Honor Courts: Revenge, Retribution, and Reconciliation in Europe and Israel after the Holocaust* (Detroit: Wayne State University Press, 2015); Dan Porat, *Bitter Reckoning: Israel Tries Holocaust Survivors as Nazi Collaborators* (Cambridge: Belknap, 2019).

26. Judt, *Postwar*, 42; Henry Rousso, *The Vichy Syndrome: History and Memory in France since 1944* (Cambridge: Harvard University Press, 1991).

27. Judt, *Postwar*, 42; István Deák and Norman M. Naimark, *Europe on Trial: The Story of Collaboration, Resistance, and Retribution During World War II* (Oxford: Routledge, 2015) 204.

28. Fabrice Virgili, *Shorn Women: Gender and Punishment in Liberation France* (Oxford: Berg, 2002).

29. Lowe, *Savage Continent*, 174, 219; Lowe, *The Fear and the Freedom*, 199; Snyder, *Bloodlands*, 313–37.

30. István Deák, "Introduction," in idem, Jan T. Gross, and Tony Judt (eds.), *The Politics of Retribution in Europe: World War II and Its Aftermath* (Princeton: Princeton University Press, 2000), 4.

31. Richard Bessel, "Death and Survival in the Second World War," in *The Cambridge History of the Second World War*, ed. Michael Geyer and Adam Tooze (Cambridge: Cambridge University Press, 2015), vol. 3, 252–76, here 269; R. M. Douglas, *Orderly and Humane: The Expulsion of the Germans after the Second World War* (New Haven: Yale University Press, 2012), 1.

32. Alf Lüdtke, "Explaining Forced Migration," in *Removing Peoples: Forced Removal in the Modern World*, ed. Richard Bessel and Claudia B. Haake (Oxford: Oxford University Press, 2009), 24.

33. Lowe, *Savage Continent*, 243; idem, *The Fear and the Freedom: How the Second World War Changed Us* (New York: Viking Press, 2017), 391.

34. Bill Niven, "Reactive Memory: The Holocaust and the Flight and Expulsion of Germans," in *Memory and Postwar Memorials: Confronting the Violence of the Past*, ed. Marc Silberman and Florence Vatan (New York: Palgrave, 2013), 64, 69. Other authors have lower numbers of overall expellees but higher numbers of dead. For example R. M. Douglas, *Orderly and Humane*, 1, speaks of 14 million and 500,000–1.5 million respectively.

35. At least 190,000 rapes by US soldiers; 50,000 by French soldiers; and 45,000 by the British. See Miriam Gebhardt, *Crimes Unspoken: The Rape of German Women at the End of the Second World War* (Cambridge: Polity Press, 2017), 2, 22; Thomas J. Kehoe and E. James Kehoe, "Crimes Committed by U.S. Soldiers in Europe, 1945-1946," *The Journal of Interdisciplinary History* 47, no. 1 (2016): 53–84, 55.

36. Gebhardt, *Crimes Unspoken*, 2, 18–19.

37. For example, Christian Goeschel, *Suicide in Nazi Germany* (Oxford: Oxford University Press, 2009), 158; Atina Grossmann, "A Question of Silence: The Rape of German Women by Occupation Soldiers," *October* 72 (Spring 1995), 42–63, 46.

38. In Berlin, where perhaps around 100,000 women were raped, 10,000 women committed suicide; see Florian Huber, *Promise Me You'll Shoot Yourself: The Downfall of Ordinary Germans in 1945* (London: Allen Lane, 2019), 75.

39. Gebhardt, *Crimes Unspoken*, 18.

40. Letter from Sammy Popush to his parents, May 1, 1945, YVA O.75/1463; cited in Robert Rozett and Iael Nidam-Orvieto (eds.), *After So Much Pain and Anguish: First Letters after Liberation* (Jerusalem: Yad Vashem, 2016), 118.
41. Ibid., 117.
42. Levin, *In Search*, 279.
43. Ibid., 276–7.
44. Ibid., 277.
45. Ibid., 264.
46. See letter from George Patton to Dwight D. Eisenhower, April 15, 1945, Dwight D. Eisenhower's Pre-Presidential Papers, Principal File, Box 91, Patton George S. Jr. (1); Eisenhower Library, NAID #12007734.
47. See the accounts of American liberators about their own emotions at liberation and the moral problems they see in hindsight: testimony of Charles Ferree (born in Prescott, AZ, 1924), March 11, 1997, VHA 26728, tape 6, seg. 164–8; testimony of Werner Ellmann (born in Bodenwöhr, Germany, 1924), June 6, 1997, VHA 29715, tape 4, seg. 113–15; testimony of Herbert Mirkin (born in Sajtt, Lithuania, 1924), Aug. 22, 1995, VHA 4076, tape 2, seg. 55–6.
48. This was reported by British and American liberators as well as liberated prisoners: testimony of Edward Ruston (born in Chatteris, UK, 1915), Oct. 10, 1996, VHA 21308, tape 5, seg. 132–4; testimony of Curtis Whiteway (born in Newburyport, MA, 1925), May 11, 1998, VHA 44111, tape 5, seg. 138–41 and tape 6, seg. 174–7; testimony of Helen Bolstok (born in Lodz, 1925), Aug. 30, 1995, VHA 6121, tape 3, seg. 79; testimony of Leon W. (born in Lodz, 1925), May 2, 1979, HVT 2, tape 3, 10 mins (concerning US soldiers who kept liberated prisoners from killing guards after one guard was killed in Buchenwald).
49. See, for example, the testimony from American liberators about executions of SS men at Dachau: testimony of Sidney Shafner (born in Philadelphia, 1921), March 31, 1998, VHA 40109, tape 3, seg. 63–6; testimony of Morris Hoffman (born in Marshalltown, IA, 1921), Dec. 3, 1998, VHA 48363, tape 3, seg. 59–60.
50. See for example, the unpublished memoir of Allen A. Cramer, a liberator of Gusen, "Half a Century Later," USHMM Allen A. Cramer collection, accession no. 2005.389, pp. 51–4. See also testimony of James Hayes (born in Istanbul, 1916), Sep. 8, 1994, VHA 93, tape 1, seg. 15–16 (about Breitenbach near Kassel); testimony of John F. Boland (born in Great Falls, 1923), April 2, 1992, USHMM RG-50.759.0015, 16–19 mins (about Mauthausen); testimony of Manfred Steinfeld (born in Germany, 1924), undated, USHMM 1989.346.70 RG-50.031.0070, 15–16 mins (about Wobbelin).
51. See, for example, testimony of Michael Morrow (born in Blakely, PA, 1923), Sept. 22, 1997, VHA 34023, tape 2, seg. 38 (about Ohrdruf); testimony of Bert Weston (born Bertram Weinstein in New York, 1919), Oct. 27, 1997, VHA 34964, tape 4, seg. 94 (about Ebensee); testimony of David Wolf (born in Brzeziny near Lodz, 1920), Jan. 28, 1998, VHA 38725, tape 3, seg. 74 (about Dora-Mittelbau); testimony of Robert Stubenrauch (born in New York, 1924), Dec. 12, 1996, VHA 24207, tape 5, seg. 144 (about Dachau).
52. Testimony of Leon Bass (born in Philadelphia, 1925), Aug. 12, 1998, VHA 44720, tape 2, seg. 49; see also tape 3, segment 70. Other interviewees expressed similar empathy, see the testimony of James Hayes, Sept. 8, 1994, VHA 93, tape 2, seg. 38; and testimony of David Olds (born in New York, 1920), July 23, 1997, VHA 32979, tape 2, seg. 53–4.
53. Testimony of Lusia Puterman (born in Lodz, 1923), March 27, 1996, VHA 12897, tape 4, seg. 19, related that when she was liberated passing as a Polish forced laborer at the Volkswagen factory in KdF Stadt (Wolfsburg) by the Americans, she told an older American officer in a

jeep: "... you must kill all the Germans on earth. And then he started crying. And he said, it's terrible for a young girl like you to say that. The rest I couldn't say to him, you know? I mean. So that was the liberation."

54. See, for example, testimony of Martin Travis (born in Warsaw, 1922), April 12, 1983, USHMM RG-50.477.1382 audio/transcript [ca. 13:00], concerning encouragement to violence of Russian liberators at Blechhammer; although this moment is highly emotional in this testimony, the episode is not mentioned in later testimony for USC, June 29, 1995, VHA 3629, tape 2, seg. 14.

55. See for example, testimony of Irene Hirschfeld (born in Krakow, 1921), Oct. 9, 1995, VHA 7556, tape 3, seg. 70–1.

56. See for example testimony of Abraham Malnik (born in Kaunas, 1927), Feb. 27, 1992, USHMM RG-50.042.0019. Liberated in Theresienstadt by the Russians, Malnik refused to take revenge himself but saw others do so (tape 3). Similarly, testimony of Michael Finkelstein (born in Radom, 1928), April 21, 1985, USHMM, 1997.A.0441.78; Finkelstein saw others engaged in revenge acts in Ebensee but did not participate (c.52–53 mins into tape).

57. For example in the photo collection of the United States Holocaust Memorial Museum.

58. Howard Blum, *The Brigade: An Epic Story of Vengeance, Salvation, and World War II* (New York: HarperCollins, 2001); Morris Beckman, *The Jewish Brigade: An Army with Two Masters, 1944-1945* (Rockville Centre: Sarpedon 1998); Lavi, "'The Jews are Coming,'" 288–92.

59. See the fictionalized autobiographical account by one of the participants, Hanoch Bartov, *The Brigade*, trans. David Segal (London: Macdonald & Co, 1968), on entering Germany as "Hebrew soldiers" from Palestine, 56, 148.

60. Porat, *Nakam*, 39.

61. On the reality of postwar violence against Jews see David Engel, "Patterns of Anti-Jewish Violence in Poland 1944–1946," *Yad Vashem Studies* 26 (1998), 43–85; Jan T. Gross, *Fear: Anti-Semitism in Poland after Auschwitz: An Essay in Historical Interpretation* (New York: Random House 2006); Karolina Panz, "'The Children Are in a State of True Panic.' Postwar Anti-Jewish Violence in Podhale and Its Youngest Victims," *Yad Vashem Studies* 46,1 (2018): 103–40; Joanna Tokarska-Bakir, "Terror in Przedbórz: The Night of 26 May 1945," *East European Politics and Societies* 37,1 (2023): 298–329 and idem, *Cursed: A Social Portrait of the Kielce Pogrom* (Ithaca: Cornell University Press, 2023).

62. Porat, *Nakam*, 175–93.

63. See for example the articles about the poisoning in *The New York Times*, April 20 (p.6) and 23, 1946 (p. 9).

64. See the testimony of Shlomo Kenet, Sept. 14, 1995, USHMM RG-50.120.0219, tape 8 (12–13 minutes into the tape).

65. See Herf, *The Jewish Enemy*; and Peter Longerich, *Antisemitismus: Eine deutsche Geschichte. Von der Aufklärung bis heute* (Berlin: Siedler, 2021), 283–369.

66. See, for example, testimony of Abraham S. (born in Vilna, 1924), Oct. 6, 1985, HVT 615, tape 6, 19 mins; testimony of Eugene N. (born in Zdanov, Czechoslovakia, 1923), Nov. 7, 1982, HVT 178, tape 2, 31–32 mins; testimony of Martin B. (born in Záluzs, Czechoslovakia, today Ukraine, in 1928), Oct. 30, 1996, HVT 1261, tape 1, 59 mins.

67. Padover, *Experiment in Germany*, 343.

68. Nikolaus Wachsmann, *KL: A History of the Nazi Concentration Camps* (New York: Farrar, Straus and Giroux, 2015), 577.

69. David Cesarani, *Final Solution: The Fate of the Jews, 1933-1949* (New York: St. Martin's Press, 2016), 762; Dan Stone, *The Liberation of the Camps: The End of the Holocaust and Its Aftermath* (New Haven: Yale University Press, 2015), 19; Wachsmann, *KL*, 577, 592 and 767 n 191.
70. Letter from Aba Tarlowski, Grodno, Aug. 17, 1944, Yad Vashem Archives [hereafter YVA] O-48/249.3; original in Russian, cited in translation in Rozett and Nidam-Orvieto, *After So Much Pain*, 25.
71. Letter from Grisha Birman, Sept. 4, 1944, YVA O.37/70; original in Yiddish, cited in ibid., 45.
72. Ibid., 46.
73. Letter from Leib Shaus, Nov. 12, 1944, YVA O.37/70; original in Yiddish, cited in ibid., 66.
74. Letter from Azriel Tunik, Aug. 28, 1944, YVA O.75/2327; original in Yiddish, cited in ibid., 30.
75. Letter from Hava Tunik, undated, YVA O.75/2327; original in Yiddish, cited in ibid., 33.
76. Letter from Azriel Tunik, Nov. 7, 1944, YVA O.75/2327; original in Yiddish, cited in ibid., 34.
77. For an English translation of some of these accounts, see Freda Hodge (ed.), *Tragedy and Triumph: Early Testimonies of Jewish Survivors of World War II* (Clayton, Victoria: Monash University Publishing 2018); see esp. 53, 86, 93, 103-104, 107, 112, 115, 118, 214-215.
78. David P. Boder's interview with Benjamin Piskorz, Sept. 1, 1946, Tradate, Italy, Illinois Institute of Technology, Voices of the Holocaust, here 51:00-51:38.
79. See for example, testimony of David Danzyger (born in Będzin, 1923), July 12, 1991, USHMM RG 50.031.0009. Danzyger did not take part in such revenge; in the testimony he noted that most such acts were committed by non-Jewish former prisoners (63 minutes into the tape).
80. *Oma & Bella* (dir. Alexa Karolinski 2012), 56:50–58:10.
81. Testimony of Hanna F., Oct. 16, 1987, HVT 971, tape 1, 45:56.
82. Testimony of Marie Lebovitz, May 31, 1995, VHA 2917, tape 2, seg. 52.
83. On haircutting as revenge see testimony of Frieda G., (born in Odrzywół, Poland, in 1923), November 9, 1986, HVT 827, a survivor of Auschwitz-Birkenau, liberated by the Soviets at Halbstadt, a sub camp of Gross-Rosen; she recounted taking revenge by cutting the hair of the SS guard who had made her life miserable and had humiliated her; tape 1, 51:13–52:54. See also testimony of Eva Bleeman (née Wolf-Buksbaum, born in Oświęcim in 1927), July 19, 1989, VHA 53927, seg. 57–60 (56:00–1:00), concerning liberated prisoners at the Parschnitz concentration and labor camp in Czechoslovakia cutting hair and humiliating German women.
84. Testimony of Marie Lebovitz (born in Kopasnovo, Czechoslovakia, 1924), May 31, 1995, VHA 2917, tape 2, seg. 52.
85. See for example, testimony of Lily Grossman (born in Sajopalfala, Hungary, 1922), Jan. 7, 1997, VHA 24544, on prisoners stepping on a corpse of a SS-Oberscharführer Meier, a guard, killed by Russian tank at liberation, tape 5, seg. 125; testimony of former US soldier Alan Peters (born in Chicago, 1911), July 30, 1997, VHA 32049, recalling that at Dachau weak prisoners beat the corpses of guards killed by US troops with gathered twigs, tape 2, seg. 54.
86. See, for example, testimony of Judith Handley (born in Budapest, 1928), March 21, 1995, VHA 1655, tape 4, seg. 97–8.
87. See for example testimony of Stella Kolin (born in Warsaw, 1926), Aug. 13, 1995, VHA 5415, tape 6, seg. 161; testimony of Linda Breder (born in Stropkov, Czechoslovakia, 1924), November 20, 1996, VHA 22979, tape 6, seg. 37–8.

88. See Rebecca Clifford, *Survivors: Children's Lives after the Holocaust* (New Haven: Yale University Press, 2020), 38, 220–5; Mary Fraser Kirsh, *The Lost Children of Europe: Narrating the Rehabilitation of Child Holocaust Survivors in Great Britain and Israel* (PhD Dissertation, University of Wisconsin, Madison, 2012), 3–4; Johannes Dieter Steinert, "A Moment in Time: The Liberation of Jewish Child Slave Laborers," in *Starting Anew: The Rehabilitation of Child Survivors of the Holocaust in the Early Postwar Years*, ed. Sharon Kangisser Cohen and Dalia Ofer (Jerusalem: Yad Vashem, 2019), 23–50, here 47–9.

89. Testimony of Flora Carasso Mihael (born in Salonica, 1935), April 5, 1995, VHA 1885; tape 3, seg. 61.

90. Padover, *Experiment in Germany*, 343; Levin, *In Search*, 264.

91. See David P. Boder's interview with Otto Feuer, Aug. 22, 1946, Paris, Illinois Institute of Technology, Voices of the Holocaust, here 41:26–41:59.

92. Testimony of Morris Rich, Aug. 12, 1996, VHA 18626, tape 7, seg. 196.

93. Ibid., tape 7, seg. 196–7.

94. Ibid., tape 7, seg. 199–200.

95. Ibid., tape 7, seg. 202. Similarly, testimony of Solomon Kaplan (born in Kovno in 1922), Jan. 20, 1997, VHA 24935, tape 4, seg. 27 and Gabriele Rosenthal, *The Holocaust in Three Generations: Families of Victims and Perpetrators of the Nazi Regime* (Leverkusen: Verlag Barbara Budrich, 2010), 75.

96. Similarly, testimony of Leon W. (born in Lodz 1925), May 2, 1979, HVT 2, tape 3, 10:26; Leon W. did not think of revenge when liberated at Buchenwald because his first priority was food.

97. See Gerhard Wettig, *Entmilitarisierung und Wiederbewaffnung in Deutschland 1943 bis 1955: Internationale Auseinandersetzungen um die Rolle der Deutschen in Europa* (Munich: R. Oldenbourg Verlag, 1967), 106. See also Philip Towle, *Enforced Disarmament: From the Napoleonic Campaigns to the Gulf War* (Oxford: Clarendon Press 1997), 152–68.

98. Elly Gotz, *Flights of Spirit* (The Azrieli Series of Holocaust Survivor Memoirs 54; Toronto: Azrieli Foundation 2018), 73–4.

99. Ibid., 74.

100. Ibid., 77–8.

101. Ibid., 78.

102. Author's interview with Elly Gotz, Oct. 27, 2023 (zoom recording).

103. Ibid.

104. Ibid.

105. Jean Améry, "Im Warteraum des Todes," in *Menschen im Ghetto* ed. Günther Deschner (Gütersloh: Bertelsmann, 1969), 11–31, here 21, translation LJ.

106. David P. Boder's interview with Otto Feuer, 43:03.

107. Ibid., 43:40.

108. Ibid., 44:18–44:21.

109. Ibid., 44:35–45:32.

110. Ibid., 43:42–43:50.

111. Author's interview with Elly Gotz, Oct. 27, 2023.

112. Gotz, *Flights of Spirit*, 78.

113. Author's interview with Elly Gotz, Oct. 27, 2023.
114. Gotz, *Flights of Spirit*, 78.
115. Author's interview with Elly Gotz, Oct. 27, 2023.
116. Gotz, *Flights of Spirit*, 78.
117. Testimony of Martin L., Oct. 19, 1983, HVT 224, tape 1, 34:46.
118. Testimony of Violet S., Sept. 25, 1991, HVT 1650, tape 1, 53–5 mins.
119. Testimony of George Tievsky, Aug. 25, 1997, VHA 33147, tape 4, seg. 117–18.
120. Speech by Zalman Grinberg at the Liberation Concert in St. Ottilien, May 27, 1945, published in Zalmen Grinberg, *Our Liberation from Dachau: Memories of a Survivor* (St. Ottilien: EOS Books 2024), 113–23, here 123.
121. Testimony of Regina Spiegel https://www.youtube.com/watch?v-hdDREztZZY (accessed May 16, 2023).
122. Testimony of Siegfried Halbreich, RG-50.042.0013), March 10, 1992, tape 3, 18 mins. Similarly the testimony of Sidney S. (born in Dolgoye, Ukraine, 1915), May 5, 1985, VHT 0580, tape 2, 48:06, after liberation from Bergen-Belsen.
123. Testimony of Rose K., HVT 355, Aug. 23, 1984, tape 3, seg. 74–5.
124. Larry Orbach and Vivien Orbach-Smith, *Soaring Underground: A Young Fugitive's Life in Nazi Berlin* (Washington, D.C: Compass Press, 1996), 330–1.
125. Testimony of Kurt Klappholz (born in Bielsko-Biala, 1927), USHMM RG-50.149.0060 (1995), tape 12, 10 mins.
126. Ibid., tape 1, 23 mins.
127. Testimony of Norbert Wollheim, Feb. 18, 1992, USHMM RG-50.042.0032, tape 3, 32:40–33:36.
128. Ibid., tape 2, 17:10–17:32.
129. Ibid., tape 3, 31:45–31:55.
130. Testimony of Abraham Malnik, May 10, 1990, USHMM RG 50.030.0145, tape 2. Similarly: testimony of Aron S. (born in Kolomyia, 1918), Nov. 26, 1991, HVT 1936, tape 2, 38:38–40:22.
131. Testimony Fred O. (born in Hrubieszow, 1909), Nov. 18, 1987, HVT 943, tape 3, 17 mins.
132. Testimony of Abraham Malnik (born in Kaunas, 1927), 1992, USHMM RG 50.042.0019, tape 3, 17 mins (transcript p. 19).
133. Testimony of Morris Rich, Aug. 12, 1996, tape 10, seg. 260–1.
134. Testimony of Erika Landon (born in Miskolc, Hungary, 1924) June 20, 2000, VHA 50943, tape 2, seg. 47. Similarly, testimony of Yetta Kleiner (born in Bedzin, 1928), Nov. 28, 1994, VHA 288, tape 3, seg. 61.
135. Yitzhak Zuckerman, *A Surplus of Memory: Chronicle of the Warsaw Ghetto Uprising*, ed. and trans. by Barbara Harshav (Berkeley: University of California Press, 1993), 635.
136. Ibid., 634.
137. Ibid., 632.
138. Ibid., 635.
139. For example, Filip Müller described Moll's exceptional brutality at Auschwitz-Birkenau in his memoir, see Müller *Eyewitness Auschwitz*, esp.125–35, 140–2.
140. Testimony of Paul P., Aug. 28, 1990, HVT 1454, tape 5, 52–3 mins.

141. For a similar conditional acceptance of revenge in the abstract, see testimony of Eva F. (born in Berlin in 1920), Dec. 14, 1995, HVT 3410, tape 2, seg. 31.
142. Yehuda Bauer's comment in *She'erit Hapletah, 1944–1948: Rehabilitation and Political Struggle*, ed. Israel Gutman and Avital Saf (Jerusalem: Yad Vashem 1990), 527.
143. Levin, *In Search*, 275.
144. Ibid., 276.
145. Ibid., 279.
146. Ibid., 276.
147. Ibid., 276.
148. Ibid., 280.
149. Ibid., 280–3.
150. This is not to suggest that in principle Jewish men did not also participate in sexual violence perpetrated by Allied soldiers at the end of World War II, but numbers are impossible to establish, see Atina Grossmann, "Gendered Perceptions and Self-Perceptions of Memory and Revenge: Jewish DPs in Occupied Postwar Germany as Victims, Villains and Survivors," in *Gender, Place, and Memory in the Modern Jewish Experience: Re-Placing Ourselves*, ed. by Judith Tydor Baumel-Schwartz (London: Vallentine Mitchell, 2003), 78–107, here 91–2.
151. See testimony of Yaffa U. (née Shayne Kowalski, born in Švenčionys, Poland, presently Lithuania, 1927), Dec. 8, 1995, HVT 3816, tape 13, seg. 122.
152. Grossmann, "Gendered Perceptions and Self-Perceptions of Memory and Revenge," 89 and Zoë Waxman, *Women in the Holocaust: A Feminist History* (Oxford: Oxford University Press, 2017), 125–8.
153. For example, testimony of Brenda H., Oct. 13, 1991, HVT 0877, 51–52 mins. This was not necessarily the case with men; survivor Lothar (Larry) Orbach recalls how he and other survivors witnessed a rape of a young German girl by a Soviet soldier without having interfered; Orbach felt scorn toward German men who, once powerful and brutal perpetrators, were now "too meek even to protect one of their own children," see Orbach and Orbach-Smith, *Soaring Underground*, 331. The contemporary account of a German woman in end-of-the-war Berlin describes German men as passive and willing to give up women to avoid being targeted by the Soviet occupiers, see Anonymous, *A Woman in Berlin: Eight Weeks in the Conquered City: A Diary*, ed. by Philip Boehm (New York: Metropolitan Books, 2005).
154. Gotz, *Flights of Spirit*, 78.
155. While this night have been the case for Gotz and other survivors, one might object that countless Nazi perpetrators also had humanistic education, were virtuosos and held PhDs and that did not prevent them from committing crimes against humanity; Max Weinreich, *Hitler's Professors; the Part of Scholarship in Germany's Crimes against the Jewish People* (New York: Yiddish Scientific Institute-YIVO, 1946).
156. Author's interview with Elly Gotz, Oct. 27, 2023.
157. See Primo Levi, "Light on the Camps," *The New Republic* 194, 7 (Feb. 17, 1986), 28–32, here 28.
158. Aryeh Sandowski (Leibek), "In the Jewish Brigade," *A Tale of One City: Piotrków Trybunalski*, ed. by Ben Giladi (New York: Shengold Publishers in cooperation with the Piotrkow Trybunalski Relief Association in New York, 1991), 284.
159. Ben Helfgott, "From Piotrkow to London—the of Genesis of the 45 Society Aid," *A Tale of One City*, 393.

160. See Eva Mozes Kor, *The Power of Forgiveness* (Las Vegas: CRP, 2016), see also Shira Diamond and Natti Ronel, "From Bondage to Liberation: The Forgiveness Case of Holocaust Survivor Eva Mozes Kor," *Journal of Aggression, Maltreatment & Trauma* 28, no. 8 (2019): 996–1016. See also Hédi Fried, *Questions I am asked about the Holocaust* (London: Scribe, 2017), 110–17; Rachel Hanan and Thilo Komma-Pöllath, *Ich habe Hass und Wut besiegte. Was mich Auschwitz über den Wert der Liebe gelehrt hat* (Munich: Heyne, 2024); Gidon Lev and Julie Grey, *Let's Make Things Better: A Holocaust Survivor's Message of Hope and Celebration of Life* (London: Macmillan, 2024).

161. Alina Bothe and Markus Nesselrodt, "Survivor: Towards a Conceptual History," *Leo Baeck Institute Year Book* 61, no. 1 (2016): 57–82; Jonathan Zait and Christopher D. Green, "'I'm Not a Person Anymore': The 'Survivor Syndrome' and William G. Niederland's Perception of the Human Being," *History of Psychology* 27, no. 2 (2024): 121–38.

162. On this shift in perception see Wieviorka, *The Era of the Witness* and Terrence des Pres, *The Survivor: An Anatomy of Life in the Death Camps* (New York: Washington Square Press, 1977).

163. See for example testimony of Norbert N. (born in Czernowitz, 1922), March 3, 1984, HVT 536, tape 3, 18:53: "I had my revenge – I survived. Yeah. And I made it"; testimony of Abraham D. (Hebrew), a member of the Sonderkommando at Auschwitz (born in Żuromin, Poland, *c*.1919), June 30, 1988, HVT 1835, tape 2, 20:50: "When I am look back, I think: how did I manage to survive all this? That's what I think. How did I have the luck to be left here alive? And that is my revenge: I am alive . . . [tears up while finishing the sentence]."

164. See, for example, the memoirs by Jenny Harrison, *Out of Poland: When the best revenge is to have survived—A Holocaust Story* (New Zealand: Lamplighter Press 2016); Ernest Feibelman, *Journeys: Survival is the best revenge* (Philadelphia: Xlibris Corporation, 2010).

165. Sutzkever, *From the Vilna Ghetto to Nuremberg*, 240.

166. Ibid., 240.

167. Ibid., 241.

168. Ibid., 241.

169. Ibid., 241.

170. Ibid., 241.

171. Ibid., 242.

172. Grossmann, *Jews, Germans, and Allies*, 213–14 and Feinstein, *Holocaust Survivors*, 150.

173. Testimony of Susan F., May 14, 1990, HVT1622, tape 2, 10 mins.

174. Testimony of Morris Rich, Aug. 12, 1996, tape 10, seg. 262. Similarly the survivor and historian Avraham Fuchs commented at a conference at Yad Vashem in October 1985: "Revenge did not mean only killing Germans. We had revenge when we saw the Germans acting as hewers of wood and drawers of water, when they arrived at Bergen-Belsen and were ready to sell anything for a piece of bread, when we saw them cleaning Jewish houses, the Jewish school I attended, buying cigarettes and paying them in gold – gold that had undoubtedly been taken from Jews. We sold them bread and coffee, and they gave everything they had." See *She'erit Hapletah, 1944–1948: Rehabilitation and Political Struggle*, ed. Gutman and Saf, 532–3.

175. Testimony of Julius O., May 16, 1987, HVT 894, tape 2, 16–18 mins.

176. Testimony of Kurt Klappholz (born in Bielsko-Biala 1927), USHMM RG-50.149.0060 (1995), tape 12, 31 mins.; similarly Roman Frister, *The Cap: The Price of a Life* (New York: Grove Press, 1999) and Avraham Fuchs's comment at a conference at Yad Vashem in

October 1985, "Revenge also meant living with German women." Fuchs was a young survivor from Transnistria who lived in Bergen-Belsen as a DP. See *She'erit Hapletah, 1944-1948: Rehabilitation and Political Struggle*, ed. Gutman and Saf, 533. Having sexual relationships with German women also stirred controversy among Jewish DPs, see Feinstein, *Holocaust Survivors*, 116-17.

177. See USHMM photo archives, photograph no. 69499 (two posters displayed in Landsberg DP camp displayed in what is probably a Purim celebration); ibid., no. 69497 (poster displayed in Landsberg DP camp with cartoon illustration of Hitler, Göring, and possibly Goebbels hanging from a swastika; caption (in Yiddish) reading "I wish you a good Purim"); ibid., no. 69491 (poster displayed in Landsberg DP camp inviting residents to a mock execution of Hitler sponsored by Bnei Akiva religious Zionist youth movement to celebrate Purim. The poster quotes the Scroll of Esther to the effect that one nation is different from all others; declares that the Bnai Akiva court has sentenced Hitler to death by burning; and invites Jews to come witness the event).

178. Ibid., no. 69500 (large poster in Landsberg DP camp displayed during Purim celebration, showing scene from the Purim story, with villain Haman wearing a hat with a swastika and a Nazi armband. The Hitler/Haman villain has a large nose, reminiscent of how the Nazis portrayed Jews in their cartoons and propaganda).

179. See Martin Paulus, Edith Raim, Gerhard Zelger (eds.), *Ein Ort wie jeder andere: Bilder au seiner deutschen Kleinstadt. Landsberg 1923-1958* (Reinbek: Rowolt 1995; see also Yehuda Fogel, "The Year we hung Hitler: A 1946 Purim Celebration in the Landsberg DP Camp," *Tablet Magazine*, March 6, 2023; Elliott S. Horowitz, *Reckless Rites: Purim and the Legacy of Jewish Violence* (Princeton: Princeton University Press, 2006), 81-106, 248-315.

180. Lucy S. Dawidowicz, *From That Place and Time: A Memoir, 1938-1947* (New York: W.W. Norton, 1989), 290; see also Tamar Lewinsky, *Displaced Poets: Jiddische Schriftsteller im Nachkriegsdeutschland, 1945-1951* (Göttingen: Vandenhoeck & Ruprecht, 2008).

181. Grossmann, *Jews, Germans, and Allies*, 137-8 and Mankowitz, *Life between Memory and Hope*, 101.

182. Sutzkever, *From the Vilna Ghetto to Nuremberg*, 251.

183. See Atina Grossmann, "Victims, Villains, and Survivors: Gendered Perceptions and Self-Perceptions of Jewish Displaced Persons in Occupied Postwar Germany," *Journal of the History of Sexuality* 11.1/2 (2002): 291-318, here 312; Avinoam J. Patt, *Finding Home and Homeland: Jewish Youth and Zionism in the Aftermath of the Holocaust* (Detroit: Wayne State University Press, 2009), 31-5, 60-5, 194-5; Leo W. Schwarz, *The Redeemers: A Saga of the Years 1945-1952* (New York: Farrar Straus and Young, 1953), 98-100. Michael Brenner, "From Julius Streicher's Farm to the Kibbutz: The Jewish World after the Holocaust," *A Short History of the Jews* (Princeton: Princeton University Press, 2010), 349-88; Jim G. Tobias, *Der Kibbuz auf dem Streicher-Hof. Die vergessene Geschichte der jüdischen Kollektivfarmen 1945-48* (Nuremberg: Dahlinger und Fuchs, 1997).

184. See Judith Tydor Baumel-Schwartz, *Kibbutz Buchenwald: Survivors and Pioneers* (New Brunswick: Rutgers University Press, 1997), 22, 27; and Meyer Levin (ed.), *Kibbutz Buchenwald: Selections from the Kibbutz Diary* (Tel Aviv, 1946).

185. Patt, *Finding Home and Homeland*, 173, 263.

186. Ivri (Selimar Frenkel), "Hatzatzah min ha-tzad" (A glimpse from the sidelines), *Nitzotz* 6 (51) (December 17, 1945), cited in Mankowitz, *Life between Memory and Hope*, 239.

187. Hannah Yablonka, "Holocaust Survivors in Israel," in *Holocaust Survivors: Resettlement, Memories, Identities*, ed. Dalia Ofer, et al. (New York: Berghahn Books, 2011), 188.

188. As we have seen in the previous chapter, this line from Bialik's poem *Al Hashkhita* (1903) was frequently cited during and after the Holocaust; it also featured prominently in an early postwar Holocaust exhibit with photographs by George Kadish, shown among Jewish DPs in January 1946; see Rachel E. Perry, "George Kadish's 'Modest but Important Beginning:' Exhibiting the Holocaust to Survivors through Photographs, 1945-1946," *The Journal of Holocaust Research* 37, 3: 244-70, here 248.

189. *Landsberger Lager Cajtung* 1, October 8, 1945, p. 3, quoted after Avinoam J. Patt, "The future of the Jewish People: Youth and Education in the DP Camps," in *Starting Anew: The Rehabilitation of Child Survivors of the Holocaust in the Early Postwar Years*, ed. Sharon Kangisser Cohen and Dalia Ofer (Jerusalem: Yad Vashem 2019), 103-43, here 111.

190. Cited in Fishman, *The Book Smugglers*, 200.

191. See Aharon Beilin's testimony at the Eichmann trial, June 7, 1961, *The Trial of Adolf Eichmann*, vol. 3, 1255.

192. According to Hanna Yablonka, of the 88,000 enlisted men and women who fought in the War of Independence, 22,300 were Holocaust survivors; Hanna Yablonka, *Survivors of the Holocaust: Israel after the War* (New York: NYU Press, 1999), 82.

193. Hannan Hever, "From Revenge to Empathy: Abba Kovner from Jewish Destruction to Palestinian Destruction," *The Holocaust and the Nakba: A New Grammar of Trauma and History*, ed. Bashir Bashir and Amos Goldberg (New York: Columbia University Press, 2019), 275-92; Hannan Hever, *Hebrew Literature and the 1948 War: Essays on Philology and Responsibility* (Leiden: Brill, 2019), 149-67. For a similar case of trauma transference, see the case of Beni Wircberg: Amos Goldberg, "Three Forms of Post-Genocidal Violence in Beni Wircberg's Memoir," in *Talking About Evil Psychoanalytic, Social, and Cultural Perspectives*, ed. Rina Lazar (London: Routledge, 2017), 50-67; Beni Wircberg, *From Death to Battle: Auschwitz Survivor and Palmach Fighter* (Jerusalem: Yad Vashem, 2017).

194. Herf, *Three Faces of Antisemitism*, 87-99.

195. Robert A. Wistrich, "Antisemitism and Holocaust inversion," in *Antisemitism before and since the Holocaust*, ed. by Anthony McElligott and Jeffrey Herf (London: Palgrave Macmillan, 2017), 37-49.

196. As the psychiatrist Shamai Davidson noted about his decades of treating Holocaust survivors: "Despite their hatred, few survivors took advantage of the helplessness of the Nazi criminals after the liberation. They had the feeling that in the destroyed cities of Germany revenge had been meted out and further revenge 'would only dirty their hands.' They wished to leave the burnt-out cemetery of Europe to go back to an unsullied old-new homeland for their own rebirth in identification with and on behalf of their lost brothers and sisters. This was in itself an act of revenge and at the same time a triumph over Hitler's image of the Jews and the fate he planned for them in the 'Final Solution.'" See Davidson, *Holding on to Humanity*, 74.

197. Grossmann, "Victims, Villains, and Survivors," 312 and 316.

198. Grossmann, *Jews, Germans, and Allies*, 226.

199. See Grossmann, *Jews, Germans, and Allies*, 188-93, 195-6; especially on children as symbolic revenge, 230-4. On the significance of children for survivors see also Sharon Kangisser-Cohn, "Survivors of the Holocaust and their children," *Journal of Modern Jewish Studies* 9, 2 (2010): 165-83. The Auschwitz survivor and writer Ka-Tzetnik (aka Yehiel De-Nur) wrote a Hebrew novel entitled revenge in which children and future generations are seen as the ultimate revenge; Ka-Tzetnik, *Nakam* (Tel Aviv: Tarmil, 1981).

200. Porat, *Nakam*, 276, 302.

201. See, for example, Werner T. Angress, *Witness to the Storm: A Jewish Journey from Nazi Berlin to the 82nd Airborne, 1920–1945* (Bloomington: Indiana University Press, 2012), 333; testimony of Celina F. Aug. 10, 1991, HVT 1954, tape 3, seg. 27; or testimony of Cela L., July 20, 1984, HVT 1071, tape 2, seg. 9–10 "What was my revenge? What did I, as an individual, do to take revenge? On the Germans? . . . I came to an understanding that I was successful in moving to a country, my homeland, to have a family and establish a family line, to have children and grandchildren. That is what they wanted to obliterate, that there won't be any more [Jewish] children in this world . . . Maybe this is my revenge, and what I stayed alive for."

202. Testimony of Irving Raab (Esther Raab's husband; born in Wojslawice in 1918), Nov. 23, 1997, VHA 35757, tape 8, seg. 232–3; and tape 9, seg. 257.

    Similarly, the survivor and historian Yaffa Eliach (née Shaynele Sonenson) remarked at a conference at Yad Vashem in October 1985: ". . . revenge is not exhausted in murder and desire to humiliate one's torturer. At the large bar mitzvah celebrations and weddings that Holocaust survivors hold, one always feels that Hitler is there and that that is their revenge. At the bar mitzvah of the son of one Holocaust survivor, a poem was read, declaring: 'Today I triumphed over Hitler and Stalin.'" See *She'erit Hapletah, 1944–1948: Rehabilitation and Political Struggle*, ed. Gutman and Saf, 533.

203. Testimony of Irving Raab, (born in Wojslawice in 1918) November 23, 1997, HVT 35757, tape 8, seg. 232–3.

204. See the PBS documentary about Samuel Willenberg entitled *Treblinka's Last Witness* (dir. Alan Tominson) aired Feb. 8, 2019 (https://www.pbs.org/video/treblinkas-last-witness-4rbuxq/, 1:30:15-1:30:50). Willenberg died in 2016. See also for example testimony of Abraham Malnik, USHMM, RG 50.042.0019, 1992, tape 3, 17 mins (transcript p. 19).

205. Garbarini, *Numbered Days*, 51.

206. Virgil, *Aeneid*, IV, 625.

207. Simon Dubnow, Introduction to Elias Tcherikower, *Antisemitism un pogromen in Ukraine, 1917-1918: tsu der geshikhte fin unkarinish-yidishe batsihungen* (Berlin: Mizrekh-Yidisher historisher arkhiv, 1923), 15.

208. Kermisz, *To Live with Honor and to die with Honor!*, 24.

209. See Laura Jockusch, *Collect and Record! Jewish Holocaust Documentation in Early Postwar Europe* (New York: Oxford University Press, 2012).

210. Philip Friedman, "Our Historic Task," Lodz 1945, AŻIH, CŻKP, KH, folder 7, 35–7, Yiddish; translated by Moishe Dolman (translation modified).

211. Testimony of Norman Salsitz, June 9, 1995, tape 3, seg. 92, tape 4, seg. 94.

212. Levi, *If This is a Man*, 523f.

213. Jean Améry, *At the Mind's Limits: Contemplations by a Survivor on Auschwitz and its Realities*, transl. Sidney and Stella P. Rosenfeld (Bloomington: Indiana University Press, 1980 (original German edition 1977), 69–71. On the personal quest for postwar justice see also Richard W. Sonnenfeldt (born in Berlin in 1923), *Witness to Nuremberg: The Many Lives of the Man who Translated at the Nazi War Trials* (New York: Arcade Publishers, 2006) and his testimony, Nov. 13, 1998, VHA 46858; Joseph Riwash (born in Vilna in 1913), *Resistance and Revenge, 1939-1949* (Mount Royal: R & R Distribution, 1981) and his testimony, August 23, 1998, VHA 46406.

214. For example testimony of Florence Lieblich (born in Czortków in 1923), August 10, 1995, VHA 5359 tape 5, seg. 123.

215. See Joshua Rubenstein, "Il'ia Ehrenburg and the Holocaust in the Soviet Press," in *Soviet Jews in World War II: Fighting, Witnessing, Remembering* ed. Harriet Murav and Gennadi Estraikh (Brighton, MA: Academic Studies Press, 2014), 36–57, 40 and Jeffrey Burds, "Sexual Violence in Europe in World War II, 1939–1945," *Politics & Society* 37, no. 1 (2009): 35–73, 49–50, 69 n60.

216. Quoted after Joseph Leftwich, *Abraham Sutzkever: Partisan Poet* (New York: T. Yoseloff, 1971), 11. See also Sutzkever, *From the Vilna Ghetto to Nuremberg*, 282–3.

217. Abraham Sutzkever, "Mayn eydes zogn in Nirnberg," *Di goldene keyt* 54 (1966), 1–14, here 6.

218. Sutzkever, *From the Vilna Ghetto to Nuremberg*, 248.

219. Sutzkever, "Mayn eydes zogn in Nirnberg," 9. See also a recording and transcript of Sutzkever's testimony: https://perspectives.ushmm.org/item/nuremberg-trial-testimony-of-avrom-sutzkever/collection/the-holocaust-and-the-moving-image.

220. Testimony of Morris Rich, tape 10, seg. 253–4.

221. Ibid., tape 11, seg. 280.

222. Ibid., tape 11, seg. 280, 281, 282.

223. Testimony of Roman Sompolinski, Dec. 7, 1995, VHA 9735, tape 2, seg. 42–3.

224. Ibid., tape 3, seg. 80–1.

225. Ibid., tape 4, seg. 111.

226. Ibid., tape 4, seg. 110.

227. Testimony of Michael Goldmann-Gilead, Oct. 28–29, 2015, USHMM RG-50.030.0832, English transcript, p. 133.

228. Josef Buzminsky's testimony at the Eichmann trial, May 2, 1961, *The Trial of Adolf Eichmann*, vol. 1, 391.

229. Testimony of Michael Goldmann-Gilead, p. 109.

230. Ibid., p. 146.

231. Ibid., p. 146.

232. Ibid., p. 149.

233. Ibid., p. 149.

234. Ibid., p. 150.

235. Segev, *The Seventh Million*, 361-5; Ben-Zvi's confirmation of the death sentence contained a reference to Amalek as in 1 Samuel 15:33.

236. See Gali Drucker Bar-Am, "The Holy Tongue and the Tongue of the Martyrs: The Eichmann Trial as Reflected in Letste Nayes," *Dapim* 28, no. 1 (2014): 17–37 and Hanna Yablonka, *The State of Israel vs. Adolf Eichmann* (New York: Schocken Books, 2004), 236–7, 239.

    The Israeli government chose to put only prison guards of non-Ashkenazi descent in charge of Eichmann, individuals with no personal ties to the Holocaust and thus considered less likely to take violent revenge on the prisoner. Eichmann's executioner, Shalom Nagar, a twenty-three-year-old prison guard of Yemenite descent, was reluctant to fulfill the task and kept it secret for most of his life. See Sam Roberts, "Shalom Nagar Dies; Reluctant Executioner of Adolf Eichmann," *The New York Times*, December 5, 2024, and Rachel Ginsberg, "Death Guard," *Mishpacha: Jewish Family Weekly*, December 3, 2024.

237. Testimony of Samuel Lerer, March 23, 1995, VHA 1609, tape 5, seg. 35.

238. Ibid., seg. 32.

239. Arad, *The Operation Reinhard Death Camps*, 427.
240. Testimony of Samuel Lerer, March 23, 1995, VHA 1609, tape 4, seg. 29.
241. Testimony of Esther Terner Raab, April 30, 1990, USHMM RG-50.030.0184, transcript p. 36.
242. Testimony of Samuel Lerer, tape 5, seg. 35.
243. Testimony of Esther Terner Raab, p. 22.
244. Ibid., p. 25.
245. See the verdict of Case No. 212a LG Berlin, May 8, 1950, in *Justiz und NS-Verbrechen*, vol. 6, 543–60, 545.
246. The men who were tried were: Hubert Gomerski and Johann Klier in Frankfurt in 1950; Kurt Bolender, Werner DuBois, Karl Frenzel, Erich Fuchs, Alfred Ittner, Robert Juehrs, Erwin Lambert, Erich Lachmann, Hans-Heinz Schuett, Heinrich Unverhau, Franz Wolf, and Ernst Zierke in Hagen in 1965–1966; and camp-commandant Franz Stangl in Duesseldorf in 1970.
247. See Katharina Stengel, "Eine jüdische Stimme vor Gericht," *Vierteljahrshefte für Zeitgeschichte* 71, no. 3 (2023): 449–81, and idem, *Die Überlebenden vor Gericht. Auschwitz-Häftlinge als Zeugen in NS-Prozessen (1950–1976)* (Göttingen: Vandenhoeck & Ruprecht, 2022) and Rebecca Wittmann, "A Lost Voice? Jewish Witnesses in the Auschwitz Trials in Germany," *Holocaust Research in Context: The Emergence of Research Centers and Approaches*, ed. David Bankier and Dan Michman (Jerusalem: Yad Vashem Press, 2010), 555-66.
248. Testimony of Esther Terner Raab, p. 19.
249. Ibid., p. 15.
250. Ibid., p. 15.
251. Ibid., pp. 21, 38.
252. Ibid., p. 35.
253. See Frenzel's sentencing, case no. 897, LG Hagen, Oct. 4, 1985, in *Justiz- und NS-Verbrechen*, vol. 46, 539–805.
254. Testimony of Esther Terner Raab, pp. 15–16.
255. Ibid., p. 35.
256. Ibid., p. 21.
257. Ibid.
258. Ibid., pp. 35, 38.
259. Ibid., pp. 37–8.
260. Ibid., p. 21.
261. See note 271.
262. Hans-Christian Jasch and Wolf Kaiser, *Der Holocaust vor deutschen Gerichten: Amnestieren, Verdraengen, Bestrafen* (Stuttgart: Reclam, 2017).
263. See for example, testimony of Anita Lasker Walfish (born in Breslau in 1925), Dec. 8, 1998, VHA 48608; Walfish describes her experiences as a trial witness at the "Bergen-Belsen trial" in Lüneburg, Sept.- Nov. 1945 (also the first Auschwitz trial, as the defendants had worked in Auschwitz before being transferred to Bergen-Belsen). Testifying made Walfish realize ". . . how impossible it was for the outside world to understand what was going on [t]here. It was a proper trial, British justice, innocent until proven guilty and I was exposed to the most ridiculous questions. . . . I would be asked questions like 'did you ever see anyone kill

anybody?' and I would say 'yes' and I would be asked 'what day was it?' and I would say 'I don't know' What time was it, was it a stick, was it a stone, . . . I could not answer these questions because a) I didn't have a watch and b) I couldn't care less . . . what date it was. . . . and you are under oath and I was a very good girl of course I was not going to invent anything . . . you immediately feel like a liar. So the whole trial seemed like a total and utter farce to me, because you cannot apply British justice, which is a very commendable thing[,] to something that is so outside anything that has ever been. . . . Admittedly, most of the people were sentenced to death. But the whole system suddenly made me realize this is stuff that will never really be understood unless you have been in it." Asked if she thought it was the right thing to hold trials, given their shortcomings, she replied: "yes, what else can you do? I mean, the alternative is lynching." From her intonation on the recording, it is clear that Walfish did not consider that an option (Tape 4, seg. 105–6).

Disappointment in the West German court system naturally extended to those who in a sense had felt there was no alternative to it during the war already, which is to say from the start: persons such as Norbert Wollheim, who already categorically rejected violent revenge on principled grounds when in Auschwitz, his wife and three-year-old son murdered. After suing I. G. Farben, Wollheim would receive some compensation for his suffering; but despite his own emphatic investment in the principles of legal redress and courtroom justice, he grew disappointed with how things were working out in practice, with lenient sentences and amnesties; Wollheim in any event was particularly disappointed at the results of the American trials at the Nuremberg Military Tribunal.

264. Chaim Brettler, "At the Trials of the Nazi Murderers in Germany," *Skala on the River Zbrucz: A History of the Former Skala Jewish Community*, ed. Max Mermelstein and Tony Hausner (United States: Skala Research Group and Skala Benevolent Society, 2009 [originally published in 1978]), 244–52, here 244.
265. Ibid., 245.
266. Ibid., 246.
267. Brettler himself refers to telling the truth about a perpetrator denying his wrongdoing as "vengeance on the German murderers." (ibid., 244).
268. Ibid., 246–7.
269. See the summary of the trial and verdict, case no.723, LG Hamburg, February 20, 1970, in *Justiz und NS-Verbrechen*, vol. 33, 393–426.
270. Brettler, "At the Trials of the Nazi Murderers in Germany," 247.
271. Ibid., 250.
272. Sutzkever's Nuremberg poem, "Farn nirnberger tribunal" (Feb. 27, 1946), Abraham Sutzkever, *Poetishe verk* (Tel Aviv: Yuval, 1963) 2 vols., vol. 1, 560; translation LJ.
273. See the testimony of Martin S. (born in Tarnobrzeg, Poland, 1933), Jan. 3, 1986, HVT 641, tape 1, 47 mins and testimony of Siegfried Halbreich, RG-50.042.0013 (born in Dziedzice, Poland, 1909), March 10, 1992, tape 3, 19 mins.
274. "Gauting," in Ulrike Puvogel/Martin Stankowski unter Mitarbeit von Ursula Graf (eds.), *Gedenkstätten für die Opfer des Nationalsozialismus: Eine Dokumentation* (Bonn: Bundeszentrale für Politische Bildung 1995), 141 and https://www.gauting.de/fileadmin/gauting-online/Dateien/downloads_pdf/Leben_in_Gauting/Friedhoefe/tafeln_gaut_02.pdf.
275. The Hebrew reads: "*Le-olam kdoshav. Itba bedam zvahav am bli'al she-ratsah hanak saraf ve-harag 6,000.000 kdoshei aheinu be-shnot tarts'ag-tasha*."
276. Porat, *The Fall of a Sparrow*, 235.
277. Ibid., 235.

278. Ibid., 236.

279. Testimony of Victor S., May 3, 1987, HVT 885, tape 1, 45:55–49:56; similarly testimony of Hanan L. (born in Traby, Poland, presently Belarus, 1924), December 6, 1994, HVT 2838, tape 3, segment 30.

280. See, example, testimony of Ernest R. (born in Nitra, Czechoslovakia, 1933), May 17, 1987, HVT 897, tape 2, seg. 19.

281. Testimony of Bart Stern (born in Uzhhorod, Hungary, then Czechoslovakia, 1926), May 20, 1984, USHMM RG-50.005.0052; tape 1, 14 mins; similarly, testimony of Larry K. (born in Zhuprany, Poland, 1925), Nov. 4, 1990, HVT 1734, tape 2, 13–16 mins.

282. For example, testimony of Kurt G. (born in Krefeld, Germany, 1927), Oct. 9, 1996, HVT 3730, tape 2, seg. 22; Kurt G. refused to accept reparations, *Wiedergutmachung*, calling it an insult.

283. Testimony of Hans N., May 9, 1988, HVT 979, tape 2 20:10–20:59.

284. Testimony of Andrew S., Aug. 21, 1984, HVT 495, tape 2, seg. 17.

285. Binyamin Zilberman "Parties and Figures," *Demblin-Modzjitz Book*, English translation by Yiddish Book Center, 2017), 130–45, here 145. Originally published as *Sefer Demblin-Modz'its*, ed. David Sztokfisz (Tel-Aviv: Irgune Demblin-Modz'its, 1969).

286. Yizroel Rozenwein, "For the Eternal Memory," *Demblin-Modzjitz Book*, 611.

287. Mordechai and Yechudit-Sara Teichman-Davidovit's memorial page for Esther Faigenboim-Zavorovsky, ibid., 622.

288. Avraham Lidovski, "Rovno Jews lie buried here," *Rowno: A Memorial to the Jewish Community of Rowno, Wolyn*, ed. Arie Avatihi (Tel Aviv: Association of Rovno Jews in Israel, 1956), 561–2 (Hebrew).

289. See the images published in ibid., 562 and in the Yad Vashem photo archives # 5649/1.

290. For example, in the memorial plaque for the Jews of *Demblin* at the Mount Zion cemetery in Jerusalem, printed in *Demblin-Modzjitz Book*, 552.

291. Rozenwein, "For the Eternal Memory," ibid., 611.

292. The list of works is long: from wartime works by Friedrich Torberg (*Die Rache ist mein*) over Jewish DP poets (Tamar Lewinsky, ed. *Ein Unterbrochenes Gedicht: Jiddische Literatur in Deutschland, 1944-1950*), over Soma Morgenstern (*Die Blutsäule*), Yehuda Amichai (*Lo me-'akhshav lo mi-kan*), Ka-Tzetnik (*Nakam*), or Edgar Hilsenrath (*The Nazi and the Barber*), to Edgar Keret (*Half-baked stories about my Dead Mom*), Max Czollek (*Desintegriert Euch*; *Gegenwartsbewältigung*) to the exploration of revenge through a graphic novel, as Ari Richter's, *Never Again will I visit Auschwitz*, to name just a few examples. Sebastian Schirrmeister is preparing a comprehensive study of literary representations of Jewish revenge during and after the Holocaust; revenge themes are also addressed throughout Rose's *Making and Unmaking Literature in the Warsaw, Lodz and Vilna Ghettos* (Waltham: Brandeis University Press, forthcoming).

293. See documentary, *Treblinka's Last Witness*.

294. See testimony of Luna K. (born in Kraków in 1926), July 5, 1988, HVT 1095, tape 2, 22–6 mins.: "I see too many people of the second generation so angry trying to pay back for us. It's the most counterproductive thing anybody can do. You can't payback for it."

295. Améry, *At the Mind's Limits*, 63.

296. Ibid., 72.

297. Ibid., 67.

298. See Bruno Quelennec, "'The Germans will never forgive the Jews for Auschwitz' (Zvi Rex). Origin, scope and limits of the concepts of "secondary anti-Semitism," *Cités* 87, no. 3 (2021), 33–50.
299. Améry, *At the Mind's Limits*, 67.
300. Ibid., 75.
301. Ibid., 68.
302. Ibid., 70.
303. Ibid., 70.
304. Ibid., 71–2.
305. Ibid., 72.
306. Ibid., 78.
307. Testimony of Edith P. (born in Michalovce, Czechoslovakia, 1920), Feb. 18, 1980, HVT 107, tape 2.
308. Primo Levi, *Collected Poems,* trans. Ruth Feldman and Brian Swann (New York: Faber & Faber, 1988), 24. An Auschwitz survivor uttered similar ideas in an "Open letter to Irma Grese," *The Palestine Post*, Oct. 29, 1945.
309. Memorial plaque https://www.gauting.de/fileadmin/gauting-online/Dateien/downloads_pdf/Leben_in_Gauting/Friedhoefe/tafeln_gaut_02.pdf

    See also People: individuals, families, groups; cemetery: Holocaust memorial, 1943–1949, Box: Case 17, Drawer 2, Folder: 167 (Gauting-15). Displaced Persons Camps and Centers Photograph Collection, RG 294.5. YIVO Institute for Jewish Research, photograph 24.

POSTSCRIPT
JEWISH REVENGE IN POSTWAR FILM

The first feature film produced in postwar Germany, Wolfgang Staudte's *Die Mörder sind unter uns* (The Murderers are Among Us), centered on revenge: albeit not "Jewish revenge," but rather a form of fantasy-revenge of a German against a German—mercifully averted by a Jew. Released in 1946 with the stamp of approval of the Soviet Military Government, the film featured an unlikely pair of apartment-mates in bombed out Berlin: Susanne Wallner, a Jewish woman who has returned from a concentration camp; and Dr. Hans Mertens, a demobilized Wehrmacht soldier and physician. Both individuals are traumatized; but they seek different paths to healing. Wallner works at rebuilding human connections: to the elderly Jewish optometrist Mr. Mondschein, who is waiting for the homecoming of his deported son; to those she meets through work—cleaning up the rubble, rebuilding a pleasant home, preparing food and caring for others, including her new roommate, Mertens. Mertens tries to heal through anger, alcohol, and revenge. He plans to shoot his former commanding officer, Ferdinant Brückner, now a successful businessman and *pater familias*, as revenge for having ordered Mertens' battalion to shoot Polish civilians on Christmas Day 1942. Mertens believes he can only return to life if he avenges Brückner's victims. Wallner, the Jewess, dissuades him through love, optimism, and care; Mertens gives up his plans to wreak vengeance on the former Nazi commander and regains a sense of purpose in life, a sense of having a place in postwar German society.

Although the film operates with realistic scenery—rubble and ruins—its plot was far from the historical reality on the ground; it involves an interesting early postwar cinematic revenge narrative reversal: Germans were, after all, highly unlikely to pursue revenge against other Germans for murdering Jews or other non-German civilians under the Nazi regime; a great many Germans feared revenge by surviving Jews—and in any case *already* viewed themselves, through destruction and defeat, as victims of "Jewish revenge." In addition, among the German Jews who survived Germany's mass murder, in the camps, in hiding, or in exile abroad, only a minute number had come back to the country with plans to somehow resume prewar lives. Although *Die Mörder sind unter uns* is a valuable reflection of Germany's postwar situation, with a memorable presentation of fantasies and images, the film is at a significant remove from the historical reality of Germany as it was in 1946.

Die Mörder sind unter uns had an interesting counterpart filmed in the American zone of occupation in 1947: the German-American coproduction, *Lang ist der Weg* (Long is the way), the only Yiddish film produced in Germany. Licensed by the American Information Control Division, it is an attempt to tell the history of the Holocaust from a

Jewish perspective. It combines the story of one family, the Jelins from Warsaw, with a narrative about the collective cataclysm of the Jewish people. Starting with the September 1939 German attack on Poland, it covers now-iconic Holocaust tropes: ghettoization, deportation to death camps, selection, escape, partisan fight, survival and loss; it also delves into postwar Jewish displacement, homelessness, search for missing family members, reunion and rebuilding; it makes a strong political plea for solving the plight of the Jewish Displaced Persons in Germany through immigration and sovereignty in Palestine. Filmed on site in the Landsberg DP camp, the film combines fictionalized scenes—played by mostly Jewish actors who were survivors themselves and some German non-Jewish actors—with documentary footage from wartime and postwar. Although the dialogues are primarily in Yiddish, with some Polish and German, the film features a German-language voiceover. In its attempt to reach not just a Jewish but also a German audience, *Lang ist der Weg* calls out Hitler, the SS, and faceless German soldiers as Holocaust perpetrators but refrains from incriminating the German population; antisemitism only seems to exist in Poland, Poles are depicted in ambivalent roles as Nazi collaborators and greedy thieves of Jewish property but also as helpers of Jews. *Lang ist der Weg* was a cooperation between Jewish and German artists: directed by Marek Goldstein, a survivor of Polish background, and Herbert B. Fredersdorf, who had worked in the film industry of the Nazi regime, the script was based on an idea by the actor Israel Becker (who also plays the leading character, David Jelin), and was co-written by Becker and Karl-Georg Külb. While Becker had escaped his native Bialystok and survived in the Soviet Union, Külb had written the scripts for Nazi entertainment films. The film follows David Jelin and his parents Hanne (Berta Litwina) and Jakob (Jakob Fischer) into the Warsaw ghetto and onto a deportation train; David saves himself by jumping off the train. While Hanne survives the selection at Auschwitz, Jakob is selected for death. David survives among hostile and helpful Poles, and by joining the Jewish partisans. He returns to Warsaw in search of his parents only to learn of his father's death and to understand that there is no place for Jews in Poland. He makes his way to a DP camp in the US zone of occupied Germany in search of his mother and seeking to rebuild his life. Along the way he falls in love with Dora Berkowitz, a German Jewish survivor (played by the non-Jewish actress Bettina Moissis), marries her, and becomes a father. Ultimately, David reunites with his mother who is slowly recovering from mental and physical collapse. The film touches upon the revenge theme in a subtle way. When David and Dora make their way from Warsaw to Munich along with other survivors, they encounter a group of ethnic Germans who have just been expelled from Poland, also seeking refuge in Germany. Hearing these Germans complain about their hardship and loss of home and property, one of the Jewish survivors gloats that they only get their just deserts: "Rightly so, now they eat from the same bowl! They used to displace others and now they are displaced themselves!" David does not share the glee and comments: "we *all* eat from the same bowl!" While the other survivor insists "but they are responsible for all this!" David elaborates "I cannot think like this. . . . Horrors were done to me . . . mother and father won't come back . . . but I do not wish what I have endured to anyone. I finally want to live in peace. How can there be peace if no one wants to stop hating?" The film thus presents a narrative in which survivors put aside their pain and negative emotions, empathize with the suffering of Germans and prepare for a life in Palestine. It ends with a scene portraying David farming the German soil—while Dora and Hanne lovingly watch the child—as preparation for a future in a sovereign Jewish state. Despite this political message, the film presents a vision of a productive transformation of vengeful impulses.

Both *Die Mörder sind unter uns* and *Lang ist der Weg* portray Jewish survivors as giving up hate, seeking peaceful coexistence, recognizing the shared humanity of Germans, Jews, Poles, and others, and as channeling their emotions and experiences into becoming productive members of society and building a better present and future for the greater good of society. While this larger than life, idealized version of "the survivor" carried through other cinematographic representations of the Holocaust in later decades, the attitude toward revenge changes from rejection to embrace, from side-plot to central story line.

On the verge of a post-survivor age, we can observe that popular cinematic culture has been quite well-informed by representations of vengeful Jews baiting and killing Nazis. In this respect, a special realm of counterfactual expression opened with Quentin Tarantino's 2009 film *Inglorious Basterds*, which projected a lurid and exciting revenge fantasy: two entangled revenge plots, one involving a secret American battalion led by Lt. Aldo Raine (Brad Pitt), which has been formed to track down and then brutally murder Nazi officers in German-occupied France; the other involving a young Jewish woman working for the French resistance, Shoshanna Dreyfus (Mélanie Laurent), who succeeds, by the time the film has ended, in avenging her murdered family by incinerating the entire Nazi leadership, Hitler and Goebbels included, in a Paris movie theater. With his film, Tarantino established a new cinematic genre: Holocaust-revenge movies that use stylized violence and subvert the moral stigmatization normally attached to revenge by celebrating it as heroic, enjoyable, and entertaining. Celebrating counterfactual history and stretching the audience's imagination to picture a role-reversal between the Nazi regime and its victims, the movie aestheticized and justified violence: payback for extreme brutality and inhumane acts with extreme brutality and inhumane acts. Tarantino's film had subtlety of offering viewers cheap and trashy wish-gratification while ironizing their enjoyment as they watched. Audiences enjoyed the film and watched it with enthusiasm because the violence was meted out by the right people to the right people for the right reasons—and because it was, after all, only a fantasy.

Inglorious Basterds was a smash hit paving the way for several Holocaust-revenge movies for cinema and TV operating with some of the same plot elements and forms of expression. These productions share elements of counterfactual, alternative historical narrative; they feature different versions of intergenerational revenge imperatives meant to be implemented by the film's protagonists, either in the immediate postwar period in Germany and Austria or decades after the Holocaust in places where Nazi criminals found refuge, in Spain, the US, Canada, and South America. All the films treat the frustration and pain of victims and survivors at the justice system's failures, and all revolve around searches for Nazi war criminals who escaped justice. Likewise, they all combine stories of personal revenge with a broader quest for vengeance in the name of the Holocaust's victims, even in the name of humanity as a whole. They tell particularist stories about Jews intent on meting out payback on Nazis for having murdered Jews—but this combined with universalist narratives about Jews and non-Jews joining forces in the payback, to punish racist crimes, and contribute to humanity's common good.

Some of these films present intergenerational narratives of sons taking revenge on Nazi perpetrators on behalf of their parents; but rather than carrying out the revenge-killings themselves they have nature—the elements—do the work for them. *This Must be the Place* (Paolo Sorrentino, Italy/France/Ireland, 2011) depicts the journey of an aging and dysfunctional rock star, Cheyenne (Sean Penn), the estranged son of a Holocaust survivor, across America, aiming to track down his father's tormentor in Auschwitz, Alois Lange. But as the film depicts him, Cheyenne mainly gains a sense of meaning and purpose not in the revenge he seeks but through the human connections he makes on his journey—including connections to both his deceased father and himself. Rather than murdering old, blind Lange with the weapon he has purchased, he confronts him and forces him to strip naked and march into the Utah salt flats, leaving him there to die. More recently, Thomas Roth's drama *Schächten / A Retribution* (Austria, 2022) follows the revenge quest of Victor Dessauer (Jeff Willbush), a young Viennese Jewish businessman whose father has died of a heart attack shortly after failing to get his former tormentor at Mauthausen, Kurt Gogel, convicted in an Austrian court, despite the solid evidence against him. As a child, Victor himself survived the war hiding in the woods in an Austrian valley. Victor hunts down Gogel—but again refrains from killing him with the gun he has purchased, instead driving him into a lonely creek located in the very valley where Victor hid as a child, leaving him to die in a landslide. Set in the early 1960s, the movie provides a glimpse into the reality of a postwar Austrian society in which perpetrators enjoyed widespread sympathies and stereotypes of Jews lived on unbroken—in which Jews were outcasts and Nazi criminals were protected and defended by their old networks.

Two cinematic contributions to this genre use the plotline of a Jewish survivor-avenger who is in fact a Nazi war criminal hiding his identity by mingling with survivors and passing as a Jew. Atom Egoyan's *Remember* (Germany/Canada, 2015) tells the story of a pair of Auschwitz survivors in a Jewish nursing home in New York, Max Rosenbaum (Martin Landau) and Zev Guttman (Christopher Plummer). Guttman suffers from dementia. After the passing of Guttman's wife Ruth, Rosenbaum convinces him to find Otto Wallisch, one of the guards who tortured them both at Auschwitz. Guttman is, Rosenbaum explains, the last person able to identify Wallisch, who has immigrated to America under the name of Rudy Kurlander. Four men can be located who go by that name and otherwise fit the description; Guttman is now sent on a road trip to seek out each of these men in turn.

The first three men Guttman visits do not seem to be Wallisch; he then enters the house of the fourth man, Rudy Kurlander (Jürgen Prochnow), whom he recognizes by his familiar voice. When Gutmann threatens Kurlander's granddaughter with a revolver,

Postscript

Kurlander confesses to his family that his real name is Kunibert Sturm—and that Zev Guttman is in fact Otto Wallisch, a fellow SS guard at Auschwitz, an unmasking to which the real Wallisch reacts by first shooting Sturm, then himself. Max Rosenbaum, it turns out, has orchestrated this revenge plot after discovering the truth about the purported Gutmann—and that real Wallisch was the only one who could identify and murder Sturm while playing the role of a demented survivor on a vengeance mission.

The motif of a Nazi war criminal posing as a vengeful Jew to escape accountability is also central to Amazon Prime's action drama *Hunters* (two seasons, 2020–2023); as in *Remember*, the identity-theft story, which is set in New York City, is complemented by figures who are actually Jews and are pursuing their own revenge plots or those of deceased relatives. In *Hunters*, the main characters are Meyer Offerman (Al Pacino), leader of a diverse group of Jewish survivors, Poles, Blacks, and Asians hunting down old Nazis, neo-Nazis, and white supremacists in America, and Jonah Heidelbaum (Logan Lerman), who has replaced his late, charismatic grandmother Ruth (Jeannie Berlin) in the group. Over the course of a highly convoluted plot full of false identities, Meyer Offerman is revealed to actually be Wilhelm Zuchs, a former SS doctor who escaped accountability by killing a Polish Jewish inmate at Auschwitz, assuming his identity and—with the help of plastic surgery—looks and becoming the charismatic leader of a secret revenge imperium. By leading the group in its hunt for hidden Nazis, Zuchs alias Offerman has eliminated all those capable of exposing his real identity and past. Jonah Heidelbaum's grandmother Ruth had been romantically tied to the real Meyer Offerman; she was murdered in her home by the false Offerman, Zuchs—a murder Jonah witnesses at the beginning of the series—because she discovered his real identity. Jonah, who turns out to be the grandson of Meyer Offerman, ultimately dispenses with violent revenge, instead leading the group in a quest to capture Nazi criminals and see them tried in court. The film culminates with the group hunting down Hitler, who did not commit suicide but lives comfortably in Argentina, kidnapping him, and bringing him to justice in Germany. Ultimately, *Hunters* tells the story of a large spectrum of outcasts representing different minority groups who were, or would have been, victimized by the German Nazis, and who oppose a world ruled by white supremacists: a group bonded together behind a mission to use vengeance as a tool for building a better, more inclusive society.

Less phantasmagorical than *Hunters* but still fictionalized are two spinoffs of the Jewish Brigade's and Nakam's revenge plots: the French/German/Canadian eight-episode TV production *Shadowplay/The Defeated* (Netflix, 2020) and the Israeli-German cinematic coproduction *Plan A*, directed by Doron and Yoav Paz (2021). *Shadowplay/The Defeated* tackled the topic of Holocaust revenge without any Jewish protagonists. It is the story of an American police officer, Max McLaughlin, helping Else Garten, a newly appointed German police superintendent, in rebuilding West Berlin's police force; he is also investigating a series of brutal murders of former Nazi perpetrators—the responsible party being, it turns out, his brother Moritz, a missing American GI and self-declared avenger of Nazi crimes. For its part, *Plan A* is a fictionalized version of the Nakam plot to murder six million Germans; also drawing on operations of the Jewish Brigade, the film presented its revenge story in a directly Jewish context, paying close attention to the plotters' loss and trauma to justify their actions and explain why they ultimately failed.

All the more recent popular film and TV representations of Holocaust revenge are aimed at viewers' consumption of a gratuitous violence that is aestheticized, made pleasurable and entertaining: a reflection of the double standard generally guiding the entertainment industry's relationship to violence. Most of the films involved offer a one-dimensional understanding of such revenge as the torturing and killing of Nazis; more subtle forms of vengeance—non-violent, imagined, unfulfilled—and the internal struggles of conscience of would-be avengers, are absent. These cinematographic representations are also counter-factual in that they suggest that revenge plots against former Nazis occurred decades after the war—when in reality, as we have seen, violent Jewish revenge only extended to the immediate postwar period, and then but rarely.

These recent film and TV presentations mostly focus on male avengers; when women do enter the picture, they have typically male roles marked by combat and violence—as we see for example in the figure of Isabel, the protagonist in the Spanish TV drama of Ramón Campos and Gema R. Neira, *Jaguar* (Netflix, 2021). The film is set in Spain in the 1960s; its plot is as follows: Isabel, a Spanish non-Jewish survivor of Mauthausen, hunts down Otto Bachmann, her former tormentor and the murderer of her family, who had found refuge in Spain. She is joined by a group of male avengers, some Jewish, who are also on a mission to find Bachmann. *Jaguar* is in fact a good example of how the entertainment industry uses Holocaust tropes and emblems having little or nothing to do with actual historical events. Good guys fight bad guys, the historical context slimmed to what is recognizable, relatable, and entertaining, as in a mediocre video-game—some victim, Jewish or not, is fighting some Nazi as payback for some gruesome crime in some awful camp in a foreign country, played by actors with vague accents. This is facile audience-intake purchased at the cost of historical precision—and any effort at historical insight. At a time when viewers, especially but not only younger ones, have increasingly little knowledge of Nazism and the Holocaust, this purchasing of cheap entertainment at the cost of any justice to a real, complex and momentous historical event, while clearly inevitable, is nonetheless questionable.

The obscurantist thrust of popular "Jewish revenge" entertainment notwithstanding: it is also the case that arguably, popular culture's phantasmagoric approach to the topic served as impetus for historians to begin acknowledging it in their research. There is now, at least, a possibility for more sober, thought-provoking explorations of the topic aimed at a broad audience. In this respect, two recent documentary films have helped lead the way: Danny Ben-Moshe's *Revenge: Our Dad the Nazi Killer* (Australia, 2023) and a German language documentary directed by Antonius Kempmann und Martin Kaul, *Shlomo—Der Goldschmied und der Nazi* (*The Goldsmith and the Nazi*, Germany, 2023). Both these films are concerned with encounters between Holocaust survivors and perpetrators in places where large numbers of both groups had reestablished themselves after the war, hoping to get away from their past. Both tell the story of state authorities who let down survivors during the Cold War by not following information they offered about where war criminals were living and by failing to prosecute them, and even by failing to furnish protection to former victims.

Ben-Moshe's *Revenge* follows Jack, Jon, and Sam Green the three sons of Boris Green, a Lithuanian-born Jewish survivor and partisan who settled in Melbourne after the war; Sam Green, a loving father and engaged member of Melbourne's survivor community, was apparently tied to the murder of a Lithuanian Nazi collaborator in Sydney in the 1950s. With the help of a private investigator, on the basis of family archives and photo albums, video testimony, and accounts of family members and friends—and in particular from scattered written statements in the papers Boris Green left behind, together with recollection of their father's lifelong struggle to cope with a traumatic past stamped by irretrievable loss—the brothers probe their complicated moral feelings concerning revenge. They experience shock and turmoil as they pursue traces of his wartime and early postwar desire for violent revenge and learn about what seem like concrete actions he took to exact it. They discover a side of their deceased survivor father that he never revealed to them during his lifetime, a side apparently incompatible with the man they had known. Ultimately, they are left with more questions than answers. For one thing: can writing a poem in Yiddish expressing a wish for revenge at the end of the war, and some random statements to that effect, brought together with the unresolved murder of a Lithuanian Nazi collaborator in the Sidney harbor, lead to the conclusion that Boris indeed committed what would have been a violent crime? For another thing: why should his sons see their father's role as a partisan fighter in a Lithuanian forest as heroic, and at the same time his alleged murder of a Lithuanian Nazi collaborator in Australia in the absence of courtroom justice as morally wrong?

Kempmann and Kaul's *Shlomo* reconstructs the story of Stanislaw (Shlomo) Szmajzner, a Polish Jewish survivor of Sobibor who rebuilt his life in Brazil after the war. In 1978, Brazilian police authorities, following Simon Wiesenthal's lead, called on Szmajzner to confirm the identity of Austrian SS-Oberscharführer Gustav Wagner, deputy commandant of Sobibor, known for his brutality and sadism by the Jewish prisoners temporarily spared from death to work for the SS guards in the murder-camp's workshops—Szmajzner survived in this way as a goldsmith. Szmajzner duly confronted Wagner, who did not deny his identity; but the authorities released him and failed to press charges. A few weeks later, Wagner was found dead in his apartment in a village outside of Atibaia. The documentary brings together interviews with Szmajzner, in which he voices some vengeful feelings, and with people who knew him closely, together with eye witness testimony from people in Wagner's community and excerpts from the local police investigation. The two journalist-directors make no inference that Szmajzner was involved in Wagner's death, as there is no conclusive evidence in that respect. Instead, they probe their own feelings of empathy with Szmajzner, the survivor, with his pain and frustration with the legal authorities—this against the backdrop of the horror of Sobibor and the monstrosity of a perpetrator like Wagner never seeing justice.

In their empathetic look at survivors' struggle to rebuild their lives, the revived trauma of encountering former tormentors now shielded by the authorities and living comfortably, these two films do not shy from complexity and nuances: the survivors may, for instance, have revealed many details about their past to families, communities, and a wider public but have kept silent about other details; and at the same time, the fact that one indulges in violent revenge fantasies does not mean one ever became a killer. Both films also look at the image held of survivors by those born after, their expectations in respect to which feelings and actions lie in a realm of toleration, even approval, which not. Neither film offers conclusive answers to the problems it raises, and neither tries to establish the truth located within a murky postwar traumatic field comprised of fantasy and fact.

CONCLUSION

The personal experiences of most European Jews murdered during the Holocaust are lost from the historical record. That is also the case for victims who engaged in violent revenge or, defiantly and desperately, issued revenge imperatives—virtually all were murdered, as were witnesses to these acts; and nearly all those who may have recorded them likewise will have perished, along with their records. For every survivor, at least two European Jews were murdered. In some parts of eastern Europe, especially in Poland, Latvia, Lithuania, Belorussia, and Ukraine, there were more than nine deaths per survivor. If, when, and how the few survivors wrote and testified about revenge depended on the postwar setting, with audiences and interviewers playing ambiguous roles—at times judging and silencing, at times facilitating survivors' acknowledgment of, or attention to, the theme. Sometimes those listening to testimony glossed the theme over, perhaps uneasy or embarrassed to probe; there are no follow-ups on details in the interviews, instead a turn to subjects thought more important. Often, interviewers did not ask about revenge and interviewees did not think it was important enough to volunteer the subject. Asked in 2023 why he did not talk about revenge in his 1987 testimony but did so thirty years later,[1] Elly Gotz explained that back in the 1980s it had not occurred to him to talk about his feelings. "To me the essence was: the facts . . . I wanted to tell the story. What happened. What was done. Something that people could grab and understand as a physical thing." Aside from these testimonial priorities, Gotz also pointed out that for decades after the war "nobody asked me, how do you feel? So . . . I saw that the more important thing was to tell the facts and not my state of mind." After decades of telling, retelling and writing his life-story, Gotz changed his attitude and added his wartime and postwar emotions to his account of the lived historical facts. "The state of mind is more important to me now because I realized that young people listen to me, and perhaps they learn something."[2] Historicizing also the emotional responses to the lived historical experience afforded Gotz the attention—and affection—of especially younger listeners of diverse cultural backgrounds. With the survivors' generation fading away, the revenge theme is fading into history as well, along with various other topics survivors have generally not addressed as too painful, or else from a presumption that others would not care to know.

Nevertheless, as we have seen, numerous sources and voices offer a history of the forms and functions of revenge, as deed and idea, during and after the Holocaust. How has the material we have surveyed illuminated our understanding of the Nazi Germany's "final solution," its perpetrators, bystanders, and victims, and its immediate aftermath?

A wide range of Germans directly and indirectly involved in the mass murder of Europe's Jewry held conspiratorial views of Jews. From the Middle Ages onward, anti-Jewish stereotypes of innate vengefulness and fantasies of Jewish vengeance had informed the Christian antisemitic imagination. Nazi antisemitism, while offering a new project of creating a "world without Jews" through physical elimination, was eclectic; it reused ideas and policies from the longstanding antisemitic arsenal, including, as a persistent leitmotif that now gained new relevance, the idea of the vengeful Jew. Revenge-focused rhetoric now served as one tool for imagining, motivating, and normalizing violence against Jews; it helped reverse the roles of victim and aggressor, exculpating Germans from intentional murderous violence against unarmed human beings while criminalizing and militarizing the Jews.

In this manner, an ideologically potent myth emerged of German victimization at the hands of "international Jewry," held responsible for international communism, defined as ruling the Soviet Union and other nations, and charged with seeking Germany's destruction: a picture, painted through a torrent of highly effective propaganda, pointing to a need for German self-defense through physically eliminating the Jews. Here a *fantasy* of Jewish aggression and revenge was used, with great skill, to legitimize the *reality* of what became a German campaign of absolute genocide. German perpetrators in killing fields and death camps operated, in a very concrete way, with the ideological construct, devoid of any reality, of German self-defense against European and world Jewry: a necessity for military security; a patriotic duty. Revenge fantasies were an integral part of the Nazi German antisemitic and genocidal worldview.

Between 1933 and 1945, rather many Germans who were *not* true Nazi believers came to embrace, or at least more or less accept, a view of Jews as avengers, this sometimes, as time went by, from fear of the results of war and mass murder, from guilt, or from shame. As Nazi Germany perpetrated its mass crimes against humanity, its victims intuitively responded by conjuring up and—rarely, as they were defenseless and powerless—carrying out violent revenge. In that respect, it is important to take note of the uni-directional causal link between German aggression and Jewish revenge: namely Jews resorted to the idea and—again, rarely—practice of revenge as a response to German aggression. German aggression against Jews was *not* a response to actual revenge acts by Jews. Predating and outlasting the Holocaust, the ideological idea of "Jewish vengeance" had nothing to do with how Jews behaved in reality.

Conspiracy-focused ideas about Jewish revenge also resonated with many non-Jews in the Nazi empire, especially among those collaborating in one or another way with the Germans. Most commonly, such ideas, harbored in a broader conceptual framework of "Judeo-Bolshevism," informed the actions of eastern European nationals wishing to themselves take revenge on Jews for alleged collaboration with the previously occupying Soviets. Later, persons who had betrayed Jews, robbed or confiscated their property in eastern Europe, out of envy and greed, feared that the former owners would return and take back what had been theirs, identify them as Nazi collaborators to their compatriots—and take revenge on their former neighbors; this led to violence against survivors: part of a larger European history of "Jewish revenge" and anti-Jewish ethnic violence beyond the scope of this book.

Conclusion

The multi-dimensional story of Jewish revenge, both conjured up and real, during and after the Holocaust sheds light on questions of response and agency under constantly worsening living conditions. Apart from a few outliers, Jews only turned to the idea of revenge when they understood the extent and systematic nature of the ongoing mass murder. They turned to revenge gradually and partially. For those who did, as Jean Améry succinctly noted, revenge emerged "at the end of a long journey through the night"[3]—when individuals believed they were left with no other options and despaired to find an expression of their pain and hopelessness. What we can broadly consider a revenge-response was manifest in a variety of forms: acts of real physical violence, defiant humiliation and mockery of Nazi perpetrators and non-German auxiliaries, written and oral revenge imperatives directed at other Jews, together with revenge imprecations aimed at the murderers themselves; and the expression of fantasies of revenge in diaries, letters, and inscriptions. Acts and fantasies existed side by side. During the war and Holocaust, fantasies and non-violent gestures by far predominated, due to the crushing nature of the circumstances; in the early postwar period, non-violent and symbolic forms of revenge was the general rule, due to both ethical principles and restoration of a civil society possessing a genuine justice system. In wartime, the threshold for enacting violent revenge was naturally lower for persons in the underground or partisan groups. But in this crisis period, all manifestations of revenge and its desire were a response to complete powerlessness and hopelessness, a coping mechanism in the face of coming murder, whether immediate or down the road.

The revenge acts and fantasies outlined in these chapters were merely one response to an unprecedented mass murder. The phenomenon, both as repetitively articulated wish and action, needs to be understood in a broader context of Jewish responses to Nazi persecution—and this not only as the genocide was unfolding but also in its aftermath. It is in any case important to note that the great variety of revenge phenomena that emerged, ranging, for example, from a defiant mother cursing those about to murder her children—and expressing full awareness of the exterminatory context in which the crime was taking place, its radical injustice—over imagining revenge while coping with mass atrocities in ghettos, camps, hiding places and death marches to the assassination of a German government official or SS guard, offers one more reason to reject the notion of Jewish passivity during the Holocaust as a myth: one not only failing to do justice to the situation facing European Jewry but simply wrong.

Confronting "Jewish revenge" from the German perspective during and immediately after the Holocaust deepens our understanding of German mentalities at this time. We see, for a start, that Germans from all walks of society had internalized the propagated myth of Jewish power, aggression, and vengefulness; in the early postwar period, the myth fueled German anxiety, in a mental context stamped by latent guilt for Nazi crimes, feelings of humiliation, and shame at defeat and failure. Germans expected vengeance from Jews. They saw the Allied bombing of German cities, military defeat, and occupation, expulsions, mass rape, and war crime trials, as manifestations of it. To be sure, German fears of "Jewish revenge" had no relation to real postwar revenge by Jews. Contemporary observers from among the Allies, most of them Jews who were aware of what Jewish survivors had gone through, in fact voiced surprise at how much restraint they were showing. Germans tended to see any acts of vengeance they experienced at the war's end from various national groups as "Jewish"; some saw Jewish commemoration of the dead, a search for justice, even reminding Germans of their Nazi past, as vengeful acts.

Detached from reality, German ideas of Jewish revenge remained static in substance throughout the prewar, wartime, and postwar years. Fueled by relentless Nazi propaganda that actually intensified toward the end of the war, stereotypes of Jews as vengeful victimizers of non-Jews were not simply confronted, deconstructed, disproven, and discarded when the Nazi regime collapsed and Germany came under Allied occupation. In a context of half-hearted de-Nazification, reeducation, and legal-judicial programs, these stereotypes, rooted in the minds of millions of Germans—and indeed of other Europeans—could not be unlearned so easily. They continued to enjoy an active afterlife, even if the rhetoric has been toned down over time and the mode of expression has changed from explicit and loud to implicit and subdued.[4]

Projecting revenge onto Jews was a convenient way—not just for Germans but for other Europeans and the Allies as well—to detach one's own national group from the inconvenient truth that in the violent transition from war to peace vengeance was a universal phenomenon. Transitioning out of the deadliest-ever global war, everyone was vengeful: Germans were vengeful against other Germans; the many different national groups who had been victimized by, occupied by, and allied with Nazi Germany were vengeful vis-à-vis Germans as well as their own nationals suspected of collaboration and betrayal; the Allied liberators and victors also engaged in vengeance, often in brutal, gendered, misogynistic ways. But this is not how the war's end and early postwar period is commonly represented and remembered. Revenge is a blind spot (Fabian Bernhardt). It is not part of the heroic narratives and images of liberation and postwar justice, nor is it part of the rites and ceremonies commemorating World War II and the Holocaust. Conveniently forgotten in public memory is the fact that all the judicial achievements of the postwar epoch, achievements that would transform international law, were accompanied by vigilantism; justice was partial and aspirational at best, compromised by shifting political interests and undermined by cursory amnesties as the victors and vanquished of World War II transitioned into the new global Cold War.

The history of Jewish revenge during and after the Holocaust also sheds light on the moral judgments cast on survivors. In the postwar years, public recognition was only gradually accorded the unprecedented persecution and mass murder inflicted on these survivors. As they made their way back from a societal fringe to something akin to a normal presence within society, people with any interest in their stories often passed self-righteous judgement on how these victims were meant to behave and feel. If victims appeared too weak they were accused of passivity; if they appeared to be rebelling for the right political reasons, they were seen as heroic resisters, without account being taken of changing circumstances. Revenge corresponded neither to passivity nor proper resistance; it remained morally stigmatized. Stigmatization implies that by engaging in revenge, survivors tainted, or even gambled away their moral status as victims of the Holocaust. This is of course a false moral calculus; survivors who embraced vengeance were no less victims, just as Nazi perpetrators who fall victim to that revenge did not become less accountable for their wartime crimes. Stigmatization makes no distinctions between different kinds of revenge phenomena, treating mere sentiments and fantasies with the same gravitas as behaviors, seeing both violent and non-violent revenge as moral transgressions. But, as we have seen, revenge phenomena had many nuances. While revenge feelings played central roles as coping reactions among Holocaust victims, they did, for the most part, not result in actions; and if they did, these actions were not always violent.

Public perception tends to perceive revenge as the antithesis of forgiveness: with revenge seen as negative and forgiveness as positive, and individuals having to forgo revenge to achieve forgiveness. However, an individual who cannot forgive a wrong does not necessarily embrace revenge; likewise, rejecting or giving up on revenge does not necessarily mean forgiving.[5] Rather, both could coexist. For example, Brenda H. (born in 1926 in Horodenka, Poland, who survived ghettoization, forced labor, and hiding), had refused to take revenge in postwar Germany despite the fact that she—along with a group of friends who had left Poland shortly after their liberation and migrated westward to the US Zone of occupied Germany with the assistance of the Bricha—had ample opportunity. "We could have killed and killed and killed . . . We were very free then . . . Not one we touched! No revenge." She rationalized that restraint explaining "we are people [of] the Bible . . . we learn from our parents that you do not kill, you don't hate . . ." One day they rescued a German woman from sexual assault by a Russian soldier, empathising with her plight; "we just couldn't watch him go rape her," she recalled. But while these actions were, perhaps, a form of practical reconciliation with individual Germans she encountered and were based on her capacity for compassion and empathy, Brenda H. seemed adamant that it was impossible for her to forget and forgive Nazi crimes. After such traumatic experiences, "how would you forget, forgive? How would you forgive?"[6] Her testimony points to the moral double standard of those pressuring survivors to forget and forgive—and judging them as vengeful if they refuse to do either. In Brenda H.'s experience, such pressure usually came from devout Christians, who did not even realize the fundamental irony that for centuries Christians had not forgotten to cast Jews in a negative light, nor forgiven them their alleged collective, ancestorial guilt as "Jesus-killers."[7] And, we should add, admonishing Jews for their alleged unforgiveness of Nazi crimes often came from those who had a vested interest since forgiving would mean not to be held accountable or be reminded of their (or their ancestors') crimes.[8]

As victims and survivors of the Holocaust gained public standing and moral clout in public discourse, they also encountered an expectation that they embrace martyrdom without accompanying negatively invested, violent emotions. Their narratives were to transmit hope, resilience, love, and model "turning the other cheek" rather than transmitting anger, aggression, despair, bitterness, and hate. Survivors were typically held to a higher moral standard than the Nazi perpetrators who were, for the most part, aging in comfort outside the public eye, most of them never investigated let alone tried. In this manner, public celebration of survivors as authority figures often came at the expense of acknowledging their complex emotions and their diversity of national, religious, and ideological outlook, their different generations and genders—all these differences affecting the way they responded to the profound injustice that they had experienced.

For their part, Jewish survivors thought and talked about revenge in complex ways right after liberation and over the following decades. Most of this discourse initially unfolded in Yiddish and within survivors' own networks and publications.[9] Mainly direct articulation of revenge fantasies and scenarios took place in the early postwar period, when emotions were raw and vivid; in later decades, beginning in the late 1970s, flourishing in the 1990s, and continuing into the 2000s, the topic became historicized, emotion making room for more distanced reflection in the forum of audiovisual-testimony projects. The great majority of testimonies in collections such as those of the USC Shoah Foundation and the Fortunoff Archive at Yale do *not* include revenge as a theme.[10] Perhaps this was because interviewers didn't ask.[11] Perhaps for the witnesses involved, revenge was not a major concern, at least at the time of the interview; but perhaps it was a concern in the past, and had meanwhile become irrelevant on the larger scale of things to be recalled and spoken about—years of traumatic experience recounted in a few hours of testimony—as, say, an erstwhile fleeting emotion or fantasy. And perhaps some witnesses refrained from raising the topic as something that might potentially taint their stories, or even conjure up antisemitic stereotypes, and inadvertently play into the hands of distorters and deniers or promote Holocaust inversion. Finally, for other survivors, certain dimensions of revenge—along with other themes, as for example infanticide, sexual activity and abuse, internecine conflict and betrayal—may have been outside discussion's limits: as what Sara Horowitz has termed "deferred narratives" concerning past experiences that defy words, only capable of being shared very late in life, if ever.[12]

Now that the age of the contemporaries is drawing to a close, historians as well as descendants are left to work with what survivors were willing to share. The graphic artist Ari Richter has recently offered a chilling exploration of the boundaries that his survivor grandfather Jack (Heinz) Honig had placed on probing the topic of revenge. In his graphic family memoir *Never Again Will I Visit Auschwitz*, Richter used Jack's unpublished memoir, photo albums, and some family anecdotes as the basis to picture Jack as a victim-turned-avenger, although he had refused to share the details of his foray into revenge during his lifetime. Richter draws out his own speculations and revenge fantasies of Jack engaging in all kinds of violent and non-violent payback when he returned to Germany in 1945 in American uniform. Jack visits his former hometown Alsenz in the Rhineland-Palatinate, along with the now liberated Dachau concentration camp where he had once been incarcerated and tortured before managing to escape to the United States. But Richter candidly confronts his own ghosts. "With all the pain he carried . . . I find it hard to believe that these not quite-war-crime-level shenanigans were the extent of Grandpa Jack's 'score settling' in Alsenz." Richter goes on to address his own emotions:

"And what does it say about me that I feel a little disappointed he didn't admit to committing acts of violent retribution? I'm not really here for Holocaust revenge fantasies ... despite appearances. Certain things are better left to the imagination."[13] Richter thus reminds us that those born after run the risk of projecting their own emotions onto the historical actors; namely, that *we* may want to see some cathartic revenge, to make *us* feel better about this past. Rather, Richter cautions us, we must always stay true to the historical record and carefully separate our own emotional desires, biases, and agendas from the sources and actors we study.

There is, in any event, a critical mass of witness testimony that does present the revenge theme—and this reflecting a range of approaches. These include acknowledging wartime emotions and past revenge acts, sometimes tied to expressions of regret and to past-centered moral qualms, as well as a principled rejection of violent and even nonviolent revenge and feelings of pride at not having engaged in either. The testimony is marked by silences, absences, pauses, missing words, and tears, together with body language revealing pain and unease.

Interviewees often seem to grapple with the problem of how to bridge an abyss between postwar reality and its ethical standards, rooted in peacetime and condemning violent revenge, on the one hand, and a lived wartime reality in which negative emotions and the revenge urge were vital, coping responses to persecution, indeed perhaps an existential necessity. Looking back from a distance of several decades, witnesses struggled with their own alienation from, and discomfit with, their revenge acts and feelings. One has the impression that talking about revenge was easier if it related to heroic contexts—anti-Nazi resistance in ghetto undergrounds and partisan fighting; or else among survivors who then turned to helping build Israel's state- sovereignty, as opposed to those occupying a diasporic reality, that of a minority seeking acceptance; or again in the context of stories tied to processes of overcoming revenge in favor of a pursuit of justice. Did narratives tied to conscious decisions to abandon violent revenge help witnesses acknowledge they had held such fantasies and urges?

Indeed, some survivors graciously shared narratives of liberating themselves from vengeful impulses and expressed positive emotions such as gratitude, relief, and pride for *not* having actualized revenge, despite having had ample opportunity and moral justification at the end of the war. "I'm very proud of myself I didn't became an animal," Agnes S. noted about her liberation in Budapest in January 1945. "I am not. I'm proud of myself and I'm proud of the other survivors who didn't became an animal. Because what we went through, it wouldn't be surprising if we would become animal."[14] Weapons were readily available but Agnes S. and other survivors did not pick them up to take revenge but focused on physical well-being and reuniting with surviving family members.

Others candidly shared both the details of their participation in revenge acts at liberation and also their regrets. Katarina Salcer (née Kellner, born in Plešivec, Czechoslovakia, in 1927) related how shortly after her liberation near Leipzig—after having survived Auschwitz-Birkenau and the Hessisch Lichtenau subcamp of Buchenwald—joined two Polish prisoners and two Jewish girls in the chasing and hanging of SS-Oberscharführer Ernst Zorbach, Hessisch Lichtenau's deputy commandant, whom they had encountered in a village near Wurzen. "The young men dragged the SS man from the village to a suitable tree," she told the anthropologist D. Z. Stone in 1999. "When the noose was around his neck, I joined in. I held my hands on the rope. I pulled with everyone. I pulled and pulled until he was yanked dead. What did I feel? Not the least bit of pity. Not a touch of remorse. No sympathy for this man, all I felt was hatred. I wanted him dead. I wanted revenge."[15] Only later that day when Salcer continued her march back to her native Czechoslovakia with a group of Jewish girls the deed began to haunt her: "I began to see the SS man's dying face. All the time. I was terrified. Afraid I had become a monster like him."[16] In her 1996 USC Shoah Foundation testimony, Salcer did not mention this revenge episode.[17] Thirteen years later when she and her husband gave extensive testimony to Stone she shared this. When Stone identified Zorbach and found a photograph—at age seventeen, Salcer did not even know his name—Salcer replied "If it's okay, I would rather not look. I do not need to see it. I still cannot forget his face."[18] In her 1996 testimony, Salcer observed that as forced laborers "we were treated and felt like animals" and that the Germans "didn't allow us any human thought or even any emotions."[19] Thus the emotions that surrounded the revenge act—hatred of a man who had brutalized the female prisoners, anxiety of becoming like him, horror, and remorse—was a form of reasserting herself as a human being who owns and contains her complex emotions but is also haunted by the past—even as she built a fulfilling postwar life.

Some survivors seem to have been reluctant to discuss revenge and yet did so. Instead of simply keeping silent, they set strict boundaries on what they were willing share, at once admitting revenge acts and burying the details. Ismar Reich related how at age nineteen he had taken revenge on a Gestapo officer who had mistreated him. Born in 1926 in Berlin to a religious upper middle class home, he had tried to pass as an "Aryan" until his arrest by the Gestapo. On September 10, 1943, he was deported to Auschwitz but managed to escape from the deportation train with the help of a saw and drill he had hidden on his body. Reich returned to Berlin, where he survived the rest of the war in hiding. In April 1945, Reich recalled, in the turmoil of the Soviet takeover of the German capital, "I fortunately found one of my Gestapo people . . . by happenstance I saw him . . . and was able to do . . . eh . . . eh . . . make sure that he was not to tell the story anymore." While the interviewer probed "Would you care to tell us what precisely you did?" Reich replied "I did away with him, that's all," refusing to give more details, smiling with discomfort and eager to move on to a different subject.[20] Others revealed even less, but still something. Born in 1900 in Strasbourg, Richard Kanter had lived in Bonn, working as a menswear salesman until, in 1935, he was fired from a department-store job, then arrested, jailed, but released following the courageous intervention of his mother. He escaped to Brazil—via Holland, Belgium, France, and Portugal—before arriving in the United States in 1938. Drafted into the American army, he was deployed to France and Germany, where he worked after the war as a translator in a camp for German POWs. Kanter's testimony for the Shoah Foundation in 1996 offers few details—but as said, still something. Kantner recalls how his younger brother, who also returned to Germany as a GI, traveled to Bonn, in the British occupation zone, in his military jeep and encountered

Conclusion

a Nazi he knew from before the war. Intending to kill him, he took him up the Venusberg, hitting him with the butt of his rifle and letting him lie there.[21] When interviewer Leah Dickstein asks Kantner: "How do you think your experiences in the war affected your life afterward?" he replies: "Well . . . I do not know what to say there . . . what do you want me to say?" When Dickstein prompts him, "About losing your mother and other family?" (Kantner's mother was deported to Theresienstadt, where she died), Kantner replies: "Well . . . I didn't treat the German prisoners too good . . . because I was mad"—with no further elaboration.[22] The overall barrenness of his account conveys a deep sadness, and a great deal of vulnerability.

Other witnesses closed conversations touching on revenge with sentences such as "I did what I did"[23]; "I did have a revenge in Lodz. I was . . . you know . . . But . . . um, well . . . that is another story,"[24] and "I remember—some things that cannot be told."[25] It would seem that a number of witnesses found it especially difficult to convey both the emotions and distinctive logic and morality of the wartime and immediate postwar period to listeners, none of whom could have had similar experiences, in faraway places decades later. Some survivors clearly feel alienated from their wartime selves that harbored vengeful emotions. Beyond this, a sense of shame sometimes comes through, even agony, caused by the reminder that one's younger self had been through things that had caused such emotions and actions.

The testimony of Rudolf F., interviewed for the Fortunoff video archive in 1987, can here serve as an example. Rudolf F. was born in Krojanke, Germany in 1922; he was able to flee to Belgium and then southern France, where he joined the resistance. In 1943 he was arrested, incarcerated at Drancy, and deported to Auschwitz, where he was selected for slave labor at Auschwitz-Monowitz. In his account, he recalls an American bombing of Buna in 1944, when only the German guards and foremen were allowed to take cover in earthen shelters while the prisoners lay flat on their bellies in the open air. Most of the prisoners were fortunate enough to be spared; some of the Germans were injured and asked the prisoners for help:

> We were told again over the loudspeakers to help all the people in the bunkers to dig them out. And I tell you very frankly—there was a terrible thing, because when there was a poor little German in there saying "uhm . . . uhm" the prisoners took a rock and helped him out. You know how they helped him out, ya? [pause] I have never seen so much hatred in my whole life. And I did it myself. He was crying because he was . . . broken arms and he [sic] took a rock and just hit him over the head and got him out of his misery.

It is striking that Rudolf F. switches from first to third person when recounting his participation in the collective act of beating the guard to death. After pausing for several seconds, he adds the following:

> It was a terrible thing . . . but . . . um . . . but . . . you know it still made you feel good. I don't know, for the first time – I killed people before [a reference to his

participation in the French resistance] – but I never got an enjoyment out of it. But there I got an enjoyment out of it and I don't understand why. [. . .] I mean, let's be honest, after what they have done to us, could you have done anything else? It was such a terrible feeling. But we had . . . eh . . . I don't know why we do . . . um . . . did it. Today I couldn't do it. When I see that a dog gets killed, it hurts me, I almost cry because I don't want anything to die anymore, but at that time, I couldn't have cared less. There was an enjoyment . . ."[26]

During this part of his testimony Rudolf F.'s voice sometimes breaks; at one time he tears up before quickly regaining control and moving on with his story. In general, speaking about revenge, whether enacted or imagined, in these testimonies often seems to trigger a breaking point in the survivor's narrative, a momentary collapse of composure: this although earlier parts of the narration may contain details concerning more gruesome and horrific endured experiences, the death of parents and children, horrendous physical violence. It seems that the question of exacting revenge, or not doing so, often deeply touched survivors' sense of their own personhood and humanity: as a test of the capacity for empathy, for feeling sorrow, pity, and regret at having been in a state in which these emotional capacities were numbed.

This loss of composure could confirm, for the survivors themselves, compassion and regret, capability for empathy and the capacity to see the shared humanity of all human beings, hence distance from the Nazi murderers. Recounting his liberation near Tutzing, Bavaria, with SS men fleeing into the woods and throwing away their weapons, Aaron S. (born in Dobrzyń nad Wisłą, Poland, in 1925) breaks down, begins to cry after stating that "there was a lot of revenge there." Under tears, struggling to regain self-control he adds: "But I couldn't do it. They gave me a gun. And I said, I can't shoot nobody. Some people did it. I said, I can't do it."[27] Possibly, Aaron S.'s tears reflected, at least in part, a depth of retrospective relief that he did not go down a path of violence—that he maintained core decency after what had been done to him. Often the emotions at work here are clearly difficult to contain at the moment of retelling the past—this sometimes combined with a manifest sense of embarrassment at crying in front of the camera, in testimony meant for future audiences. This is especially evident among male witnesses. Martin S. thus breaks down for a moment while stating that trying to survive in the Skarżysko-Kamienna and Buchenwald forced labor and concentration camps as a child and young teenager brought out what he called an "animalistic" side in him. Before explaining that by "animalistic" he means that he came to care only about himself and refused to share bread, addresses a question to the interviewer: "I guess, I can't ask them to turn this off, can I?" referring to the cameramen; he then regains composure, adding this assessment: "No, no keep it running. It should be documented. I sometimes think I was made too inhuman. Because I didn't care about anybody else."[28] Thus Martin S. reveals scathing self-judgement—after all he was "too animalistic" or "too inhuman" in relation to his own moral and ethical standards and sense of self—and conveys an intrinsic sense of guilt for his drive for self-preservation, for having survived. In his testimony, while acknowledging his emotional urge for violent revenge, Martin S. refuses to share details about the revenge he took; he indicates that what he calls his "animalistic" behavior declined as he came back to life after the war, securing adequate food and decent shelter and thinking about the future.

An anonymous witness describes his survival of ghettoization, hiding, and internment at Buchenwald and Theresienstadt as guided by a strong sense of self-preservation, perseverance, and optimism, dismisses revenge as a thoughtless affect that cannot possibly constitute a level-headed principled response to the Holocaust. "Revenge can only happen on the spur of the moment, but not when one thinks about it, not when one reflects upon it because the most important and the most sacred thing is human life, is the human being." His experience of human evil had caused him to cherish the universal value of a human life and to promote the human capacity for goodness. Testifying in the early 1990s under the impression of interethnic violence and war in Yugoslavia, he emphasized that the "lesson of the Holocaust is that we must care for other human beings. And we are not doing it. We are back to square one. And I really agonize once again to see that we haven't learned enough." Yet he refused to give up his optimism "I still believe that in spite of what is happening at the moment, . . . we will . . . prevail, but unfortunately it will . . . be at a cost; people will have to suffer first before they realize that they have gone the wrong way. And this is the tragedy of it all. But . . . I have always believed that the only way we can live on this planet is to have . . . tolerance . . . and try to . . . understand other human beings."[29]

Survivor testimony, along with many other historical sources, as we have seen, account for a powerful historical development: during the Holocaust revenge as an emotional state, a fantasy, and a form of behavior was a vital coping measure; it gave individuals a glimpse of hope after all hope had died, a sense of agency in total powerlessness. After the war, for the most part, these urges were not acted out for practical and ethical reasons. Radical revenge plots such Nakam's were outliers and remained a fantasy. Most Jews found other ways to arrive at emotional balance and cope with survival, setting boundaries in their postwar interactions with Germans. Over time, however, survivors lost their taste for revenge, even its symbolic forms.

Ultimately closely considering the different dimensions of Jewish revenge during and after the Holocaust humanizes the mass murder's victims and survivors. Revenge is, among other things, a universal and uniquely human response to injustice, violence, oppression, and trauma. Revenge as a response to such phenomena is present in all cultures and time periods; it has a distinct evolutionary function in a context where, in the words of the political scientist Anthony C. Lopez "deterrence and reputation management [are] essential for survival, reinforcing behaviors that imposed costs on harmful individuals."[30] Seen in that light, in approaching the history of the wartime and postwar actions and perspectives of Holocaust victims, what is called for is a sober acknowledgment of the complexity and range of human responses to experiencing an unprecedented mass crime—and sensitivity to the enduring brokenness and frailty of survivors—what Lawrence Langer has termed "afterdeath."[31] It is the case that many survivors succeeded in building meaningful and successful postwar lives; but it would be naïve to imagine that the trauma, loss, and grief was ever absent. This is the backdrop for approaching both an entirely normal postwar desire for revenge—a desire that, as James Kimmel Jr. has observed, is a deeply embedded neurological coping response to grievance in which pain is compensated by pleasure that may become an addictive cycle[32]—and the striking fact that survivors did not become addicted to it. As intense as feelings tied to revenge were in the immediate aftermath of fathomlessly traumatic events, various survivor accounts have made clear that the feelings were often tempered and regulated by values inherited from a civil world existing before Nazi occupation, and by the expectations tied to once again being part of a functioning civil society. At the same time, the grievance-compensation effect of revenge feelings that Kimmel analyzes seems to have been quite limited in the case of many Holocaust survivors; one additional reason for the fading of such feelings that some survivors spoke of may well have been the sheer weight of enduring pain, irretrievable loss. Revenge does not offer an uplifting, redemptive path from the Holocaust; it is neither sweet nor cathartic. This would seem to be an uncomfortable truth about the limits to any trauma-processing after genocide.

Notes

1. Testimony of L. Elly Gotz, June 15, 1987, VHA 54119 and April 29, 2018, VHA 57261; Elly Gotz, *Flights of Spirit* (Toronto: Azrieli Foundation, 2018).
2. Author's interview with Elly Gotz, Oct. 27, 2023 (zoom recording).
3. Améry, "Im Warteraum des Todes," 21; translation LJ.
4. Peter Longerich, *Antisemitismus: Eine deutsche Geschichte: Von der Aufklärung bis heute* (Munich: Siedler, 2021), 373–83.
5. See Ira Gäbler and Andreas Maercker, "Revenge and Trauma," 58–9.
6. Testimony of Brenda H., Oct. 13, 1991, HVT 0877, seg. 9. She relates the lasting impact of pain and loss on her life as she married, had children, got a college degree and an education and what she calls a "normal life" in the United States (seg. 10).
7. Ibid., seg. 9.
8. For example clemency requests for Germans who had been sentenced in Allied war crime trials often invoked humanitarian arguments and Christian motives of mercy and forgiveness, which were self-serving, denied responsibility for Nazi crimes, and disregarded the continued pain, loss, and trauma experienced by the victims; see Katharina von Kellenbach, *The Mark of Cain: Guilt and Denial in the Post-War Lives of Nazi Perpetrators* (Oxford: Oxford University Press, 2013).
9. Even in the context of video testimony, survivors might switch to Yiddish when talking about revenge; see Hannah Pollin-Galay, "The History of My Voice: Yiddish at the Seams of Holocaust Video Testimony," *Prooftexts* 35 no. 1, (2016): 58–97, here 78.
10. Of the 54,211 testimonies from Jewish survivors in the USC Shoah Foundation collection, 1,822 (that is 3.3 percent of the entire collection) include references to revenge in the broadest sense (by Jews; against Jews by Germans and other national groups); 256 testimonies refer to individual decisions regarding revenge; 421 to German anti-resistance measures and partisan reprisals. Of the 573 testimonies from Allied liberators, 99 discuss revenge acts by various groups. In the Fortunoff Archive, which contains 4,400 testimonies,

mostly from Jewish survivors, 594 (that is 13 percent of the entire collection) mention revenge in the broadest sense of the term. There might be more testimonies with such references but not indexed as such.

11. The role of interviewers must be crucial; only 3.3 percent of testimonies in the USC Shoah Foundation address revenge as opposed to 13 percent in the Fortunoff collection, which might be a reflection of Fortunoff interviewers' openness to breech the topic. It might also be an result of timing, as the Fortunoff collection begins in 1979, USC Shoah Foundation fifteen years later; although willingness to talk about revenge is not linear. Rebecca Clifford claims that over time, interviewers stopped asking child survivors about revenge, see *Survivors*, 225.

12. Sara R. Horowitz, "'If He Knows to Make a Child . . .' Memories of Birth and Baby-Killing in Deferred Jewish Testimony Narratives," in Norman J.W Goda (ed.), *Jewish Histories of the Holocaust: New Transnational Approaches* (New York, Oxford: Berghahn Books 2014), 135–51.

13. Ari Richter, *Never Again Will I Visit Auschwitz: A Graphic Family Memoir of Trauma and Inheritance* (Seattle: Fantagraphics Books, 2024), 173.

14. Testimony of Agnes S. (born in Budapest, 1925), July 23, 1980, HVT 103, tape 1, seg. 57–8; similarly, Aron S. (born in Kolomyia in 1918) believed that it was a distinctly Jewish trait in which he took great pride, not to have engaged in large scale revenge by killing Germans, HVT 1936, Nov. 26, 1991, tape 2, seg. 17; and Claire F. (born in Bratislava in 1926) consciously refrained from revenge because she believed that as a decent person she could not have lived with herself had she engaged in revenge, HVT 1919, Dec. 17, 1991, tape 2, seg. 14.

15. D. Z. Stone, *No Past Tense: Love and Survival in the Shadow of the Shoah* (Elstree: Vallentine Mitchell, 2019), 66.

16. Ibid., 67.

17. Testimony of Katarina Salcer, Aug. 6, 1996, VHA 18263. She appears in her husband's interview William Zeev Salcer, Aug. 6, 1996, VHA 18264.

18. Stone, *No Past Tense*, 67.

19. Testimony of Katarina Salcer, VHA 18263, tape 4, seg. 29.

20. Testimony of Ismar Reich, Feb. 7, 1995, VHA 826, tape 4, seg. 20.

21. Testimony of Richard Kanter, Aug. 19, 1996, VHA 18752, tape 1, seg. 26.

22. Ibid., tape 2, seg. 31.

23. Testimony of Alexander B., May 22, 1998, HVT 4004, tape 6, seg. 20. Alexander B., born in Bratislava in 1925; although acknowledging satisfaction at beating guards immediately after liberation, Alexander B. refrains from delving into his emotions and declines to share some details of what he did.

24. Anonymous testimony, HVT.

25. Testimony of Martin S. (born in Tarnobrzeg, Poland, in 1933), Jan. 3, 1986, HVT 641, tape 1 (48 mins).

26. Testimony of Rudolf F., November 11, 1987, HVT 1262, tape 1, seg. 10.

27. Testimony of Aaron S. June 10, 1991, HVT 1533, tape 2 (22 mins).

28. Testimony of Martin S. (born in Tarnobrzeg, Poland, in 1933), Jan. 3, 1986, HVT 641, tape 1 (27–28 mins). More on what he means by "animalistic" in tape 1, 40 and 47 mins and tape 2, 27–28 mins.

29. Anonymous testimony, HVT.
30. Cited in Thomas B. Edsall, "Revenge is a Dish best Served from the White House," *The New York Times* (Jan. 14, 2025); see also Anthony C. Lopez and Rose McDermott, Pete Hatemi, "'Blunt not the heart, enrage it': The Psychology of Revenge and Deterrence," *Texas National Security Review* 1, no. 1 (Dec. 2017), 69–88.
31. Lawrence Langer, *The Afterdeath of the Holocaust* (Cham, Switzerland: Palgrave Macmillan, 2021), 1–14, 37–86, 145–67.
32. Cited in Edsall, "Revenge is a Dish best Served from the White House"; see also James Kimmel and Michael Rowe, "A Behavioral Addiction Model of Revenge, Violence, and Gun Abuse," *The Journal of Law, Medicine & Ethics* 48, no. 4 (2020): 172–8; Kimmel, *The Science of Revenge*.

SOURCES AND BIBLIOGRAPHY

Archival Sources

Bundesarchiv, Koblenz
Zsg. 109 Theo Oberheitmann Collection

Central Zionist Archives, Jerusalem
S 26 Rescue Committee of the Jewish Agency for Palestine

Dwight D. Eisenhower Presidential Library, Abilene, Kansas
Pre-Presidential Papers of Dwight D. Eisenhower

Fortunoff Archives of Holocaust Testimony, Yale University
HVT 1 Eva B., May 2, 1979
HVT 2 Leon W., May 2, 1979
HVT 22 Rudy F., Aug. 7, 1979
HVT 36 Celia K., Feb. 25, 1980
HVT 61 Joseph K., Dec. 2, 1979
HVT 69 Hillel K., May 3, 1980
HVT 71 Eva L., May 12, 1982
HVT 103 Agnes S., July 23, 1980
HVT 107 Edith P., Feb. 18, 1980
HVT 178 Eugene N., Nov. 7, 1982
HVT 224 Martin L., Oct. 19, 1983
HVT 227 Janet B., Dec. 19, 1983
HVT 355 Rose K., Aug. 23, 1984
HVT 423 Erika J. and Marvina E., May 1, 1983
HVT 495 Andrew S., Aug. 21, 1984
HVT 536 Norbert N., March 3, 1984
HVT 580 Sidney S., May 5, 1985
HVT 615 Abraham S., Oct. 6, 1985
HVT 641 Martin S., Jan. 3, 1986
HVT 670 Eve F., Feb. 10, 1986
HVT 827 Frieda G., Nov. 9, 1986
HVT 833 Allen S., Dec. 14, 1986
HVT 877 Brenda H., Oct. 13, 1991
HVT 885 Victor S., May 3, 1987
HVT 894 Julius O., May 16, 1987
HVT 897 Ernest R., May 17, 1987

Sources and Bibliography

HVT 943 Fred O., Nov. 18, 1987
HVT 971 Hanna F., Oct. 16, 1987
HVT 979 Hans N., May 9, 1988
HVT 1071, Cela L., July 20, 1984
HVT 1095 Luna K., July 5, 1988
HVT 1175 Manfred K., Nov. 10, 1987
HVT 1261 Martin B., Oct. 30, 1996
HVT 1262 Rudolf F., Nov. 11, 1987
HVT 1286 Regina G., Nov. 13, 1989
HVT 1454 Paul P., Aug. 28, 1990
HVT 1533 Aaron S., June 10, 1991
HVT 1622 Susan F., May 14, 1990
HVT 1650 Violet S., Sept. 25, 1991
HVT 1734 Larry K., Nov. 4, 1990
HVT 1835 Abraham D., June 30, 1988
HVT 1919, Claire F., Dec. 17, 1991
HVT 1936 Aron S., Nov. 26, 1991
HVT 1954 Celina F., Aug. 10, 1991
HVT 2838 Hanan L., Dec. 6, 1994
HVT 3410 Eva F., Dec. 14, 1995
HVT 3563 Masha P., July 22 and 29, Oct. 29, Nov. 9 and 19, 1993, Feb. 1, 1994
HVT 3730 Kurt G., Oct. 9, 1996
HVT 3816 Yaffa U., Dec. 8, 1995
HVT 4004 Alexander B., May 22, 1998
HVT 4085 Dietrich G., Nov. 7, 1996

Harvard Law School Library, Cambridge, Massachusetts

Nuremberg Trials Project

Illinois Institute of Technology, Chicago

David Boder Interviews, Voices from the Holocaust:
Kalman Eisenberg, July 31, 1946
Otto Feuer, August 22, 1946
Benjamin Piskorz, September 1, 1946

Jewish Historical Institute, Warsaw

Central Committee of Polish Jews / Central Historical Commission

Leo Baeck Institute, New York

AR 360 Bernhard Kolb Collection

United States Holocaust Memorial Museum, Washington DC

RG-50.005.0052 Oral history interview with Bart Stern, May 20, 1984
RG-50.030.0066 Oral history interview with Chaim Engel, July 16, 1990
RG 50.030.0145 Oral history interview with Abraham Malnik, May 10, 1990

RG-50.030.0184 Oral history interview with Esther Terner Raab, April 30, 1990
RG-50.030.0185 Oral history interview with Chil Rajchman, Dec. 7, 1988
RG 50.030.0478 Oral history interview with Edgar Krasa, Sept. 9, 2003
RG-50.030.0832 Oral history interview with Michael Goldmann-Gilead, Oct. 28–29 2015
RG-50.031.0009 Oral history interview with David Danzyger, July 12, 1991
RG-50.031.0070 Oral history interview with Manfred Steinfeld, undated
RG-50.042.0013 Oral history interview with Siegfried Halbreich, March 10, 1992
RG-50.042.0019 Oral history interview with Abraham Malnik Feb. 27, 1992
RG-50.042.0032 Oral history interview with Norbert Wollheim, Feb. 18, 1992
RG-50.120.0219 Oral history interview with Shlomo Kenet, Sept. 14, 1995
RG-50.120.0321 Oral history interview with Emrich Gonczi, Jan. 16, 1997
RG-50.149.0060 Oral history interview with Kurt Klappholz, 1995
RG-50.477.1382 Oral history interview with Martin Travis, April 12, 1983
RG-50.549.02.0009 Oral history interview with Lisa Derman and Aron Derman, Nov. 22, 1997
RG-50.549.02.0014 Oral history interview with Chaim Engel and Selma Saartje Engel, March 30, 1998
RG-50.641.0001 Oral history interview with George Kadish, c.1997
RG-50.694.0151 Oral history interview with Sidney Simon, July 31, 1994
RG-50.759.0015 Oral history interview with John F. Boland, April 2, 1992
RG-60.5044 Claude Lanzmann Shoah Collection
RG-2012.318.1 Rachel Zonszajn Benshaul Collection
RG 2014.406.2 Ben Zion Kalb Papers
RG 2017.103.1 Tamar Lazerson-Rostovsky's Diaries
Accession Number 1995.A.1067.1 Michael J. Kraus Papers
Accession Number 1997.A.0441.78 Oral history interview with Michael Finkelstein, April 21, 1985
Accession Number 2005.389 Allen A. Cramer Collection

USC Shoah Foundation, Los Angeles

VHA 93 James Hayes, Sept. 8, 1994
VHA 288 Yetta Kleiner, Nov. 28, 1994
VHA 826 Ismar Reich, Feb. 7, 1995
VHA 1609 Samuel Lerer, March 23, 1995
VHA 1655 Judith Handley, March 21, 1995
VHA 1885 Flora Carasso Mihael, April 5, 1995
VHA 2917 Marie Lebovitz, May 31, 1995
VHA 3331 Norman Salsitz, June 9, 1995
VHA 3629 Martin Travis, June 29, 1995
VHA 4076 Herbert Mirkin, Aug. 22, 1995
VHA 5359 Florence Lieblich, Aug. 10, 1995
VHA 5415 Stella Kolin, Aug. 13, 1995
VHA 6121 Helen Bolstok, Aug. 30, 1995
VHA 7556 Irene Hirschfeld, Oct. 9, 1995
VHA 9735 Roman Sompolinski, Dec. 7, 1995
VHA 12897 Lusia Puterman, March 27, 1996
VHA 18263 Katarina Salcer, Aug. 6, 1996
VHA 18264 William Zeev Salcer, Aug. 6, 1996
VHA 18626 Morris Rich, Aug. 12, 1996
VHA 18752 Richard Kanter, Aug. 19, 1996
VHA 20848 Lusia Haberfeld, Oct. 13, 1996
VHA 21308 Edward Ruston, Oct. 10, 1996

Sources and Bibliography

VHA 22979 Linda Breder, Nov. 20, 1996
VHA 24207 Robert Stubenrauch, Dec. 12, 1996
VHA 24544 Lily Grossman, Jan. 7, 1997
VHA 26728 Charles Ferree, March 11, 1997
VHA 29715 Werner Ellmann, June 6, 1997
VHA 32049 Alan Peters, July 30, 1997
VHA 32979 David Olds, July 23, 1997
VHA 33147 George Tievsky, Aug. 25, 1997
VHA 34023 Michael Morrow, Sept. 22, 1997
VHA 34964 Bert Weston, Oct. 27, 1997
VHA 35757 Irving Raab, Nov. 23, 1997
VHA 38725 David Wolf, Jan. 28, 1998
VHA 40109 Sidney Shafner, March 31, 1998
VHA 43411 Faye Schulman, June 21, 1998
VHA 44111 Curtis Whiteway, May 11, 1998
VHA 44720 Leon Bass, Aug. 12, 1998
VHA 46406 Joseph Riwash, Aug. 23, 1998
VHA 46858 Richard Sonnenfeld, Nov. 13, 1998
VHA 47399 Isaac Brecher, Nov. 19, 1998
VHA 48363 Morris Hoffman, Dec. 3, 1998
VHA 48608 Anita Lasker Walfish, Dec. 8, 1998
VHA 50943 Erika Landon, June 20, 2000
VHA 53927 Eva Bleeman, July 19, 1989
VHA 54119 L. Elly Gotz, June 15, 1987
VHA 55650 Miriam Brysk, March 12, 2012
VHA 57261 L. Elly Gotz, April 29, 2018

Yad Vashem, Jerusalem

O.6 Poland Collection
O.33 Various Testimonies, Diaries and Memoirs Collection
O.37 Displaced Persons Collection (She'erit Hapletah)
O.48 Miscellaneous Documents Collection
O.75 Letters and Postcards Collection
M.11 The Bialystok Ghetto Underground Archive (Mersik-Tenenbaum Archive)

YIVO Institute for Jewish Research, New York

RG 294.5 Displaced Persons Camps and Centers

Published Legal Records

Justiz und NS-Verbrechen, ed. Rüter, C.F., and D.W. de Mildt. Amsterdam: Amsterdam University Press, 2010.
Nazi Conspiracy and Aggression, ed. Office of United States Chief of Counsel for Prosecution of Axis Criminality. Washington, DC: United States Government Printing Office 1946–1948, 11 vols.

Sources and Bibliography

The Trial of Adolf Eichmann: Record of Proceedings in the District Court of Jerusalem. Jerusalem: The State of Israel, Ministry of Justice, 1992.

Trial of the Major War Criminals before the International Military Tribunal, Nuremberg, 14 November 1945–1 October 1946, ed. International Military Tribunal. Nuremberg, Germany: International Military Tribunal, 1947–1949, 22 vols.

Trials of War Criminals before the Nuremberg Military Tribunals under Control Council Law No. 10, ed. Nuremberg Military Tribunals. Washington, DC: US Government Printing Office, 1946–1949.

Films

Der Ewige Jude (Fritz Hipper, 1940)
Die Mörder sind unter uns (Wolfgang Staudte, 1946)
Harlan in the Shadow of Jud Süss (Felix Moeller, 2008))
Inglorious Basterds (Quentin Tarantino, 2009)
Jaguar (Netflix, 2021)
Jud Süss (Veit Harlan, 1940)
Lang ist der Weg (Marek Goldstein and Herbert B. Fredersdorf, 1947)
Oma & Bella (Alexa Karolinski, 2012)
Remember (Atom Egoyan, 2015)
Revenge: Our Dad the Nazi Killer (Danny Ben-Moshe, 2023)
Schächten / A Retribution (Thomas Roth, 2022)
Shadowplay/The Defeated (Netflix, 2020)
Shlomo—Der Goldschmied und der Nazi (Antonius Kempmann und Martin Kaul, 2023)
The Hunters (Amazon Prime, 2020–2023)
The Memory of Justice (Marcel Ophuls, 1976)
This must be the Place (Paolo Sorrentino, 2011)
Treblinka's Last Witness (PBS, 2014)
Yehuda Bacon: Glück ist eine Möglichkeit (ARD Mediathek, 2024)

Bibliography

Abramovitsh, Dodl, and Mordekhay V. Bernshtayn, eds. *Pinkes Byten: Der Oyfkum un Untergang fun a yidisher kehile*. Buenos Aires: Bitener Landslayt in Argentine, 1954.

Abramsky, Samuel et al. "Amalekites." *Encyclopaedia Judaica*, ed. by Michael Berenbaum and Fred Skolnik, 2nd ed., vol. 2 (Macmillan Reference USA, 2007), 28–31.

Adler, Stanislaw. *In the Warsaw Ghetto 1940–1943 an Account of a Witness the Memoirs of Stanislaw Adler*. Jerusalem: Yad Vashem, 1982.

Adorno, Theodor W. "Schuld und Abwehr," *Soziologische Schriften* II, in idem, *Gesammelte Schriften*, vol. 9, no. 2. Frankfurt am Main: Suhrkamp, 1997.

Afterman, Adam and Gedaliah Afterman. "Meir Kahane and Contemporary Jewish Theology of Revenge." *Soundings* 98, 2 (2015): 192–217.

Allen, William Sheridan. *The Nazi Seizure of Power: The Experience of a Single German Town, 1922–1945*, revised edition. Brattleboro: Echo Point Books & Media, 2014.

Améry, Jean. *At the Mind's Limits: Contemplations by a Survivor on Auschwitz and its Realities*, transl. Sidney and Stella P. Rosenfeld. Bloomington: Indiana University Press, 1980.

Améry, Jean. "Im Warteraum des Todes." In *Menschen im Ghetto* ed. Günther Deschner Gütersloh: Bertelsmann, 1969, 11–31.

Sources and Bibliography

Andreas-Friedrich, Ruth. *Der Schattenmann. Tagebuchaufzeichnungen: 1938–1945*. Berlin: Suhrkamp Verlag, 1947.

Andrieu, Claire. *When Men Fell from the Sky: Civilians and Downed Airmen in Second World War Europe*. New York: Cambridge University Press, 2023.

Angress, Werner T. *Witness to the Storm: A Jewish Journey from Nazi Berlin to the 82nd Airborne, 1920–1945*. Bloomington: Indiana University Press, 2012.

Anonymous, *A Woman in Berlin: Eight Weeks in the Conquered City: A Diary*, ed. by Philip Boehm. New York: Metropolitan Books, 2005.

Arad, Yitzhak. *Ghetto in Flames: The Struggle and Destruction of the Jews in Vilna in the Holocaust*. Jerusalem: Yad Vashem, 1980.

Arad, Yitzhak. *The Holocaust in the Soviet Union*. Lincoln: University of Nebraska Press, 2009.

Arad, Yitzhak. *The Operation Reinhard Death Camps: Belzec, Sobibor, Treblinka*. Bloomington: Indiana University Press, 2018.

Arad, Yitzhak, Israel Gutman, and Avraham Margaliyot, eds. *Documents on the Holocaust: Selected Sources on the Destruction of the Jews of Germany and Austria, Poland, and the Soviet Union*. Lincoln: University of Nebraska Press, 1999.

Arendt, Hannah. *Eichmann in Jerusalem: A Report on the Banality of Evil*. New York: Viking Press, 1963.

Arnold, Jörg. *The Allied Air War and Urban Memory: The Legacy of Strategic Bombing in Germany*. Cambridge: Cambridge University Press, 2011.

Auerbach, Rachel. *Schriften aus dem Warschauer Ghetto* ed. Karolina Szymaniak. Berlin: Metropol Verlag, 2022.

Avatihi, Arie, ed. *Rowno: A Memorial to the Jewish Community of Rowno, Wolyn*. Tel Aviv: Association of Rovno Jews in Israel, 1956.

Bacharach, Walter Zwi, ed. *Last Letters from the Shoah*. Jerusalem: Yad Vashem, 2013.

Bachrach, Susan D. Edward J. Phillips, and Steven Luckert. *State of Deception: The Power of Nazi Propaganda*. Washington, D.C: United States Holocaust Memorial Museum, 2009.

Bajohr, Frank and Dieter Pohl. *Der Holocaust als offense Geheimnis: Die Deutschen, die NS-Führung und die Alliierten*. Munich: C.H. Beck, 2006.

Bankier, David. *The Germans and the Final Solution: Public Opinion under Nazism*. Oxford: B. Blackwell, 1992.

Bankier, David. "The Use of Antisemitism in Nazi Wartime Propaganda," in *The Holocaust and History: The Known, the Unknown, the Disputed, and the Reexamined*, ed. Michael Berenbaum and Abraham J. Peck. Bloomington: Indiana University Press, 1998: 41–55.

Bar-Zohar, Michael. *The Avengers*. New York: Hawthorn Books, 1967.

Barash, David P. and Judith Eve Lipton. *Payback: Why We Retaliate, Redirect Aggression, and Take Revenge*. New York: Oxford University Press, 2011.

Barkai, Avraham. *"Wehr dich!": Der Centralverein deutscher Staatsbürger jüdischen Glaubens (C.V.) 1893–1938*. Munich: Beck, 2002.

Bartov, Hanoch. *The Brigade*, trans. David Segal. London: Macdonald & Co, 1968.

Bartov, Omer. "Defining Enemies, Making Victims: Germans, Jews, and the Holocaust." *The American Historical Review* 103, 3 (June 1998): 771–816.

Bartov, Omer. *Hitler's Army: Soldiers, Nazis, and War in the Third Reich*. New York: Oxford University Press, 1991.

Bass, Gary Jonathan. *Stay the Hand of Vengeance: The Politics of War Crime Tribunals* Princeton: Princeton University Press, 2000.

Bauer, Yehuda. *Rethinking the Holocaust*. New Haven: Yale University Press, 2001.

Baumel-Schwartz, Judith Tydor. *Kibbutz Buchenwald: Survivors and Pioneers*. New Brunswick: Rutgers University Press, 1997.

Bazyler, Michael. *Holocaust, Genocide, and the Law: A Quest for Justice in a Post-Holocaust World*. New York: Oxford University Press, 2016.

Beckman, Morris. *The Jewish Brigade: An Army with Two Masters, 1944-1945*. Rockville Centre: Sarpedon, 1998.

Benard, Stephen. Long Doan, D. Adam Nicholson, Emily Meanwell, Eric L. Wright, and Peter Lista, "An 'Eye For an Eye' Versus 'Turning The Other Cheek'? The Status Consequences of Revenge and Forgiveness in Intergroup Conflict," *Social Forces* 102, no. 3 (2024): 1200-19.

Bender, Sara. "Life Stories as Testament and Memorial: The Short Life of the Neqama Battalion, an Independent Jewish Partisan Unit Operating during the Second World War in the Narocz Forest, Belarus." *East European Jewish Affairs* 42, 1 (2012): 1-24.

Bender, Sara. *The Jews of Białystok during World War II and the Holocaust*. Waltham: Brandeis University Press, 2008.

Beorn, Waitman Wade. "All the Other Neighbors." In *A Companion to the Holocaust*, ed. Earl and Gigliotti, 153-72.

Beorn, Waitman Wade. *The Holocaust in Eastern Europe: At the Epicentre of the Final Solution*. London: Bloomsbury Academic, 2018.

Berg, Mary. *The Diary of Mary Berg: Growing up in the Warsaw Ghetto*. London: Oneworld Publications, 2018.

Berg, Nicolas, Elisabeth Gallas, Aurélia Kalisky. "'Unschuldige Wörter'? Jüdische Sprachkritik und historische Erkenntnis." *Zeithistorische Forschungen/Studies in Contemporary History* 20, no. 2 (2023): 187-203.

Bergen, Doris L. *War and Genocide: A Concise History of the Holocaust*. Lanham: Rowman & Littlefield, 2016.

Berglas, Rebecca. *Hillel Seidmann: A reassessment*. MA Thesis, University of Haifa, 2012.

Berkowitz, Michael. *The Crime of My Very Existence: Nazism and the Myth of Jewish Criminality*. Berkeley: University of California Press, 2007.

Bernhardt, Fabian. *Rache: Über einen blinden Fleck der Moderne*. Berlin: Matthes und Seitz, 2021.

Bessel, Richard. "Death and Survival in the Second World War." *The Cambridge History of the Second World War*, ed. Michael Geyer and Adam Tooze. Cambridge: Cambridge University Press, 2015. Vol. 3, 252-76.

Bessel, Richard. *Germany 1945: From War to Peace*. New York: HarperCollins, 2009.

Bessel, Richard. "Murder amidst Collapse: Explaining the Violence of the Last Months of the Third Reich." In *Years of Persecution, Years of Extermination: Saul Friedlander and the Future of Holocaust Studies*, ed. Christian Wiese and Paul Betts. London: Bloomsbury, 2010, 255-68.

Bessel, Richard. "The End of the Volksgemeinschaft." In *Visions of Community in Nazi Germany: Social Engineering and Private Lives*, ed. Martina Steber and Bernhard Gotto. Oxford: Oxford University Press, 2014, 281-94.

Bettelheim, Bruno. *The Informed Heart : Autonomy in a Mass Age*. New York: Avon Books, 1971.

Biddiscombe, Perry. *Werwolf! The History of the National Socialist Guerrilla Movement, 1944-1946*. Toronto: University of Toronto Press, 1998.

Biess, Frank. *German Angst: Fear and Democracy in the Federal Republic of Germany*. Oxford: Oxford University Press, 2020.

Biess, Frank. *Homecomings: Returning POWs and the Legacies of Defeat in Postwar Germany*. Princeton: Princeton University Press, 2006.

Biess, Frank, and Robert G. Moeller, eds. *Histories of the Aftermath: The Legacies of the Second World War in Europe*. New York: Berghahn Books, 2010.

Bikont, Anna. *The Crime and the Silence: Confronting the Massacre of Jews in Wartime* Jedwabne. New York: Farrar, Straus and Giroux, 2015.

Blatman, Daniel. *For Our Freedom and Yours: The Jewish Labour Bund in Poland 1939-1949*. Portland: Valentine Mitchell, 2003.

Blatman, Daniel. *The Death Marches: The Final Phase of Nazi Genocide*. Cambridge: Harvard University Press, 2011.

Sources and Bibliography

Blum, Howard. *The Brigade: An Epic Story of Vengeance, Salvation, and World War II.* New York: HarperCollins, 2001.
Bor, Josef. *The Terezín Requiem.* New York: Knopf, 1963.
Borowski, Tadeusz. *This Way to the Gas, Ladies and Gentlemen.* New York: Penguin Books, 1976.
Bothe, Alina, and Markus Nesselrodt. "Survivor: Towards a Conceptual History." *Leo Baeck Institute Year Book* 61, 1 (2016): 57–82.
Bowman, Jackson. "Turning a War Crime into a Weapon." *Central Europe* 5 (2024): 27–38.
Brenner, Michael. *A Short History of the Jews.* Princeton: Princeton University Press, 2010.
Brettler, Marc. "Destroying Amalek," The Future of the Past Blog (University of Minnesota), published March 22, 2024, https://sites.google.com/umn.edu/future-of-the-past/blog/destroying-amalek (accessed Aug. 14, 2025).
Browning, Christopher R. *Ordinary Men: Reserve Police Battalion 101 and the Final Solution in Poland.* New York: HarperCollins, 1992.
Browning, Christopher R., and Jürgen Matthäus. *The Origins of the Final Solution: The Evolution of Nazi Jewish Policy, September 1939–March 1942.* Lincoln: University of Nebraska Press, 2004.
Burds, Jeffrey. "Sexual Violence in Europe in World War II, 1939–1945." *Politics & Society* 37, no. 1 (2009): 35–73.
Burrin, Philippe. *Nazi Anti-Semitism: From Prejudice to the Holocaust.* New York: New Press, 2005.
Buruma, Ian. *Year Zero: A History of 1945.* New York: The Penguin Press, 2013.
Brot, Rivka. *Be-ezor ha-afor: ha-kapo ha-Yehudi ba-mishpat: mishpatim shel Yehudim meshatfe peʻulah ʻim ha-Germanim.* Raʻananah: Lamda, 2019.
Brysk, Miriam. *Amidst the Shadows of Trees.* Ann Arbor: Yellow Star Press 2007.
Bytwerk, Randall L. "The Argument for Genocide in Nazi Propaganda." *The Quarterly Journal of Speech* 91, 1 (2005): 37–62.
Bytwerk, Randall L. *Julius Streicher.* New York: Stein and Day, 1982.
Bytwerk, Randall L., ed. *Landmark Speeches of National Socialism.* College Station: Texas A&M University Press, 2008.
Bytwerk, Randall L. "The Argument for Genocide in Nazi Propaganda." *The Quarterly Journal of Speech* 91, no. 1 (2005): 37–62.
Carey, Maddy. *Jewish Masculinity in the Holocaust: Between Destruction and Construction.* New York: Bloomsbury Academic, 2017.
Cesarani, David. *Final Solution: The Fate of the Jews, 1933–1949.* New York: St. Martin's Press, 2016.
Chatwood, Kirsty. "Schillinger and the Dancer: Representing Agency and Violence in Holocaust Testimonies." In *Sexual Violence against Jewish Women during the Holocaust*, ed. by Sonja M. Hedgepeth and Rochelle G. Saidel. Waltham, Mass: Brandeis University Press, 2010, 67–79.
Christensen, Kit Richard. *Revenge and Social Conflict.* Cambridge: Cambridge University Press, 2016.
Cienciala, Anna M. "Poles and Jews under German and Soviet Occupation, September 1, 1939–June, 22 1941." *The Polish Review* 46, 4 (2001): 391–402.
Clifford, Rebecca. *Survivors: Children's Lives after the Holocaust.* New Haven: Yale University Press, 2020.
Cohen, Rich. *The Avengers.* New York: Knopf, 2000.
Cohn, Haim Hermann. "Blood-Avenger," *Encyclopaedia Judaica*, ed. Michael Berenbaum and Fred Skolnik, 2nd ed. Macmillan Reference USA, 2007, vol. 3, 772–3.
Confino, Alon. *A World Without Jews: The Nazi Imagination from Persecution to Genocide.* New Haven: Yale University Press, 2014.
Crago, Laura. "Łódź," *The United States Holocaust Memorial Museum Encyclopedia of Camps and Ghettos 1933–1945*, vol. 2, 75–82.
Czollek, Max. *Versöhnungstheater.* Munich: Hanser 2023.

Czollek, Max. *De-Integrate! A Jewish Survival Guide for the 21st Century*. Amherst, MA: Restless Books, 2023.

Czollek, Max, Erik Riedel, and Mirjam Wenzel, eds. *Revenge: History and Fantasy*. Berlin: Hanser Verlag, 2022.

Dafni, Reuven, and Yehudit Kleiman, eds. *Final Letters from Victims of the Holocaust*. New York: Paragon House, 1991.

Davidson, Shamai and Israel W. Charny. *Holding on to Humanity—The Message of Holocaust Survivors: The Shamai Davidson Papers*. New York: New York University Press, 1992.

Dawidowicz, Lucy S. *From That Place and Time: A Memoir, 1938-1947*. New York: W.W. Norton, 1989.

Deák, István, and Norman M. Naimark. *Europe on Trial: The Story of Collaboration, Resistance, and Retribution During World War II*. Oxford: Routledge, 2015.

Deák, István, Jan T. Gross, and Tony Judt, eds. *The Politics of Retribution in Europe: World War II and Its Aftermath*. Princeton: Princeton University Press, 2000.

Dean, Carolyn J. *The Moral Witness: Trials and Testimony after Genocide*. Ithaca, New York: Cornell University Press, 2019.

Dean, Martin. *Collaboration in the Holocaust: Crimes of the Local Police in Belorussia and Ukraine, 1941-44*. New York: St. Martin's Press, 2000.

Dean, Martin. *Investigating Babyn Yar: Shadows from the Valley of Death*. Lanham: Lexington Books, 2024.

Dean, Martin. "Local Collaboration in the Holocaust in Eastern Europe." In *The Historiography of the Holocaust*, ed. Dan Stone. Houndmills, Basingstoke, Hampshire: Palgrave Macmillan, 2004, 120-40.

Debreczeni, József. *Cold Crematorium: Reporting from the Land of Auschwitz*. New York: St. Martin's Press, 2023.

DeKoven Ezrahi, Sidra. "My mother taught me Jews are above vengeance. The Israel-Hamas war is finally making me doubt her." *Forward*, Oct. 27, 2023.

Desbois, Patrick. *The Holocaust by Bullets: A Priest's Journey to Uncover the Truth behind the Murder of 1.5 Million Jews*. New York: Palgrave Macmillan, 2008.

Des Pres, Terrence. *The Survivor: An Anatomy of Life in the Death Camps*. New York: Washington Square Press, 1977.

Dietrich, John. *The Morgenthau Plan: Soviet Influence on American Postwar Policy*. New York: Algora Pub., 2013.

Diewerge, Wolfgang. *Der Fall Gustloff: Vorgeschichte und Hintergründe der Bluttat von Davos*. Munich: F. Eher, 1936.

Doerfer, Achim. *"Jemand musste die Täter ja bestrafen: Die Rache der Juden, das Versagen der deutschen Justiz nach 1945 und das Märchen deutsch-jüdischer Versöhnung*. Cologne: Kippenhauer und Witsch, 2021.

Dörner, Bernward. *Die Deutschen und der Holocasut: Was niemand Wissen wollte, aber jeder Wissen konnte*. Berlin: Popyläen, 2007.

Douglas, Lawrence. *The Right Wrong Man: John Demjanjuk and the Last Great Nazi War Crimes Trial*. Princeton: Princeton University Press, 2016.

Douglas, Lawrence. "Was Damals Recht War: Nulla Poena and the Prosecution of Crimes against Humanity in Occupied Germany." In *Jus Post Bellum and Transitional Justice*, ed. Larry May and Elizabeth Edenberg. Cambridge University Press, 2013, 44-73.

Douglas, R. M. *Orderly and Humane: The Expulsion of the Germans after the Second World War*. New Haven: Yale University Press, 2012.

Dreifuss, Havi. "The Leadership of the Jewish Combat Organization during the Warsaw Ghetto Uprising: A Reassessment." *Holocaust and Genocide Studies* 31, 1 (2017): 24-60.

Dreifuss, Havi. *The People's Uprising and the Fall of the Warsaw Ghetto, April 1942-June 1943*. Waltham: Brandeis University Press, forthcoming.

Sources and Bibliography

Earl, Hilary. *The Nuremberg SS-Einsatzgruppen Trial, 1945-1958: Atrocity, Law, and History*. New York: Cambridge University Press, 2009.
Edsall, Thomas B. "Revenge is a Dish best Served from the White House." *The New York Times*, January 14, 2025.
Eichmann, Adolf. *Ich, Adolf Eichmann: ein historischer Zeugenbericht*. Ed. by Rudolf Aschenauer. Leoni am Starnberger See, Germany: Druffel Verlag, 1980.
Elkins, Michael. *Forged in Fury*. New York: Ballantine Books, 1971.
Engel, David. "A Sustained Civilian Struggle: Rethinking Jewish Responses to the Nazi Regime." In *A Companion to the Holocaust*, ed. Simone Gigliotti and Hilary Earl. Chichester, UK: John Wiley 2020, 233–45.
Engel, David. "On the Bowdlerization of a Holocaust Testimony: The War Time Journal of Calek Perechodnik." *Polin* 12 (1999): 316–29.
Engel, David. "Patterns of Anti-Jewish Violence in Poland 1944–1946." *Yad Vashem Studies* 26 (1998): 43–85.
Feibelman, Ernest. *Journeys: Survival is the Best Revenge*. Philadelphia: Xlibris Corporation, 2010.
Feinstein, Margarete Myers. *Holocaust Survivors in Postwar Germany, 1945-1957*. Cambridge: Cambridge University Press, 2010.
Feinstein, Margarete Myers. "Reconsidering Jewish Rage After the Holocaust." *The Palgrave Handbook of Holocaust Literature and Culture* ed. Victoria Aarons and Phyllis Lassner. Cham: Palgrave Macmillan, 2020: 743–60.
Feldman, Nira. *Der Stürmer: The Power of a Hate Magazine*. Jerusalem: Carmel 2023, Hebrew.
Finder, Gabriel, and Alexander Prusin. "Collaboration in Eastern Galicia: The Ukrainian Police and the Holocaust." *East European Jewish Affairs* 34, 2 (2004): 95–118.
Finkel, Evgeny. *Ordinary Jews: Choice and Survival during the Holocaust*. Princeton: Princeton University Press, 2017.
Fish, Morris J. "An Eye for an Eye: Proportionality as a Moral Principle of Punishment." *Oxford Journal of Legal Studies* 28, no. 1 (2008): 57–71.
Fishman, David. *The Book Smugglers: Partisans, Poets, and the Race to Save Jewish Treasures from the Nazis*. Lebanon, NH: ForeEdge, 2017.
Fogel, Yehuda. "The Year we hung Hitler: A 1946 Purim Celebration in the Landsberg DP Camp." *Tablet Magazine*, March 6, 2023.
Forger, Deborah and Susannah Heschel "Christianity and Antisemitism." In *The Routledge History of Antisemitism*, ed. Robert J. Williams, James Wald, and Mark Weitzman. London: Routledge, 2024, 247–54.
Frank, Anne. *The Diary of Anne Frank: The Critical Edition*, ed. David Barnouw and Gerrold van der Stroom. New York: Doubleday, 2003.
Frank, Leonhard. *Die Jünger Jesu. Ein Roman aus dem Deutschland der Nachkriegszeit*. Amsterdam: Querido Verlag, 1949.
Frankl, Viktor E. *Man's Search for Meaning*. Boston: Beacon Press, 2006.
Frankfurter, David. "I Killed a Nazi Gauleiter." *Commentary* 9 (1950): 133–41.
Frankfurter, David. *Ich tötete einen Nazi*, ed. Sabina Bossert and Janis Lutz. Wiesbaden: S. Marix Verlag, 2022.
Franklin, Ruth. *The Many Lives of Anne Frank*. New Haven: Yale University Press, 2025.
Frei, Norbert, ed. *Transnationale Vergangenheitspolitik: Der Umgang mit deutschen Kriegsverbrechern in Europa nach dem Zweiten Weltkrieg*. Göttingen: Wallstein, 2006.
Fried, Hédi. *Questions I am asked about the Holocaust*. London: Scribe, 2017.
Friedländer, Saul. *Kurt Gerstein: The Ambiguity of Good*. New York: Knopf, 1969.
Friedländer, Saul. *Nazi Germany and the Jews*. New York: HarperCollins, 1997.
Frister, Roman, *The Cap: The Price of a Life*. New York: Grove Press, 1999.
Fritz, Stephen G. *Endkampf: Soldiers, Civilians, and the Death of the Third Reich*. Lexington: University Press of Kentucky, 2004.

Fritzsche, Peter. "Babi Yar, but Not Auschwitz: What Did Germans Know about the Final Solution?" In *The Germans and the Holocaust*, ed. Schrafstetter, Susanna, and Alan E. Steinweis. New York: Berghahn, 2016, 85–106.

Frymer-Kensky, Tikva. "Tit for Tat: The Principle of Equal Retribution in Near Eastern and Biblical Law." *The Biblical Archaeologist* 43, 4 (1980): 230–341.

Fullbrook, Mary. *Reckonings: Legacies of Nazi Persecution and the Quest for Justice*. New York: Oxford University Press, 2018.

Gäbler, Ira and Andreas Maercker. "Revenge and Trauma: Theoretical Outline," Michael Linden and Andreas Maercker (eds.), *Embitterment: Societal, Psychological, and Clinical Perspectives* (Vienna: Springer, 2011), 42–69.

Garbarini, Alexandra. *Numbered Days: Diaries and the Holocaust*. New Haven: Yale University Press, 2006.

Gebhardt, Miriam. *Crimes Unspoken: The Rape of German Women at the End of the Second World War*. Cambridge: Polity Press, 2017.

Geis, Jael. "'Ja, man muss seinen Feinden verzeihen, aber nicht früher, als bis sie gehenkt werden': Gedanken zur Rache für die Vernichtung der europäischen Juden im unmittelbaren Nachkriegsdeutschland." *Menora: Jahrbuch für deutsch-jüdische Geschichte* 9 (1998): 155–80.

Geis, Jael. *Übrig sein, Leben "danach": Juden deutscher Herkunft in der britischen und amerikanischen Zone Deutschlands 1945–1949*. Berlin: Philo, 1999.

Gelbart, Mendl, ed. *Sefer ḳehilat Yehude Dombrovah Gurnitsheh ṿe-ḥurbanah*. Tel Aviv: Irgun yots'e Dombrovah Gurnitsheh be-Yiśra'el, 1971.

Gerlach, Christian. *The Extermination of the European Jews*. Cambridge: Cambridge University Press, 2016.

Gerwarth, Robert. *Hitler's Hangman: The Life of Heydrich*. New Haven: Yale University Press, 2011.

Geyer, Michael. "Endkampf 1918 and 1945. German Nationalism, Annihilation and Self-Destruction." In *No man's Land of Violence: Extreme Wars in the 20th Century*, ed. Alf Lüdke and Bernd Weisbrod. Göttingen: Wallstein 2006, 36–67.

Giladi, Ben, ed. *A Tale of One City: Piotrków Trybunalski*. New York: Shengold Publishers in cooperation with the Piotrkow Trybunalski Relief Association in New York, 1991.

Gilbert, Gustave M. *Nuremberg Diary*. New York: Farrar, Straus, 1947.

Gilbert, Shirli. *Music in the Holocaust: Confronting Life in the Nazi Ghettos and Camps*. Oxford: Oxford University Press, 2005.

Goebbels, Joseph. *Das eherne Herz: Reden und Aufsätze aus den Jahren 1941/42*. Munich: F. Eher, 1943.

Goebbels, Joseph. *Das eherne Herz: Rede vor der Deutschen Akademie*. Munich: Zentralverlag der NSDAP, 1942.

Goebbels, Joseph. *Der steile Aufstieg: Reden und Aufsätze aus den Jahren 1942/43*. Munich: F. Eher, 1944.

Goebbels, Joseph. *The Goebbels Diaries, 1939–1941*. Ed. and trans. Fred Taylor. New York: G.P. Putnam's Sons, 1983.

Goebbels, Joseph. *The Goebbels Diaries 1942–1943*. Ed. and trans. Louis P. Lochner. Garden City, New York: Doubleday & Company, Inc., 1948.

Goeschel, Christian. *Suicide in Nazi Germany*. Oxford: Oxford University Press, 2009.

Goldberg, Amos. "Jews' Diaries and Chronicles." In *Oxford Handbook of Holocaust Studies*, ed. Peter Hayes and John K. Roth. New York: Oxford University Press, 2010, 397–413.

Goldberg, Amos. "Rumor Culture among Warsaw Jews under Nazi Occupation: A World of Catastrophe Reenchanted." *Jewish Social Studies* 21, no. 3 (2016): 91–125.

Goldberg, Amos. "Rumors in the Ghettos: A Case Study of Cultural History." *Lessons and Legacies XII* (2017): 67–86.

Sources and Bibliography

Goldberg, Amos. "Three Forms of Post-Genocidal Violence in Beni Wircberg's Memoir." In *Talking About Evil Psychoanalytic, Social, and Cultural Perspectives*, ed. Rina Lazar. London: Routledge 2017, 50–67.

Goldberg, Amos. *Trauma in First Person: Diary Writing during the Holocaust*. Bloomington: Indiana University Press, 2017.

Gonzalez-Crussi, Frank, *The Body Fantastic*. Boston: MIT Press, 2021.

Gotz, Elly, *Flights of Spirit*. Toronto: Azrieli Foundation, 2018.

Govier, Trudy. *Forgiveness and Revenge*. London: Routledge, 2002.

Gradowski, Zalmen. *The Last Consolation Vanished: The Testimony of a Sonderkommando in Auschwitz*. Chicago: University of Chicago Press, 2022.

Graf, Philipp. *Die Bernheim-Petition 1933: Jüdische Politik in der Zwischenkriegszeit*. Göttingen: Vandenhoeck & Ruprecht, 2008.

Greif, Gideon. *We Wept without Tears: Testimonies of the Jewish Sonderkommando from Auschwitz*. New Haven: Yale University Press, 2005.

Griech-Polelle, Beth A. *Anti-Semitism and the Holocaust: Language, Rhetoric, and the Traditions of Hatred*. London: Bloomsbury Academic, 2017.

Grinberg, Zalmen. *Our Liberation from Dachau: Memories of a Survivor*. St. Ottilien: EOS Books, 2024.

Gross, Jan T. *Fear: Anti-Semitism in Poland after Auschwitz: An Essay in Historical Interpretation*. New York: Random House, 2006.

Gross, Jan T. *Neighbors: The Destruction of the Jewish Community in Jedwabne, Poland*. Princeton University Press, 2000.

Grossmann, Atina. "A Question of Silence: The Rape of German Women by Occupation Soldiers." *October* 72 (Spring 1995): 42–63.

Grossmann, Atina. "Gendered Perceptions and Self-Perceptions of Memory and Revenge: Jewish DPs in Occupied Postwar Germany as Victims, Villains and Survivors." In *Gender, Place, and Memory in the Modern Jewish Experience: Re-Placing Ourselves*. Ed. by Judith Tydor Baumel-Schwartz (London: Vallentine Mitchell, 2003), 78–107.

Grossmann, Atina. *Jews, Germans, and Allies: Close Encounters in Occupied Germany*. Princeton: Princeton University Press, 2009.

Grossmann, Atina. "Victims, Villains, and Survivors: Gendered Perceptions and Self-Perceptions of Jewish Displaced Persons in Occupied Postwar Germany." *Journal of the History of Sexuality* 11.1/2 (2002): 291–318.

Gruner, Wolf. *Resisters: How Ordinary Jews Fought Persecution in Hitler's Germany*. New Haven: Yale University Press, 2023.

Gruner, Wolf. "'Worse Than Vandals': The Mass Destruction of Jewish Homes and Jewish Responses during the 1938 Pogrom," *New Perspectives on Kristallnacht: After 80 Years, the Nazi Pogrom in Global Comparison*, ed. Wolf Gruner et al., West Lafayette: Purdue University Press, 2019, 25–50.

Guenter, Anna Celina. *Jewish Revenge in Postwar Vienna*. MA thesis, University of Missouri, 2023.

Gutman, Israel. *Resistance: The Warsaw Ghetto Uprising*. Boston: Houghton Mifflin, 1994.

Gutman, Israel, and Avital Saf, eds. *She'erit Hapletah, 1944–1948: Rehabilitation and Political Struggle*. Jerusalem: Yad Vashem, 1990.

Gutman, Israel, and Avital Saf, eds. *The Nazi Concentration Camps: Structure and Aims, the Image of the Prisoner, the Jews in the Camps*. Jerusalem: Yad Vashem, 1984.

Haase, Norbert. "Justizterror in der Wehrmacht am Ende des Zweiten Weltkrieges." In *Terror nach Innen: Verbrechen am Ende des Zweiten Weltkrieges*, ed. Cord Arendes, Edgar Wolfrum, and Jörg Zedler. Göttingen: Wallstein, 2006.

Hahn, Fred, and Günther Wagenlehner. *Lieber Stürmer: Leserbriefe an das NS-Kampfblatt 1924 bis 1945: eine Dokumentation aus dem Leo-Baeck-Institut, New York*. Stuttgart: Seewald, 1978.

Hall, Kevin T. *Terror Flyers: The Lynching of American Airmen in Nazi Germany*. Bloomington: Indiana University Press, 2021.

Hanan, Rachel, and Thilo Komma-Pöllath, *Ich habe Hass und Wut besiegte. Was mich Auschwitz über den Wert der Liebe gelehrt hat*. Munich: Heyne, 2024.

Hanebrink, Paul A. *A Specter Haunting Europe: The Myth of Judeo-Bolshevism*. Cambridge, Mass.: Harvard University Press, 2018.

Hansen, Jennifer. "The Art and Science of Reading Faces: Strategy of Racist Cinema in the Third Reich." *Shofar*, vol. 28, no. 1 (2009): 80–103.

Harrison, Jenny. *Out of Poland: When the best revenge is to have survived—A Holocaust Story*. New Zealand: Lamplighter Press, 2016.

Hartung, Günter. *Deutschfaschistische Literatur und Ästhetik: Gesammelte Studien*. Leipziger Universitätsverlag, 2001.

Hass, Amira. "Arriving again at the Cycle of Vengeance," *Haaretz*, Oct. 10, 2023.

Hayes, Peter. *Why? Explaining the Holocaust*. New York: W.W. Norton and Company 2017.

Hebert, Valerie. "Disguised Resistance? The Story of Kurt Gerstein." *Holocaust and Genocide Studies* 20, 1 (2006): 1–33.

Hedgepeth, Sonja M., and Rochelle G. Saidel, eds. *Sexual Violence against Jewish Women during the Holocaust*. Waltham, Mass: Brandeis University Press, 2010.

Herf, Jeffrey. *The Jewish Enemy: Nazi Propaganda During World War II and the Holocaust*. Cambridge, Harvard University Press, 2006.

Herf, Jeffrey. "The 'Jewish War': Goebbels and the Antisemitic Campaigns of the Nazi Propaganda Ministry." *Holocaust and Genocide Studies* 19, 1 (2005): 51–80.

Herf, Jeffrey. *Three Faces of Antisemitism*. London: Routledge, 2024.

Hever, Hannan. "From Revenge to Empathy: Abba Kovner from Jewish Destruction to Palestinian Destruction." In *The Holocaust and the Nakba: A New Grammar of Trauma and History*, ed. Bashir Bashir and Amos Goldberg. New York: Columbia University Press, 2019, 275–92.

Hever, Hannan. *Hebrew Literature and the 1948 War: Essays on Philology and Responsibility*. Leiden: Brill, 2019, 149–67.

Hiemer, Ernst. *Der Giftpilz*. Nuremberg: Der Stürmer, 1938.

Hilberg, Raul. *The Destruction of the European Jews*. 3rd ed. New Haven: Yale University Press, 2003.

Hillesheim, Jürgen, and Elisabeth Michael. *Lexikon nationalsozialistischer Dichter: Biographien, Analysen, Bibliographien*. Würzburg: Königshausen und Neumann 1993.

Hitler, Adolf *Mein Kampf*. English translation, New York: Houghton Mifflin, 1969.

Hitler, Adolf. *Mein Kampf: Eine kritische Edition*, ed. by Christian Hartmann, Thomas Vordermayer, Othmar Plöckinger, Roman Töppel, and Edith Raim. Munich: Institut für Zeitgeschichte, 2016.

Himka, John-Paul. "The Lviv Pogrom of 1941: The Germans, Ukrainian Nationalists, and the Carnival Crowd." *Canadian Slavonic Papers* 53, 2–4 (2011): 209–43.

Hirschmann, Ira Arthur. *The Embers Still Burn: An Eye-Witness View of the Postwar Ferment in Europe and the Middle East and our Disastrous Get-Soft-With-Germany Policy*. New York: Simon and Schuster, 1949.

Hodge, Freda, ed. *Tragedy and Triumph: Early Testimonies of Jewish Survivors of World War II*. Clayton, Victoria: Monash University Publishing, 2018.

Hornshøj-Møller, Stig, and David Culbert. "'Der Ewige Jude' (1940): Joseph Goebbels' Unequaled Monument to Anti-Semitism." *Historical Journal of Film, Radio, and Television* 12, 1 (1992): 41–67.

Horowitz, Elliott S. *Reckless Rites: Purim and the Legacy of Jewish Violence*. Princeton: Princeton University Press, 2006.

Horowitz, Sara R. "'If He Knows to Make a Child . . .' Memories of Birth and Baby-Killing in Deferred Jewish Testimony Narratives." In *Jewish Histories of the Holocaust: New*

Transnational Approaches, ed. Norman J. W Goda. New York, Oxford: Berghahn Books, 2014, 135–51.

Höss, Rudolf. *Commandant of Auschwitz: The Autobiography of Rudolf Hoess*, transl. Constantine Fitz Gibbon. London: Weidenfeld and Nicolson, 1959.

Huber, Florian. *Promise Me You'll Shoot Yourself: The Downfall of Ordinary Germans in 1945*. London: Allen Lane, 2019.

Humburg, Martin. *Das Gesicht des Krieges. Feldpostbriefe von Wehrmachtssoldaten aus der Sowjetunion 1941–1944*. Wiesbaden and Opladen: Westdeutscher Verlag, 1998.

Huth, Peter, ed. *Die letzten Zeugen: Der Auschwitz-Prozess von Lüneburg 2015; eine Dokumentation*. Stuttgart: Reclam, 2015.

Imonti, Felix, and Miyoko. *Violent Justice: How Three Assassins Fought to Free Europe's Jews*. Amherst: Prometheus Books, 1994.

Inon, Maoz. "Hamas murdered my Parents. Six Months later Israel's War of Revenge threatens us all." *Haaretz*, April 7, 2024.

International Military Tribunal. *Trial of the Major War Criminals before the International Military Tribunal, Nuremberg, 14 November 1945–1 October 1946*. Nuremberg, Germany: International Military Tribunal, 1947–1949, 22 vols.

Jäckel, Eberhard. *Hitler's World View: A Blueprint for Power*. Cambridge, Mass: Harvard University Press, 1981.

Jacoby, Susan. *Wild Justice: The Evolution of Revenge*. New York: Harper & Row, 1983.

Jalowicz Simon, Marie. *Underground in Berlin: A Young Woman's Extraordinary Tale of Survival in the Heart of Nazi Germany*. New York: Little, Brown and Company, 2015.

Jarausch, Konrad H., ed. *Reluctant Accomplice. A Wehrmacht Soldier's Letters from the Eastern Front*. Princeton: Princeton University Press, 2011.

Jardim, Tomaz. *Ilse Koch on Trial: Making the "Bitch of Buchenwald"*. Cambridge: Harvard University Press, 2023.

Jasch, Hans-Christian and Wolf Kaiser. *Der Holocaust vor deutschen Gerichten: Amnestieren, Verdraengen, Bestrafen*. Stuttgart: Reclam, 2017.

Jockusch, Laura. *Collect and Record! Jewish Holocaust Documentation in Early Postwar Europe*. New York: Oxford University Press, 2012.

Jockusch, Laura. "Justice at Nuremberg? Jewish Responses to Nazi War-Crime Trials in Allied-Occupied Germany," *Jewish Social Studies* 19, no. 1 (2012): 107–47.

Jockusch, Laura, ed. *Khurbn-Forshung: Documents on Early Holocaust Research in Postwar Poland*. Göttingen: Vandenhoeck & Ruprecht, 2021.

Jockusch, Laura, and Gabriel Finder (eds.), *Jewish Honor Courts: Revenge, Retribution, and Reconciliation in Europe and Israel after the Holocaust*. Detroit: Wayne State University Press, 2015.

Joskowicz, Ari. *Rain of Ash: Roma, Jews, and the Holocaust*. Princeton: Princeton University Press, 2023.

Judt, Tony. *Postwar: A History of Europe since 1945*. London: Penguin Books, 2005.

Jung, Michael. *Liederbücher im Nationalsozialismus Band 2: Dokumente*. PhD thesis, University of Frankfurt, 1989.

Kallis, Aristotle A. *Nazi Propaganda and the Second World War*. Basingstoke: Palgrave Macmillan, 2005.

Kangisser-Cohn, Sharon. "Survivors of the Holocaust and their children." *Journal of Modern Jewish Studies* 9, 2 (2010): 165–83.

Kaplan, Chaim A. *Scroll of Agony: The Warsaw Diary of Chaim A. Kaplan*. New York: Macmillan, 1965.

Kaplan, Israel. *The Jewish Voice in the Ghettos and Concentration Camps: Verbal Expression under Nazi Oppression*, ed. Zeev W. Mankowitz, trans. Jenny Bell and Dianne Levitin. Jerusalem: Yad Vashem, 2018.

Kaplan, Marion. *Between Dignity and Despair: Jewish Life in Nazi Germany*. New York: Oxford University Press, 1998.

Kaplan, Thomas Pegelow. *The Language of Nazi Genocide: Linguistic Violence and the Struggle of Germans of Jewish Ancestry*. New York: Cambridge University Press, 2009.

Kaplan, Thomas Pegelow, and Wolf Gruner, *Resisting Persecution: Jews and their Petitions during the Holocaust*. New York: Berghahn Books, 2020.

Karas, Joža. *Music in Terezín 1941-1945*. New York: Beaufort Books, 1985.

Kassow, Samuel D. *Who Will Write Our History? Emanuel Ringelblum, the Warsaw Ghetto, and the Oyneg Shabes Archive*. Bloomington: Indiana University Press, 2007.

Katz, Jacob. *From Prejudice to Destruction: Anti-Semitism, 1700-1933*. Cambridge: Harvard University Press, 1980.

Katzenelson, Yitzhak. *Vittel Diary (22.5.43-16.9.43)* transl. Myer Cohen. Lohame HaGetaòt: Ghetto Fighters' House, 1964.

Ka-Tzetnik, *Nakam*. Tel Aviv: Tarmil, 1981.

Kay, Alex J. *Empire of Destruction: A History of Nazi Mass Killing*. New Haven: Yale University Press, 2021.

Kehoe, Thomas J., and E. James Kehoe. "Crimes Committed by U.S. Soldiers in Europe, 1945-1946." *The Journal of Interdisciplinary History* 47, no. 1 (2016): 53-84.

Kellenbach, Katharina von. *The Mark of Cain: Guilt and Denial in the Post-War Lives of Nazi Perpetrators*. Oxford: Oxford University Press, 2013.

Keller, Sven. *Volksgemeinschaft am Ende: Gesellschaft und Gewalt 1944/45*. Berlin: De Gruyter, 2013.

Kermisz, Joseph, ed. *To Live with Honor and Die with Honor! Selected Documents from the Warsaw Ghetto Underground Archives "O.S."* Jerusalem: Yad Vashem 1986.

Kershaw, Ian. "'Working towards the Führer': Reflections on the Nature of the Hitler Dictatorship." In idem, *Hitler, the Germans, and the Final Solution*. New Haven: Yale University Press 2008, 29-48.

Kessler, Edmund, Kaziemierz Kalwinski, and Lusia Sicher. *The Wartime Diary of Edmund Kessler: Lwow, Poland 1942-1944*. Boston: Academic Studies Press, 2010.

Kimmel, James Jr., and Michael Rowe. "A Behavioral Addiction Model of Revenge, Violence, and Gun Abuse." *The Journal of Law, Medicine & Ethics* 48, 4 (2020): 172-8.

Kimmel, James Jr. *The Science of Revenge: Overcoming the World's Deadliest Addiction—and How to Overcome It*. New York: Harmony Books, 2025.

Kipp, Michaela. "The Holocaust in the Letters of German Soldiers on the Eastern Front (1939-44)." *Journal of Genocide Research* 9, 4 (2007): 601-15.

Kipp, Michaela. *Großreinemachen im Osten: Feindbilder in deutschen Feldpostbriefen im Zweiten Weltkrieg*. Frankfurt am Main: Campus, 2014.

Kirsh, Mary Fraser. *The Lost Children of Europe: Narrating the Rehabilitation of Child Holocaust Survivors in Great Britain and Israel*. PhD Dissertation, University of Wisconsin, Madison, 2012.

Klee, Ernst, Willi Dressen, and Volker Riess, eds. *"The Good Old Days": The Holocaust as Seen by Its Perpetrators and Bystanders*. New York: Free Press, 1991.

Klemperer, Victor. *I Will Bear Witness: A Diary of the Nazi Years, 1933-1941*, transl. by Martin Chalmers. New York: Modern Library, 1999.

Klemperer, Victor. *I Will Bear Witness: A Diary of the Nazi Years, 1942-1945*, transl. by Martin Chalmers. New York: Modern Library, 1999.

Klemperer, Victor. *LTI; Notizbuch eines Philologen*. Berlin: Aufbau-Verlag, 1947.

Klemperer, Victor. *The Language of the Third Reich: LTI, Lingua Tertii Imperii: A Philologist's Notebook*. London: Athlone Press, 2000.

Klinger, Chaika. *I Am Writing These Words to You: The Original Diaries, Bedzin 1943*, ed. Avihu Ronen, transl. Anna Brzostowska and Jerzy Giebułtowski. Jerusalem: Yad Vashem, 2017.

Sources and Bibliography

Klüger, Ruth. *Zerreißproben. Kommentierte Gedichte*. Vienna: Zsolnay, 2013.

Kochavi, Arieh J. *Prelude to Nuremberg : Allied War Crimes Policy and the Question of Punishment*. Chapel Hill: University of North Carolina Press, 1998.

Kogon, Eugen. *Der SS-Staat: Das System der deutschen Konzentrationslager*. Munich: Heyne, 1994.

Kopówka, Edward, and Laura Crago. "Siedlce." In *The United States Holocaust Memorial Museum Encyclopedia of Camps and Ghettos, 1933–1945*, ed. Martin Dean and Mel Hecker, vol. 2: *Ghettos in German-Occupied Eastern Europe*. Bloomington: Indiana University Press, 2012, 428–32.

Kopstein, Jeffrey, and Jason Wittenberg. *Intimate Violence: Anti-Jewish Pogroms on the Eve of the Holocaust*. Ithaca: Cornell University Press, 2018.

Kor, Eva Mozes. *The Power of Forgiveness*. Las Vegas: CRP, 2016.

Kosman, Admiel. "Vengeance in the Tanakh, Mishnah, and Talmud: A Brief Introduction," in Czollek et al., *Revenge: History and Fantasy*, 39–46.

Koss, Andrew. "Byteń," *The United States Holocaust Memorial Museum Encyclopedia of Camps and Ghettos 1933–1945*, vol. 2, 1172–4.

Krakowski, Shmuel and Ilya Altman. "The testament of the last prisoners of the Chelmno death camp." *Yad Vashem Studies* 21 (1991): 105–23.

Kramen, Alexandra. "Justice versus Revenge, or Justice as Revenge? A Case Study of Holocaust Testimony." *AJS Perspectives* (Fall 2022): 80–1.

Kramer, Aaron. "Creative defiance in a death camp," *The Journal of Humanistic Psychology* 38, no.1 (1998): 12–24.

Kruglov, Alexander, and Ray Brandon. "Czortków," *The United States Holocaust Memorial Museum Encyclopedia of Camps and Ghettos 1933–1945*, vol. 2, 770–2.

Kruglov, Alexander, and Samuel Schalkowsky. "Kowel," in *The United States Holocaust Memorial Museum Encyclopedia of Camps and Ghettos 1933–1945*, vol. 2, 1388–90.

Kruk, Herman. *The Last Days of the Jerusalem of Lithuania: Chronicles from the Vilna Ghetto and the Camps 1939–1944*, ed. Benjamin Harshav. New Haven: Yale University Press, 2002.

Kugler, Gili. "Metaphysical Hatred and Sacred Genocide: The Questionable Role of Amalek in Biblical Literature," *Journal of Genocide Research* 23, no. 1 (2021): 1–16.

Kühne, Thomas. *Belonging and Genocide: Hitler's Community, 1918–1945*. New Haven: Yale University Press, 2010.

Kühne, Thomas. *The Rise and Fall of Comradeship : Hitler's Soldiers, Male Bonding and Mass Violence in the Twentieth Century*. Cambridge: Cambridge University Press, 2017.

Kulka, Otto Dov. *Landschaften der Metropole des Todes. Auschwitz und die Grenzen der Erinnerung und der Vorstellungskraft*. Berlin: DVA, 2013.

Kulka, Otto Dov, and Eberhard Jäckel, eds. *The Jews in the Secret Nazi Reports on Popular Opinion in Germany, 1933–1945*. New Haven: Yale University Press, 2010.

Kulke, Christine. "Lwów," *The United States Holocaust Memorial Museum Encyclopedia of Camps and Ghettos 1933–1945*, vol. 2, 802–5.

Lambert, Raymond-Raoul. *Diary of a Witness: 1940–1943*. Chicago: Ivan R. Dee, 2007.

Landry, Olivia. "Jewish Revenge on the German Screen." *New German Critique* (2025) 52, no. 1 (154): 107–29.

Landsmann, Carolina. "In Pursuit of Revenge, Israel No longer Knows what it is thinking." *Haaretz*, Aug. 29, 2024.

Landsmann, Carolina. "Israel Is Living in a Tarantino Film. We Have Become the Inglourious Basterds." *Haaretz*, Jan. 10, 2025.

Lang, Berel. "Holocaust Memory and Revenge: The Presence of the Past," *Jewish Social Studies* 2, no. 2 (1996): 1–20.

Lang, Berel. *Post-Holocaust: Interpretation, Misinterpretation, and the Claims of History*. Bloomington: Indiana University Press, 2005.

Lang, Berel. *The Future of the Holocaust: Between History and Memory*. Cornell University Press, 2018.

Langbein, Hermann. *People in Auschwitz*. ed. by Harry Zohn, and Henry Friedlander. Chapel Hill, NC: University of North Carolina Press, 2004.

Langer, Lawrence. *The Afterdeath of the Holocaust*. Cham, Switzerland: Palgrave Macmillan, 2021.

Lanzmann, Claude. *Shoah: An Oral History of the Holocaust. The Complete Text of the Film; preface by Simone de Beauvoir*. New York: Pantheon Books, 1985.

Latzel, Klaus. *Deutsche Soldaten—nationalsozialistischer Krieg? Kriegserlebnis— Kriegserfahrung 1939-1945*. Munich: Schöningh, 1998.

Lavi, Shai. "'The Jews Are Coming': Vengeance and Revenge in Post-Nazi Europe." *Law, Culture and the Humanities* 1, no. 3 (2005): 282–301.

Leoni, Eliezer, ed. *Kovel: Sefer 'edut ve-zikaron le-kehilatenu she-'alah 'aleha ha-koret*. Tel Aviv: Irgun Yots'e Ḳovel be-Yiśra'el, 1957.

Leftwich, Joseph. *Abraham Sutzkever: Partisan Poet*. New York: T. Yoseloff, 1971.

Lerner, Roni. *National Vengeance as a Component of Jewish Resistance during the Holocaust, 1939-1945*. Bar Ilan University, Ramat Gan, 2018.

Lewin, Abraham. *A Cup of Tears: A Diary of the Warsaw Ghetto*, ed. Antony Polonsky. Oxford: Basil Blackwell, 1988.

Lev, Gidon, and Julie Grey, *Let's Make Things Better: A Holocaust Survivor's Message of Hope and Celebration of Life*. London: Macmillan, 2024.

Levi, Primo. *Collected Poems*, trans. Ruth Feldman and Brian Swann. New York: Faber & Faber, 1988.

Levi, Primo. *If this is a Man / The Truce*, transl. Stuart Woolf. London: Abacus, 2013.

Levi, Primo. "Light on the Camps." *The New Republic* 194, no. 7 (February 17, 1986): 28–32.

Levin, Meyer. *In Search: An Autobiography*. New York: Horizon Press 1950.

Levin, Meyer, ed. *Kibbutz Buchenwald: Selections from the Kibbutz Diary*. Tel Aviv, 1946.

Levitt, Ruth, ed. *Pogrom November 1938: Testimonies from "Kristallnacht"*. London: Souvenir Press, 2015.

Levy, Richard S. "Antisemitism in Germany 1890-1933: How Popular as it?" in *The Germans and the Holocaust: Popular Responses to the Persecution and Murder of the Jews*, ed. Schrafstetter, Susanna, and Alan E. Steinweis. New York: Berghahn, 2016, 17–40.

Lewin, Abraham. *A Cup of Tears: A Diary of the Warsaw Ghetto*, ed. Antony Polonsky. Oxford: Basil Blackwell, 1988.

Lewinsky, Tamar. *Displaced Poets: Jiddische Schriftsteller im Nachkriegsdeutschland, 1945–1951*. Göttingen: Vandenhoeck & Ruprecht, 2008.

Lipiński, Edward. "נקם, nāqam," *Theological Dictionary of the Old Testament*, ed. G. Johannes Botterweck, Helmer Ringgren, and Heinz-Josef Fabry. Grand Rapids: Eerdmans, 1999, vol. 10, 1–9.

Lohse, Alexandra. *Prevail until the Bitter End: Germans in the Waning Years of World War II*. Ithaka: Cornell University Press, 2021.

Longerich, Peter. *Antisemitismus: Eine deutsche Geschichte: Von der Aufklärung bis heute*. Munich: Siedler, 2021.

Longerich, Peter. *"Davon haben wir nichts gewusst!": Die Deutschen und die Judenverfolgung 1933–1945*. Munich: Siedler 2006.

Longerich, Peter. *Die Sportpalastrede 1943: Goebbels und der "totale Krieg"*. Munich: Siedler, 2023.

Longerich, Peter. *Holocaust: The Nazi Persecution and Murder of the Jews*. Oxford: Oxford University Press, 2010.

Lopez, Anthony C., and Rose McDermott, Pete Hatemi. "'Blunt not the heart, enrage it': The Psychology of Revenge and Deterrence." *Texas National Security Review* 1, 1 (December 2017): 69–87.

Lowe, Keith. *Savage Continent: Europe in the Aftermath of World War II*. New York: Picador, 2013.

Sources and Bibliography

Lowe, Keith. *The Fear and the Freedom: How the Second World War Changed Us*. New York: Viking Press, 2017.

Lower, Wendy. "Pogroms, Mob Violence and Genocide in Western Ukraine, Summer 1941: Varied Histories, Explanations and Comparisons." *Journal of Genocide Research* 13, no. 3 (2011): 217–46.

Lower, Wendy. *The Ravine: A Family, a Photograph, a Holocaust Massacre Revealed*. Boston: Houghton Mifflin Harcourt, 2021.

Lüdtke, Alf. "Explaining Forced Migration." In *Removing Peoples: Forced Removal in the Modern World*, ed. Richard Bessel and Claudia B. Haake. Oxford: Oxford U.P. 2009, 13–32.

Luettig, Frank, and Jens Lehmann, eds. *Die Letzten NS-Verfahren*. Baden-Baden: Nomos, 2017.

Lutjens, Richard. *Submerged on the Surface: The Not-So-Hidden Jews of Nazi Berlin 1941–1945*. New York: Berghahn Books, 2018.

Magilow, Daniel H. "Jewish Revenge Fantasies in Contemporary Film." *Jewish Cultural Aspirations*, ed. Bruce Zuckerman et al. West Lafayette: Purdue University Press, 2013: 89–110.

Mallmann, Klaus-Michael, Volker Rieß and Wolfram Pyta, eds. *Deutscher Osten 1939–1945. Der Weltanschauungskrieg in Photos und Texten*. Darmstadt: Wissenschaftliche Buchgesellschaft, 2003.

Mankowitz, Zeev W. *Life between Memory and Hope: The Survivors of the Holocaust in Occupied Germany*. New York: Cambridge University Press, 2002.

Mannes, Stefan. *Antisemitismus im nationalsozialistischen Propagandafilm: Jud Süss und Der ewige Jude*. Cologne: Teiresias, 1999.

Manoschek, Walter, ed. *Es gibt nur eines für das Judentum: Vernichtung. Das Judenbild in deutschen Soldatenbriefen 1939–1944*. Hamburg: Hamburger Edition, 1995.

Mark, Bernard, and Isaiah Avrech, eds. *The Scrolls of Auschwitz*. Tel Aviv: Am 'Oved Pub. House, 1985.

Mark, Natan, and Shimon Friedlander, eds. *Sefer yizkor; mukdash le-yehudei ha-ayarot she-nispu ba-shoa be-shanim 1939–44, Linsk, Istrik, Beligrod, Litovisk veha-sevivah*. Tel Aviv, 1964.

Marrus, Michael R. "Jewish Resistance to the Holocaust." *Journal of Contemporary History* 30, 1 (1995): 83–110.

Marrus, Michael R. "The Strange Story of Herschel Grynszpan." *The American Scholar* 57, 1 (Winter 1988): 69–79.

Matthäus, Jürgen. "Kaunas." *The United States Holocaust Memorial Museum: Encyclopedia of Camps and Ghettos 1933–1945*, vol. II, part B, 1066–9.

Matthäus, Jürgen, Mark Roseman, Emil Kerenji, Alexandra Garbarini, Jan Lambertz, Avinoam J. Patt, and Leah Wolfson, eds. *Jewish Responses to Persecution*, vols. 1–5. Lanham, Md: AltaMira Press, 2010–2015.

Mauriello, Christopher. *Forced Confrontation: The Politics of Dead Bodies in Germany at the End of World War II*. Lanham: Lexington Books, 2017.

Mendes-Flohr, Paul, and Jehuda Reinharz, eds. *The Jew in the Modern World: A Documentary History*. New York: Oxford University Press, 2011.

Mermelstein, Max, and Tony Hausner, eds. *Skala on the River Zbrucz: A History of the Former Skala Jewish Community*. United States: Skala Research Group and Skala Benevolent Society, 2009 [originally published in 1978].

Meyer, Linda Ross. "The New Revenge and the Old Retribution: Insights from Monte Cristo." *Studies in Law, Politics and Society* 31 (2003): 119–42.

Meyer, Martin. *Auge um Auge, Zahn um Zahn: Der jüdische und der deutsche Holocaust*. Frankfurt am Main: Haag + Herchen, 1992.

Meyer, Michael. *The Politics of Music in the Third Reich*. Peter Lang, 1991.

Michalczyk, John J., Michael Bryant, and Susan A. Michalczyk, eds. *Hitler's "Mein Kampf" and the Holocaust: A Prelude to Genocide*. London: Bloomsbury, 2022.

Michlic, Joanna B. "The Soviet Occupation of Poland, 1939–41, and the Stereotype of the Anti-Polish and Pro-Soviet Jew." *Jewish Social Studies* 13, 3 (2007): 135–76.

Michlic, Joanna B. *Poland's Threatening Other: The Image of the Jew from 1880 to the Present.* Lincoln: University of Nebraska Press, 2006.

Mickiewicz, Adam. "Forefathers' Eve." *The Slavonic Review* 3, 9 (1925): 499–523.

Miller, William Ian. *Eye for an Eye.* New York: Cambridge University Press, 2006.

Minow, Martha. *Between Vengeance and Forgiveness: Facing History after Genocide and Mass Violence.* Boston: Beacon Press, 1998.

Mintzker, Yair. *The Many Deaths of Jew Süss: The Notorious Trial and Execution of an Eighteenth-Century Court Jew.* Princeton, New Jersey: Princeton University Press, 2017.

Moeller, Robert G. *War Stories: The Search for a Usable Past in the Federal Republic of Germany.* Berkeley: University of California Press, 2001.

Morris, Douglas. "The Lawyer Who Mocked Hitler, and Other Jewish Commentaries on the Nuremberg Laws." *Central European History* 49, 3/4 (2016): 383–408.

Moss, Candida. *The Myth of Persecution: How Early-Christians Invented a Story of Martyrdom.* San Francisco: HarperOne, 2013.

Mortensen, Erik. "The Mode of Lynching: One Method of Vigilante Justice," *Canadian Review of American Studies* 48, no.1 (2018): 20–39.

Müller, Filip. *Eyewitness Auschwitz: Three Years in the Gas Chambers.* Chicago: Ivan R. Dee, 1999.

Munk, Yascha. *Stranger in My Own Country: A Jewish Family in Modern Germany.* New York: Farrar, Straus and Giroux, 2015.

Namysło, Aleksandra. "Dąbrowa Górnicza." *The United States Holocaust Memorial Museum Encyclopedia of Camps and Ghettos 1933–1945*, 149–52.

Nansen, Odd. *From Day to Day: One Man's Diary of Survival in Nazi Concentration Camps.* Nashville: Vanderbilt University Press, 2016.

Neitzel, Sönke and Harald Welzer, eds. *Soldaten on Fighting, Killing, and Dying: The Secret World War II Transcripts of German POWs.* New York: Alfred A. Knopf, 2012.

Neumann, Franz, Herbert Marcuse, Otto Kirchheimer, Raffaele Laudani, *Secret Reports on Nazi Germany: The Frankfurt School Contribution to the War Effort.* Princeton: Princeton University Press, 2013.

Neustadt, Mordechai. *Sefer Druyah u-ḳehilot Miyor, Droisḳ, ye-Le'onpol.* Tel-Aviv? Be-hotsa'at Yots'e Druyah yeha-sevivah be-Yiśra'el, 1973.

Nirenberg, David. *Anti-Judaism: The Western Tradition.* New York: W.W. Norton, 2013.

Niven, Bill. "Reactive Memory: The Holocaust and the Flight and Expulsion of Germans." In *Memory and Postwar Memorials: Confronting the Violence of the Past*, ed. Marc Silberman and Florence Vatan. New York: Palgrave 2013, 51–69.

Novitch, Miriam, ed. *Sobibor: Martyrdom and Revolt.* New York: Holocaust Library, 1980.

NSDAP, *Liederbuch der Nationalsozialistischen Deutschen Arbeiter-Partei.* Munich: Zentralverlag der NSDAP, 1938.

Orbach, Larry and Vivien Orbach-Smith. *Soaring Underground: A Young Fugitive's Life in Nazi Berlin.* Washington, D.C: Compass Press, 1996.

Ostrower, Chaya. *It Kept Us Alive: Humor in the Holocaust.* Jerusalem: Yad Vashem, 2014.

Overmans, Rüdiger. *Deutsche militärische Verluste im Zweiten Weltkrieg.* Munich: Oldenbourg, 1999.

Padover, Saul Kussiel. *Experiment in Germany: The Story of an American Intelligence Officer.* New York: Duell, Sloan and Pearce, 1946.

Panz, Karolina. "'The Children Are in a State of True Panic.' Postwar Anti-Jewish Violence in Podhale and Its Youngest Victims." *Yad Vashem Studies* 46, 1 (2018): 103–40.

Patt, Avinoam J. *Finding Home and Homeland: Jewish Youth and Zionism in the Aftermath of the Holocaust.* Detroit: Wayne State University Press, 2009.

Patt, Avinoam J. *The Jewish Heroes of Warsaw: The Afterlife of the Revolt.* Detroit: Wayne State University Press, 2021.

Paulus, Martin, Edith Raim, Gerhard Zelger, eds. *Ein Ort wie jeder andere: Bilder au seiner deutschen Kleinstadt. Landsberg 1923–1958.* Reinbek: Rowolt, 1995.

Sources and Bibliography

Peifer, Douglas Carl. *Hitler's Deserters: Breaking Ranks with the Wehrmacht.* New York: Oxford University Press, 2025.

Pendas, Devin. *The Frankfurt Auschwitz Trial, 1963–1965: Genocide, History, and the Limits of the Law.* Cambridge: Cambridge University Press, 2006.

Pendas, Devin. "Perpetrators on Trial." In *Cambridge History of the Holocaust*, vol. 4. Ed. Laura Jockusch and Devin Pendas. Cambridge: Cambridge University Press, 2025.

Perechodnik, Calel. *Am I a Murderer?: Testament of a Jewish Ghetto Policeman*, ed. Frank Fox. Boulder, CO: Westview Press, 1996.

Perry, Rachel E. "George Kadish's 'Modest but Important Beginning:' Exhibiting the Holocaust to Survivors through Photographs, 1945–1946." *The Journal of Holocaust Research* 37, 3: 244–70.

Pick, Aharon. *Notes from the Valley of Slaughter: A Memoir from the Ghetto of Siauliai, Lithuania.* Bloomington: Indiana University Press, 2023.

Polian, Pavel, ed. *Briefe aus der Asche: Die Aufzeichnungen des jüdischen Sonderkommandos Auschwitz.* Freiburg i. B.: WBG Theiss, 2024.

Polian, Pavel. "Das Ungelesene Lesen: Die Aufzeichnungen von Marcel Nadjari, Mitglied Des Jüdischen Sonderkommandos von Auschwitz-Birkenau, Und Ihre Erschließung," *Vierteljahrshefte Für Zeitgeschichte* 65, no. 4 (2017): 597–619.

Pollin-Galay, Hannah. 'A Rubric of Pain Words': Mapping Atrocity with Holocaust Yiddish Glossaries." *Jewish Quarterly Review* 110, 1 (2020): 161–93.

Pollin-Galay, Hannah. "The History of My Voice: Yiddish at the Seams of Holocaust Video Testimony." *Prooftexts* 35 no. 1, (2016): 58–97.

Porat, Dan. *Bitter Reckoning: Israel Tries Holocaust Survivors as Nazi Collaborators.* Cambridge: Belknap, 2019.

Porat, Dina. *Nakam: The Holocaust Sturvivors Who Sought Full-Scale Revenge.* Stanford: Stanford University Press, 2022.

Porat, Dina. *The Fall of a Sparrow: The Life and Times of Abba Kovner*, transl. and ed. Elizabeth Yuval. Stanford: Stanford University Press, 2010.

Przyrembel, Alexandra, and Jörg Schönert, eds. *"Jud Süß": Hofjude, literarische Figur, antisemitisches Zerrbild.* Frankfurt am Main: Campus, 2006.

Puvogel, Ulrike, Martin Stankowski, Ursula Graf, eds. *Gedenkstätten für die Opfer des Nationalsozialismus: Eine Dokumentation.* Bonn: Bundeszentrale für Politische Bildung, 1995.

Quelennec, Bruno. "'The Germans will never forgive the Jews for Auschwitz' (Zvi Rex). Origin, scope and limits of the concepts of "secondary anti-Semitism." *Cités* 87, 3 (2021), 33–50.

Rabinbach, Anson, and Sander Gilman, eds. *The Third Reich Sourcebook.* Berkeley: University of California Press, 2013.

Rajchman, Chil. *Treblinka: A Survivor's Memory 1942-1943*, transl. Solon Beinfeld. London: MacleHose Press, 2011.

Reichmann, Hans. *Deutscher Bürger und verfolgter Jude: Novemberpogrom und KZ Sachsenhausen 1937 bis 1939.* Munich: R. Oldenbourg, 1998.

Rein, Leonid. "Local Collaboration in the Execution of the 'Final Solution' in Nazi-Occupied Belorussia." *Holocaust and Genocide Studies* 20, 3 (2006): 381–409.

Richter, Ari. *Never Again Will I Visit Auschwitz: A Graphic Family Memoir of Trauma and Inheritance.* Seattle: Fantagraphics Books, 2024.

Ringelblum, Emanuel. *Ksovim fun geṭo.* Warsaw: Yidish bukh, 1961.

Ringelblum, Emanuel. *Notes from the Warsaw Ghetto: The Journal of Emmanuel Ringelblum.* New York: McGraw-Hill, 1958.

Riwash, Joseph. *Resistance and Revenge, 1939-1949.* Mount Royal: R & R Distribution, 1981.

Rojowska, Elżbieta et al. "Wilno." In *The United States Holocaust Memorial Museum Encyclopedia of Camps and Ghettos 1933–1945*, ed. Martin Dean and Mel Hecker, vol. 2. Bloomington: Indiana University Press, 2012, 1148–52.

Rosenberg, Alfred. *Dietrich Eckart: Ein Vermächtnis*. Munich: Zentralverlag der NSDAP, 1935.

Rosenberg, Alfred. *The Political Diary of Alfred Rosenberg and the Onset of the Holocaust*, ed. Jürgen Matthäus and Frank Bajohr. Lanham, Maryland: Rowman & Littlefield, 2015.

Rosenthal, Gabriele. *The Holocaust in Three Generations: Families of Victims and Perpetrators of the Nazi Regime*. Leverkusen: Verlag Barbara Budrich, 2010.

Roseman, Mark. "'. . . but of revenge not a sign.' Germans' Fear of Jewish Revenge after World War II." *Jahrbuch fuer Antisemitismusforschung* 22 (2013): 79–98.

Roseman, Mark. "'No Herr Führer!' Jewish Revenge after the Holocaust: Between Fantasy and Reality." In *Revenge, Retribution, Reconciliation: Justice and Emotions Between Conflict and Mediation, a Cross-Disciplinary Anthology*, ed. Laura Jockusch, Andreas Kraft, and Kim Wünschmann. Jerusalem: Hebrew University Magnes Press, 2016, 69–90.

Roskies, David and Naomi Diamant. *Holocaust Literature*. Waltham: Brandeis University Press, 2012.

Rossoliński-Liebe, Grzegorz. "Der Verlauf und die Täter des Lemberger Pogroms vom Sommer 1941: Zum aktuellen Stand der Forschung." *Jahrbuch für Antisemitismusforschung* 22 (2013): 207–43.

Rousso, Henry. *The Vichy Syndrome: History and Memory in France since 1944*. Cambridge: Harvard University Press, 1991.

Rozett, Robert, and Iael Nidam-Orvieto, eds. *After So Much Pain and Anguish: First Letters after Liberation*. Jerusalem: Yad Vashem, 2016.

Rubenstein, Joshua. "Il'ia Ehrenburg and the Holocaust in the Soviet Press." In *Soviet Jews in World War II: Fighting, Witnessing, Remembering*. Ed. Harriet Murav and Gennadi Estraikh. Brighton, MA: Academic Studies Press, 2014, 36–57.

Rubenstein, Joshua, and Ilya Altman. *The Unknown Black Book: The Holocaust in the German-Occupied Soviet Territories*. Bloomington: Indiana University Press, 2008.

Rudolph, Katharina. *Rebell im Maßanzug. Leonhard Frank: Die Biographie*. Berlin: Aufbau, 2020.

Sack, John. *An Eye for an Eye*. New York: Basic Books, 1993.

Sagi, Avi. "The Punishment of Amalek in Jewish Tradition: Coping with the Moral Problem." *The Harvard Theological Review* 87, no. 3 (1994): 323–46.

Sakowicz, Kazimierz. *Ponary Diary 1941–1943: A Bystander's Account of a Mass Murder*, ed. Yitzhak Arad. New Haven: Yale University Press, 2005.

Salsitz, Norman, and Richard Skolnik. *A Jewish Boyhood in Poland: Remembering Kolbuszowa*. Syracuse, NY: Syracruse University Press, 1992.

Salsitz, Norman, and Amalie Petranker Salsitz. *Against All Odds: A Tale of Two Survivors*. New York: Holocaust Library, 1990.

Salsitz, Norman, and Stanley Kaish. *Three Homelands: Memories of a Jewish Life in Poland, Israel, and America*. New York: Syracuse University Press, 2002.

Schabas, William A. *An Introduction to the International Criminal Court*. New York: Cambridge University Press, 2001.

Schalkowsky, Samuel. *The Clandestine History of the Kovno Jewish Ghetto Police*. Bloomington: Indiana University Press, 2014.

Schelvis, Jules. *Sobibor: A History of a Nazi Death Camp*. Bloomsbury Academic, 2014.

Schleunes, Karl A. *The Twisted Road to Auschwitz: Nazi Policy Toward German Jews, 1933–1939*. Urbana: Univ. of Illinois Press, 1970.

Schulman, Faye. *A Partisan's Memoir: Woman of the Holocaust*. Toronto: Second Story Press, 1995.

Schwarz, Leo W. *The Redeemers: A Saga of the Years 1945–1952*. New York: Farrar Straus and Young, 1953.

Schwarz-Friesel, Monika, and Jehuda Reinharz. *Inside the Antisemitic Mind: The Language of Jew-Hatred in Contemporary Germany*. Waltham: Brandeis University Press, 2017.

Segev, Tom. *Simon Wiesenthal: The Life and Legends*. London: Jonathan Cape, 2010.

Segev, Tom. *The Seventh Million: Israelis and the Holocaust*. New York: Henry Holt, 2000.

Sources and Bibliography

Seidman, Hillel. *The Warsaw Ghetto Diaries*. Southfield, MI: Targum Press, 1997.

Seidman, Naomi. "Elie Wiesel and the Scandal of Jewish Rage." *Jewish Social Studies* 3, no. 1 (autumn 1996), 1–19.

Shahar Pinsker, "On Jewish Revenge: What might a people subjected to unspeakable historical suffering, think about the ethics of vengeance once in power?," *Aeon* (May 17, 2024).

Shmidman, Joshua H. "Vengeance," *Encyclopaedia Judaica*, vol. 20, 498–9.

Sierakowiak, Dawid. *The Diary of Dawid Sierakowiak: Five Notebooks from the Łódź Ghetto*. New York: Oxford University Press, 1996.

Smith, Bradley F., and Agnes F. Peterson, eds. *Heinrich Himmler: Geheimreden, 1933 bis 1945, und andere Ansprachen*. Frankfurt/M: Propylaen, 1974.

Smith, David Livingstone. *Making Monsters: The Uncanny Power of Dehumanization*. Cambridge: Harvard University Press, 2021.

Sneh, Perla. "Khurbn Yiddish: An Absent Absence," *Lessons and Legacies* XII (2017): 215–31.

Snyder, Timothy. *Bloodlands: Europe between Hitler and Stalin*. New York: Basic Books, 2010.

Sonnenfeldt, Richard W. *Witness to Nuremberg: The Many Lives of the Man who Translated at the Nazi War Trials*. New York: Arcade Publishers, 2006.

Soussan, Julian-Chaim. "Indeed, where revenge is necessary, it is a great thing." In *Revenge: History and Fantasy*, ed. Max Czollek, Erik Riedel, and Mirjam Wenzel. Berlin: Hanser Verlag, 2022, 47–55.

Stasiulis, Stanislovas. "The Holocaust in Lithuania: The Key Characteristics of Its History, and the Key Issues in Historiography and Cultural Memory." *East European Politics and Societies* 34, 1 (2020): 261–79.

Steinert, Johannes Dieter. "A Moment in Time: The Liberation of Jewish Child Slave Laborers." In *Starting Anew: The Rehabilitation of Child Survivors of the Holocaust in the Early Postwar Years*, ed. Sharon Kangisser Cohen and Dalia Ofer. Jerusalem: Yad Vashem, 2019, 23–50.

Steinke, Ronen. *The Politics of International Criminal Justice: German Perspectives from Nuremberg to the Hague*. Oxford and Portland: Hart Publishing, 2011.

Stengel, Katharina. *Die Überlebenden vor Gericht. Auschwitz-Häftlinge als Zeugen in NS-Prozessen (1950–1976)*. Göttingen: Vandenhoeck & Ruprecht, 2022.

Stengel, Katharina. "Eine jüdische Stimme vor Gericht." *Vierteljahrshefte für Zeitgeschichte* 71, no. 3 (2023): 449–81.

Stern, Frank. *The Whitewashing of the Yellow Badge: Antisemitism and Philosemitism in Postwar Germany*. Oxford: Vidal Sassoon International Center for the Study of Antisemitism SICSA, the Hebrew University of Jerusalem, 1992.

Stone, Dan. *The Liberation of the Camps: The End of the Holocaust and Its Aftermath*. New Haven: Yale University Press, 2015.

Stone, D. Z. *No Past Tense: Love and Survival in the Shadow of the Shoah*. Elstree: Vallentine Mitchell, 2019.

Strimple, Nick. "Music as Resistance." In *Jewish Resistance Against the Nazis*, ed. Patrick Henry. Washington: Catholic University of America Press 2014, 319–38.

Sutzkever, Abraham. *From the Vilna Ghetto to Nuremberg: Memoir and Testimony*, ed. and transl. Justin D. Cammy. Montreal: McGill-Queen's University Press, 2021.

Sutzkever, Abraham. "Mayn eydes zogn in Nirnberg." *Di goldene keyt* 54 (1966): 1–14.

Sutzkever, Abraham. *Poetishe verk*. Tel Aviv: Yuval, 1963, 2 vols.

Szarota, Tomasz. *On the Threshold of the Holocaust: Anti-Jewish Riots and Pogroms in Occupied Europe. Warsaw – Paris – The Hague – Amsterdam – Antwerp – Kaunas*. Frankfurt: Peter Lang, 2015.

Tamari, Moshe. *Kehilat Lenin: Sefer zikaron*. Tel Aviv: Va'ad yots'ey Lenin be-Yi´sra'el, 1956.

Tausendfreund, Doris. *Erzwungener Verrat. Jüdische „Greifer" im Dienst der Gestapo 1943– 1945*. Berlin: Metropol, 2006.

Tcherikower, Elias. *Antisemitism un pogromen in Ukraine, 1917–1918: tsu der geshikhte fin unkarinish-yidishe batsihungen*. Berlin: Mizrekh-Yidisher historisher arkhiv, 1923.
Tec, Nechama *Defiance*. Oxford: Oxford University Press, 2009.
Tegel, Susan. *Jew Süss: Life, Legend, Fiction, Film*. London: Continuum, 2011.
Tegel, Susan. *Nazis and the Cinema*. London: Hambledon Continuum, 2007.
Teter, Magda. *Blood Libel: On the Trail of an Antisemitic Myth*. Cambridge: Harvard University Press, 2020.
Tobias, Jim G. *Der Kibbuz auf dem Streicher-Hof: Die vergessene Geschichte der jüdischen Kollektivfarmen 1945–48*. Nuremberg: Dahlinger und Fuchs, 1997.
Tobias, Jim G., and Peter Zinke. *Nakam: Jüdische Rache an NS-Tätern*. Hamburg: Konkret Literatur Verlag, 2000.
Tokarska-Bakir, Joanna. *Cursed: A Social Portrait of the Kielce Pogrom*. Ithaca: Cornell University Press, 2023.
Tokarska-Bakir, Joanna. "Terror in Przedbórz: The Night of 26 May 1945." *East European Politics and Societies* 37, 1 (2023): 298–329.
Tomkiewicz, Monika, and Steven Seegel. "Druja." *The United States Holocaust Memorial Museum Encyclopedia of Camps and Ghettos 1933–1945*, vol. 2, 1180–2.
Towle, Philip. *Enforced Disarmament: From the Napoleonic Campaigns to the Gulf War*. Oxford: Clarendon Press, 1997.
Trepp, Gunda. *Gebrauchsanweisung gegen Antisemitismus*. Darmstadt: WBG, 2022.
Trunk, Isaiah. *Jewish Responses to Nazi Persecution: Collective and Individual Behavior in Extremis*. New York: Stein and Day, 1979.
Trunk, Isaiah. *Łódź Ghetto: A History*, ed., trans., and annotated by Robert Moses Shapiro. Bloomington: Indiana University Press, 2006.
Tryczyk, Mirosław, and Frank Szmulowicz. *The Towns of Death: Pogroms Against Jews by Their Neighbors*. Lanham: Lexington Books, 2021.
Virgili, Fabrice. *Shorn Women: Gender and Punishment in Liberation France*. Oxford: Berg, 2002.
Volkov, Shulamit. "The Written Matter and the Spoken Words: On the Gap between Pre-1914 and Nazi Antisemitism." In *Unanswered questions: Nazi Germany and the Genocide of the Jews*. Ed. François Furet. New York: Schocken Books, 1989, 33–53.
Von Kardorff, Ursula. *Berliner Aufzeichnungen: 1942 bis 1945*. Munich: DTV, 1997.
Wachsmann, Nikolaus. *KL: A History of the Nazi Concentration Camps*. New York: Farrar, Straus and Giroux, 2015.
Walke, Anika. *Pioneers and Partisans: An Oral History of Nazi Genocide in Belorussia*. New York: Oxford University Press, 2015.
Waxman, Zoë. *Women in the Holocaust : A Feminist History*. Oxford: Oxford University Press, 2017.
Webb, Chris. *The Sobibor Death Camp: History, Biographies, Remembrance*. Stuttgart: Ibidem-Verlag, 2017.
Weckel, Ulrike. "'Jüdische Rache'?: Wahrnehmungen des Nürnberger Hauptkriegsverbrecherprozesses durch Angeklagte, Verteidiger und die deutsche Bevölkerung 1945/46," *Jahrbuch für Antisemitismusforschung* 22 (2013): 57–78.
Weckel, Ulrike. *Beschaemende Bilder: Deutsche Reaktionen auf alliierte Dokumentarfilme über befreite Konzentrationslager*. Stuttgart: Franz Steiner Verlag, 2012.
Weitz, Eric D. *A Century of Genocide: Utopias of Race and Nation*. Princeton: Princeton University Press, 2003.
Welch, David. *The Third Reich: Politics and Propaganda*. London: Routledge, 1993.
Wettig, Gerhard. *Entmilitarisierung und Wiederbewaffnung in Deutschland 1943 bis 1955: Internationale Auseinandersetzungen um die Rolle der Deutschen in Europa*. Munich: R. Oldenbourg Verlag, 1967.

Sources and Bibliography

Wildman, Sarah. "The Israeli Hostage who Refused to Embrace Revenge." *The New York Times*, June 10, 2025.

Willenberg, Samuel. *Surviving Treblinka*. Oxford: Basil Blackwell, 1989.

Wircberg, Beni. *From Death to Battle: Auschwitz Survivor and Palmach Fighter*. Jerusalem: Yad Vashem, 2017.

Wiesel, Elie. *All Rivers Run to the Sea: Memoirs*. New York: Schocken Books, 1995.

Wiesel, Elie. "To a Young Palestinian Arab." In idem., *A Jew Today*. New York: Random House, 1978.

Wiesel, Elie. *Un di velt hot geshvign. Dos Poylishe Yidnţum* 117. Buenos Aires: Tsenţral-Farband fun Poylishe Yidn in Argenţine, 1956.

Wieviorka, Annette. *The Era of the Witness*. Ithaca, N.Y: Cornell University Press, 2006.

Wittmann, Rebecca. "A Lost Voice? Jewish Witnesses in the Auschwitz Trials in Germany." *Holocaust Research in Context: The Emergence of Research Centers and Approaches*, ed. David Bankier and Dan Michman. Jerusalem: Yad Vashem Press, 2010.

Wittmann, Rebecca. *Beyond Justice: The Auschwitz Trial*. Cambridge: Harvard University Press, 2005.

Yablonka, Hanna. "Holocaust Survivors in Israel." *Holocaust Survivors: Resettlement, Memories, Identities*, ed. Dalia Ofer, et al. New York: Berghahn Books, 2011.

Yablonka, Hanna. *Survivors of the Holocaust: Israel after the War*. New York: NYU Press, 1999.

Yablonka, Hanna. *The State of Israel vs. Adolf Eichmann*. New York: Schocken Books, 2004.

Yelton, David K. *Hitler's Volkssturm: The Nazi Militia and the Fall of Germany, 1944–1946* Lawrence: University Press of Kansas, 2002.

Yuval, Israel. *Two Nations in Your Womb: Perceptions of Jews and Christians in Late Antiquity and the Middle Ages*. Berkeley: University of California Press, 2006.

Zabransky, Florian. *Jewish Men and the Holocaust: Sexuality, Emotions, Masculinity. An Intimate History*. Berlin/Boston: Walter de Gruyter, 2024.

Zait, Jonathan, and Christopher D. Green. "'I'm Not a Person Anymore': The 'Survivor Syndrome' and William G. Niederland's Perception of the Human Being." *History of Psychology* 27, no. 2 (2024): 121–38.

Zapruder, Alexandra, ed. *Salvaged Pages: Young Writers' Diaries of the Holocaust*. New Haven: Yale University Press, 2002.

Zbirohowski-Koscia, Witold, ed. *Marcel Nadjari's Manuscript, November 3 1944: Conservation and Legibility Enhancement through Multispectral Imaging*. Auschwitz: Auschwitz-Birkenau State Museum, 2020.

Zegenhagen, Evelyn, and Christoph Dieckmann. "Kauen Main Camp." In *The United States Holocaust Memorial Museum Encyclopedia of Camps and Ghettos 1933–1945*, vol. 1, 847–53.

Zuckerman, Yitzhak. *A Surplus of Memory: Chronicle of the Warsaw Ghetto Uprising*, ed. and trans. by Barbara Harshav. Berkeley: University of California Press, 1993.

INDEX

Note: References in *italic* refer to figures. References followed by "n" refer to notes.

Adorno, Theodor W. 151–2
aerial bombings 55, 62, 113, 150, 239
afterdeath 241
Alexander, Karl 38
Al Hashkhita (Bialik) 124, 146n227, 183, 216n188
al-Hussaini, Amin 185
Allach 169
Allies/Allied forces 13, 102
    Adorno's interviewees on 152
    as agents of future vengeance 116
    bombings and invasion of Germany 47–57, 113, 122, 130–1, 150, 233–4
    courts 17n4
    gendered perspective 157
    Nuremberg trials 57–63, 177, 180, 189–91, 197
    rape committed by 154
    summary executions 154
    vigilante justice 157
Alma-Ata 161
Almelo 123
Alsenz 236
Amalek/Amalekites 6, 185
American Jewish Joint Distribution Committee 122
Amsterdam 13
Améry, Jean 167–8, 189, 201–2, 233
Andreas-Friedrich, Ruth 35
Anielewicz, Mordechai 88
antisemitism 4–8, 28–32. *See also* Nazis
armed resistance 86–7
Aryans 14, 26, 29, 42
Atlas, Gina 103
Atlas, Reuven 103
Auerbach, Rachel 117–18
Auschwitz (camp complex) 1–2, 12, 106, 188–9, 191–2, 199, 239
    "family camp" 96, 126–7, 132
    Sonderkommando 85, 93, 96–7, 99, 115, 119–20, 149
    uprising 101, 133

B., Alexander 243n23
B., Eva 12
Babi Yar massacre 42, 70n81
baby boom 186. *See also* Jewish Displaced Persons (DP)
Bacon, Yehuda 132
Barbakow, Fania 109–10

Baretzki, Stefan 69n62
Bass, Leon 157
Bauer, Erich 193–4
Bauer, Yehuda 173
Becker, Israel 224
Bedzin 91, 121
Beilin, Aharon 106, 133–4, 184
Belsen trial 191–2
Belzec 31, 95–6, 101–2, 112
Ben-Gurion, David 159
Ben-Moshe, Danny 228, 229. *See also Revenge* (film, 2023)
Berg, Mary 132
Bergen-Belsen 12–13, 165, 168–9, 191
Berlin 35, 40–1, 55, 92, 95, 170, 177–8, 187, 193, 223
Berliner, Meier 84–5, 90
Bettelheim, Bruno 134
Between Dignity and Despair (Kaplan) 66n26
Biala, Max 84–5
Bialik, Chaim Nachman 124
    Al Hashkhita 124, 146n227, 183, 216n188
Bialystok 110–11
Bielski brothers 90
Birkenau boys 127
Birman, Zipora 110–11
Błażewski, Władysław 129
Blechhammer 170
Boder, David P. 10–11, 162–3
Bonn 238
book burnings (May 1933) 1
Bradley, Omar 155, *155*
Bratislava 107
Brettler, Marc 19n31, 196–7, 220n267
Browning, Christopher 77n203
Brudzew 86
Brysk, Miriam 89, 90
Buchenwald 10, 92, 125, 157, 166, 168, 170, 241
Budapest 237
Bundism 116, 119
Budzyn 89, 199
Bunzlau 50
Bureau 06 192
Buzminsky, Josef 192
Byten 108–9

Campos, Ramón 228
Champetier de Ribes, Auguste 58–9

Index

Chelmno death camp 9, 31
    prisoners testament 9
Chemnitz 51
children
    German 48, 130, 163, 165, 168
    Jewish (*See* Jewish children)
Christianity/Christians 4, 235
    churches 7
    divine vengeance 6
    injustice and 6
    revenge and 6–7
Chronicles from the Vilna Ghetto (Kruk) 115–16
churches 7
cinema. *See* films
Clifford, Rebecca 243
collaborators 42–3, 108. *See also* Ukrainian auxiliaries / Lithuanian auxiliaries
collective punishment 61–2
communism 8, 42, 50
confrontations with Nazi perpetrators 94–9
Czestochowa 187
Czollek, Max 15
Czortkow 112

Dabrowa-Gornica 110
Dachau 10, 105, 154, 166, 171, 173, 190–1, 200, 236
Danzyger, David 210n79
Das Reich 40
Das Schwarze Korps 35–6
Davidson, Shamai 15, 216n196
Davos 79
Dean, Carolyn J. 12
Dean, Martin 70n81
death camps 31. *See* Auschwitz, Belzec, Chelmno, Majdanek, Sobibor, Treblinka
death marches 56, 134
Deblin 200
Debreczeni, József 134
deferred narratives 236
Der ewige Jude 39–40, 69n63
Der Fall Gustloff (Diewerge) 80
Der Giftpilz (Hiemer) 59, 66n15, 72n100
Der Stürmer 25, *36, 37, 43,* 48, 50–2, *52,* 59, *82,* 92
Deutschkron, Inge 131
Deutschland Erwache ("Awaken, Germany") 33
diaries 111–21
"Die Juden sind schuld!" 40
Die Jünger Jesu ("The Disciples of Jesus") (Frank) 1–2
Die Mörder sind unter uns/The Murderers are Among Us (film, 1946) 223, 225
Dietrich, Otto 49
Diewerge, Wolfgang 80
Dora-Mittelbau 134, 162–3, 168
Dragomiresti 92
Drancy 122, 130, 239
dreams 134, 170
Dresden 13–14

Dreilich, Ernst 50
Druja 109–10
Dubnow, Simon 187

Ebensee 199
Eckart, Dietrich 33, *34*
Egoyan, Atom 226
Eichmann trial 62, 64, 106, 118, 124
    Arendt on 206n25
    ashes 193
    Beilin's testimony 106, 133–4, 184
    Bureau 06 192
    Buzminsky's testimony 192
    execution and cremation 192
    Goldman-Gilead's testimony 192–3
    Israeli intellectuals on sentencing 193
    Levi's poem 204
    reluctant executioner 218n236
    sentencing/death sentence 192–3
Eisenberg, Kalman 125
Eisenhower, Dwight D. 155, *155, 156*
Eliach, Yaffa 217n202
Ellersleben 165
Ellrich-Juliushuette 92
Elsnig 169
emasculation 128, 178
Endkampf 56
Endphaseverbrechen 56
Engel, Artur 196
Engel, Chaim 86–7, 101, 122
ethnic violence 42–3, 153–4
Eule 134
Exodus (film, 1960) 17n3

F., Hanna 164
F., Rudolf 239–40
F., Susan 178
fantasies 9
    diaries 111–20
    survivors 198–204
Feldafing *181*
Feuer, Otto 10, 168–9
films 15. *See also specific film*
    Holocaust-revenge 15, 225–30
    postwar 223–9
final solution 13, 29–31, 45, 133, 150, 159
    Frank's understanding 1–2
    Gerstein on 95
Finkel, Evgeny 15
Flossenbourg 91, 170
"For Adolf Eichmann" (Levi's poem, 1960) 204
Fort Breendonk 168
Fort IX 106
Fortunoff Archive 12, 236, 239, 242–3nn10–11
Frank, Anne 13, 14
Frank, Leonhard 1–2
Frankfurt am Main 55, 81

Index

Frankfurter, David 79–81, 83, 135n1, 135n3
Frankl, Viktor Emil 131
Fredersdorf, Herbert B. 224
French Revolution 7
Frenkel, Selimar 182
Friedland 169
Friedman, Philip 188
Froehling, Martin 48
Fuchs, Avraham 214–15n176, 214n174
Fun Letztn Khurbn 162

G., Frieda 210n83
G., Kurt 149–50
G., Regina 134–5
Gansser, Hans *34*
Garbel, Salomon 102
Gauting cemetery obelisk 198, 204
gender-based violence 175. *See* sexual violence
Gebirtig, Mordechai vi
German children 48, 130, 163, 165, 168
German criminal code 63, 82
German women 48, 62, 170, 213n153
    Nazi propaganda and 29, 41
    sexual assault or rape of 154, 173–4, 207n38
    sexual relationships with Jewish men 178, 214–15n176–7
Gerstein, Kurt 95–6
Gertner, Alla 101
Gerwarth, Robert 72n94
Gilbert, Gustave M. 58
Gitterman, Yitzhak 122–3
Gläser, Johannes 51, 74n135
Gleiwitz 173
Globocnik, Odilo 101
Goebbels, Joseph 30, 33–5, 38–41, 45–8, 53, 55, 80, 152, 178, 185
Goldap 51
Goldman-Gilead, Michael (Micki) 192–3
Goldstein, Marek 224
Göring, Hermann 30, 48–9, 80, 190
Gorny, Yekhiel 121
Gotz, Elly 167–9, 175, 231
Gradowski, Zalmen 85, 90, 96–8, 119, 132, 133, 158–9
    prediction for the German nation 149
grandchildren 44, 186
great purge 47
Green, Boris 229
Green, Jack 229
Green, Jon 229
Green, Sam 229
grievances 2, 3, 242. *See also* revenge
Griffith-Jones, Mervyn 59
Grinberg, Zalman 169
Gringauz, Samuel 183, 184
Grodno 161
Gröning, Oskar 76n167

Grossman, Vassily 126, 140n91
Grossmann, Atina 185–6
Grutman, S. N. 103
Grynszpan, Herschel 34–5, 37, 79–81, *81*, 83, 135n3
Gunzenhausen 123
Gusen 158
Gustloff, Wilhelm 79, 80
Gutman, Israel 134

H., Brenda 235, 242n6
Hagen 195
haircutting 153, 165, 210n83
Halbreich, Siegfried 170
Haman 38, 179
Hamburg 196
Hannover 96, 199
Harlan, Veit 38–9, 69n63. *See also Jud Süß* (film, 1940)
Hausner, Gideon 62, 192
Heath, James 44
Hebrew Bible
    neighborly love and mutual care 6
    revenge in 5
Hecker, Friedrich 33
Herf, Jeffrey 65n10
Hessisch Lichtenau 237
Heydrich, Reinhard 46–7, 72n94
Hiemer, Ernst 37, 59
Der Giftpilz 59, 66n15, 72n100
Hilberg, Raul 15, 30
Himmler, Heinrich 30, 38, 40, 44–7, 72nn94–5, 72n101, 185
Hippler, Fritz 39. *See Der ewige Jude*
Hirschmann, Ira Arthur 11
Hitler, Adolf 25, 28, 30–1, 32–3, 151
    Frank's anger against 13, 14
    Grinberg on 169
    Gustloff's funeral speech 80
    January 1939 speech 37–8, 40
    Mein Kampf 33, 144n183, 179, *182*
    mocking 178, 179, *180*, *181*
    prophesy 39, 40, 45, 50, 70n67
    revenge addiction 24n86
    September 1922 speech 32
Hoffmann, Irma (Irmgard) 170
Holocaust 8. *See also* Jewish revenge; Nazis; survivor(s) (of Holocaust)
    intensification 27
    scholarship 15
Holocaust-revenge movies 225–30
Holz, Karl 25–6
Honig, Jack (Heinz) 236
Horowitz, Sara 236
Höss, Rudolf 72n101, 150–1
House of Dolls (Ka-Tzetnik) 17n3
Huber, Engelbert 41
humor 93–4, 131
Hunters (TV drama, 2020–2023) 227

Index

If This is a Man (Levi) 75n146
Inglorious Basterds (film, 2009) 15, 225
inscriptions 102–6
    Kadish's photographs document 105–6
    Kovel synagogue walls 102–4
intergenerational revenge 127–8
International Military Tribunal (IMT) trial at Nuremberg. *See* Nuremberg trials
Islam 4

Jackson, Robert H. 58
Jacoby, Susan 7, 22–3n74, 28
Jaguar (TV drama, 2021) 228
Jeckeln, Friedrich 44
Jedwabne, Poland 42
Jerusalem 46, 64
Jew(s)
    as aggressors 25–6
    communism and 8
    dehumanizing 4
    genocidal measures against 7
    as race 26, 27, 28
    stereotypes 4
    victimization 7–8
Jewish Antifascist Committee 124
Jewish Brigade 157–8, 175, 227
Jewish children 125–30, 185–7
    Germanization 47
    killing/murder of 47
Jewish death in Holocaust 83, 125
Jewish Displaced Persons (DP) 11, 150, 177, 224
    Adorno's interviewees/interviews 151–2
    baby boom 186
    Gauting cemetery obelisk 198, 204
    nation-building 182–5
    Purim celebrations 178–9, *180, 181,* 215n177–8
    symbolic meaning for Nazism 180
Jewish Fighting Organization. *See* ŻOB
Jewish men 128–9
Jewish Museum, Frankfurt 23n81
Jewish question 40, 51, 55, 133
Jewish revenge 79–135
    ambiguities 120–5
    diaries 111–20
    face-to-face confrontation 94–9
    fantasies 111–20, 132–5
    gender roles 127–30
    generational imperatives 125–30
    humor 93–4, 131
    inscriptions 102–6
    last letters 106–11
    sarcasm 93–4
    signs and scenarios 130–5
    singing 92–3
    struggle for survival 117–20
Jewish women 62, 88, 91–101, 108, 99, 168–70
    acts of revenge 9–10, 44, 85, 163–4

feminine revenge 129
male or masculine role and acts 129
Nazi propaganda and killing 43, 44, 45
rape 35, 174
sexual exploitation 17n3
suicide 207n38
Joskowicz, Ari 22n74
Jösting, Erwin 54
Judaism
    cultures shaping 4
    literature 4–5
    revenge in 5
Judeo-Bolshevism 8, 29, 42, 160
Jud Süß (film, 1940) 38–9, 68–70n66
justice 3, 4, 61, 157, 172
    survivors seeking 189–98
    vigilante 157
Justice, not Vengeance (Wiesenthal) 11

K., Celia 122
K., Joseph 91
K., Rose 170
Kadish, George 104, 104–6, *107,* 216n188
Kaiserwald 94
Kalb, Ben Zion 119, 133
Kaltenbrunner, Ernst 60
Kanter, Richard 238–9
Kaplan, Chaim Aron 94, 114, 128, 152
Kaplan, Marion 66n26
kapo (prisoner functionary) 63, 157, 206–7 n 25
Kapo (film, 1960) 17n3
Karlsbad 92
Karolinski, Alexa 163–4
Karolinski, Regina 164
Kassel 178
Katyn 47–8, 52
Katz, Bella 164
Katzenelson, Yitzhak 130, 132
Ka-Tzetnik 216n199
    House of Dolls 17n3
    Piepel 17n3
Kaufering 154–6, 167, 169, 173, 182–3
Kaufmann, Kurt 60–1
Kaul, Martin 228, 229. *See also Shlomo* (film, 2023)
Kedainai 130
Keitel, Wilhelm 72–3n106
Kempmann, Antonius 228, 229. *See also Shlomo* (film, 2023)
Kempner, Vitka 10, 12, 158, 199
Kenet, Shlomo 159–60
Kezmarok 133
Kibbutz Buchenwald 181
Kibbutz Nili 180
Kiev 42–3
Kimmel, James, Jr. 24n86, 242
Kipp, Michaela 74n138
Kishinev. *See* Bialik, Chaim Nachman

Index

Klappholz, Kurt 170–1
Klemperer, Victor 13–14, 22n71, 80, 143n151, 147n264
Klinger, Chaika 91, 119, 121
Klüger, Ruth 132
Kolbuszowa 92, 101, 115
Kor, Eva Mozes 175
Kovel synagogue wall inscriptions 102–4
Kovner, Abba 10, 11–12, 158–9, 172, 185, 198, 199
Kovno 43, 104–5, 119, 131, 161, 175
Krajowa, Armia 129
Krakow 164
Kramer, Josef 191–2
Krasa, Edgar 92–3
Krasnik 199
Kraus, Karel 126–7
Kraus, Lotte 126–7
Kraus, Michal (Michael) 126–7, *127*
Kreidl, Paul 22n71
Kristallnacht. *See* pogrom of November 1938
Krojanke 239
Kruk, Herman 115–17
Kühne, Thomas 67n33
Külb, Karl-Georg 224
Kulka, Otto Dov 132–3, 158–9

L., Martin 169
Lambert, Raul Raymond 122
Landau, Dov 17n3
Landsberg 174, 179–80
Lang, Berel 23n78
Langbein, Hermann 148n278
Langer, Lawrence 241
Lang ist der Weg/Long is the way (film, 1947) 17n3, 223–5
Lanzmann, Claude 131
Laternser, Hans 61
Lavi, Shai 15–16
Lawrence, Geoffrey 59
Lazerson, Tamara 119
Leipzig 51, 237
Lerer, Samuel 193–4
Lerner, Roni 24n85
letters
    by Germans 50–5
    by Jews 106–11, 160–1
Levi, Primo
    as a chemist 75n146
    "For Adolf Eichmann" 204
    on hatred 175
    If This is a Man 75n146
    The Truce/*La tregua* 188–9
Levin, Meyer 22n56, 153, 154, 166, 173–4
Levit, Max 140n91
Lewin, Abraham 114, 124, 128, 152
lex talionis (law of talion) 3, 5

Ley, Robert 58
Lida 89
Lidice and Lezaky massacres 46–7
Lidski, Isaak 106
Liethen, Alois J. *155*
Lithuanian auxiliaries 94–5, 98, 105–6, 108, 122, 229
Lodz 9, 99–100, 112, 123–4
Lopez, Anthony C. 241
Lubetkin, Zivia 88, 124, 172
Ludoph, Julius 199
Lvov 43, 95–6

Majdanek 31, 89, 134, 162, 164
Malnik, Abraham 172, 209n56
Mann, Franceska 9–10, 85, 90
Marx, Hans 59–60
mass atrocities 4
Mattner, Walter 45
Mauthausen 131, 134, 199
Mein Kampf (Hitler) 33, 144n183, 179, *182*
Melk 131, 199
Mengele, Josef 175
Mersik-Tennebaum archive 111
Mielec 91
Mihael, Flora Carasso 165
Mikhoels, Solomon 124
Mikolajow 125
Mikulov 173
Minsk 44
Mogilev 45
Moll, Otto 173
Molotov Brigade 89
Morgenthau, Henry, Jr. 205n13
Morgenthau plan 205n13
Moscow 120, 177
Muehlheim an der Ruhr 149–50
Müller, Filip 96
Munich 14, 33, 180

N., Hans 199
Nachod 126
Nadjari, Marcel 119–20
Nagar, Shalom 218n236
Nakam 10, 11–12, 159
Nakba 185
national revenge 15–16
Natke 110
Nazis 25–64. *See also* Allies/Allied forces
    antisemitism and anti-jewish policies 28–32
    fantasies 49–57
    genocidal rhetoric and practice 32–40
    Holz's editorial 25–6
    Jewish revenge (*See* Jewish revenge)
    motives in killing fields 40–9
Neira, Gema R. 228
Netanyahu, Benjamin 21n48
Never Again Will I Visit Auschwitz (Richter) 236–7

Index

Nir, Arie 193
Nitzotz 182
Novy Hrozenkov 132
Nowy Sacz 96
Nuremberg 10, 35
Nuremberg trials 57–63, 177–8, 180, 189–91, 197

O., Julius 178
obelisk. *See* Gauting cemetery obelisk
Oberaltstadt 170
Ohlendorf, Otto 44, 45, 185
Ohrdruf 154–5, *156, 157*
Oma & Bella (film, 2012) 164
Operation Barbarossa 66n27
Operation Reinhard 47, 96. *See also* Belzec, Sobibor, Treblinka
Ophuls, Marcel 73n115
Oppenheimer, Joseph Süß 38–9
Orbach, Lothar (Larry) 170, 213n153
Otwock 113, 129
Oyneg Shabbes archive 187

P., Masha 88
P., Paul 173
P., Rudy 131
Padover, Saul Kussiel 11, 151–3, 166
Palestine (British Mandate) 111, 114, 157, 159, 161, 184, 224
Palestinians 21n48, 185
Paper Brigade 86
Paris 13, 79
partisans 46, 8
    Jewish 89–90, 105, 122
Patterson, Orlando 66n26
Patton, George S. 155, *155, 156*
Pelckmann, Horst 61
Perechodnik, Bezalel (Calel or Calek) 113, 116–18, 120, 128–30, 132, 158–9
Person, Katarzyna 24n82
Petlura, Simon 139n75
Petlura Days 139n75
Pick, Aharon 130
Piepel (Ka-Tzetnik) 17n3
Piskorz, Benjamin 134, 162–3
Plan A (film, 2021) 227–8
Plaszow 164
Pleikershof 180
Plesivec 237
Poale Zion movement 116, 121
poems/poetry 199
pogrom of November 1938 34–5, 55, 80–1
Poland 31, 50, 79, 191–2
    antisemitism 224
    German attack and occupation 37, 84, 187, 224
    She'erit Hapletah 188
    Soviet occupation 70–1n84, 94
Poles 42, 152–3, 159

Polish Supreme National Tribunal 150-1
Poniatowa 89
Pontecorvo, Gillo 17n3
Porat, Dina 15
Post-Holocaust (Lang) 23n78
POWs 10, 46, 53–4, 150, 153–5, 159, 164
Ponary 94, 102, 105, 108, 115, 170
Prague 164
Preminger, Otto 17n3
property destruction 165
Przemysl 192
Purim 37, 39, 178–9, *180, 181,* 215nn177–8
Puterman, Lusia 208–9n53

Quackernack, Walter 9

Raab, Esther 186–7, 194–6
Raab, Irving 187
race 26, 27, 28, 46
Radom 169
Rajchman, Chil 126
Rasch, Otto 44
Raseinai 104
Ravensbrück 134
Reich, Ismar 238
Reichenau, Walter von 42
Reinharz, Shulamit 145n218
Remember (film, 2015) 226–7
reproduction 185–7
resistance 16, 85–94
    armed 86–7
    collective goals 89
    cultural 86
    forms 86
retaliation 2–3
retribution 2
revenge 1–17. *See also* Jewish revenge; Nazis
    as an anthropological constant 2
    as an emotional state 2
    as antithesis of forgiveness 235
    appropriate and inappropriate 5–6
    Christianity/Christians and 6–7
    as a criminal offense 3
    desires and practices 2
    justice and 3, 4
    memory 4
    modern societies 3
    national 15–16
    negative social behavior 3
    as a personality trait 2
    phenomena, range of 3
    plotted 10
    as a post-traumatic response 3
    as reactive 4
    resistance *vs.* (*See* resistance)
    as self-empowering 4
    short-term benefits 3

Index

symbolic 27
time and temporality 4
vengeance *vs.* 2
vigilantism *vs.* 3
as violence 3
Revenge: History and Fantasy (exhibition, 2022) 23n81
Revenge (film, 2023) 228–30
Rex, Zvi (Franz) 201
Richter, Ari 236–7
Ringelblum, Emanuel 113–14, 116, 117, 121–3, 132, 187
Robota, Róża 101
Roma 152
Rosenberg, Alfred 41
Roth, Thomas 226
Rothschild, Max Michael 123
Rozavlea 92
Rutschaisky, Moishe 131, 166–7, 178, 190–1

S., Agnes 237
S., Allen 125–6
S., Aron 243n14
S., Martin 240–1
S., Violet 169
Sachsenhausen 10, 170–1
Sakowicz, Kazimierz 94–5
Salcer, Katarina 237–8
Saleschuetz, Isaak 101
Salsitz, Norman 126
Salonika 119
Sanok 110
Sandowski, Aryeh 175
Sapir, Regina 101
sarcasm 93–4
Sauckel, Fritz 61
Schächten / A Retribution (film, 2022) 226
Schächter, Rafael 92–3
Schillinger, Josef 9
Schirrmeister, Sebastian 24n82, 221n292
Schlegel, Horst 51
letter to the editor of *Der Stürmer* 51, *52*
Schloss, Peyse 115
Schnapps, Nahman 141n117
Schulman, Faye 89
Schulz, Erwin 44
Schwartz, Asher 110
Schwarzbard, Sholem 135n3, 139n75
Schwerin 172
screaming. *See* confrontations with Nazi perpetrators
Seidman, Hillel 112, 115, 124
Seidman, Naomi 12
Servatius, Robert 61–2, 64
sexual violence 35, 107–8, 173–5 2, 17n3
Seyss-Inquart, Artur 62–3
Shadowplay/The Defeated (TV production, 2020) 227

Shaus, Leib 161
Shavli 130, 161
Shawcross, Hartley 58
Shekhter, Yehuda 103
Shema (prayer) 101
Shlomo (film, 2023) 228–30
Shumer, Leon 101
Shylock 197
Siberia 163
Siedlce 98–9, 118–19
Sierakowiak, Dawid 123–4
Silbermann, Moses 96
Simon, Sidney 89–90
singing 92–3
Širviai 108
Skala-Podilska 196
Skarzysko-Kamienna 240
slurs. *See* confrontations with Nazi perpetrators
Sobibor (extermination camp) 31, 101, 194–5, 193–5, 229
uprising on October 14, 1943 86–7, 194
socialism 116, 123
Sokal 43
Sompolinski, Roman 191–2
Sonderkommando. *See* Auschwitz and SS-Einsatzgruppen
Sonderkommando 1005 (Janowska) 90
songs 33–4, 80, 93
Soviet Union
German attack on 31, 40–54
Goebbels on Jewry in 41
occupation of Poland 70–1n84, 94
Speer, Albert 47–8
Spiegel, Regina 12, 169–70
SS-Einsatzgruppen 31, 41–5, 106
SS women 97
St. Ottilien 167, 169, 190
Stalin, Joseph 47
Stalingrad 53, 130
Stanislawow 112
Starachowice-Wierbnik 125
Staudte, Wolfgang 223
Stauffenberg, Claus Count Schenk von 13
Steinbauer, Gustav 62–3
Stimson, Henry L. 205n13
Stolpce 161
"Storm Song" (song, 1919) 33, *34*, 80
Strasbourg 238
Streicher, Julius 33–7, 58–60, 180–1
Stroop, Jürgen 88
Stutthof 105, 127, 131
Sudetenland 163
suicidal revenge 186
suicide 119, 130
survivor(s) (of Holocaust) 235–6
absence of revenge acts 10–11
conflicted emotions 176

275

Index

documentation/witness accounts 187–9
fantasy and utopia 198–204
as moral authority figures 11
as moral witnesses 12–13
reappropriating property and institutions 180–1
seeking justice 189–98
Sutzkever, Abraham 86, 102, 120, 124, 142n130, 177, 183–4, 189–90, 197–8
symbolic revenge 27
Szmajzner, Stanislaw (Shlomo) 229. *See also Shlomo* (film, 2023)

Tarantino, Quentin 15, 225
Tarlowski, Aba 161
Tashkent 161
Tehlirian, Soghomon 135n3
Thal, Bernhard 152
Theresienstadt (Terezin) 92–3, 126, 131–2, 239, 241
This Must be the Place (film, 2011) 226
Tievsky, George 169
Trawniki 89
Tradate 162
Travis, Martin 209n54
Treblinka 31, 84, 89, 113, 125–6, 128–9, 162
The Truce/La tregua (Levi) 188–9
Tunik, Azriel 161–2
Tutzing 240

U., Yaffa 174–5
Ukrainians (auxiliaries) 45, 87, 90, 94–8, 102–3, 112
Ulm 44
Un di velt hot geshvign (Wiesel) 12
Unger, Eliezer 107
UNRRA 11
Uris, Leon 17n3
USC Shoah Foundation 236, 238, 242–3n10–11

verbal confrontation. *See* confrontations with Nazi perpetrators
Vienna 45, 131–2, 167
vigilante justice 157
vigilantism 3, 18n8. *See also* revenge
Vilna 105, *107*, 115, 164, 183
Vilna Jews, mass shooting of 94
Vinnitsa 48
Vittel 130
Völkischer Beobachter 180
Volkov, Shulamit 65n8
Volksgemeinschaft 48, 56, 151
volkssturm 56
vom Rath, Ernst 34–5, 37, 79–80
von Kardorff, Ursula 55
von Ludighausen, Otto Freiherr 60

von Ribbentrop, Joachim 58
von Rothkirch und Trach, Edwin Graf 54
von Stauffenberg, Claus Count Schenk 13
Voss, Peter 97

Wagner, Gustav 229
Wald, Moshe 110
Walfish, Anita Lasker 219–20n263
war crimes trials 57–64, 150
Warsaw 84, 113, 117–18, 123, 128–9, 162, 224
Warsaw ghetto uprising (1943) 87–9, 130
Warsaw uprising (1944) 129
Wehrmacht 39, 41–2, 50–1, 53–4, 56, 131, 172
Weimar Republic 28, 33
Weisblum, Esther 101
Weiss-Felenbaum, Hella 101–2
Weizmann, Chaim 159
Weliczka 91
Wiesel, Elie 11, 12, 22n58
Wiesenthal, Simon 11
Wieviorka, Annette 11
Willenberg, Ada 187
Willenberg, Samuel 187, 201, 217n204
Willenberg-Giladi, Orit 201
Winter, Shmuel 118
Winter Olympics 80
Wirth, Christian 96
Wishniatsky, Moyshe 108
Wishniatsky, Zlatka 108–9
witnessing 187–9
Wollheim, Norbert 171–2, 219–20n263
women
    acts of solidarity 175
    Aryan 29, 38
    German (*See* German women)
    Jewish (*See* Jewish women)
    taking revenge on women 165
    violence against 174–5
Worms 43
Würzburg 1
Wurzen 238

Yablonka, Hanna 183, 216n192
yelling. *See* confrontations with Nazi perpetrators
Yishuv 16, 159, 175, 177, 180, 183
Yizker books 200

Zgierz 191
Zionism 16, 114–15, 182, 185–6
Zonszajn, Cypora "Cypa" 98–9, 118–19
ŻOB 88–9, 91, 119, 122, 162
Zorbach, Ernst 237–8
Zuckerman, Yitzhak 88, 172–3